AF811606

Beyond the Gavel: A Paradigm Shift in Global Criminal Justice

G. S. Bajpai • Beulah Shekhar • M. Priyamvadha
Editors

Beyond the Gavel: A Paradigm Shift in Global Criminal Justice

In Honor of Professor K. Chockalingam

Springer

Editors
G. S. Bajpai
National Law University, Delhi
New Delhi, Delhi, India

M. Priyamvadha
Department of Criminology
University of Madras
Chennai, Tamil Nadu, India

Beulah Shekhar
Department of Criminology &
Forensic Science
Parul University
Vadodara, Gujarat, India

ISBN 978-981-95-4486-8 ISBN 978-981-95-4487-5 (eBook)
https://doi.org/10.1007/978-981-95-4487-5

© The Editor(s) (if applicable) and The Author(s), under exclusive license to Springer Nature Singapore Pte Ltd. 2026

This work is subject to copyright. All rights are solely and exclusively licensed by the Publisher, whether the whole or part of the material is concerned, specifically the rights of translation, reprinting, reuse of illustrations, recitation, broadcasting, reproduction on microfilms or in any other physical way, and transmission or information storage and retrieval, electronic adaptation, computer software, or by similar or dissimilar methodology now known or hereafter developed.
The use of general descriptive names, registered names, trademarks, service marks, etc. in this publication does not imply, even in the absence of a specific statement, that such names are exempt from the relevant protective laws and regulations and therefore free for general use.
The publisher, the authors and the editors are safe to assume that the advice and information in this book are believed to be true and accurate at the date of publication. Neither the publisher nor the authors or the editors give a warranty, expressed or implied, with respect to the material contained herein or for any errors or omissions that may have been made. The publisher remains neutral with regard to jurisdictional claims in published maps and institutional affiliations.

This Springer imprint is published by the registered company Springer Nature Singapore Pte Ltd.
The registered company address is: 152 Beach Road, #21-01/04 Gateway East, Singapore 189721, Singapore

If disposing of this product, please recycle the paper.

Preface

Great minds that contribute significantly and add value to society are invaluable treasures who should be celebrated with great reverence. With utmost pleasure and immense respect, we present this Festschrift to celebrate the legacy of Prof. Dr. K. Chockalingam on his 80th birthday. This volume serves as a tribute to an exceptional academician whose contributions have enriched and shaped the fields of Criminal Justice, Criminology, and Victimology. In honor and recognition of his significant contributions, this book will serve as a resource for scholars who seek to advance in the above-mentioned fields.

Albert Einstein once remarked, "Strive not to be a success, but rather to be of value." In line with this quote, Prof. Dr. Chockalingam's journey is a testament to his strong will, hard work, and dedication. Being the harbinger of change in the domain of Victimology in India, he established the Indian Society of Victimology and served as its founder President for 13 years. During this tenure, he built a solid groundwork for learning and practice that has been a beacon for students, scholars, and professionals. With a career lasting over fifty years in teaching and research, Prof. Dr. Chockalingam's influence reaches far beyond national boundaries. He has lectured and worked with prestigious institutions like the University of Madras, Harvard, and Oxford and Tokiwa University. He has also been actively participating in global discussions about criminal justice.

This Festschrift foregrounds the exemplified achievements of Prof. Dr. Chockalingam. This volume is divided into four sections: Criminal Justice, Criminology, Victimology, and Criminal Law, each addressing pertinent issues in contemporary society. It includes studies on evolving law enforcement strategies, challenges to fair trials, and the influence of globalization on crime. It also highlights the often-overlooked voices of victims, emphasizing their stories, rights, and the support to be built up. These contributions showcase the diverse approach Dr. Chockalingam has supported and championed all these years.

This edited volume is also a testament to Prof. Dr. Chockalingam's unwavering commitment to academic excellence and institution-building. As the Vice-Chancellor of Manonmaniam Sundaranar University, he introduced remarkable changes in transformative reforms, which established a culture of innovation and academic rigor. His legacy encompasses not only scholarly achievements, but also inspiration for countless generations of students, colleagues, and administrators to relentlessly strive for "Excellence in Everything."

Prof. Dr. Chockalingam's distinguished contributions have been recognized globally, earning him numerous awards for his exceptional work, some of which include the Distinguished International Scholar Award from the American Society of Criminology and the Tamil Nadu Scientist Award. The Indian Society of Victimology has also honored him by establishing the "Professor K. Chockalingam Award," which will ensure that his legacy will endure for many more generations to come.

This Festschrift has compiled excellent studies and thereby unveils a multitude of insights. Researchers from within the domain have addressed various key issues such as open discussions regarding the criminal process, the global impacts of Somali piracy rooted in local lawlessness, crime victim compensation since the twentieth century, the history and current scenario of victim rights in China, food crimes that lead to financial, health, and ethical consequences, advocating for developing a cold case center in India, critiques on the Dialectics of Law advocating for dialogic criminal proceedings, discussion on how criminology, victimology, and forensic science have changed the way we perceive criminal justice, advances in youth, the complexity of psychopathic sexual offenses, the tension between cultural traditions, human rights, and local laws in addressing moral offenses in Aceh, Participatory Action Research (PAR) to empower marginalized victims, improvement of support systems in India, the transition from punitive to rights-based approaches to combating human trafficking, the role of Victim Impact Statements (VIS) in the criminal justice system, the assessment of global victim rights, strategies to reduce violence, the role of victimologists, and the exploration of factors driving recidivism in young adult offenders.

This Festschrift is enriched with profound insights from distinguished scholars across diverse fields, greatly influenced by Prof. Dr. Chockalingam's pathbreaking works. We extend our heartfelt gratitude to the contributors for their efforts, and we, Prof. Dr. G.S. Bajpai, Prof. Dr. Beulah Shekhar, and Prof. Dr. M. Priyamvadha, are greatly honored to have been presented with the opportunity to curate this significant volume in celebration of an extraordinary academician.

As we wholeheartedly dedicate this work to Prof. Dr. Chockalingam, we celebrate his resounding success and substantial contributions to Criminal Justice and honor the values of kindness, honesty, and mentorship that he embodies. We hope that this Festschrift will serve as both a worthy tribute to his legacy and a source of inspiration for future generations of scholars and practitioners.

New Delhi, Delhi, India — G. S. Bajpai
Vadodara, Gujarat, India — Beulah Shekhar
Chennai, Tamil Nadu, India — M. Priyamvadha

Contents

About the Editors

G. S. Bajpai serves as Vice-Chancellor of National Law University Delhi, India. He has previously served as Vice-Chancellor at the Rajiv Gandhi National University of Law (RGNUL), Punjab, and Registrar at National Law University Delhi. He also served as Convenor of the Committee for Reforms in Criminal Laws set up by the Ministry of Home Affairs, Government of India, tasked with spearheading historic reforms in Criminal Laws in India. The Ministry of Consumer Affairs, Government of India, has nominated Prof. G.S. Bajpai as Member of the committee for conferring statutory status to the "Right to Repair" under the statutory framework of the Consumer Protection Act, 2019. Having more than thirty years of professional experience as a researcher, teacher, and administrator, Prof. Bajpai has authored twenty-two books/monographs, more than sixty papers, and over a hundred op-eds in leading Indian newspapers like the *Indian Express*, *The Hindu*, and *The Tribune*. He is the Vice President of Victim Support Asia and the President of the Indian Society of Victimology and credited with designing and pioneering the expression: "Critical Criminal Law in India," which is now an LL.M. course in many universities. He is also credited to have conceptualized the novel paradigms of "Victim Justice," "Victim Jurisprudence," and "Wrongful Prosecution" in the Indian context. Prof. G.S. Bajpai was appointed as *Amicus Curiae* in various cases by the High Court of Delhi. His areas of interest include victim justice, critical criminal law, criminal procedure, empirical legal research, and criminology and victimology.

Beulah Shekhar is Professor of Criminology at Lok Nayak Jayprakash Narayan National Institute of Criminology and Forensic Science and Emeritus Professor of Criminology at Karunya Institute of Technology and Sciences, Coimbatore, India. She was Head of the Department of Criminology and Criminal Justice Sciences at Manonmaniam Sundaranar University and coordinated UGC sponsored programs on victimology and victim assistance and human rights and duties education. Prof. Shekhar has also served as Juvenile Justice Board Member for the three districts of the Indian state of Tamil Nadu, and as Director of the Childline Nodal agency and the Sahodari Family Counselling Center Project at Tirunelveli. Prof. Shekhar's research focuses on inequalities in various areas, including vulnerability and denied access to justice for excluded groups like women, dalits, children, transgender persons, victims of crime, and abuse of power. She focuses on developing partnerships between researchers, policymakers, program developers, agency personnel, and community groups to conduct basic and applied research and evaluation in sociological concerns and various aspects of victimology, crime, criminology, law, and justice.

M. Priyamvadha is Professor in the Department of Criminology at the University of Madras, Chennai, India. She has received numerous awards, including *Commendation Disc* from the Bureau of Police Research and Development in 2023, *International Visitors Leadership Award 2023* from the US Government, the Achiever's Award in 2014, and the *Fellowship Award* from the Indian Society of Victimology in 2018. Prof. Priyamvadha has published numerous research articles on the rights of children, women, and aged people and has conducted research projects funded by various government agencies. She has co-edited a book on victim assistance. In 2022, she participated in the International Visitor Leadership Program "Road to Safe Social Media Space for Girls and Young Women."

Beyond the Gavel: A Paradigm Shift in Global Criminal Justice—In Honor of Professor K. Chockalingam

G. S. Bajpai

1 Introduction

The criminal justice system incorporated both enforcement and punishment and restoration practices right from its founding date. Recent global shifts across criminal justice systems have created operational structures that unite human rights standards with rehabilitative efforts and restorative justice approaches alongside current technology frameworks. Studies from diverse disciplines resulted in both legal changes and social-legal actions to establish humanistic and advanced crime and justice models. Underdeveloped nations should implement this change because their judiciary operates with structural problems alongside access concerns and fair practice difficulties. Professor K. Chockalingam has been a pioneer in the study of victimology, human rights, and criminal justice reform, contributing significantly to the discourse on justice beyond mere legal adjudication. His work has underscored the need for a victim-centric approach in criminal justice, advocating for restorative measures that prioritize healing and rehabilitation. This volume, *Beyond the Gavel: A Paradigm Shift in Global Criminal Justice*, seeks to honor his contributions by exploring the shifts in criminal justice paradigms across the world, highlighting innovative practices, policy transformations, and theoretical advancements that align with his vision.

G. S. Bajpai (✉)
National Law University Delhi, Delhi, India
e-mail: vc@nludelhi.ac.in

© The Author(s), under exclusive license to Springer Nature Singapore Pte Ltd. 2026

G. S. Bajpai et al. (eds.), *Beyond the Gavel: A Paradigm Shift in Global Criminal Justice*, https://doi.org/10.1007/978-981-95-4487-5_1

2 The Evolution of Criminal Justice Paradigms

Historically, criminal justice systems fostered punitive measures because deterrence and retribution served as their core approaches to maintain law enforcement. The traditional justice system designed accountability procedures before starting punishment without examining who committed the crimes. The crime reduction strategies in recent decades failed because they omitted criminal cause drivers while producing significant prison overcrowding that mainly affected lower-income communities. Criminal justice systems today have transitioned entirely to restore justice through a combination of restorative justice, victimology, therapeutic jurisprudence, and community-based corrections. New approaches in criminal investigation show that justice now encompasses social circumstances, human psychological features, and economic metrics for assessing criminal activities. Protective global human rights, along with international agreements and present-day socio-legal principles, led to necessary reforms within traditional criminal justice systems.

3 The Victim Perspective in Criminal Justice Reform

Traditionally, victims of crime were relegated to the periphery of legal proceedings, with little consideration given to their psychological, emotional, and financial needs. Victimology emerged as an independent discipline to transform perspective through victim need-focused approaches that also involve victims in legal procedures. Legislative systems require modern structures that acknowledge victim trauma while promoting victim involvement across judicial procedures.

Victims often experience secondary victimization through legal procedures that fail to recognize their rights and concerns. Many justice systems historically prioritized the prosecution of offenders while overlooking the needs of victims, leaving them without adequate support or recourse. In earlier criminal trial proceedings, victims officially stood outside the courtroom. Victims did not get adequate assessment of their mental health together with financial stability and emotional wellness. Victimology emerged as an autonomous discipline by changing this perspective through recognition of victim requirements during legal proceedings and active victim participation. Justice procedures need updated law structures that simultaneously recognize victim trauma and offer solutions that boost their participation in legal processes.

Restorative justice, a concept that has gained global traction, aligns with this perspective by facilitating dialogues between offenders and victims, encouraging reconciliation, and fostering community involvement in justice processes. Several jurisdictions have successfully implemented restorative justice programs, demonstrating their efficacy in reducing recidivism and promoting societal healing. A study by Bonta et al. (2006) reported that offenders participating in restorative justice programs had a recidivism rate of 15% after 1 year, compared to 38% for those on probation. Another analysis (Bahna 2022) found that victim-offender mediation participants had a 19% recidivism rate over 1 year, while counterparts undergoing traditional court sentencing exhibited a 28% rate.

The significance of victim-centric justice has been acknowledged by various scholars and international bodies. Prominent victimologist Ezzat A. Fattah has argued that traditional criminal justice systems often revictimize individuals by excluding them from key legal processes and denying them adequate restitution. This perspective is supported by various victimological studies that emphasize the need for a victim-centered approach within the justice system, especially exclusion from the legal process and inadequate restitution and punitive measures leaving victims without proper compensation for their losses. Similarly, the United Nations Declaration of Basic Principles of Justice for Victims of Crime and Abuse of Power (1985) underscores the rights of victims to fair treatment, restitution, and access to justice. The South African Truth and Reconciliation Commission demonstrates how victim-centered practices affect justice systems in a relevant manner. Established postapartheid, the Truth and Reconciliation Commission (TRC) provided a platform for victims of major rights abuses to disclose their stories while obtaining compensation. Victims can access reparations, and they can also join restorative justice processes. Reports indicate that the program received statements from 21,000 victims who earned both financial payments and counseling services support. Through its operations, the TRC proved why including victims strengthens justice structures. The procedures of the TRC offer valuable guidance to justice system modernizers around the world.

The justice system uses a victim compensation scheme together with support services and participatory justice models as additional ways to strengthen victims' position. Such approaches empower victims in two ways: first by recognizing their pain and second by giving them the opportunity to participate in the justice process. In 2018, victim compensation programs in the United States disbursed over $400 million to support victims and their families, underscoring the significant role these programs play in victim assistance. However, in 2022, a survey revealed that while over $300 million was paid to crime victims and their families, many individuals in need did not receive aid, indicating room for improvement in reaching all affected parties. Different victim support systems, like victim impact statements along with victim advocacy groups and specialized victim support units, have gained more recognition. Global authorities are implementing law provisions that require victims to participate during sentencing hearings and parole decisions to make their perspectives part of judicial decisions. Research conducted in Australia revealed that three female survivors of sexual assault considered the courtroom process to be more disturbing than their crime of assault because of insufficient trauma understanding and intrusive questions combined with feelings of being left alone.

4 Criminal Law: Navigating the Jurisprudential Landscape

Legal interpretation of criminal law is significantly based on shifting social values and interpretations. The advancement of justice theory now avoids the traditional retributive model. Crime models transform into rehabilitative approaches along with proportionate action models while simultaneously addressing public safety threats. The modern judicial system follows restorative and human-rights-based jurisprudential methods for issuing its guidelines For reform efforts.

Reports from the United Nations Office on Drugs and Crime (UNODC) indicate a global trend towards alternatives to incarceration, with over 70% of surveyed countries adopting community-based sentencing programs. Furthermore, studies by the World Justice Project highlight that access to legal representation significantly impacts judicial outcomes, with countries emphasizing public defender systems experiencing lower wrongful conviction rates. Landmark cases, *Miranda v. Arizona (1966),* demonstrated how legal doctrine perpetually influences criminal statutes. In a parallel development, the Indian Supreme Court issued its judgment in *Bachan Singh v. State of Punjab (1980).* The "rarest of rare" doctrine established its precedent in capital punishment during the State of Punjab (1980) decision because this created space for judges to exercise proper discretion when delivering sentences. The criminal law system remains in continuous evolution because it adapts to changing justice principles through new decisions and legal innovations.

5 Technological Advancements and Criminal Justice

Modern society has accomplished new advancements in criminal justice through digital transformation processes, for crime detection, evidence gathering, and judicial decision-making. With the advent of artificial intelligence, crime detection abilities have improved through the adoption of big data analytics and forensic science. Also digital platforms now provide people with easier avenues to obtain legal assistance as well as justice services. However, these innovations in technology bring privacy risks together with problems in data security protection, and ethical considerations in law enforcement. The intersection of technology has identified the requirement to establish ethical rules and regulatory systems. Innovation requires proper attention to fundamental human rights preservation. The digitalization of legal processes, virtual courtrooms, and electronic case management systems have enhanced operational efficiency despite their creation. There is an urgent need to put forward the discourse regarding how automated systems affect accessibility while addressing fairness and detecting possible biases.

6 Conclusion

The evolution of criminal justice is a dynamic process shaped by legal reforms, societal changes, and technological advancements. The festschrift *Beyond the Gavel: A Paradigm Shift in Global Criminal Justice* serves as a tribute to Professor K. Chockalingam's contributions to this ever-evolving field. The book examines modern justice systems through analysis of four central themes, which include criminal justice alongside criminology and victimology and criminal law. The criminal justice system navigates an evolving environment while managing pressing matters which consist of cybercrimes alongside transnational cases and human rights protections. The delivery of justice demands that organizations achieve harmony between police operations, prison rehabilitation, and societal fairness principles. Through his research, Professor Chockalingam advocates for a flexible legal infrastructure that combines restorative justice practices with alternative dispute resolution and technological improvements for security forces, whereas criminology acts as an academic field that focuses on examining both criminal behavioral origins and their manifestation patterns. The research volume demonstrates the relevance of mixing academic disciplines for both crime control strategies and public policy development. The book examines new tendencies by analyzing how digital environments affect illegal actions. Victimology works to increase victim voices in criminal matters and protect those rights independently. The book addresses modern criminal challenges, starting with the effects of violence on offenders during globalization to victim services and crime-root-level analysis and fair trial complexities together with social and psychological victim effects, which highlight an urgent need for extensive legal victim defense services.

The evolution of criminal justice is a dynamic process shaped by legal reforms, societal changes, and technological advancements. *Beyond the Gavel: A Paradigm Shift in Global Criminal Justice* serves as a tribute to Professor K. Chockalingam's contributions in the field of Criminology. Through the exploration of four key themes—criminal justice, criminology, victimology, and criminal law—this volume provides critical insights into the challenges and transformations shaping modern justice systems. The criminal justice system operates in a rapidly changing landscape, addressing complex issues such as cybercrime, transnational offenses, and human rights concerns. Ensuring justice requires a balance between law enforcement, rehabilitation, and social equity. This volume highlights the importance of interdisciplinary approaches in crime prevention and policymaking. It explores emerging trends, including the role of digital spaces in shaping criminal activities. Victimology focuses on amplifying the voices of crime victims and advocating for their rights.

References

Bahna M (2022) https://pitjournal.unc.edu/2023/03/22/impacts-of-restorative-justice-on-recidivism/
Bonta J, Jesseman R, Rugge T, Cormier R (2006) Restorative justice and recidivism: promises made, promises kept? In: Sullivan D, Tifft L (eds) Handbook of restorative justice. Routledge
United Nations (1985) Declaration of basic principles of justice for victims of crime and abuse of power. United Nations General Assembly

Criminology: Unveiling the Mechanisms of Deviance

Food Fraud from a Victimological Perspective: Financial, Health, and Ethical Implications

Pamela Kerschke-Risch

Abstract Food crime is a global and pervasive problem that harms consumers in many ways. The aim of the article is firstly to illustrate the impact food fraud can have. Secondly, demands for an adequate visualization of the victims are substantiated. However, criminology and victimology have only recently begun to deal with these effects. Using various examples of fraud, the financial, health, and ethical consequences for those affected are presented and discussed against the background of victimological issues. Of particular relevance here is the universal human right to food (see United Nations, Article 11 of the International Covenant on Economic, Social and Cultural Rights [ICESCR], 1999) which explicitly formulates the demand for food that also takes into account non-nutrient-based requirements in ethical or ideological terms. It also discusses why there is hardly any public awareness of the problem of food fraud and why the damage can hardly be quantified in monetary terms. It calls for those affected by serious food fraud to be given help in the form of victims' assistance and for their status as victims to be recognized.

Keywords Food fraud · Victim assistance · Human rights · Recognition of victim status · Moral convictions · Justice

1 Introduction

"Food should be safe for human consumption and free from adverse substances" (OHCHR & FAO, 2010: p. 3). And: "Cultural or consumer acceptability implies the need also to take into account, as far as possible, perceived non-nutrient-based values attached to food and food consumption and informed consumer concerns regarding the nature of accessible food supplies" (United Nations 1999, p. 4). The

P. Kerschke-Risch (✉)
Faculty of Business, Economics and Social Sciences, University of Hamburg, Hamburg, Germany
e-mail: pamela.kerschke-risch@uni-hamburg.de

© The Author(s), under exclusive license to Springer Nature Singapore Pte Ltd. 2026

G. S. Bajpai et al. (eds.), *Beyond the Gavel: A Paradigm Shift in Global Criminal Justice*, https://doi.org/10.1007/978-981-95-4487-5_2

UN's demands therefore state that, in addition to sufficient food, it should also satisfy individual cultural needs and moral beliefs as well as being safe. Or, to put it simply: People should be given the food that meets their individual needs.

But food fraud can violate these rights in numerous ways, as the following examples will illustrate. The aim of this article is to use various examples to show that offenses in the food sector can harm consumers in different ways. However, these harms are rarely obvious and unambiguous. The examples show that food fraud is an offense that can also compromise the goal of respecting personal values in relation to food as formulated in Article 11 of the International Covenant on Economic, Social and Cultural Rights (United Nations, 1999).

2 Food Fraud History

Food fraud has existed since people have been trading in food and is therefore not a new phenomenon (Hargin 1996; Visciano and Schirone 2021). In the past, due to a lack of technical possibilities, fraud was mostly limited to manipulating the weight or, for example, replacing expensive ingredients with cheaper ones (Meerza et al. 2020). Higher weights were also feigned by adding stones or lumps of lead to bales of tea or musk (Hart 1952, p. 5). As almost all foods at that time were unprocessed, such as whole grains or unground spices, there were fewer opportunities for fraud. Honey and olive oil, on the other hand, were and are adulterated more frequently, as fraud is less noticeable with these products. Nowadays, fraud is more sophisticated and more difficult to detect (Kennedy 2021).

As early as 300 BC fraud in specific types of food was prohibited (Hart 1952; Kennedy 2021), followed by further laws in the Middle Ages and subsequent centuries (Shears 2010). In the Middle Ages, bakers in Europe who adulterated bread were punished with sometimes draconian punishments (Kerschke-Risch 2016).

3 Consequences of Food Fraud

Nowadays, there are specific regulations and laws around the world that are intended to guarantee the safety of food for consumers. However, the problem today is that long supply chains and an unmanageable number of products can hardly be controlled effectively, especially in view of the fact that only a ridiculously small proportion of the sales price is spent on controls (Shears 2010).

It can be assumed that food fraud is a billion-dollar business (Yiannaka 2023) and occurs worldwide. As early as 2016, PWC estimated the financial damage worldwide at 30–40 billion dollars, while the EU Commission estimates the damage caused by economically motivated food fraud in Europe alone at 8–12 billion euros per year (European Commission 2020).

The consequences of food fraud can be of a financial (Harris 2004), health (Barnhoorn et al. 2015; Marchand et al. 2010), or ethical/moral nature (Gutman 1999; Clarke et al. 2008), although there can be overlaps. Food fraud is only committed for economic reasons; the perpetrators want to maximize their profits or avoid losses. The perpetrators consciously or unconsciously accept the possible harm to consumers associated with the fraud. However, harm is not the aim of the fraud, only personal gain.

It is therefore all the more surprising that food fraud has only come into the focus of criminology in recent years, although it is a worldwide and ubiquitous phenomenon that affects everyone (Kerschke-Risch 2016). Previous studies have mainly focused on the offenses and perpetrators, with consumer reactions only partially examined (for example, Yamoah and Yawson 2014). Victimological issues in connection with food fraud, on the other hand, have so far only been addressed sporadically (Levy and Kerschke-Risch 2020, 2022). This is all the more surprising as those affected are harmed in various ways, sometimes with serious health or even fatal consequences.

The following definition summarizes the most important aspects of food fraud:

> Food fraud is a collective term used to encompass the deliberate and intentional substitution, addition, tampering, or misrepresentation of food, food ingredients, or food packaging; or false or misleading statements made about a product for economic gain (Spink and Moyer 2011).

In this context, it is important to emphasize that although possible damage is accepted, it is not the aim of the fraud (Coleman 1987). The following examples are used to show how consumers can be harmed in financial, health and/or ethical terms. The questions arising in this context are discussed against the background of victimological considerations. This results in demands for greater awareness of food fraud and better protection for aggrieved consumers, as well as support for severely injured victims.

Consumers can only recognize fraud themselves in the rarest of cases. False designations of origin, substituted ingredients, unauthorized colorants and preservatives, pesticide, and antibiotic residues, or even allegedly organically produced food can only be detected through sometimes extremely complex analyses (Everstine et al. 2021). It is also important to be aware that only those substances can be found in analyses that are explicitly searched for and for which the technical testing options are available. This also applies, for example, to the DNA of other species, as in the horsemeat scandal. As long as there was no suspicion, products declared as beef were not tested for horsemeat (Kerschke-Risch 2017).

The following examples are used to illustrate the possible consequences for consumers:

4 Financial Consequences: Oil, Honey, and Fish

Financial losses are the most common direct consequences of food fraud (Harris 2004), but in most cases, those affected are not even aware of the fraud. Furthermore, these financial losses are usually only seen as "trivial matters" (Croall 2009, p. 128).

False indications of origin can primarily harm customers financially. Products from certain regions are sometimes considered to be of a higher quality than those from others, and accordingly, a higher price can be charged. One example of this is olive oil, which is generally considered to be very healthy (Guillaume et al. 2021). Italian olive oil from Tuscany is regarded as of particularly high quality and is sold at a correspondingly high price. For example, high-quality organic olive oil from Tuscany is sold to end consumers at prices ranging from 20 to more than 50 euros per liter (see, for example, Rovial Group Srl 2024). The wholesale price of conventional Italian extra virgin olive oil was on average 55% more expensive than Tunisian oil of the same category in November 2024 (Oleista.com 2024). Wholesale prices vary according to the origin of the oil, in addition to the quality. According to market data, it should be noted that the price of olive oil can vary considerably, but it can generally be assumed that organic oils are on average 20 to 30% more expensive than conventional oils (Ruggeri and Gambin 2024).

However, if this olive oil has a completely different origin, is mixed with olive oil from other Italian regions or even foreign oil, for example from Turkey or Tunisia, this supposedly Tuscan oil can be sold at a higher price than it is actually worth. Provided that the oil does not contain any harmful substances, customers are only harmed financially. If not only the designation of origin is incorrect, but the oil contains undeclared or even harmful substances, this can pose a health risk. Elderly and sick people, small children, pregnant women, or allergy sufferers can be particularly affected.

It should be noted that the financial loss suffered cannot be precisely quantified. For example, how high is the proportion of falsely declared oil? How should this oil be valued? While Tuscan oil costs around 7 euros a liter, the price for oil of the same quality from the Puglia region in Italy was only 5.85 euros (oliottaviani.com 2024). It is therefore difficult to determine the actual price for the respective oil components, which means that the difference to the sales price is unknown. In addition, it must also be taken into account that food is generally sold at different prices, regardless of whether it is counterfeit or of the best quality. This is another reason why possible losses cannot be precisely quantified.

This leads to the question of how the exact price and quality of a counterfeit product can be determined in contrast to a non-counterfeit product.

5 Honey

Honey was and is a product that is repeatedly counterfeited or adulterated. The fact that glucose is often added to honey was already mentioned by Ward (1952). It is difficult to detect impurities, additives or substitutes, for which special analytical methods and appropriate laboratories are required. For example, the European coordinated action "From the Hives" has found "that a significant part of honey imported into the EU is suspicious of not complying with the provisions of the "Honey Directive"" (European Commission 2023). In India, 77% of the honey samples tested in 2020 contained illegally added sugar syrup (CSE 2020). Honey, which is quite expensive and is said to have special health properties, is counterfeited particularly frequently, as the profit rates are very high. During the COVID-19 pandemic, for example, many Indians bought honey to strengthen their immune system. However, this supposedly particularly healthy honey was often mixed with cheap glucose syrup. Consumers were financially damaged because they paid too much for an inferior product. In countries where the average income is relatively low, the financial damage caused by food fraud is relatively more serious for individual consumers than in wealthy countries.

Counterfeit honey can cause damage in two ways: First, financially, as consumers pay too much for an inferior product, and secondly, in terms of health, as the beneficial effects of the honey are not or not fully given or may even harm consumers' health due to the high sugar content. However, irrespective of possible damage, fraud can erode consumer confidence in healthy and natural products.

6 Fish

Fish is regarded as a high-quality food, as it contains a high protein content as well as health-promoting substances such as omega-3 fatty acids. Global demand for fish, which is considered healthy, has risen continuously in recent years, with annual fish production reaching 200 million tons in 2021 (Ritchie and Roser 2021). However, this also has ecological consequences, such as overfishing, the use of trawl nets, which has a variety of negative consequences for the seabed and bycatch (turtles, dolphins, sharks, etc.). But the increasing importance of aquaculture also has negative consequences for the ecosystem. For example, animal welfare aspects are being disregarded, antibiotics are used, the water is overfertilized and mangrove forests are destroyed. Wild-caught fish, such as salmon, are generally more expensive and considered healthier than aquaculture fish. Certain types of fish are also more expensive than others, such as sole as opposed to plaice. However, fillets of these fish are almost indistinguishable, and restaurants often offer inferior fillets as high-quality sole fillets.

Silva et al. (2021) state that seafood is susceptible to a variety of fraudulent practices, including species substitution. False declarations of origin or the unauthorized use of the MSC label, which is supposed to guarantee sustainable fishing, are common practices.

7 Health Consequences: Oil, Milk, and Alcohol

The best-known cases of fraud in recent decades that have resulted in serious damage to health are the Spanish oil scandal or *Toxic Oil Syndrome* (TOS) in 1981 (Doeg 2005; Gelpi 2002) and the Chinese milk scandal in 2008 (Cheng 2012).

8 Oil

In the Spanish oil scandal, oil was sold by street vendors, mainly in areas with a poorer population. Around 100,000 people were affected by the scandal (Reuters 2021). After consuming this oil, a number of people fell ill, with the number of deaths ranging from 350 to 600. 25,000 more suffered serious and sometimes irreparable damage to their health and lifelong disabilities (Gelpi et al. 2002). To this day, it has not been clearly proven which harmful substances this oil contained that led to the outbreak of *Toxic Oil Syndrome*. The Spanish justice system and the authorities have often been accused of never having properly investigated the case. While this case aroused great interest from a scientific point of view and a search was made for the toxic substances that caused the disease, the perspective and situation of those affected from a victimological point of view have not yet been examined.

Those affected joined together in the victims' organization "*Seguimos viviendo*" to assert their rights. After a trial in 1989, in which only a few companies were sentenced to minor penalties, Carmen Cortés, the chairwoman of the victims' organization "*Seguimos viviendo*," told the press, "that the verdict was a disgrace" [...] "We were treated as second-class people in court. We were poisoned because we shopped where we shouldn't have. Even a high official blamed the victims: We had just bought cheap oil" (Macher 2019 /translated by the author). It should be noted that more than 40 years ago, the density of supermarkets in Spain was still very low, and it was therefore quite common to buy food at markets or from small traders.

9 Milk

In the Chinese milk scandal (2008), melamine was added to diluted milk for profit in order to simulate a higher protein content in analyses. However, if melamine is ingested with food, this can lead to kidney damage. 300,000 babies and toddlers who consumed this adulterated milk were affected; many became seriously ill and six babies died. The perpetrators were severely punished. In the understanding of a "just world" (Pemberton 2012; Lerner et al. 1966), the babies and toddlers are "innocent" victims, as they are not or cannot be responsible for the harm they have suffered.

10 Alcohol

Despite the dangers of addiction and health risks, alcohol is considered a legal stimulant in most countries around the world and is often part of the lifestyle. Muslim countries, on the other hand, restrict or even completely ban consumption for religious reasons. However, alcohol is taxed in almost all countries. In order to obtain cheap alcohol, it is sometimes distilled illegally, which can be dangerous to health if it contains methanol. Methanol has serious health effects that can lead to blindness and death, among other things. Illegally distilled alcohol repeatedly leads to serious poisoning, with poorer men in particular consuming it. Especially in Eastern European countries or Russia, poisoning by alcohol containing methanol occurs again and again. But even in Indian states such as Gujarat, where alcohol is banned, there are repeated tragic cases of poisoning with dozens of deaths and a number of people, some with serious health problems. In 2022, at least 36 people died from poisoned alcohol, and more than 50 people had to be hospitalized (Gupta and Mogul 2022).

However, consumers of illicitly distilled alcohol are not seen as innocent as babies or small children. They are not "ideal victims" in the sense of Nils Christie (1986), but can be seen as people who act responsibly. They can therefore be regarded as "guilty" in the sense of "victim blaming" because they did something forbidden. If untaxed alcohol is knowingly consumed, this is tax fraud, albeit on a small scale. If there is a ban on alcohol in a country, as is the case in many Muslim countries or some Indian states, for example, this is a violation of state laws and/or religious regulations.

Therefore, although it is not at all tolerable in such cases, it is understandable that the injured parties are not granted victim status. According to the logic of the country concerned, a reversal of blame can therefore take place. This can be illustrated by the example of victims who wanted to seek medical help with severe symptoms of poisoning but were denied it (Jones 2019). For humanitarian reasons, medical assistance must be provided to all people with life-threatening and serious health problems, regardless of whether or not they are at fault.

11 Evidence of Damage to Health?

It is relatively easy to prove health effects if, for example, there is bacterial contamination with Salmonella that leads to diarrhea. In such cases, the causal link can be proven directly if, for example, several people fall ill after eating food from a commercial kitchen, and Salmonella can be detected. The consequences are also clear in the case of allergic reactions to undeclared or incorrectly declared ingredients. On the other hand, it is difficult to clearly prove links between increased residues of pesticides or drug residues in animal products and health problems (Croall 2009).

The long-term effects of consuming contaminated food vary from person to person and depend on a wide range of individual factors. As no individual can trace back what he or she has eaten in the course of their life and what possible pollutants they have been exposed to through the food they have eaten, it is not possible to establish a clear link to possible health problems ex post. Similarly, it is not possible to prove that exposure to harmful substances occurred a long time ago, nor is it possible to establish a clear causal relationship between past or present consumption of products and health problems that will only occur in the future.

The example of honey adulterated with syrup shows how difficult it is to prove clear causal relationships. In contrast to serious poisoning, the effects of adulterated honey are less serious and not immediately detectable. Consumers were harmed, albeit not directly and seriously, in terms of their health. However, it should be emphasized that high sugar consumption can damage health in various ways. For example, sugar causes obesity and diabetes, but it can also weaken the immune system. Sunita Narain, the director general of the Center for Science and Environment, even feared that high sugar consumption could weaken the immune system during the COVID 19 pandemic (CSE 2020).

12 Ethical Consequences

In contrast to financial and health damage caused by food fraud, moral and ethical damage or damage to religious feelings is even more difficult to classify. When consumers buy food with a fake organic label for environmental and animal welfare reasons, they are harmed financially because organic products are more expensive. They are also harmed ethically, as these products have not been produced according to the criteria that are important to these consumers. This applies in particular to animal products.

If religious regulations are not observed and halal or kosher certificates are falsified, religious consumers are particularly harmed and can feel guilty. In December 2020, whistleblowing in Malaysia revealed that halal labels had been falsified for a long time, possibly even for four decades. Horse, kangaroo and pork were being sold as halal-certified meat to the predominantly Muslim population (Adam 2021). Here, too, the question arises as to how these damages should be assessed.

13 Why Has Little Attention Been Paid to Food Fraud in Criminology and Victimology to Date?

In this context, it is important to consider similarities and differences to other offenses. One reason is that offenses in the food sector are often not even noticed. Accordingly, those affected cannot feel that they have been cheated. In many cases, therefore, it may remain with unpleasant feelings, or these feelings are suppressed. The idea that something as essential to life as daily food could be hazardous to health would be disturbing, and therefore, most people do not want to admit or know this. This can be explained by the fact that there can hardly be any absolutely safe alternatives to counterfeit or adulterated food. This is not only due to increasingly complex international supply chains, but also to the fact that in modern societies, it is not at all possible to be 100% self-sufficient in food. Trust is a basic prerequisite in nutrition—but if this trust is shaken, consumers have only a few different options—either to relativize the dangers and think that the food will be okay, to buy other products or brands, to rely on government seals of approval or to avoid certain foods altogether. If someone has been harmed, he or she must be given justice, regardless of any co-responsibility that may be assigned to them by public opinion.

The main interest of criminology lies in mainstream crime. So-called "invisible" crime still remains irrelevant and receives only marginal attention. Less spectacular crimes, in which the victims are not as obviously harmed as is the case with violent crimes, are less likely to be heard. One reason for this is that the media have little interest in crimes where there are no clearly identifiable victims and where the perpetrators are unknown. An olive oil bottle with a false indication of origin is neither memorable nor spectacular. A couple sitting at dinner, for example, who have used this mislabeled oil for their meal will not arouse any sympathy. This also applies, for example, to guests in restaurants who consume falsely declared luxury products. The consequences of violent or street crime can easily be seen, whereas victims of food fraud are, in most cases invisible and uninteresting.

14 Victimological Aspects

Eating and drinking are the basic requirements for human life. One of the UN's goals is to ensure that all people have access to sufficient food and water of impeccable quality. If people acquire certain foods because of their religious, ethical, and moral beliefs or health needs, it must be ensured that they receive them (United Nations 1999).

In recent decades, the perspective on victimological issues has steadily broadened. This means that if people are harmed by food fraud, they must be recognized as victims. Victims have rights, regardless of the offense that caused them harm. There can be no good or bad, guilty, or innocent victims: All victims must have their status recognized.

The just world hypothesis can explain why people blame or sympathize with victims for the harm done to them (Lerner and Simmons 1966; Pederson and Ströwall 2013). Nevertheless, it is unusual to use the term victim in connection with affected consumers or offenses in the food sector, if there are no incidents with serious health consequences or even fatalities. In the media, the term victim is used in connection with food-related offenses with fatal consequences, as was the case with counterfeit alcohol or the Spanish Toxic Oil Syndrome, for example, The Guardian wrote on February 11, 2019: "Toxic alcohol 'laced with methanol' kills at least 99 people in India. Many *victims* in Uttar Pradesh and Uttarakhand left writhing in pain after consuming liquor." Therefore, it must be a victimological goal to make the suffering of those affected visible. And the victims of food-related offenses and defrauded consumers must be given a voice.

In addition to the severity of the damage suffered, it is important to consider the individual circumstances as well as the socioeconomic status: Some offenses primarily affect the poorest, as is the case with the Spanish Toxic Oil Syndrome or the again and again occurring poisoning of alcohol containing methanol. Therefore, victims' assistance is needed: For example, victims of adulterated alcohol have the right to appropriate treatment. This must of course also apply to marginalized groups or people in societies where alcohol is restricted or forbidden. Everyone has the human right to get help. Many serious food crimes affect the poor in particular. These crimes tend to affect socioeconomically disadvantaged groups of people who are also disadvantaged in other areas and hardly have a voice in public.

The oil scandal of 1981 is an exception. This case was reported in all the media, and public interest was very high, not only in Spain. This can probably be explained on the one hand by the large number of people affected and on the other by the serious and obvious damage. While those affected by the Spanish oil scandal have joined together in a victims' organization ("*Seguimos viviendo*"), the situation is different for victims of illegally distilled alcohol.

Although there are always deaths caused by alcohol containing methanol, the people affected here differ from other food fraud cases. Deliberately consuming illegally produced alcohol also means evading taxes, albeit on a small scale. In other words, those who drink this alcohol are acting unlawfully. In most cases, the consumers are adult men and not women or children, who would tend to be regarded as innocent victims in a just worldview. Whether it can be assumed that the consumers concerned are aware of the risk that illegally distilled alcohol generally represents a health hazard would have to be investigated on a case-by-case basis.

As home-distilled alcohol is primarily consumed by economically disadvantaged people, they often receive no, too late or inadequate medical help in the event of poisoning. It is particularly problematic when this alcohol is consumed in countries where there is a strict ban on alcohol. In these cases, those affected are not only breaking existing laws, but also violating religious rules, which makes them guilty per se according to the prevailing moral concept. As a result, they cannot be regarded as victims, let alone innocent victims, in the self-image of these countries. However, it must be borne in mind that alcohol is an addictive drug. Those affected often need the drug alcohol because of their addiction. While the economically better-off can easily buy the more expensive nontoxic alcohol, this is not the case for the poor.

Although toxic alcohol has a clear impact on health and consumption leads to serious long-term illness and death, those affected do not have a voice. These are mostly individual cases; there are no mass poisonings like the Spanish oil scandal or the Chinese milk scandal. As those affected usually have neither economic nor social capital, they cannot afford lawyers, mobilize the media or set up victims' organizations.

15 Conclusion

As the examples presented have shown, food fraud can have financial, environmental, and health consequences. However, these harms were not intended by the perpetrators, but tacitly accepted (Coleman 1987). From a victimological perspective, the question arises as to how these injuries should be viewed. Should we feel sorry for the couple at a candlelight dinner in an expensive restaurant, enjoying overpriced "sole," which in reality is just cheap fillet? What happens to consumers if they eat fish contaminated with heavy metals? What possible damage to health can this cause? What about particularly vulnerable groups, such as pregnant women or children?

But ethical and moral damage is also conceivable in the case of false indications of origin: Consumers who attach importance to regionality (for ecological reasons and support of the regions) can be shaken in their trust and also feel morally responsible if, for example, they have bought a special offer. Or they feel guilty if they find out that they have eaten products such as fish or seafood that do not meet their ecological and ethical standards. And, as Elliot states, "There is always the potential for food fraud to lead to severe illness, or in the worst case, death due to consumption of contaminated food or food that is not what it claims to be" (Elliot 2014, p. 12). Croall also points out, that: "while all consumers are at risk, the impact of consumer crime, like other forms of crime, reflects wider patterns of structural inequality and falls most severely on the most disadvantaged" (Croall 2009, p. 127).

What does it mean regarding victimhood? In the context of food fraud, it is not only important whether those affected see themselves as victims (Levy and Kerschke-Risch 2022), but also how they are perceived by the public. Everyone has a right to receive food that corresponds to their personal convictions. It must be guaranteed by the state or authorities that food complies with the declarations. Based on human rights, as outlined in Article 11 of the International Covenant on Economic, Social and Cultural Rights (United Nations 1999), all people must have the right to receive the food that meets their wishes and needs. In this context, different religious, moral, and ethical convictions must be taken into account. And the victims of food crime must be recognized as "real" victims, as the following quote makes clear.

Carmen Cortés, Chairwoman of the Victims' Organization "*Seguimos viviendo*" said:

> "What hurts us most is the lack of moral compensation. We want the same recognition that every victim gets in other cases" (Macher 2019/translated by the author).

References

Adam A (4 January 2021) How Malaysia's 'meat cartel' scandal unfolded: A timeline. malayamail. https://www.malaymail.com/news/malaysia/2021/01/04/how-malaysias-meat-cartel-scandal-unfolded-a-timeline/1937007

Barnhoorn IEJ, Van Dyk JC, Genthe B, Harding WR, Wagenaar GM, Bornman MS (2015) Organochlorine pesticide levels in Clarias gariepinus from polluted freshwater impoundments in South Africa and associated human health risks. Chemosphere 120:391–397

Cheng H (2012) Cheap capitalism. A sociological study of food crime in China. Br J Criminol 52:254–273

Christie N (1986) The ideal victim. In: Fattah EA (ed) From crime policy to victim policy. Reorienting the justice system. Macmillen Press, pp 17–30

Clarke N, Cloke P, Barnett C, Malpass A (2008) The spaces and ethics of organic food. J Rural Stud 24(3):219–230

Coleman JW (1987) Toward an integrated theory of white collar-crime. Am J Sociol 93(2):406–439

Croall H (2009) White collar crime, consumers and victimization. Crime Law Soc Chang 51(1):127–146. https://doi.org/10.1007/s10611-008-9147-z

CSE (Center for Science and Environment) (2020) Food Fraud. CSE. Retrieved December 10, 2024, from https://www.cseindia.org/food-fraud-10493

Doeg C (2005) Crisis Management in the Food and Drinks Industry. A practical approach, 2nd edn. Springer

Elliot C (July 2014) Elliott review into the integrity and assurance of food supply networks—final Report. A national food crime prevention framework. July 2014. His Majesty's Government. Retrieved December 10, 2024, from www.gov.uk/government/uploads/system/uploads/attachment_data/file/350726/elliot-review-final-reportjuly2014.pdf

European Commission, Knowledge Centre for Food Fraud and Quality (14 January 2020) Food Fraud. European Commission. Retrieved December 10, 2024, from https://knowledge4policy.ec.europa.eu/food-fraud-quality/topic/food-fraud_en

European Commission (2023) EU coordinated action "From the hives". Sampling, investigations and results. https://food.ec.europa.eu/document/download/eb8aaddd-0e2a-463a-bd3d-d7ba63375b78_en?filename=official-controls_food-fraud_2021-2_honey_report_euca.pdf

Everstine K, Hellberg RS, Sklare SA (2021) Introduction to food fraud. In: Hellberg RS, Everstine K, Sklare SA (eds) Food fraud: a global threat with public health and economic consequences. Academic Press, pp 1–7

Gelpí E, de la Paz MP, Terracini B, Abaitua I, de la Cámara AG, Kilbourne EM, Lahoz C, Nemery B, Philen RM, Soldevilla L, Tarkowski S, WHO/CISAT Scientific Committee for the Toxic Oil Syndrome. Centro de Investigación para el Síndrome del Aceite Tóxico (2002) The Spanish toxic oil syndrome 20 years after its onset: a multidisciplinary review of scientific knowledge. Environ Health Perspect 110(5):457–464. https://doi.org/10.1289/ehp.110-1240833

Guillaume C, Miller P, Cantrill R (2021) Fraud in fats and oil. In: Hellberg RS, Everstine K, Sklare SA (eds) Food fraud: a global threat with public health and economic consequences. Academic Press, pp 151–175

Gupta S, Mogul R (27 July 2022) Dozens dead after drinking bootleg alcohol in western India. CNN World. https://edition.cnn.com/2022/07/27/india/india-bootleg-alcohol-deaths-gujarat-intl-hnk/index.html

Gutman BN (1999) Ethical eating: applying the kosher food regulatory regime to organic food. Yale Law J 108(8):2351–2384

Hargin KD (1996) Authenticity issues in meat and meat products. Meat Sci 43:277–289

Harris L (2004) Hamburger hell. In: Leiss W, Powell DA (eds) Mad cows and mother's Milk: the perils of poor risk communication, 2nd edn. McGill-Queen's University Press, pp 77–98

Hart FL (1952) A history of the adulteration of food before 1906. Food Drug Cosmetic Law J 7(1):5–22

Jones A (6 Oct 2019) Methanol poisoning: Death by ignorance and taboo. BBC News 6. https://www.bbc.com/news/world-asia-46423180

Kennedy SP (2021) History of food fraud and mitigation requirements and standards. In: Hellberg RS, Everstine K, Sklare SA (eds) Food fraud: a global threat with public health and economic consequences. Academic Press, pp 9–22

Kerschke-Risch P (2016) The ideal victims? Consumers and economically motivated food fraud. ErnährungsUmschauInternational9:192–197.https://www.ernaehrungs-umschau.de/fileadmin/ErnaehrungsUmschau/pdfs/pdf_2016/09_16/EU09_2016_Special_Kerschke_Risch_en.pdf

Kerschke-Risch P (2017) The horsemeat scandal: the unknown victims of economically motivated crime. J Victimol 5:63–84

Lerner MJ, Simmons CH (1966) Observer's reaction to the "innocent victim": compassion or rejection? J Pers Soc Psychol 4(2):203–210

Levy I, Kerschke-Risch P (2022) Attitudes toward food fraud, food safety concerns, national culture, and self-labeling as a victim. Israel Aff 28(3):501–522. https://doi.org/10.1080/13537121.2022.2066868

Levy I, Kerschke-Risch P (2020) Attitudes toward food fraud in Israel and Germany. Br Food J 122(7):2219–2232. https://doi.org/10.1108/BFJ-10-2019-0785

Macher J (20 May 2019) Urteile im Prozess um vergiftetes Olivenöl in Spanien. Deutschlandfunk. https://www.deutschlandfunk.de/vor-30-jahren-urteile-im-prozess-um-vergiftetes-olivenoel-100.html

Marchand MJ, Pieterse GM, Barnhoorn IEJ (2010) Sperm motility and testicular histology as reproductive indicators of fish health of two feral fish species from a currently DDT sprayed area, South Africa. J Appl Ichthyol 26(5):707–714

Meerza SIA, Giannakas K, Yiannaka A (2020) Economic impacts of food fraud. Cornhusker Econ 1051

Office of the United Nations High Commissioner for Human Rights (OHCHR). (2010). The right to adequate food: Fact sheet No. 34. https://www.ohchr.org/sites/default/files/Documents/Publications/FactSheet34en.pdf

Oleista The olive oil trading marketplace (2024) Olive Oil Prices at Origin. Oleista. Retrieved November 29, 2024, from https://oleista.com/en/prices

Oliottaviani (17 May 2024) Prices of Extra Virgin Olive Oil in Italy in 2024: Trends, Changes and Forecasts. Oliottaviani. Retrieved December 10, 2024, from https://www.oliottaviani.com/en/blogs/news/prezzi-dellolio-extra-vergine-di-oliva-in-italia-nel-2024-tendenze-variazioni-e-previsioni

Pedersen SH, Strömwall LA (2013) Blame, sexism and just-world beliefs: a cross-cultural comparison. Psychiatry Psychol Law 20(6):932–941

Pemberton A (2012) Just world Victimology: revisiting Lerner in the study of victims of crime. In: Morosawa H, Dussich JJP, Kirchhoff GF (eds) Victimology and human security: new horizons. Wolf Legal Publishers

Reuters (19 October 2021) Fake olive oil scandal that caused Spain's worst food poisoning epidemic in 1981. Reuters. https://www.reuters.com/world/europe/fake-olive-oil-scandal-that-caused-spains-worst-food-poisoning-epidemic-1981-2021-10-19/

Ritchie H, Roser M (2021) Fish and Overfishing. How are fish stocks changing across the world? How much is overfished? Our World in Data. Retrieved December 10, 2024, from https://ourworldindata.org/fish-and-overfishing

Rovial Group Srl (2024) Extra Virgin Olive Oil Bio. Rovial Group Srl. Retrieved November 29, 2024, from https://www.oliveoilsitaly.com/extra-virgin-oil/extra-virgin-olive-oil-bio-franci-500ml.html

Ruggeri R, Gambin E (2024) Here is the estimated average price for olive oil 2024/2025. Developed using a "linear regression statistical model". OlivoNews. Retrieved December 10, 2024, from https://olivonews.it/en/here-is-the-estimated-average-price-for-olive-oil-2024-2025

Silva AJ, Hellberg RS, Hanner RH (2021) Seafood. In: Hellberg RS, Everstine K, Sklare SA (eds) Food fraud: a global threat with public health and economic consequences. Academic Press, pp 109–137

Shears P (2010) Food fraud—a current issue but an old problem. Br Food J 112(2):198–213

Spink J, Moyer DC (2011) Defining the public health threat of food fraud. J Food Sci 76(9):R157–R163

The Guardian (11 Feb 2019) Toxic alcohol 'laced with methanol' kills at least 99 people in India. The Guardian. https://www.theguardian.com/world/2019/feb/11/toxic-alcohol-methanol-india-uttar-pradesh-uttarakhand

United Nations Economic and Social Council. (1999). Substantive issues arising in the implementation of the International Covenant on Economic, Social, and Cultural Rights: General Comment 12 (Twentieth Session) The Right to Adequate Food (art. 11). https://documents.un.org/doc/undoc/gen/g99/420/12/pdf/g9942012.pdf

Visciano P, Schirone M (2021) Food frauds: global incidents and misleading situations. Trends Food Sci Technol 114:424–442

Yamoah FA, Yawson DE (2014) Assessing supermarket food shopper reaction to horsemeat scandal in the UK. Int Rev Manag Mark 4(29):98–107

Yiannaka A (2023) Food fraud: a persistent problem that demands a comprehensive approach. J Consum Prot Food Saf 18(4):359–360

The Trafficking Discourse: From Punitive to Rights-Based Approach

Dipa Dube and Ankita Chakraborty

Abstract This chapter explores the evolution of international responses to human trafficking, tracing the shift from punitive actions to a rights-based approach. Initially, international frameworks like the Suppression of Traffic in Persons and of the Exploitation of the Prostitution of Others, 1949, predominantly embraced an abolitionist stance, often conflating trafficking with consensual prostitution. Modern advancements are embodied in the Palermo Protocol, which, while prioritizing criminalization, recognizes trafficking as a human rights violation and stresses the importance of protecting victims alongside prosecuting offenders. The authors extend the discussion to India's specific legal responses to sex trafficking through the Immoral Traffic Prevention Act, 1956 (hereinafter, ITPA/PITA, 1956). However, the PITA, 1956, is criticized for its vague and often punitive measures toward sex workers, rather than offering genuine protection or rehabilitation for trafficking victims. The authors advocate for a nuanced understanding of sex trafficking that prioritizes the dignity and rights of the victims as a focal point of all credible actions. They recommend incorporating community-based rehabilitation and comprehensive victim support services that emphasize victim empowerment and integration rather than criminalization. This transition not only safeguards individual autonomy but also addresses the fundamental socio-economic causes driving sex trafficking. It promotes a holistic and empathetic approach to both prosecuting and preventing the crime, as well as protecting and rehabilitating the victims.

Keywords Sex trafficking • Abolitionist approach • Palermo Protocol • Criminalization • Community-based rehabilitation • Victim support services

D. Dube (✉)
RGSOIPL, IIT Kharagpur, Kharagpur, West Bengal, India

A. Chakraborty
Xavier Law School, St. Xavier's University, Kolkata, West Bengal, India

© The Author(s), under exclusive license to Springer Nature Singapore Pte Ltd. 2026
G. S. Bajpai et al. (eds.), *Beyond the Gavel: A Paradigm Shift in Global Criminal Justice*, https://doi.org/10.1007/978-981-95-4487-5_3

1 Introduction

Human trafficking stands as one of the gravest violations of human rights globally, intertwining complexities of unlawful migration, coerced labor, and sexual exploitation. This complex crime has evolved in its definition and recognition under international law, reflecting a broader understanding of its multifaceted nature and the various forms it takes. Since the late 1990s, concerted efforts by the international community have led to a clearer distinction of trafficking from other practices such as irregular migration and slavery, culminating in the adoption of the Palermo Protocol in 2000, under the aegis of the United Nations (Bryson Clark and Poucki 2018, pp. 10–11).

The turning point in the legal response to human trafficking emerged with the United Nations Convention on Transnational Organized Crime and its accompanying Palermo Protocol, which introduced a universally recognized definition. The protocol articulates trafficking through three core components: the act (the actions involved), the means (the methods employed), and the purpose (the intent behind it). This comprehensive framework emphasizes that trafficking can occur without the need for cross-border movement and highlights the exploitation of the victims as the core motive, irrespective of the victim's consent (UNHR 2014, pp. 3–4).

In South Asia, and particularly in India, trafficking remains a pervasive issue, deeply entwined with socio-economic inequalities and cultural attitudes. India, a major source and destination for trafficked persons, faces challenges exacerbated by its vast population and significant economic disparities. To combat trafficking and prosecute traffickers, India has made significant progress in aligning its domestic laws with international standards. This is evident in the enactment of the Immoral Traffic Prevention Act of 1956 and the recent amendments to sections 370 and 370A of the Indian Penal Code of 1860.

The ITPA of 1956 is organized into several key areas, such as defining crucial terms related to trafficking and prostitution, establishing punitive measures for those involved in running brothels or trafficking individuals for commercial sexual exploitation, outlining enforcement, institutional mechanisms, etc. The act does not aim to eradicate prostitution or eliminate sex workers/prostitutes; rather, it targets the commercial vice known as "traffic in women and girls for the purpose of prostitution." As a result, the act distinguishes between mere sexual gratification, which falls beyond the extent of the act, and the exploitation or abuse of individuals for commercial gain (Immoral Traffic Prevention Act 1956a, b, s.2(f)). Nevertheless, the act strongly opposes organized prostitution due to its inherent connection with the commercial aspects of trafficking (Bai Shanta v. State of Gujarat 1967). The underlying logic is that sexual engagement of a woman, by definition, is using or exploiting her. Prostitution is often viewed as an institution of coercion, construing women engaged in selling sex as "sex slaves" and victims of exploitation (IWRAW AP 2017, pp. 8–9). All early transnational conversations about prostitution embedded it in the language of "exploitation," hence requiring sex work abolitionism (IWRAW AP 2017, p. 10). To achieve this, ITPA (1956) limits the opportunities for women engaged in prostitution to interact with the public and entice them into sexual activities (Kataria and Saeed 2019). As the ITPA, 1956, stands today, although prostitution is not criminalized per se, activities surrounding it, like soliciting in the streets or engaging in prostitution in a public place, attract criminal sanctions. Hence, ITPA, 1956 ended up with a legislative ambiguity which conformed to standardized narratives delimiting the discursive field, prescribing an approach dominated by "overcriminalization" and "intensified policing" as the preferred strategies to combat the menace of trafficking (Vanwesenbeeck 2017, p. 1631). While criticizing the 1956 law, the authors highlight the urgent need for a revised approach that centers on the rights and rehabilitation of victims, aligning more closely with international human rights standards. They advocate for a victim-centered approach in enforcement strategies that extends beyond simple detention in the protection homes, incorporating comprehensive support services such as psychological counseling, legal aid, and vocational training to facilitate the effective re-integration of victims into society. They argue that for India to effectively enhance its efforts against sex trafficking and align its laws with international standards, it must balance prevention, protection, and prosecution while emphasizing the human rights aspects of the victims.

2 International Concerns Toward Human Trafficking

2.1 Historical Perspectives

The global concern about eradicating human trafficking dates back to 1949, when the first anti-trafficking document was drafted by the Commission on the Status of Women in 1946 under the United Nations Economic and Social Council (Women's Rights in India-An Analytical Study-The United Nations Convention on the Elimination of All Forms of Discrimination Against Women (CEDAW) and The Indian Constitution, Legislations, Schemes, Policies, and Judgments 2021 n.d., p. 18). Prior to the 1949 Convention, human trafficking was predominantly conceptualized through the lens of slavery and the slave trade. The key international instrument that defined slavery and the slave trade was the Slavery Convention of 1926 (Allain 2012, p. 28). Broadly speaking, the basis of the understanding had commonality with human trafficking in the sense that the idea was deep-rooted in ownership or control over another human being in such a manner wherein he/she was reduced to a mere commodity (Obokata 2006, p. 13).

Interestingly, the origins of the International Agreement for the Suppression of White Slave Traffic of 1904 and the International Convention for the Suppression of White Slave Traffic of 1910 can be linked with the concerns about venereal disease, rooted in Victorian paternalism during the late nineteenth century (Allain 2017, pp. 2–3). This era sought to regulate women, particularly in response to communicable diseases affecting troops involved in Europe's colonial endeavors. According to historian Judith Walkowitz, the genesis of the white slave traffic can be ascertained in the reaction of the Ladies National Association, founded in the United Kingdom in 1869 (Obokata 2006, p. 3). This organization campaigned for the repeal of the Contagious Diseases Act of the 1860s, asserting that it was unconstitutional, discriminatory, and fostered male immorality while subjecting women to humiliating internal examinations. The act was viewed as an effort to control women, with prostitution being "organized" and "regulated" to meet the needs of the colonial troops. In 1873, the International Medical Congress officially abolished the state-regulated brothels and prostitution (Obokata 2006, p. 13).

The International Agreement for the Suppression of White Slave Traffic of 1904 and the International Convention for the Suppression of White Slave Traffic of 1910 were designed to prevent the enslavement of White women in Europe for the purpose of prostitution (Obokata 2006, p. 13). The term "white slave," however, restricted the agreement's effectiveness by excluding women and girls of non-White races (Obokata 2006, p. 13). Thereafter, by the end of World War I, two other international agreements on trafficking were adopted under the aegis of the League of Nations, namely, the International Convention for the Suppression of Traffic in Women and Children, 1921 (International Convention for the Suppression of the Traffic in Women and Children 1921) and the International Convention for the Suppression of Traffic in Women of Full Age, 1933 (UN 1933). Under both of these instruments, prostitution and sexual exploitation were considered significant components of trafficking. The 1933 Convention distinguished between adult women and female children and departed from the earlier agreements by criminalizing "procurement" for prostitution, even if it was consensual (Coontz and Griebel 2004, p. 49). Keeping in mind the use of preferential language found in the former White slave traffic treaties, the new instruments abstained from repeating the same mistake.

Over time, all the documents were rendered ineffective (Obokata 2006, p. 16). This necessitated international action to both abolish brothels and prosecute and punish those who manage them (Obokata 2006, p. 16). Following World War II, work continued on the 1937 draft convention of the League of Nations, leading to the adoption of the Convention for the Suppression of Traffic in Persons and of the Exploitation of the Prostitution of Others in 1949 (Obokata 2006, p. 16). The Convention preserved an abolitionist approach toward human trafficking and fortified it to associate it with both consensual and nonconsensual prostitution (Gallagher 2001, p. 1002). However, the 1949 Convention did not hold victims of trafficking and prostitution criminally liable. Instead, it called on member states to penalize those who recruit, entice, or coerce others into prostitution (Marcovich n.d., p. 4). Correspondingly, it prohibited the state parties from regulating prostitution in any manner by either making it a legal practice or by imposing administrative control over it (Convention for the Suppression of the Traffic in Persons and of the Exploitation of the Prostitution of Others 1949). The Convention advocated penalty for those who "keep/manage/knowingly finance a brothel" or "knowingly lets or rents a building or other place/part thereof for such purpose, and imposes the burden of proof on the perpetrators of the crime" (Convention for the Suppression of the Traffic in Persons and of the Exploitation of the Prostitution of Others 1949, art.1 &

2). The 1949 Convention obligated ratifying states to adopt stringent measures to prevent trafficking while prioritizing the protection and rehabilitation of victims. This included provisions for repatriation for those who wished to return to their home countries (Convention for the Suppression of the Traffic in Persons and of the Exploitation of the Prostitution of Others 1949, art.16 & 19(2)).

However, the 1949 Convention was primarily criticized on the grounds that it failed to differentiate between consensual prostitution and trafficking (Birendra 2011, p. 483). The Convention assumed that the elimination of organized prostitution would terminate human trafficking, which in turn, reaffirmed the legal stance against all forms of prostitution, but did not take into account the numerous causes for which trafficking might take place, like forced labor, surrogacy, organ trading, etc. (Birendra 2011, p. 483). Additionally, even though the Convention urged state parties to suppress trafficking, it abstained from creating a monitoring system for the implementation and supervision of the principles laid down in the treaty (Obokata 2006, p. 17). The inherent ambiguity in the 1949 Convention weakened the purpose for which it was initially drafted and set the ground for other international instruments.

2.2 *Palermo Protocol*

In the late 1990s, the resurgence of trafficking as a pressing issue was driven by factors such as the global expansion of the sex industry, the forces of globalization, and the aftermath of the Soviet Union's collapse (Coontz and Griebel 2004, pp. 49–50). Concerns mounted over the transnational scope of the crime and its intricate connections to other organized criminal activities, such as money laundering, drug trafficking, arms smuggling, and the illegal trade of human organs (Coontz and Griebel 2004, pp. 49–50). In December 1998, the United Nations General Assembly formed an intergovernmental ad hoc committee, tasking it with the responsibility of creating a new international legal framework to combat transnational organized crime (Gallagher 2001, pp. 975–976). Following extensive deliberations involving more than 120 states, the committee finalized its efforts with the adoption of the Convention Against Transnational Organized Crime in 2000. This convention is supported by three additional protocols addressing the smuggling of migrants (UN 2000a), Trafficking in Persons-Especially Women and Children (UN 2000b), and Trafficking in Firearms (UN 2001). The 2000 Convention Against Transnational Organized Crime serves as the foundational agreement, with its provisions extending to three supplementary protocols collectively referred to as the Palermo Protocol. The 2000 Convention targets five key offenses perpetrated by individuals or corporations: participation in organized criminal groups, money laundering, corruption, obstruction of justice, and other forms of organized crime (Gallagher 2001, p. 978). Prior to the 2000 Convention, no other Convention provided a rigorous international retort to the dangers posed by transnational organized crimes (Fitzpatrick 2003, p. 1148).

The 2000 Protocol on Trafficking in Persons defines trafficking as the act of recruiting, transporting, transferring, harboring, or receiving individuals through coercion, fraud, deception, abuse of power, or other means, with the inherent purpose of exploitation (UN 2000b, art.3(a)). The protocol specifically addresses the "three Ps": prosecuting perpetrators, protecting victims, and preventing trafficking (UNODC n.d.-a). The protocol acknowledges trafficking victims as individuals subjected to human rights violations and calls on state parties to address their needs by providing care, support, relief, and repatriation. During the drafting of the protocol, numerous NGOs and intergovernmental organizations, including the United Nations High Commissioner for Refugees (UNHCR) and the Office of the United Nations High Commissioner for Human Rights (OHCHR), advocated for the protection of the human rights of trafficked individuals. Although the protocol emphasizes addressing the needs of trafficking victims, it is primarily a crime control measure focused on preventing and combating trafficking, rather than a human rights treaty. In crux, the protocol encourages member states to develop strategies aimed at tackling the root causes of trafficking as a preventive discourse (UNODC n.d.-b). In addition, member states are urged to carry out awareness campaigns, strengthen law enforcement capabilities, and implement measures to minimize vulnerabilities (UNODC n.d.-a, -b, p. 10). It is also emphasized that the internationally recognized human rights of trafficked individuals must be safeguarded, and the views and concerns of the victims should be properly represented throughout all stages of the criminal proceedings (UNHR 2000, art. 6(2)). The protocol mandates that the repatriation of a victim to their country of nationality must be voluntary when a state party seeks to return them (UNHR 2000, art. 8(2)).

While the UN Trafficking in Persons Protocol is relatively comprehensive, it has shortcomings from both feminist and human rights perspectives (Coontz and Griebel 2004, p. 52). It is argued that the pivot of the protocol is criminalization and not victim protection. While the articles addressing the criminal aspects of trafficking are framed in strong, binding language, imposing serious obligations on the states, those concerning the protection of trafficked victims are expressed in more advisory and nonbinding terms. "*In appropriate cases and to the extent possible under its domestic law*" the states are obligated to address the needs of trafficked victims by ensuring their physical and psychological well-being, providing care, support, suitable housing, victim protection, and assistance, among other measures (UNHR 2000, art. 6).

Another aspect of the protocol, which was controversial, was related to the question of whether consensual prostitution should essentially be viewed as forced, or should it be perceived as a legitimate occupational choice. The International Human Rights Network considers all forms of prostitution, whether voluntary or coerced, to be a violation of human rights. They argue that structural and economic inequalities often force women into the sex trade, particularly in many developing and transitioning economies (Fitzpatrick 2003, p. 1153). The Human Rights Caucus, however, contends that a distinction exists between forced prostitution and voluntary prostitution. They argued that by incorporating elements that negate consent in the definition of trafficking for adults, the trafficking protocol overlooks the existence of voluntary adult migrant sex work (Coontz and Griebel 2004, p. 51). The debate was ultimately resolved by agreeing that the phrase "consent of the victim shall be irrelevant" would prevent traffickers from avoiding conviction by claiming that the victim had given prior consent (UNHR 2000, art. 3(b)).

2.3 *Other Associated Conventions*

In between 1949 and 2000, the Convention on Elimination of All Forms of Discrimination against Women, 1979 (hereinafter, CEDAW), the UN Convention on the Rights of Child, 1989 (hereinafter CRC), and the Supplementary Convention on the Abolition of Slavery, Slave Trade and Institutions and Practices of Slavery, 1956 are of relevance. CEDAW, 1979, cautiously reinstated the abolitionist and protective language prevalent in the other Conventions with nondiscriminatory lingo. The drafters of CEDAW, 1979, view trafficking in women through the lens of sex discrimination and gender bias. By asserting that discriminatory practices against women are real and prevalent, the thirty articles outlined in CEDAW aim to secure equal rights for women. The Convention emphasizes prohibiting activities that discriminate based on sex, implicitly making trafficking in women a violation of their equality rights. The Convention explicitly urges state parties to adopt legislative and other appropriate measures to address trafficking in women and the exploitation of prostitution (Convention on Elimination of All Types of Discrimination Against Women 1979, art.6).

The CRC, 1989, emphasizes the need for special safeguards, care, and adequate legal protection to ensure the well-being of every child (UN 1989, Preamble). The Convention urges state parties to implement necessary measures to prevent the abduction, sale, and trafficking of children in any form or for any purpose (UN 1989, art.35). The optional protocol on the sale of children, child prostitution and child pornography complimenting CRC, explains the terminologies (UN 2002, art.2) and requires state parties to incorporate specific activities, such as sexual exploitation of children, organ transfer, forced labor, and child prostitution, into their penal laws (UN 2002, art.3). The 1989 protocol mandates that state parties must prohibit the sale of children, child prostitution, and child pornography (UN 2002, art.1) and emphasizes the need to support child victims of trafficking in their repatriation and social re-integration efforts (UN 2002, art.10). The Supplementary Convention on the Abolition of Slavery, Slave Trade, and Institutions and Practices of Slavery, 1956, condemns various slavery-like practices such as forced marriage and debt bondage. It further requires the state parties to enact legislation establishing a minimum legal age for marriage (Banode 2007, p. 10).

2.4 Regional Treaties

To combat the prevalent issue of trafficking in the South Asian region, Asia's first regional treaty addressing human trafficking was adopted in 2002. The SAARC Convention on Preventing and Combating Trafficking in Women and Children for Prostitution marked a significant step in increasing political awareness and promoting collaboration among South Asian nations to address and prevent trafficking (Jahan Farhana and Easin 2015, p. 69). Article 4 of the Convention emphasizes the need for state parties to establish procedures for the repatriation of trafficking victims and mandates that specific circumstances of trafficking be considered as aggravating factors (South Asian Association for Regional Cooperation, SAARC Convention on Preventing and Combating Trafficking in Women and Children for Prostitution, 1997, art.9). Aggravating factors outlined in the Convention include instances where the offender employs violence or weapons, participates in international criminal activities or organized crime, abuses a position of authority or trust, commits the offense within a custodial or educational institution, or when the victim is a child, among other circumstances (SAARC 1997, art.4).

It is crucial to acknowledge that human trafficking is not only a criminal offense but also a violation of human rights under international law, following an examination of the specific international instruments designed to combat it. Hence, state parties must address the issue within a criminal justice framework that prioritizes both the prosecution of offenders and the protection and rehabilitation of trafficked individuals, whose human rights have been profoundly violated. Article 28 of the Universal Declaration of Human Rights, 1948, asserts that everyone is entitled to a social order that ensures the full realization of the rights outlined in the Declaration (UN 1948). The act of trafficking violates multifarious rights mirrored in the Declaration including Article 1 which talks about equal freedom and dignity of all human beings, Article 2, which elaborates on the prohibition of discrimination, and Article 3, which maintains that every person is entitled to the basic right of life, liberty, and security. Alongside the core Declaration, the International Covenant on Civil and Political Rights, 1976, also upholds similar principles to ensure that the fundamental human rights of all individuals are respected. The Declaration prohibits practices that are linked with trafficking, like forced labor, slavery, and servitude (UN 1976a, art.8). The International Covenant on Economic, Social, and Cultural Rights, 1976, guarantees the right to both physical and mental health for all individuals (UN 1976a, b, art.12), and specifies that special measures should be taken to protect children and young people (UN 1976a, b, art. 10.3).

3 Inherent Contradictions Within the Global Anti-trafficking Discourse

The wave of international law and policy around trafficking reflects an international legal consensus. This consensus results from various, sometimes conflicting frameworks, in relation to the rights and protection of trafficking victims. For example, despite widespread acceptance of the definition of "trafficking" in the anti-trafficking protocol of 2000, its parameters are contested on grounds of criminal justice focus and fragile human rights protection for victims (Gallagher 2015). During the drafting of the Palermo Protocol, states involved in the negotiation process faced significant disagreements on various issues, eventually reaching consensus by adopting a complex definition (Gallagher 2015). However, while accepting the protocol's qualified victory, it would be unjust not to place the contrary views about the protocol's sparse and feeble human rights protection.

3.1 Criminal Justice Framework

The criminalization of human trafficking is the main approach adopted by countries globally, as political leaders view it as both a criminal act and a security concern (Farrell and Kane 2019, pp. 2–3). The international community collaborated to create an instrument that recognizes trafficking as a transnational crime, necessitating both criminalization and cross-border cooperation. Therefore, the Palermo Protocol primarily adopts a criminal justice approach to address trafficking, although many international scholars criticize the protocol for its limited and weak human rights protections (Gallagher 2015, p. 19). A criminal justice framework views trafficking as a crime issue involving malicious perpetrators who are part of transnational criminal networks and exploit vulnerable individuals (Farrell and Kane 2019, p. 71). It requires a strong national legal framework to serve as the foundation and support for an effective and appropriate criminal justice response (Gallagher and Holmes 2008, pp. 321–322). It is contended that criminalization of trafficking can either be achieved by passing a special legislation, or by amending the existing laws, especially the Penal Laws, so that all aspects of trafficking are dealt with as a crime (Gallagher and Holmes 2008, pp. 321–322). In fact, a robust legal framework to criminalize trafficking also addresses related crimes such as forced labor, forced marriage, illegal recruitment, debt bondage, involvement in international organized crime, and money laundering. The framework treats trafficking as a severe human rights violation, with traffickers employing methods that inflict serious physical, sexual, and psychological harm, as well as deprivation of liberty. A criminal justice approach to trafficking requires that sanctions be proportionate, effective, and deterrent. It also mandates mandatory minimum custodial sentences or, in extreme cases, provisions for capital punishment, depending on the severity of the crime.

There is broad agreement that a criminal justice response to human trafficking represents a significant advance by the anti-trafficking community. However, there is also a counterargument that the creation of such laws fails if criminal justice organizations do not implement institutional measures to enforce them (Pfeffer 2018, p. 4). Institutional and cultural changes are necessary to enable the identification of criminal behavior and the enforcement of laws against it (Pfeffer 2018, p. 4). When trafficking is approached solely from a criminal law perspective aimed at punishing perpetrators, victim protection is limited to the extent that victims are deemed relevant for law enforcement purposes only. Therefore, the ultimate goal should be to develop a victim-centered criminal justice response to trafficking, as standard protection mechanisms for victims and witnesses in criminal proceedings are insufficient to offer adequate protection for trafficked individuals. This idea contributed to a new framework concerning human trafficking.

3.2 Gendered Framework

A gender-sensitive approach to trafficking in persons assumes that most of the anti-trafficking interventions are not only gender-insensitive but are unsustainable and tend to reinforce the vulnerability of the trafficked persons. Such an approach defies the misconception that *"men migrate, but women are trafficked"* and recognizes the similarities and differences in the trafficking experiences of men, women, and children (D'Cunha n.d., p. 8). The approach considers that women are perceived as more likely to be victimized by the crime of trafficking; but public and policy conversations around trafficking should acknowledge that men, too, are trafficked. However, given the lack of information on trafficked men, it is difficult to apprehend what factors are considered in identifying and assisting trafficked men (*Beyond Borders: Exploring Links between Trafficking and Gender, GAATW Working Papers Series*, 2010, p. 10). The approach also highlights that focusing solely on women as "victims of trafficking" obscures the other roles women may play in the trafficking process, such as traffickers, recruitment agents, or exploiters who benefit from the exploitation (Beyond Borders: Exploring Links between Trafficking and Gender, GAATW Working Papers Series 2010, p. 10).

This approach views men, women, and children as different categories of victims with specific needs. Such an approach requires the adoption of a framework that responds to the tailored needs of these groups. The ongoing discussion between anti-trafficking and human rights advocates across different sectors highlights the need for a fundamental shift in the current rhetoric of the anti-trafficking movement, as its core objective (Chang and Kim 2007, p. 342). Advocates of a gender-sensitive anti-trafficking framework argue that the current framework often overlooks aspects related to trafficking, such as people's experiences with migration and work. As a result, trafficking has become disconnected from the broader social factors that are interconnected with it. It is viewed solely as a crime rather than as a complex social issue from both gender and human rights perspectives.

The framework also assumes that discrimination against women heightens their vulnerability to trafficking. However, an excessive focus on women's vulnerability, rather than on women's rights, can further worsen the situation. Anti-trafficking measures that further restrict the mobility of a woman are criticized on the grounds that they assume that a woman's vulnerability is an inherent part of being a woman, rather than the discriminatory context she is in. The core principles of the framework advocate for rethinking human trafficking within a broader context that includes human rights, women's rights, sexual and reproductive health rights, and labor migration rights (Chang and Kim 2007, p. 326). The minimum requirements of this framework include replacing law-enforced raids and rescues with community-based responses to support trafficking victims; addressing the underlying issues, such as class, race, ethnicity, caste, gender, sex, and sexual orientation; and rejecting the notion that trafficking is solely associated with sex, thereby focusing on issues like globalization, labor migration, and trafficking (Chang and Kim 2007, p. 343).

3.3 *Victim-Oriented Human-Rights Framework*

The development of a new legal framework to address human trafficking has been profoundly shaped by the growing importance and influence of international human rights law. This framework situates trafficking within a broader context and lays the groundwork for a cross-sectoral agreement to challenge conventional approaches to addressing human trafficking (Chang and Kim 2007, p. 319). Until recently, trafficking laws primarily focused on crime control rather than victims' rights. The small number of victims who were identified were seen as potential sources of information, and those who were not willing to help law enforcement were often prosecuted (Adams 2011, p. 202). Tackling the issue of trafficking requires adopting a rights-based approach grounded in a human rights perspective. Such a tactic identifies the specific rights of the right-holders (trafficked persons or victims at risk), their entitlements (compensation, after-care, rehabilitation, restoration, etc.), and corresponding responsibilities of the duty-bearers (states) (UNHR n.d., p. 9). In terms of realizing human rights, the state holds the primary responsibility for safeguarding and assisting trafficked individuals (Farrokhzad 2017, p. 133). This approach prioritizes the victims and the protection of their rights, differing from the criminal justice approach, which emphasizes punishing offenders (Adams 2011, p. 211). Here, the criminal measures are seen as a means to protect and uphold the rights of victims. A human-rights approach to trafficking asserts that trafficking victims should be provided with appropriate services such as counseling, medical aid, legal aid, victim compensation, repatriation services etc., firstly, because they are in dire need of those services, and secondly, since without adequate victim services, there is a high risk of getting re-trafficked (Adams 2011, p. 211).

A human-rights-based approach considers exploitation in human trafficking as a fundamental violation of an individual's human rights. Trafficking infringes upon various inalienable rights, including the rights to life, health, liberty, dignity, equality, and security. Key among these violations are the breaches of personal and physical dignity, the right to freedom and security, and the principle of nondiscrimination (Rijken 2009, p. 215). Within a human-rights framework, trafficking should not be narrowly defined as merely a migration issue, a public order challenge, or a problem of organized crime (Farrokhzad 2017, pp. 133–144). The emphasis should be on implementing a human-rights-based approach or mechanism to tackle trafficking, recognizing it as both a cause and an outcome of human rights violations. The 2010 Principles and Guidelines on Human Rights and Human Trafficking, prepared by the UN High Commissioner, outline the "human-rights approach to trafficking." This approach is described as a "means" to integrate anti-trafficking efforts with human rights responses. It ensures that at every stage of addressing the issue, laws, policies, practices, and measures are implemented with the needs of trafficked victims or those vulnerable to trafficking in mind (UN OHCHR 2010, p. 3). In fact, the principles emphasize the need for a soft-law framework to integrate a human-rights-based approach into all anti-trafficking interventions (UN OHCHR 2010, pp. 24–25).

Ideally speaking, this kind of approach is intrinsically integrated with a gender-responsive orientation of the trafficked victims.

4 Legal Response to Trafficking in India

The Indian legal framework on trafficking has evolved through two main strands of criminal law: the general criminal law under the Indian Penal Code (IPC), 1860, and specific legislation such as the Immoral Traffic Prevention Act (ITPA), 1956, which amended and renamed the Suppression of Immoral Traffic in Women and Girls Act, 1956. The Indian Penal Code 1860 contains several provisions which directly or indirectly deal with slavery, prostitution or illicit intercourse. The practice of habitual dealing in slaves is criminalized under sec.371 of the IPC 1860, wherein all acts of import, export, buying, selling, and trafficking of slaves are considered. Again, to curb forced prostitution, the Indian Penal Code, 1860, criminalizes procuration of a minor girl for illicit intercourse (sec. 366A IPC 1860), importation of a girl under 21 years from a foreign country for illicit intercourse (sec. 366B IPC 1860), selling or hiring a minor for the purpose of prostitution or illicit intercourse (sec-372 IPC 1860), and buying a minor for the purpose of prostitution or illicit intercourse (sec. 373 IPC 1860). Additionally, following the 2013 Amendment, sec.370 of the 1860 Code, encompasses the act of buying or disposing of any person for various kinds of exploitation, including physical exploitation, sexual exploitation, slavery or practices like slavery, organ removal, servitude etc. (Pai 2013; The Indian Penal Code 1860, sec. 370) in determining the offense of trafficking, the consent of the person is deemed irrelevant. Additionally, the section mandates enhanced punishment for repeat offenders, offenders who traffic multiple persons concurrently, and offenders who are in a position of power, like public servants or police officers. The new section furthermore differentiates between the trafficking of majors and minors by providing a separate penalty for each and a higher mandatory minimum for trafficking in minors.

Although the general criminal law contains provisions for penalizing trafficking, it is the special law enacted in response to India's commitment to the United Nations Convention for the Suppression of Traffic in Persons and of the Exploitation of Prostitution of Others, 1949, that raises significant questions.

In evaluating the Bill on Immoral Traffic in Women and Girls, the legislature focused on the essential issue of penalizing the sale and purchase of sex to combat prostitution. One group argued that prostitution involves a private transaction between two consenting parties (buyer and seller) and that the state should not intervene, especially without providing effective rehabilitation for prostitutes. Conversely, the other group contended that prostitution is a social evil that must be prevented and suppressed. Ultimately, the legislature clarified its position by ensuring that the scope of the Act aligns with the international principles outlined in the 1949 Convention. It was also noted that while prostitution itself is not penalized, the exploitation of prostitution of others is discouraged by preventing it from operating on a commercial scale (Gajendragadkar 1975, p. 9).

The Suppression of Immoral Traffic in Women and Girls Act (1956) (SITA) was enacted by the Parliament under Article 35 of the Indian Constitution with the aim of combating immoral trafficking in women and girls and prescribing penalties for such offenses. It was the first initiative of its kind in India to address trafficking. It aimed at the eradication of the evil of prostitution in India by penalizing activities incidental to sex work. It provided for the prevention of corrosion of public morals, rescue of the victims, punishment of the perpetrators, detaining a woman or girl for prostitution or living out of her earnings, etc.

However, SITA was found to be problematic on various grounds, which led to its first amendment in 1978, and thereafter, in 1986. The move was toward shifting the focus from suppression to prevention (Gangoli and Solanki 1996, pp. 3298–3299). Margaret Alva, while advocating for the amendment, noted that "several gaps and deficiencies were identified in the conceptualization of the Act." The aim of the amendment was to broaden its scope, introduce stricter penal provisions, and establish minimum standards for correctional treatment and rehabilitation (Gangoli and Solanki 1996, pp. 3298–3299). Additionally, there was a need to revise its outdated nomenclature. Thus, by Sec. 3 of the SITA (Amendment) Act, 1986 (Suppression of Immoral Traffic in Women and Girls (Amendment) Act 1956), the nomenclature of the Act was changed to the Immoral Traffic (Prevention) Act, 1956 (hereinafter ITPA) (Immoral Traffic Prevention Act 1956b).

4.1 The Immoral Traffic Prevention Act, 1956, and Its Anti-victim Stance

Under the present law, sex work has an ambiguous legal status. For example, consensual prostitution in a private place where exploitation of the "person of another" or "trafficking" is not involved is not considered illegal per se, but certain activities associated with street prostitution, like soliciting and/ or seducing in public, are considered illegal. Thus, open manifestation of prostitution is illegal, and women who solicit or practice prostitution may be penalized under secs. 7, 8, and 20 of the act. These sections are based on the principle that while women in prostitution should not be criminalized, once they are found soliciting, they must be removed from the area and provided with rehabilitative care. As a result, the act fails to recognize sex workers as "victims of trafficking" while addressing prostitution

(Kotiswaran 2001, p. 168). While the objective of ITPA is the elimination of commercial sex, it does not provide any guidelines for intervention or law enforcement, ultimately ending up criminalizing the victims. Kotiswaran argues that *"the unclear legislative intent of permitting sex work while prohibiting certain essential acts surrounding sexual gratification has given the police significant discretion, leading to rent-seeking behavior, including monetary and sexual bribes"*(Kotiswaran 2018, p. 3).

In the entire act, there is no definition of terms like "trafficking" or "trafficker" even though the title of the act refers to trafficking (Bhatty 2018, p. 19). While India is a signatory to the Protocol to Prevent Trafficking in Persons, which offers a clear definition of human trafficking, this definition has yet to be integrated into the national legislation (Immoral Traffic Prevention Act 1956a, b; Patel 2013, p. 181). The primary focus is on defining brothels and penalizing those who facilitate commercial sexual exploitation within them. Additionally, defining a brothel as a place for the mutual benefit of two prostitutes effectively criminalizes voluntary commercial sex workers, who then face prosecution (Birendra 2011, p. 56). There is also significant uncertainty about whether the offense pertains to engaging in prostitution itself or to trafficking for the purpose of prostitution (Bhatty 2018). This ambiguity leaves many offenders involved in the transportation and harboring of potential sex trafficking victims unaddressed (Bhatty 2018).

Ironically, in an attempt to deter prostitution and to protect society from the evils of prostitution, PITA bars a prostitute from working in public places and indirectly forces her to work in segregated areas of the city, subjecting her to live a criminal-like life under constant fear of arrest or removal from that place. While the motto of the Act was to prohibit trafficking in women, none of the provisions could be invoked for the said purpose. The 182nd Report on the Immoral Traffic (Prevention) Amendment Bill, 2006, by the Standing Committee on Human Resource Development (hereinafter the 2006 Committee), recommended adding a new section to define trafficking in persons (Standing Committee 182nd Report, Parliament of India, Rajya Sabha n.d.).

The act categorizes trafficking victims as offenders, requiring their detention in Protective Homes and Corrective Institutions. Based on her Action research, A.K. Jayasree asserts that *"the anti-trafficking interventions in India, including raid, rescue and rehabilitation efforts, either criminalize or victimize sex workers and that the Law enforcement agencies often misinterpret the ITPA or target sex workers rather than focusing on traffickers"* (Jayasree 2004, pp. 59–60). In fact, the term "corrective institution" too is a cruel irony based on the hypothetical immorality of the persons earning out of prostitution (Ram Prakash 2003, pp. 110–111).

The act considerably fails on grounds of human rights perspectives of the prostitutes. For example, section 20 of the act grants a magistrate the authority to order the removal of a prostitute from any area within their jurisdiction and to bar her from returning if it is deemed essential for the public interest. A prostitute so removed shall be sent to another jurisdiction within or without the local limits of the Magistrate who gave the order.

The constitutional validity of the section was challenged on the grounds of arbitrariness and unreasonable restriction. However, the Supreme Court ruled that the section did not grant the magistrate arbitrary power, as it was subject to revision under Sections 435 and 439 of the CrPC 1973, and it did not impose unreasonable restrictions on the rights of the prostitute (State of Uttar Pradesh v Kaushailya 1964). The court further added that in exercising this power, the magistrate must act judicially, taking into account factors such as whether the woman is engaged in prostitution and whether her removal from her current residence or frequented location is in the public interest. Additionally, there is a clear and evident distinction between a prostitute who poses a nuisance and one who does not.

Even after the judicial interpretation, the section stands problematic in the sense that, first, on the basis of a mere information, a person is evicted from a place and barred from reentering the same; and secondly, the merely because a person is a prostitute, it should not disentitle her from the basic right of residence in an area of her choice, and thirdly, there is no specific guideline to determine whether a prostitute is nuisance or not. Furthermore, the onus is placed on the woman to prove that she is not a prostitute. The provision is not only a form of surveillance but is callously framed and vaguely worded.

Additionally, multiple studies have shown that the sections of the ITPA, 1956, which were intended to target traffickers and exploiters are underutilized, while Section 8 of the ITPA, 1956, is gravely misused, leading to the arrest, prosecution, and conviction of victims for soliciting in public (Kotiswaran 2014; Patel 2013, p. 184). The act failed to address the fact that a person may be made to solicit under coercion, duress, or threat. In such cases, the section should target the perpetrators of the crime, such as procurers, agents, and pimps, rather than the victims themselves. A major law enforcement challenge that India must address is distinguishing between culpable traffickers and innocent victims (Patel 2013, p. 184). Biradavolu maintains that, regarding the ITPA, the Indian police hold both the legal authority and social power to enforce rules arbitrarily or selectively on sex workers, resulting in an imbalance within the current regulatory system (Rao Biradavolu et al. 2009, p. 1544).

Additionally, the act itself operates against a woman by targeting her family. For example: If a child is found with a woman practicing prostitution, the child is presumed to have been used for the purposes of prostitution and is arbitrarily removed from the custody of the mother during rescue operations. Similarly, if the disabled partner, old parent, or adult disabled child is dependent on the income of the prostitute for survival, it will be deemed that they have been living off the earnings of the prostitute, thus liable to prosecution. No distinction is made between "living off" the earnings and "on the" earnings of a prostitute, as also recommended by the 2006 Committee on its 182nd Report (Standing Committee 182nd Report, Parliament of India, Rajya Sabha n.d., p. 211). The Committee believed that while "legal safeguards should be established to prevent extortion of money from a prostitute, her right to voluntarily incur expenses should be subject to an exception clause" (Standing Committee 182nd Report, Parliament of India, Rajya Sabha n.d., p. 211).

The raid–rescue—rehabilitation model frequently falls short in addressing trafficking, often victimizing adult consenting sex workers by misclassifying them as offenders. This institutionalized model is fraught with flaws, including the violation of victims' rights, the inability to differentiate between trafficked individuals and consenting sex workers, and inadequate access to support services following raids (Bruxvoort 2013). The World Health Organization and the Global Coalition on Women and AIDS documented in their 2005 Informational Bulletin on violence against women that raids on sex establishments often result in violence against sex workers themselves. The Bulletin noted that in countries such as India and Indonesia, these raids and rescue operations have *"exacerbated violence against sex workers and compromised their safety"* (WHO n.d., p. 3). In 2011, the Supreme Court of India issued comprehensive recommendations to combat trafficking and support the rehabilitation of sex workers. One key suggestion was the creation of a *"community-based rehabilitation mechanism"* as an alternative to state-run or state-supported shelters (Budhadev Karmaskar v State of West Bengal 2011).

Additionally, section 17(2) of the ITPA, 1956, based on the presumption of lack of consent, permits a woman rescued during raid and rescue operations to be placed in the safe custody of her husband, parents, or guardians, subject to the magistrate's satisfaction regarding their background and suitability (Pai et al. 2018, p. 3). Sec-17(2) includes adult consenting sex workers who may have been living independently of parents and families. In other cases, the families might not be aware of their sex work at all, or they might belong to broken families, impossible to trace. If the reintegration process fails, the persons are detained in the Protective Homes or Corrective Institutions forever. Such arbitrary detention, without the consent of the victims, and with no consideration to rehabilitative aspects like counseling, legal aid, alternative livelihood, vocational training, etc., appears to be a medieval approach together. Even if the victims are released from the Protective Homes or Corrective Institutions after a specific period, with no means to sustain their rehabilitation and with no opportunity of alternative livelihood, they tend to fall back into the same loop from where they were earlier rescued.

In landmark cases like *Dr. Upendra Baxi v. State of Uttar Pradesh* (Dr. Upendra Baxi v. State of Uttar Pradesh 1983), *Vishal Jeet v. Union of India* (Vishal Jeet v. Union of India 1990), and *Gaurav Jain v. Union of India* (Gaurav Jain v. Union of India 1998), the Apex Court has consistently stressed the need for rehabilitating victims of commercial sexual exploitation, urging the Government to provide comprehensive care, protection, development, and treatment for their well-being. The court further directed the setup of a Central Advisory Committee in this regard and the appointment of trained personnel in rehabilitation Homes (Vishal Jeet v. Union of India 1990). In fact, the Central Government was instructed to rectify deficiencies in the laws, systems, and institutions addressing trafficking and to enact the necessary amendments (Vishal Jeet v. Union of India 1990).

Lastly, the rights of the victims have not been clearly defined under the law, nor have the protection nor the welfare measures. Even if some welfare measures are mentioned, they do not clarify how they adhere to the specific rights of the victims. None of the welfare measures talks about legal support, psychological well-being, health, educational support, vocational training, etc. In fact, rehabilitation in Protective Homes is not even a statutory requirement. After making an application under sec. 19, the magistrate shall consider the prospects of rehabilitation and other antecedents of the victims and cross-check everything through a probation officer before sending the persons to Protective Homes or Corrective Institutions, etc. Thus, there is an option to reject the application if the magistrate does not consider it necessary to send the applicant to a rehabilitative institution.

The act falls short in effectively preventing and addressing trafficking. The international mandate under the protocol (UN 2000b) which requires the member states to formulate strategies to address the root causes of trafficking and to prevent vulnerable persons from being trafficked have been totally ignored. The act does not talk about a holistic, multidisciplinary, and inter-agency approach giving space to an outreach so as to create a strong anti-trafficking networking scheme. To address trafficking effectively, it must be approached as an organized crime with far-reaching international implications.

5 The Way Ahead

The discourse on human trafficking has moved from a punitive approach toward a victim centric rights-based approach. While making way for stringent prosecution and penalization of the offenders engaged in recruiting, transporting, harboring, and exploiting persons for commercial sexual exploitation or associated evils, the law must make way for a robust victim response system based on respect for individual choice, autonomy, decriminalization and community support.

A rights-based approach to combating human trafficking places human rights at the core of prevention, protection, and prosecution efforts. While coercion, deception, and exploitation are common means used by traffickers to force victims into prostitution, it is crucial to acknowledge that voluntary engagement in sex work, free from coercion, should be decriminalized to uphold the rights and dignity of those who engage in it. Further, this approach acknowledges individual autonomy, while also addressing the vulnerabilities that may lead some individuals to engage in the trade due to socio-economic disparities or limited opportunities. In no situation, however, should the instrument of criminal law be utilized to sanitize the society of the vices of immorality pervaded through prostitution.

In addition to respecting individuals' autonomy, it is important to create a robust support and assistance mechanism for survivors of trafficking. A community-based-rehabilitation model can be adopted as an alternative to more institutionalized methods like protection homes or shelter homes, where victim survivors feel confined and trapped within the four walls, making their experience no different from brothels (Basu 2022, p. 852). Community-based rehabilitation models concentrate on holistic approaches involving governmental and non-governmental support to address survivors' needs and to ensure their access to public services

(Basu 2022, pp. 852–853). They prioritize civic rehabilitation along with psychological and medical support to ensure survivor rehabilitation.

It is therefore recommended that every district should have a Victim Support Services Unit (VSSU) as an integral part of a community-based rehabilitation program. The VSSU will be responsible for providing Rapid Response Comprehensive Support (RRCS) to victims rescued via raid-rescue interventions or otherwise.

Each VSSU should consist of specialized personnel like local NGO representatives, advocates, medical doctors, therapists, counselors, women support groups from the district, and such other persons required for smooth rehabilitation and reintegration of the victim survivors within the community. All members should have adequate experience, training, and sensitivity with regard to the special needs of the sex trafficked survivors. The VSSU shall facilitate rehabilitation and relief services for the victims, including victim compensation, re-integration, safety, care, protection, etc. of the victim survivors. The VSSU shall also engage in community-based initiatives to raise awareness about trafficking, challenge stigma and discrimination against survivors, and promote gender equality and social inclusion. By fostering a supportive and inclusive environment, the VSSU can contribute to creating protective environments that reduce individuals' vulnerability to exploitation.

After the victims are rescued via raid-rescue interventions or otherwise, the anti-trafficking units functioning at the district level should coordinate with the VSSU operating in that district for RRCS of the victims. The VSSU, along with AHTU and local police, will ensure that the person rescued is a victim of sex trafficking, before producing her to the Child Welfare Committee (CWC) in case the victim is a child or the magistrate, in case the victim is an adult.

The victim must be produced before the appropriate authority without any delay and within 24 h from the time of rescue.

According to the applicable laws, for cases involving children, the Child Welfare Committee shall, after determining the age of the rescued victim, issue an order for their care and protection. This decision should be made in consultation with the VSSU. The child's best interests should serve as the foremost guiding principle in all such cases. Where the child is placed with parents/family or where the child is to be kept away from home in community-managed rehabilitation centers, the VSSU, in coordination with the district AHTU, shall play a crucial role in conducting thorough risk assessments to ensure victim safety. The risk assessment reports (named as consolidated social assessment report) must be submitted with the district AHTU and magistrate in a timely manner. This shall include evaluation of the dangers of re-trafficking, victim manipulation, and assessment of the family's ability to provide a safe environment. The VSSU members shall continuously monitor the victim's well-being and facilitate services like legal aid, psychological counseling, vocational training, interim and final compensation etc., to ensure that the victims do not turn hostile or go missing during depositions in the court.

In case the victim is an adult, she should be given an option to exercise her choice. Where the woman prefers to be integrated into a community, the adult victim shall be placed in a safe community within the place of rescue through VSSU which will provide victim services including victims need assessment, referral to psychological counseling, medical treatment, legal representation, legal aid, assistance in accessing governmental schemes like Prajwala, assistance in applying for victim compensation through the District Legal Services Authority (DLSA), access to transitional housing (like one stop centers) for emergency accommodation (if needed), food, clothing, education, skill development, job training, and any other basic survival needs which will ensure safe and smooth transition of the victim survivors into the community. The NGO members placed with the VSSU should ensure the survivor's safety when moving a victim into community placement and continue with assessment and reassessment of survivor needs on a periodic basis. In case the adult victim wants to return to her own family (for example, the place from where she was trafficked), the VSSU working in that district shall effectively engage with the family, assess the possibilities of victim welfare, and assist her in the re-integration process. In case the victim faces economic and psychological challenges, the VSSU shall take efforts to keep her away from potentially exploitative situations. All VSSUs should have drop-in counseling centers that offer victim support and assess their social, economic, medical, and psychological needs. These centers should also maintain ongoing coordination with the district AHTU and local NGOs dedicated to the cause.

6 Concluding Remarks

Discussions on human trafficking for sexual exploitation have witnessed a notable transition from a punitive perspective to a rights-based approach. This shift signifies a nuanced understanding of the complexities involved, with greater focus on upholding the rights, dignity, and protection of victims. It is crucial as it recognizes the inherent humanity and agency of individuals affected by trafficking, while emphasizing the need for prevention, protection, and rehabilitation of victims.

The punitive approach, characterized by criminalization and victimization, often fails to adequately address the underlying issues driving human trafficking while further marginalizing and stigmatizing victims. Instead of offering support and protection, victims are frequently treated as criminals or commodities, subjected to detention, deportation, and re-traumatization. This approach not only undermines victims' rights and dignity but also hinders efforts to effectively combat trafficking by perpetuating fear and distrust within affected communities. International efforts have significantly advanced in recognizing and adopting a human rights-based approach. However, India needs to adopt a more human-centered approach that emphasizes empowering victims and recognizing their agency as rights holders, entitled to protection, support, and compassionate care. By transitioning from a focus on criminalization to one of protection, India can create a more equitable and compassionate approach to human trafficking—prioritizing human rights and driving impactful change at individual, community, and societal levels.

References

Adams C (2011) Re-trafficked victims: how a human rights approach can stop the cycle of re-victimization of sex trafficking victims. George Washington Int Law Rev 43(1):201–234
Allain J (2012) The international legal regime of slavery and human exploitation and its obfuscation by the term of art: "slavery-like practice". Esclavage et Travail Forcé 10:27–42
Allain J (2017) White slave traffic in international law. J Trafficking Human Exploitation 1:1–40
Bai Shanta v. State of Gujarat, 211 AIR ___ (High Court of Gujarat 1967)
Banode MM (2007) Legal framework against human trafficking. Int J Law Legal Jurisprudence Stud 2(4):1–20
Basu S (2022) A study on the rehabilitation mechanisms of the victims of trafficking with special focus on commercial sexual exploitation of women in West Bengal. Int J Creative Res Thoughts 10(5):849–857
Beyond Borders: Exploring Links between Trafficking and Gender (2010) GAATW Working Papers Series. https://www.gaatw.org/publications/WP_on_Gender.pdf
Bhatty K (2018) A review of the immoral traffic prevention act, 1956. Indian Police J 65(4):1–7
Birendra KG (2011) Trafficking and the law, 2nd edn, pp 1–515
Bruxvoort D (2013) Raids, rescues and rehabilitation: rethinking anti-trafficking interventions. Josef Korbel School of International Studies. https://encompass.eku.edu/cgi/viewcontent.cgi?article=1323&context=honors_theses
Bryson Clark J, Poucki S (2018) Human trafficking and modern-day slavery, 1st edn
Budhadev Karmaskar v State of West Bengal (Supreme Court 2011)
Chang G, Kim K (2007) Reconceptualizing approaches to human trafficking: new directions and perspectives from the field(s). Stanford J Civil Rights Civil Liberties 3(2):317–345
Convention for the Suppression of the Traffic in Persons and of the Exploitation of the Prostitution of Others (1949) UNHR. https://www.ohchr.org/en/instruments-mechanisms/instruments/convention-suppression-traffic-persons-and-exploitation
Convention on Elimination of All Types of Discrimination Against Women (U.N.T.S 1249) (1979)
Coontz P, Griebel C (2004) International approaches to human trafficking: the call for a gender-sensitive perspective in international law. Women's Health J 4:47–58
D'Cunha J (n.d.) Trafficking in persons: a gender and rights perspective, expert group meeting on "trafficking in women and girls" no. 2002. UN ORG. Retrieved May 7, 2023, from https://www.un.org/womenwatch/daw/egm/trafficking2002/reports/EP-DCunha.PDF
Dr. Upendra Baxi v. State of Uttar Pradesh, 2SCC 308 SCC ___ (Supreme Court 1983)
Farrell A, Kane B (2019) The Palgrave international handbook of human trafficking. Springer Nature
Farrokhzad A (2017) Human trafficking: a human rights oriented approach. Int Law Res 6(1):132–137. https://doi.org/10.5539/ilr.v6n1p132
Fitzpatrick J (2003) Trafficking and a human rights violation: the complex intersection of legal frameworks for conceptualizing and combating trafficking. Mich J Int Law 24(4):1143–1165
Gajendragadkar PB (1975) 64th Law Commission of India Report. https://opac.svpnpa.gov.in/cgi-bin/koha/opac-detail.pl?biblionumber=15348
Gallagher A (2001) Human rights and the new UN protocols on trafficking and migrant smuggling: a preliminary analysis. Hum Rights Q 23(4):975–1004
Gallagher AT (2015) Two cheers for the trafficking protocol. Anti Trafficking Rev 4:14–32
Gallagher A, Holmes P (2008) Developing an effective criminal justice response to human trafficking. Int Criminal Justice Rev 18(3):318–343
Gangoli G, Solanki G (1996) The official discourse around PITA. Econ Polit Wkly 31(51):3298–3300
Gaurav Jain v. Union of India, 2848 A.I.R ___ (Supreme Court 1998)
Immoral Traffic Prevention Act, Pub. L. No. No. 104, Acts of Parliament (1956a)
Immoral Traffic Prevention Act, Pub. L. No. 104, 104 (1956b)

International Convention for the Suppression of the Traffic in Women and Children (9 L.N.T.S. 415) (1921). https://www.whatconvention.org/en/convention/307#:~:text=The%20High%20Contracting%20Parties%20agree%20to%20take%20all%20measures%20to,Convention%20of%204%20May%201910
IWRAW AP (2017) Framework on Rights of Sex Workers and CEDAW. www.iwraw-ap.org
Jahan Farhana R, Easin M (2015) SAARC trafficking convention and human trafficking crisis in Bangladesh: a critical appraisal. IOSR J Humanities Soc Sci 20(12):67–73
Jayasree AK (2004) Searching for justice for body & self in a coercive environment: sex work in Kerala, India. Reprod Health Matter 12(23):58–67. https://doi.org/10.1016/s0968-8080(04)23111-1
Kataria R, Saeed M (2019) Law relating to prevention of immoral traffic in India, 3rd edn
Kotiswaran P (2001) Preparing for civil disobedience: Indian sex workers and the law. Boston College Third World Law J 21(2):161–242
Kotiswaran P (2014) Beyond the allures of criminalization: rethinking the regulation of sex work in India. Criminol Criminal Just Sage 14(5):1–16
Kotiswaran P (2018) How did we get here? Or a short history of the 2018 trafficking bill. Econ Polit Wkly 53(29):1–10
Marcovich M (n.d.) Guide to the UN Convention of 2 December 1949. Nordic Model Now. Retrieved July 11, 2023, from chrome-extension://efaidnbmnnnibpcajpcglclefindmkaj/https://nordicmodelnow.org/wp-content/uploads/2020/05/attachment.pdf
Obokata T (2006) Trafficking of human beings from a human rights perspective: towards a holistic approach, 1st edn. Martinus Nijhoff Publishers. https://books.google.co.in/books?id=YWkUoiKOksUC&printsec=frontcover&source=gbs_ge_summary_r&cad=0#v=onepage&q&f=false
Pai A (2013) Section 370, Indian Penal Code Amendments and advocacy to prevent conflation of trafficking and sex work, 2013. http://sangram.org/resources/Amending-section-370-IPC-verma-commission-clarifies-intention-behind-legislation.pdf
Pai A, Seshu MS, Murthy L (2018) In its haste to rescue sex workers, anti-trafficking is increasing their vulnerability. Econ Polit Wkly 53(28):1–7
Patel R (2013) The trafficking of women in India: a four-dimensional analysis. Georgetown J Gender Law 14:159–187
Pfeffer R (2018) Reframing human trafficking: from a criminal justice problem to a social justice problem. J Fam Strengths 18(1):1–11. https://doi.org/10.58464/2168-670X.1391
Ram Prakash R (2003) Delinking prostitution: a look at India's immoral traffic prevention act. Canadian Women's Stud J 22(3/4):110–113
Rao Biradavolu M, Burris S, George A (2009) Can sex workers regulate police? Learning from an HIV prevention project for sex workers in southern India. Soc Sci Med 68(8):1541–1547. https://doi.org/10.1016/j.socscimed.2009.01.040
Rijken C (2009) A human rights based approach to trafficking in human beings. Brill 20(3):212–222
SAARC (1997) South Asian Association for Regional Cooperation, SAARC Convention on Preventing and Combating Trafficking in Women and Children for Prostitution. https://www.saarc-sec.org/index.php/resources/agreements-conventions/50-saarc-convention-on-preventing-and-combating-trafficking-in-women-and-children-for-prostitution/file#:~:text=The%20State%20Parties%20to%20the%20Convention%20shall%20establish%20protective%20homes,care%20facilities%20for%20the%20victims
Standing Committee 182nd Report, Parliament of India, Rajya Sabha (n.d.) Retrieved February 4, 2022, from chrome extension://efaidnbmnnnibpcajpcglclefindmkaj/https://prsindia.org/files/bills_acts/bills_parliament/2006/scr1167481607_standing_committee_report.pdf
State of Uttar Pradesh v Kaushailya, 416 AIR ___ (Supreme Court of India 1964)
Suppression of Immoral Traffic in Women and Girls (Amendment) Act, Pub. L. No. 104 (1956)
The Indian Penal Code, 1860, 45 (1860)
UN (11 October 1933) International convention for the suppression of traffic in women of full age. United Nations Treaty Collection. https://treaties.un.org/Pages/ViewDetails.aspx?src=TREATY&mtdsg_no=VII-5&chapter=7&clang=_en

UN (1948) Universal Declaration of Human Rights, (A/RES/217A)
UN (1976a) International Covenant on Civil and Political Rights (A/RES/ 2200A (XXI))
UN (1976b) International Covenant on Economic, Social and Cultural Rights (A/RES/ 2200A (XXI))
UN (1989) United Nations Convention on Rights of Child (U.N.T.S 1577)
UN (12 December 2000a) Protocol Against the Smuggling of Migrants by Land, Sea and Air, Supplementing the United Nations Convention Against Transnational Organized Crime. chrome-extension://efaidnbmnnnibpcajpcglclefindmkaj/https://www.unodc.org/documents/middleeastandnorthafrica/smuggling-migrants/SoM_Protocol_English.pdf
UN (12 December 2000b) Protocol To Prevent, Suppress and Punish Trafficking in Persons Especially Women and Children, Supplementing The United Nations Convention Against Transnational Organized Crime. https://www.ohchr.org/en/instruments-mechanisms/instruments/protocol-prevent-suppress-and-punish-trafficking-persons
UN (11 July 2001) Protocol against the Illicit Manufacturing of and Trafficking in Firearms, Their Parts and Components and Ammunition, supplementing the United Nations Convention Against Transnational Organized Crime. chrome-extension://efaidnbmnnnibpcajpcglclefindmkaj/https://treaties.un.org/doc/source/recenttexts/18-12_c_e.pdf
UN (2002) United Nations Human Rights, Optional Protocol to the Convention on the Rights of the child on the sale of children, child prostitution and child pornography (A/RES/54/263)
UN OHCHR (2010) Recommended Principles And Guidelines On Human Rights And Human Trafficking Commentary. https://www.ohchr.org/Documents/Publications/Commentary_Human_Trafficking_en.pdf
UNHR (15 November 2000) Protocol to Prevent, Suppress and Punish Trafficking in Persons Especially Women and Children, supplementing the United Nations Convention against Transnational Organized Crime. https://www.ohchr.org/en/instruments-mechanisms/instruments/protocol-prevent-suppress-and-punish-trafficking-persons
UNHR (2014) Fact sheet no. 36, human rights and human trafficking. Office of the High Commissioner. https://www.ohchr.org/en/publications/fact-sheets/fact-sheet-no-36-human-rights-and-human-trafficking
UNHR (n.d.) Human Rights and Human Trafficking, Fact Sheet No. 36. https://www.ohchr.org/Documents/Publications/FS36_en.pdf
UNODC (n.d.-a) India: Government Ratifies Two UN Conventions Related to Transnational Organized Crime and Corruption. Retrieved February 8, 2022, from https://www.unodc.org/southasia/frontpage/2011/may/indian-govt-ratifies-two-un-conventions.html
UNODC (n.d.-b) Recommended principles and guidelines on human rights and human trafficking: Text presented to the Economic and Social Council as an addendum to the report of the United Nations. Retrieved November 23, 2023, from chrome-extension://efaidnbmnnnibpcajpcglclefindmkaj/https://www.ohchr.org/sites/default/files/Documents/Publications/Traffickingen.pdf
Vanwesenbeeck I (2017) Sex work criminalization is barking up the wrong tree. Arch Sex Behav 46(6):1631–1640
Vishal Jeet v. Union of India, 1412 A.I.R ___ (Supreme Court 1990)
WHO (n.d.) Violence Against Women and HIV/AIDS: Critical Intersections, Information Bulletin Series, Number 3. Retrieved January 4, 2023, from https://www.who.int/gender-equity-rights/knowledge/sexworkers.pdf?ua=1
Women's Rights in India-An Analytical Study-The United Nations Convention on the Elimination of All Forms of Discrimination Against Women (CEDAW) and The Indian Constitution, Legislations, Schemes, Policies, and Judgments 2021 (n.d.) National Human Rights Commission. Retrieved December 2, 2023, from https://nhrc.nic.in/sites/default/files/Women%E2%80%99s%20Rights%20in%20India%20complete_compressed.pdf

Criminal Justice: Navigating the Dynamic Landscape

Feminization of the Police Force in India: Evaluating the Access and Redressal in Cases of Sexual Violence Against Women

Upma Gautam, Deeksha Bajpai Tewari, and Priya Das

Abstract Indian criminal justice system has always been posed with complex implementation challenges about the substantive and procedural legal framework, wherein the interests of the survivors of sexual violence could be addressed in the best humanistic way possible. Despite several amendments in the Indian substantive and procedural penal laws in the last decade, the reality of increased incidents and proportionately low convictions remains unaltered.

In a study conducted by the authors in 2020, the role of socioeconomic correlates in understanding the legal policies for curbing sexual assaults against women in India was analyzed (Tewari & Gautam, *Vulnerability of women in contemporary times: A socio legal perspective*. 2020). The study revealed the positive role of improved monitoring and surveillance in curbing sexual assaults, and it was concluded that the number of police personnel per lakh of population and the number of police personnel per 100 km^2 impact the rates of rape in the country.

Against the backdrop of the aforesaid finding, the present study analyzes the impacts of the female police officers in the police force as well as women help desks in the rape case reporting thereby understanding and evaluating the access and responsiveness of criminal justice administration toward the incidents of sexual assaults. One of the biggest efforts to feminize police force in India were setting up

---

U. Gautam
University School of Law and Legal Studies(USLLS), Guru Gobind Singh Indraprastha University, New Delhi, India
e-mail: upma@ipu.ac.in

D. B. Tewari (✉)
Department of Geography, Dyal Singh College, University of Delhi, New Delhi, India
e-mail: deekshabajpai@dsc.du.ac.in

P. Das
Campus Law Centre, Faculty of Law, University of Delhi, Delhi, India

© The Author(s), under exclusive license to Springer Nature Singapore Pte Ltd. 2026
G. S. Bajpai et al. (eds.), *Beyond the Gavel: A Paradigm Shift in Global Criminal Justice*, https://doi.org/10.1007/978-981-95-4487-5_4

of Mahila Thanas in every district where women victims of violence can report incidents to women police officers. The study also evaluates the impact of establishment of all women police units (AWPUs) in states of India on the rape cases registered.

It is found that increased feminization of the police force improves the reporting of incidents of gendered sexual violence faced by women. This addresses the problem of underreporting of such crimes and paves a long way in reaffirming the faith in criminal justice administration.

Keywords Mahila Thana · Sexual violence · Socio-economic correlates · Female police officials · Women help desks

1 Introduction

The definition of "consent" in the provision of rape was included within the letter of the Indian Penal Code, 1860, post-2013 under section 375, Explanation 2, and the said definition remains unaltered in the newly enacted Bharatiya Nyaya Sanhita, 2023. Additionally, multiple changes were introduced post-2013 by amending the substantive and procedural law, wherein the legislature adopted a stringent approach toward the wrongdoer while filling up the gaps in the legal framework. The intent of the legislature was centered around the objective of making the legal framework and the resultant functioning of the state machinery more friendly and less biased while responding to the complainant/survivor of the sexual assault. But the judicial interpretation of the term "consent" in *Mahmood Farooqui v. State (Govt of NCT of Delhi) and Vikas Garg v. State of Haryana* are illustrative examples wherein the underlying objective and intention of the legislature behind defining the term "consent" was negated. The High Courts of Delhi, Punjab, and Haryana overlooked the reforms in the legal framework and reopened the entire discourse surrounding the concept of consent in sexual assaults. It was contended academically that the said judgment shifted the focus in its entirety from what women conveyed to what men understood. Apart from the courts, the police/investigating agency and the prosecutor play an instrumental role in maintaining the robustness of the legislative framework around sexual violence and the accompanying criminal process.

The first interface between the victim and the criminal justice machinery is the investigating agency/police, and the registration of offense forms an essential interaction between them. Police stations and police officers therein are perceived as a primary redressal agency by members of society and are approached at the very first instance for reporting any sexual aggression. The sensibilities of the police officers and their unbiased response are of utmost importance. If the investigating officer endorses myths around sexual assaults, the possibility of the victim being discouraged from reporting the matter and delayed progression of the investigation, even if the matter gets reported, cannot be denied (Garza and Franklin 2021). Further, in the backdrop of inherent discretions vested with the investigating officer during the investigation till the time of filling of the charge sheet as to the contents of the police report and the evidence filled therein, secondary victimization becomes a possibility if the police officer considers the victim "not so" ideal (Venema 2018).

The response of the investigating agency to the complaint determines the experience of the victim (Healy 2019; Kilcommins et al. 2018; Orth 2002; Campbell and Raja 1999; Campbell et al. 2001). It has been documented that more than often, the criminal justice system particularly the interaction with police leads to secondary victimization of the victim (Symonds 1975; Fattah 1997; Campbell et al. 2001; Koss 2000), which usually takes the form of lack of empathy, cooperation, slut shaming, victim blaming, and delayed investigation (Aborisade 2023) has a negative influence on the self-esteem, trust, and faith of the victim (Orth 2002).

1.1 Perception of Police and Non-registration of Offense

Secondary victimization at the hands of the investigating agency in most matters is shaped by the stereotypical sociocultural perception of "ideal" rape and "ideal" victim (Dellinger Page 2008; Page 2007, 2010). Police officers are often influenced by social stereotypes and rape myths in their perception of rape victims, resulting in a lackadaisical approach to registering the matters in cases of sexual aggression.

It has also been found that attributes and behavior of a victim such as nonconventional display of emotions while reporting the matter to a police officer impacts her credibility (Jordan 2004; Bachman 1998) thereby leading to non-registration of such incidents. The Hon'ble Supreme Court in *Lalita Kumari* set the mandate to mandatorily register an FIR in case of reporting of a cognizable offense. Further, the concept of zero FIR which now finds a place in Bharatiya Nagarik Suraksha Sanhita, 2023, under section 173 wherein irrespective of the jurisdiction the police have to register an FIR if the facts reveal the commission of the cognizable offense will surely have a positive impact wherein the non-reporting will decrease as the matters of sexual assaults will be registered irrespective whether such matters are falling within the jurisdiction of the police station or not. Non-registration of offense by the investigating agency silences the grievance of the victim and deprives them from accessing justice. Non-registration of offense also undermines the faith of the victim in the criminal justice system and deters other "prospective" victim from reporting the matter in the future.

1.2 Dark Figure of Sexual Offenses

The decision to report an offense is influenced by a combination of individual, social, situational, and structural barriers that cooperate with each other to create a mesh of resistance in reporting the offense (Hardy 2019). Research evidence suggests that faith in the police predominantly determines reporting (Soares 2004; Baumer 2002) while the confidence in police is shaped by the victim's prior experience with the police. Negative experience or receiving an insufficient response affects a victim's confidence in the police and reduces the likelihood of reporting another incident in the future (Aborisade 2023; Boateng 2018; Taylor and Gassner 2010; Kelly and Lovett 2009). It has been affirmed by studies that the satisfaction of the victim is dependent on procedural justice as well as the outcome of the criminal justice process (Tyler and Huo 2002; Lind and Tyler 1988). The perception of being deemed as culpable or held responsible for the incident disincentivizes reporting (Campbell 2014; Tarling and Morris 2010). Alternatively, incidents with "believable" characteristics are more likely to be reported to the police (Fisher et al. 2003).

The unreported cases (alternatively called as the "dark figure") of sexual violence in India constitutes 99.1% of the total sexual violence cases. It is pertinent to state that reporting of offense facilitates the visibility of the victim to the criminal justice machinery, which is essential for delivering justice and for policy considerations as well (Boateng 2016). A lesser gap between reported and actual cases also improves the accuracy of intelligence and policy and budget decisions (Baumer and Lauritsen 2010; Slocum et al. 2010; Terente et al. 2017). The reduced gap between actual and reported cases also indicates the people's faith in the legitimacy of the police and the criminal justice machinery's capacity to dispense justice (Tyler 2006; Sunshine and Tyler 2003). To further improve access to police stations and police services, the policymakers, in the backdrop of the findings of the studies (Nyul and Kende 2021; Fakunmoju et al. 2020; Johnson et al. 1997), have found that among the general population the acceptance of rape myths is lower among females than males; globally the number of female police officers within the police officers is proposed to be increased. Police reforms centered around a particular gender are proposed frequently in almost all legal systems for addressing the concern of non-reporting of gendered violence. In the Indian legal framework, the procedural law post-2013 provides for the recording of the information, as far as possible, by a female police officer. It is contended that the setting up of Mahila Thanas in states as well as establishing dedicated spaces for women help desks in the police stations encourages the reporting of sexual assaults thereby reducing the number of non-reported incidents of sexual violence.

Therefore, it becomes a vital query to investigate—whether feminization of the police force improves the numbers and consequently response to reported instances of sexual aggression. The present study, in the backdrop of the studies conducted on the endorsement of rape myths among police officers and its collateral impact on their responsiveness, statistically tests the following hypotheses:

Null hypothesis	Alternative hypothesis
There is no correlation between the Strength of the Woman Police Force and *Rape Cases Registered*	There is a significant correlation between the Strength of the Woman Police Force and the *Rape Cases Registered*
There is no correlation between *Total Number of Woman Police Stations* and *Rape Cases Registered*	There is a significant correlation between the *Total Number of Woman Police Stations* and *Rape Cases Registered*
There is no correlation between the Number of Police Stations with the *Women Help Desk* and the *Rape Cases Registered*	There is a significant correlation between the Number of Police Stations with the *Women Help Desk* and *Rape Cases Registered*

2 Review of Literature

Eliminating gender discrimination across the justice chain is critical for protecting women's economic assets, bodily integrity, voice, and agency (Duncan and Broadber 2015). There are gender gaps in access to justice worldwide. The factors contributing to the underreporting and underutilization of the criminal justice system are numerous and interconnected. These include the fear of male retaliation, social stigma, financial difficulties, and the potential negative consequences for children. Women may also perceive violence as a form of self-defense and believe that it is the responsibility of men to provide for and protect them. Moreover, law enforcement officials frequently display hostility or indifference toward complaints of gender-based violence, resulting in low arrest and conviction rates that erode public trust in the system (Amaral et al. 2021; Boesten 2012; Iyer et al. 2012). One concerted effort at addressing this global issue is the establishment of Women Police Stations, which have now become a relatively common feature in several countries, especially those situated in the global South. WPS are staffed with female officers specialized in handling crimes against women, and the station chief is typically a woman (Natarajan 2008).

Studies have been conducted to evaluate the functioning and efficiency of "Women—Police Stations" (WPS) or "All—Women Police Stations (AWPS)." They are described as "group-specific institutions" established on the assumption that by separating/segregating women from male—dominated spaces and patriarchal practices, their interests will be better served (Jassal 2020). In the case of WPS across the world, work done has brought forth the "paradox of separate spheres." On one hand, the idea of separate spheres, earlier used to reinforce gender norms and a gendered division of labor, has been reclaimed to create womenonly spaces to expand their choice and the space to speak and act freely, therefore being touted as the "backdoor to equality"; on the other hand, they've been seen as spaces that have deepened the gender divide by physically separating the two, hindering the professionalization of police women. The idea dates back to the late nineteenth century in the United States, where separate police stations called Women's Bureaus in American cities were created to accommodate victims of sexual violence and to engage women in the police force (Owings 1925; Schulz 2004). Women police stations in India were first opened in Kerala in 1973. The use of specialized police to deal with crimes of a sensitive nature, such as those committed against women have been recommended since the National Police Commission of 1977 (Natarajan 2008). Tamil Nadu introduced WPS in 1992, creating an exceptional density of WPS, with WPS constituting 40% of all police stations. There were 745 women police stations in India till 2022. WPS are headed by a female inspector, employ only female officers, and are tasked to primarily handle cases related to violence committed against women.

According to research from the Global North, the inclusion of female police officers can increase the likelihood of women seeking help from law enforcement (Meier and Crotty 2006; Riccucci et al. 2014). Studies suggest that the presence of policewomen in the force is connected to higher rates of arrests for sexual assault, particularly when they have front-line authority (Andrews and Johnston Miller 2013). Moreover, it has been found that women are more likely to report crimes to female police officers.

But, in a highly patriarchal, mostly in the Global South, such a direct association is not visible, and the interrelation is often very complicated. Studies have found that feminization of the police force does not improve sensitivity toward women's issues (Karim et al. 2018). It also does not improve the quality of policing, nor does the women police officers are any more ethical or reliable (Jassal 2021). There are also studies that reveal that more women in the police force and having separate spheres improve levels of professionalism in women police officers and have a positive impact on addressing women's issues. Also, an increasing number of women police personnel also positively impact women-related crimes, especially dowry deaths, domestic violence, and the number of rapes registered (Amaral et al. 2021; Natarajan 2005).

Over the years, different case studies on women police stations in different states of India have been undertaken to assess the efficiency, effectiveness, and drawbacks of "gendered policing model" adopted by India (Mukherjee 2022; Jassal 2020; Natarajan and Babu 2020). Such studies have brought out a bird's-eye view of ground reality, including various lacunae, bottlenecks, stereotypes that women police personnels and women police stations face. Detailed discussions with women police personnel reveal their efforts at sharing the double burden, both at home and police stations, their need for male police personnel for holding and arresting a male offender, etc. These empirical studies reveal that women police personnel believe that recently inducted women police officers should not be sent to WPS, for doing so will limit their experience to just crimes against women—related cases very early on in their careers and affect chances of professional progress in the future. They refer to these stations as "gender ghettos" serving as impediments in the mainstreaming and true inclusion of women in the police. These studies also bring forth effective suggestions for improving the efficiency of WPS. Suggestions include engaging women in mobile patrolling and other activities that require public—police interface to enhance the visibility of policewomen among the larger society. A critical point that all such studies reveal is that, due to the vastness of the area that the WPS caters to, it becomes difficult for victims/complainants to access them as they have to travel considerable distances to be able to do so. Thus, establishing one women's police station in each district is at best an insufficient step toward creating an atmosphere of ease of filing a complaint for women victims, the overarching argument in favor of establishing WPS.

Tamil Nadu is the state with the highest number of Women Police Stations in the country. In the year 2022, it constituted about 27% of the total women police stations in the country. In 1997, Tamil Nadu made use of labor law legislation to mandate the recruitment of 33% of women into the police force (Natarajan and Babu 2020). As a result, NCRB and BPR&D data confirm that the representation of women in the Tamil Nadu police increased from 5.7% (in 2000) to 12.9% (in 2017). At the same time, there was an increase in the number of WPS (from 58 in 2000 to

203 in 2017). A study (Natarajan 2006) using a qualitative, comparative study approach with standard questionnaires and personal interviews to comment on the working of all—women police units (AWPUs) in Tamil Nadu was undertaken. To assess the performance trajectory of all—women police units over a time period, three distinct years—1994, 2000, and 2003 were selected. The first AWPU opened in the "Thousand Lights" area of Madras on 13th April, 1992. Between then and 1994, the state managed to increase the number of AWPUs to 29. While studying AWPUs in the given year, the study focused on the perceived advantages and disadvantages of the units, reasons behind establishing them, nature of workload and the differences, if any, in the roles and responsibilities performed by women officers stationed there vis-a-vis those working at general stations.

Studies have been undertaken to understand the status of WPSs in India (Amaral et al. 2021). Impact of WPSs on incidence of violence against women, crime deterrence, proactive behavior toward violence and arrests made in response to VAW complaints. On comparing the many metropolitan cities across the country, it was found that cities having WPS in the vicinity reflected an improved rate of reporting of crimes committed against women as compared to those that lacked the same services in and around them. Generally, a 22% increase was observed in reported crime against women, following the opening of women police stations, and this increase has been considered a result of improvements in the reporting of cases of female kidnapping and domestic violence, in particular. Furthermore, a positive correlation has been drawn between enhanced willingness and the development of proactive behavior, enabling the reduction of violence against women, one of them being the increased likelihood of women to seek support from social networks and formal services.

During the latter part of the nineteenth century, the feminist movement in the United States called for separate spheres for women, which led to the establishment of institutions exclusively for women in a range of sectors, including healthcare, finance, politics, legal services, and education, in order to empower women (Craig 1994). In this period, the Women's Peace Party, which comprised only women, was considered to be more effective in voicing the policy preferences of women (Craig 1994). Similarly, Women's Bureaus—separate police stations in various American cities were believed to be highly effective in providing a secure environment for victims of sexual violence, while also encouraging the participation of female police officers in the force (Owings 1925; Schulz 2004). Countries in the Global South, such as Argentina, Nicaragua, Bolivia, Ecuador, Ghana, Kosovo, Sierra Leone, and the Philippines, have set up specialized police stations for women. These stations cater to female victims of violence, ensuring a safe and supportive environment staffed by policewomen, free from patriarchal attitudes (Perova and Reynolds 2017). Brazil has created hundreds of all-women police stations called *Delegacia de Defesa da Mulherbrings* (Jassal 2020).

The first women police station in Brazil, known as the "Delegacia da Mulher" (DDM), was established in the year 1985 as a specialized unit meant to investigate cases of crimes against women while being run entirely by women officials (Nelson 1996; Santos 2004). The DDM came to be due to the existing political state of affairs—that of redemocratization—which led to feminist groups and organizations demanding that violence against women to be treated as a crime, no longer being viewed as a private or normal issue. Similar to the WPS in India, DDMs in Brazil were proposed on the assumption that women police officers would "naturally" be better placed to and sensitive in dealing with instances of violence/crime against women, irrespective of their training and this separatist strategy faced the same critique as highlighted earlier. The 1980s saw the beginning of the emergence of a "feminist police" in Brazil. Over the years, the trajectory of WPSs in Brazil have shifted from being pro-feminist to anti-feminists to once again being pro-feminists changing with the approach of the heads of these WPSs. Perhaps a parallel can be drawn between attitude toward WPSs between 1990 and 1993 in Brazil (Santos 2004) and those made in Jassal's work (2020, 2021) since they both imply that instead of facilitating a more active role for women in the police, women police stations have, in fact, become mechanisms for sidelining them and, in a way, set them back. The year 1994 served as another watershed and saw the beginning of alliances between feminist organizations and the women police, yet again. This tradition was taken forward, between 1995 and 2001. This explains the complex and dynamic political relationships that tend to influence views on and the functioning of WPS in Brazil, and the effects of having policewomen work in tandem with feminist scholars and organizations.

Comparisons across the Latin American countries bring forth the complexities of understanding WPSs as "women only" enclaves or "segregated spaces" (Carrington et al. 2022; Jubb et al. 2006). In all of the four countries, the collective impact of feminist's movements and women's organizations; the coming about of a regional and global rights framework; and redemocratization processes was reflected in the creation of WPS. While in Brazil, Peru, and Nicaragua, WPS exist as specialized police stations, in Ecuador, they take the form of "justice administration entities" (Jubb et al. 2008). In terms of absolute numbers, each country is reported to have witnessed a considerable growth in the number of such units, between 1985 and 2010—475 in Brazil, 34 in Ecuador, 59 in Nicaragua, and 27 in Peru (Jubb et al. 2006).

Generally, it is the "essentialist assumption" behind the establishment of Women Police Stations that has been criticized in almost all cases (Jassal 2020, 2021; Nelson 1996; Santos 2004). This assumption that essentializes the difference between men and women is rooted in the belief that policewomen, being women, will "naturally" be better placed to sympathize and deal with female victims of violence. However, observations have debased and falsified the same. Being a woman doesn't automatically enable one to understand and be sympathetic to what makes the general population of women vulnerable to gender-based violence. What needs to be recognized is that the policewomen stationed at WPS are trained in the same space as their male counterparts, being subjected to similar patriarchal norms and conditions, albeit in ways that are either subtly or explicitly different, therefore making women equally likely to think within the confines of the same stereotypical notions that are found prevailing in male-dominated spaces. Instances of policewomen being apathetic and business—like while hearing out female victims' narratives; them considering some of the forms of violence against women, especially wife beating (in Haryana, UP, India), to be normal and therefore unworthy of registering cases against; believing such cases to have been made up by women out of spite; not treating them as "real crimes," all serve as evidence for and justification of the criticism that is leveled against the said assumption (Jassal 2020, 2021; Jubb et al. 2006; Natarajan and Babu 2020). Despite the common, collective criticism leveled against the aforesaid essentialism, the response to the creation of WPS in the backdrop of this assumption has been different between countries of the Global North and those of the Global South. While it has failed to hold ground and has been rejected in the United States and largely in the West too, it has shown to have considerable support and standing in the East (or, the Global South). This can be attributed to the cultural, social, and political differences between the two regions.

Finally, with respect to their functional efficiency and impact on violence against women, WPS have been found to have several shortcomings—deflection of cases of gendered violence from general stations to women police stations, forcing complainants to travel longer distances, entailing higher costs, thereby limiting their timely access to justice (Jassal 2020, 2021) and; a lack of resources such as toilet facilities, patrolling vehicles, etc. (Carrington et al. 2020, 2022; Natarajan and Babu 2020); the trend of choosing counseling and negotiation (with the intention of "saving" the marriage and family), over upholding women's right to protect themselves against violence and seek justice in the aftermath of the same (Jassal 2020, 2021; Jubb et al. 2006; Nelson 1996); serving as mechanisms for sidelining and setting policewomen back, professionally—the specialized and therefore limited roles and requirements of WPS are seen as hindrances in the path of gaining experience and consequent professional progress /promotion, which has also resulted in women officers regarding transfers to WPS as punishments or the end of their career (Jassal 2020, 2021; Mukherjee 2022; Natarajan and Babu 2020), and; their limited availability and vast jurisdictional area, which leads to the victim's access to such institutions and their services more difficult (Jassal 2021; Jubb et al. 2006; Mukherjee 2022). Further, lack of professional training and courses (on counseling and mediation) for policewomen stationed at these stations to help them unlearn their biases and enable them to act in support of the requirements of the victim, which also forces them to rely simply on the experience acquired by working on the said matters unaided, doing no real good in the process (Duncan and Broadber 2015; Natarajan and Babu 2020; Santos 2004; Schulz 2004), lacking national bodies to oversee and manage their functioning and having no integrated networks in place to ensure one-point availability of different services required by women survivors of violence (Duncan and Broadber 2015; Jubb et al. 2006). There have been studies that point out that they were also found to have no real or positive to very small impact on women's access to justice when studied in terms of changes in the number of registered cases, charges, and arrests made (Jassal 2020, 2021; Jubb et al. 2006).

The long list of deficiencies cannot overshadow the various positive impacts that WPSs have been able to generate. They've been found to have served as safe spaces for women to share their experiences, discuss them at length (Jassal 2021; Natarajan

2005). These institutions have been said to be playing the role of "surrogate panchayats," where women find sympathetic ears for venting their experiences to, as opposed to family and village panchayats primarily headed by males, giving decisions in favor of the man while instructing the concerned woman to adjust and not create disputes (Natarajan 2005; Natarajan and Babu 2020). A few select studies have also reported an increase in the number of cases being registered, thereby enhancing reporting of VAW and generating deterrence against similar acts (Amaral et al. 2021; Natarajan 2005). Finally, they've also been found to have played an effective role in expanding job opportunities for women and in enabling women gain power in society (Carrington et al. 2022; Santos 2004).

3 The Current Study

Gender-based violence (GBV) is a growing concern worldwide, with underreporting being a nearly universal issue. To address this problem, gender-targeted police reforms are often proposed to increase the accessibility and availability of police services to women. Two specific sets of reforms are proposed: first, increasing the presence of women in the police force and second, creating gender-segregated services, especially all-women police stations (*Mahila Thanas*). The first set derives their acceptance from the theories of representative bureaucracy, which espouse the importance of the presence of members of marginalized groups in the public agency so that citizens can view them favorably because they share their background characteristics (Dolan and Rosenbloom 2016; Miller and Keiser 2021). A demographically and socioculturally representative police force is seen as necessary. Studies on this approach have yielded mixed results, with some research showing an increase in reporting and arrests for sexual assaults due to the presence of female officers (García-Moreno et al. n.d.; Meier and Crotty 2006; Robinson et al. 2014) while others have found a lack of sensitivity among female officers toward victims due to the prevailing male-dominated police force culture or even blaming the victim for the incident (Jassal 2020; Wagner et al. 2017). The second approach relies on the perception of safe spaces being created through gender-segregated service provisions. It is predicated on the notion that women would feel more at ease in the absence of male police officers and, consequently, be more inclined to report instances of violence at all women's police stations. However, studies on this approach have produced inconclusive findings, ranging from female police officers experiencing reduced stress in environments free from patriarchal norms to a lackadaisical attitude toward recording cases of gender-based violence in mixed-gender police stations, which further exacerbates the marginalization of women and obstructs the reporting of such cases (Amaral et al. 2021; Carrington et al. 2022; Jassal 2020).

The current study evaluates two key approaches to gender-focused reforms in policing through data from reports published by the National Crime Research

Bureau (NCRB) and the Bureau of Police Research and Development (BPR&D). Specifically, the investigation assesses three interrelated aspects that are of great significance:

1. Role of increased representation of female officers in the police force in reporting the cases of sexual assaults.
2. Role of segregated police stations (women police stations) in reporting the cases of sexual assaults.
3. Role of the mainstreamed approach of establishing women help desks (WHD) in all gender police stations in reporting cases of sexual assaults.

Women's access to justice is to be understood expansively and comprehensively. Women face barriers and bottlenecks that extend from familial, and social pressures to administrative indifference (Iyer et al. 2012; Roychowdhury 2021). In cases of sexual assaults, reporting is replete with various bottlenecks, social stigma, family "honor" and consequent women's hesitancy is just one of them. Police administration is marred with severe resource and capacity constraints on one hand and is saddled with the existing patriarchal policing norms, and reported political interference which often results in police personnel promoting reconciliation to victims rather than making efforts for the protection of the rights of women (Mitra 2008).

4 Data Methods and Methodology

In this study, the impact of three significant gender-related reforms on policing in India, which aim to make the police force more responsive to gender issues, was assessed in terms of their influence on rape cases reported across Indian states. Specifically, the study endeavors to determine the extent of correlation between the number of women in the police force, the number of all-women police stations (Mahila Thanas), the number of women helpdesks (WHD) established in police stations across Indian states, and the number of rape cases reported in the country. The three aspects have been carefully selected, one relating to the feminization of the police force by increasing the number of women personnel in the police force, the second pertaining to the study of the impact of the creation of gender-segregated spaces in terms of all women police stations and third referring to study the impact of an amalgamative and mainstreamed approach of establishing women help desks in already established all gender police stations. This analysis intends to further elaborate on whether implementing the strategy of establishing at least one all-women police station in each district of the country or creating additional women help desks in already established police stations and further creating a network of reach to the women complainant is a more feasible solution for developing an effective and gender-sensitive police force in our country.

5 Results and Findings

The Pearson correlation analysis disclosed a strong, positive correlation between the actual strength of women's police and rape cases reported. This correlation was found to be statistically significant (r (34) = 0.57, $p < 0.001$). This suggests that there is a significant positive association between the feminization of the police force and reported cases of rape. This indicates that, typically, as the actual strength of women's police increases, rape cases reported also tend to increase, and vice versa. Therefore, an increased number of women in the police force could potentially lead to a reduction in the non-reporting of rape incidents in the country (Table 1).

The result of the correlation calculated between number of women helpdesks and number of rape cases reported showed that there was a high, positive correlation between the *Women Help Desk* and *Rape Cases Registered*. The correlation between *Women Help Desk* and *Rape Cases Registered* was statistically significant, $r(34) = 0.62, p = <0.001$. This means that, generally, as *Women Help Desk* increases, *Rape Cases Registered* also tend to increase and vice versa. This further strengthens the case for adopting a mainstreamed and inclusive approach toward building a gender-driven reform which makes space for women both the police officials as well as complainants and victims, within their structure. It also further paves the way for a more coexisting work environment, both for men and women police officials. The introduction of women helpdesks consists of the following: first, private spaces for women complainants within the police stations, adopting a standard procedure of registering cases and providing assistance to women visitors, and assigning a female officer to head the women helpdesk. Such an inclusive approach augers well for building a humane police force that addresses women's issues with much-needed dignity, diligence, and dedication.

The result of the Pearson correlation calculated between the total number of women police stations and the number of rape cases reported a low positive correlation coefficient which was not statistically significant, $r(34) = 0.2, p = 0.237$. Thus,

Table 1 Correlation matrix: Strength of women police, number of women helpdesks, number of all-women police stations and number of rape cases reported

	Actual strength of women police	Number of women helpdesks	Number of all-women police stations	Rape cases reported
Actual strength of women police	1	0.58[a]	0.61[a]	0.57[a]
Number of women helpdesks	0.58[a]	1	0.57[a]	0.62[a]
Number of all-women police stations	0.61[a]	0.57[a]	1	0.20
Rape cases reported	0.57[a]	0.62[a]	0.20	1

[a] Significant $p < 0.001$

the null hypothesis that there is no correlation between the total number of women police stations and the number of rape cases reported in the population is therefore not rejected. In an expansive country like India, where the average size of a district in a state ranges from 12,000 square kilometers in Andhra Pradesh, the largest in the country to 1300 square kilometers in Tripura, the smallest in the country, covering the physical distance to the nearest all-woman police station becomes an almost insurmountable task for any victim of sexual assault. In addition to the physical distance, the victim has to traverse an even higher social distance, which makes the ordeal multiple times tedious. In addition, the population range of a district in India ranges from 1123 lakhs in Maharashtra to about 6 lakhs in Sikkim (Explained: How the Number and Size of Districts Vary from State to State 2019). To enhance the efficacy of policing, a greater number of all-women police stations need to be established in each district. At the current status, the number of such police stations is severely inadequate both in terms of the distance to be covered to access them and the average population that each such police station has to serve. Also, such gender-segregated services and information about their location are difficult to access for the population in general, thus defeating the very purpose for which they are established. Instead of allocating separate structures for establishing all-women police stations, gender-inclusive, and sensitization of the police personnel may pave the way for building a society where concerns of women are concerns for all police force and not just the women police force.

6 Conclusions

The increased rate of crimes against women poses a severe security threat and either directly or directly hampers the social and economic growth of any civilized society. Police reforms and effective policing have always been considered as an effective means to create deterrence amongst the wrongdoers, thereby not only preventing the commission of such crimes but also decreasing recidivism. But, in cases of sexual assaults, the issues involved are multifarious, and among all policymakers face the challenge of dealing with unreported cases of such incidents on account of varied factors. Police stations in almost all countries are male-dominated spaces that have their role to play when the matter is about reporting of sexual assault. Apart from the attached social stigma, the possibility of secondary victimization by reporting the matter to the police is the prime bottleneck in controlling sexual violence against women. Globally, the police reforms are centered around improved female representation in the police force have proved to be an effective model whereby the reporting of such incidents has significantly increased. The improved access to justice and effective redressal mechanism post establishment of dedicated spaces for women help desks in every police station and all-women police stations in Indian states have also confirmed that improved models of policing in accordance with the typology of crime to be dealt with make a positive impact. It is to be further stated that stereotyped notions about "ideal" rape, "real" victim, and associated trauma are not gender specific, thereby meaning that gender sensitization and related regular training of even female officers are required. Regular training which reduces the harshness of the profession among female police officers, will collaterally equip them to deal with the victims of sexual assaults with empathy and will serve the needs of therapeutic justice.

References

Aborisade RA (2023) On the 'darkness of dark figure' of sexual crimes: survivors' rape reporting experiences with the Nigerian police. Int J Law Crime Justice 73:100576

Amaral S, Bhalotra S, Prakash N (2021) Gender, crime and punishment: evidence from women police stations in India. www.iza.org

Andrews R, Johnston Miller K (2013) Representative bureaucracy, gender, and policing: the case of domestic violence arrests in England. Public Adm 91(4):998–1014. https://doi.org/10.1111/padm.12002

Bachman R (1998) The factors related to rape reporting behavior and arrest. Crim Justice Behav 25:8–29

Baumer EP (2002) Neighborhood disadvantage and police notification by victims of violence. Criminology 40(3): 579–616. https://doi.org/10.1111/j.1745-9125.2002.tb00967.x.

Baumer EP, Lauritsen JL (2010) Reporting crime to the police 1973–2005: a multivariate analysis of the long term trends in the National Crime Survey (NCS) and National Victimization Survey (NCVS). Criminology 48(1):131–185

Boateng FD (2016) Crime reporting behavior: do attitudes toward the police matter? J Interpers Violence 17:432–456

Boateng FD (2018) Crime Reporting Behavior: Do Attitudes Toward the Police Matter? Journal of Interpersonal Violence, 33(18), 2891–2916. https://doi.org/10.1177/0886260516632356.

Boesten J (2012) The state and violence against women in Peru: intersecting inequalities and patriarchal rule. Soc Polit 19(3):361–382. https://doi.org/10.1093/sp/jxs011

Campbell R, Raja S (1999) Secondary victimization of rape victims: insights from mental health professionals who treat survivors of violence. Violence Vict 14:261–275

Campbell R, Wasco SM, Ahrens CE, Sefl T, Barnes HE (2001) Preventing the 'second rape': rape survivors' experience with community service providers. J Interpers Violence 16:1239–1259

Carrington K, Guala N, Victoria Puyol M, Sozzo M (2020) How Women's Police Stations Empower Women, Widen Access to Justice and Prevent Gender Violence. https://doi.org/10.3316/informit.125101787654007

Carrington K, Sozzo M, Ryan V, Rodgers J (2022) Women-led police stations: reimagining the policing of gender violence in the twenty-first century. Polic Soc 32(5):577–597. https://doi.org/10.1080/10439463.2021.1956925

Craig (1994) The Woman's Peace Party and Questions of Gender Separatism. Peace & Change 19 (4): 373–98.

Dellinger Page A (2008) Gateway to reform? Policy implications of police officers' attitudes toward rape. Am J Crim Just 33:44–58

Dolan J, Rosenbloom DH (2016) Representative bureaucracy: classic readings and continuing controversies. Routledge. https://doi.org/10.4324/9781315541471

Duncan B, Broadber T-A (2015) FPI-women's access to justice. www.unwomen.org

Explained: How the number and size of districts vary from state to state (16 August 2019). https://indianexpress.com/article/explained/how-the-number-and-size-of-districts-vary-from-state-to-state-5908798/

Fakunmoju SB, Gyan TA, Maphosa N, Gutura P (2020) Rape myth acceptance: gender and cross-National Comparisons across the United States, South Africa, Ghana and Nigeria. Sex Culture 25:18–38

Fattah EA (1997) Toward a victim policy aimed at healing, not suffering. In: Davis RC, Lurigio AJ, Skogan WG (eds) Victims of crime. Sage, Thousand Oaks, CA, pp 257–272

Fisher BS, Daigle LE, Cullen FT, Turner MG (2003) Reporting sexual victimization to the police and others: results from a National-level Study of college women. Crim Justice Behav 30(1)

García-Moreno C, World Health Organization, London School of Hygiene and Tropical Medicine, & South African Medical Research Council (n.d.) Global and regional estimates of violence against women : prevalence and health effects of intimate partner violence and non-partner sexual violence

Garza AD, Franklin CA (2021) The effect of rape myth endorsement on police response to sexual assault survivors. Violence Against Women 27(3–4):552–573. https://doi.org/10.1177/1077801220911460

Hardy SJ (2019) Layers of resistance: understanding decision-making processes in relation to crime reporting. Int Rev Victimol 25(3)

Healy D (2019) Exploring victim's interaction with the criminal justice system: a literature review. Department of Justice and Equality: Research and Data Analytics

Iyer L, Mani A, Mishra P, Topalova P (2012) The power of political voice: women's political representation and crime in India. Am Econ J Appl Econ 4(4):165–193. https://doi.org/10.1257/app.4.4.165

Jassal N (2020) Gender, law enforcement, and access to justice: evidence from all-women police stations in India. Am Polit Sci Rev 114(4):1035–1054. https://doi.org/10.1017/S0003055420000684

Jassal N (2021) Segregation as efficiency? Group-specific institutions in North India. In: Journal of Asian studies, vol 80(3). Cambridge University Press, pp 631–661. https://doi.org/10.1017/S0021911820004635

Johnson BE, Kuch DL, Schander PR (1997) Rape myth acceptance and socio-demographic characteristics: a multi-dimensional analysis. Sex Roles 36:693–707

Jordan J (2004) Beyond belief?: police, rape and women's credibility. Criminol Crim Just 4(1)

Jubb N, Camacho G, Angelo AD, De La Borda GY, Hernández K, León IM, Santos CM, Molina Y, Pasinato W (2006) Regional mapping study of women's police stations in Latin America. www.idrc.ca

Jubb N, Camacho G, D'Angelo A, Yanez De La Borda G, Hernandez K, Macassi Leon I, MacDowell Santos C, Molina Y, Pasinato W (2008) Regional Mapping Study of Women's Police Station in Latin America. Project: Access to Justice for Women in situations of violence: A Comparative study of Women's Police Station in Latin America.

Karim S, Gilligan MJ, Blair R, Beardsley K (2018) International gender balancing reforms in postconflict countries: lab-in-the-field evidence from the Liberian national police. Int Stud Q 62(3):618–631. https://doi.org/10.1093/isq/sqy009

Kelly L, Lovett J (2009) Different systems, similar outcomes? Tracking attrition in reported rape cases in eleven countries. University of North London, Child and Women Abuse Studies Unit, London

Kilcommins S, Leahy S, Spain E (2018) The victim in the Irish criminal process. Manchester University Press

Koss MP (2000) Blame, shame and community: justice responses to violence against women. Am J Psychoanal 55:1332–1343

Lind EA, Tyler TR (1988) The social psychology of procedural justice. Plenum Press

Meier KJ, Crotty JN (2006) Gender, representative bureaucracy, and law enforcement: Th e case of sexual assault. Public Admin Rev, November–December:850–860

Miller SM, Keiser LR (2021) Representative bureaucracy and attitudes toward automated decision making. J Public Adm Res Theory 31(1):150–165. https://doi.org/10.1093/jopart/muaa019

Mitra SK (2008) The puzzle of India's governance: culture, context and comparative theory. Routledge
Mukherjee T (2022) Institutional Effectiveness, Access to Justice, and the Governance of Women Police Stations in West Bengal. In: Policing in Global South
Natarajan M (2005) Women police stations as a dispute processing system: the Tamil Nadu experience in dealing with dowry-related domestic violence cases. Women Criminal Justice 16(1–2):87–106. https://doi.org/10.1300/J012v16n01_04
Natarajan M (2006) Dealing with domestic disputes/violence by women police in India: results of a training program in Tamil Nadu. In: International journal of criminal justice sciences, vol 1(1)
Natarajan M (2008) Women police in a changing society: Back door to equality. Ashgate Publishing Limited
Natarajan M, Babu D (2020) Women police stations: have they fulfilled their promise? Police Pract Res 21(5):442–458. https://doi.org/10.1080/15614263.2020.1809827
Nelson S (1996) Constructing and negotiating gender in women's police stations in Brazil. Lat Am Perspect 23(1):131–148
Nyul B, Kende A (2021) Rape myth acceptance as a relevant psychological construct in a gender-unequal context: the Hungarian adaptation of the updated Illinois rape myths acceptance scale. Curr Psychol 42:3098–3111
Orth U (2002) Secondary victimization of crime victims by criminal proceedings. Soc Justice Res 15:313–325
Owings C (1925) Women police: a study of the development and status of the women police movement. Frederick H. Hitchcoc
Page AD (2007) Behind the blue line: investigating police officers' attitudes toward rape. J Police Crim Psych 22:22–32
Page AD (2010) True colors: police officers and rape myth acceptance. Fem Criminol 5(4):315–334. https://doi.org/10.1177/1557085110384108
Perova E, Reynolds SA (2017) Women's police stations and intimate partner violence: evidence from Brazil. Soc Sci Med 174:188–196. https://doi.org/10.1016/j.socscimed.2016.12.008
Riccucci NM, Van Ryzin GG, Lavena CF (2014) Representative bureaucracy in policing: does it increase perceived legitimacy? J Public Adm Res Theory 24(3):537–551. https://doi.org/10.1093/jopart/muu006
Robinson S, MacCulloch R, Arentsen V (2014) The effects of gender and country on stress and resilience: a comparative study of police academy recruits from Australia, China and Canada. Police J 87(4):245–257. https://doi.org/10.1350/pojo.2014.87.4.678
Roychowdhury P (2021) Capable Women, Incapable States: Negotiating Violence and Rights in India
Santos CMD (2004) En-gendering the police: women's police stations and feminism in Sã o Paulo. Lat Am Res Rev 39(3):29–55. https://doi.org/10.1353/lar.2004.0059
Schulz DM (2004) Breaking the Brass ceiling: women police chiefs and their paths to the top. Praeger Publishers Inc
Slocum L, Taylor TJ, Brick BT et al (2010) Neighborhood structural characteristics, individual-level attitudes, and youths' crime reporting intentions. Criminology 48(4):1063–1100
Soares (2004) Crime Reporting as a measure for institutional development. Economic Development and Cultural Change 2(4): 851–871. https://doi.org/10.1086/420900
Sunshine J, Tyler TR (2003) The role of procedural justice and legitimacy in shaping public support for policing. Law Soc Rev 37(3):513–548
Symonds M (1975) Victims of violence: psychological effects and aftereffects. Am J Psychoanal 35:19–26
Tarling R, Morris K (2010) Reporting crime to the police. Br J Criminol 50(3):474–490
Taylor CS, Gassner L (2010) Stemming the flow: challenges for policing adult sexual assault with regard to attrition rates and underreporting of sexual offences. Police Pract Res 11(3):240–255
Terente D, Gallo P, Oltra C (2017) Comparing crime reporting factors in EU countries. Eur J Criminal Police Res 23(2):153–174

Tewari DB, Gautam U (2020) Legal policies for curbing sexual assault against women: correlating the missing socio -economic links. In: Singh KD, Goswami S (eds) Vulnerability of women in contemporary times: a socio legal perspective, 1st edn, pp 51–75

Tyler TR (2006) Restorative justice and procedural justice: dealing with rule breaking. J Soc Issues 62(2):307–326

Tyler TR, Huo YJ (2002) Trust in the law: encouraging the public cooperation with the police and courts. Russell Sage Foundation

Venema RM (2018) Police officers' rape myth acceptance: examining the role of officer characteristics, estimates of false reporting, and social desirability bias. Violence Vict 33(1):176–200. https://doi.org/10.1891/0886-6708.VV-D-15-00016

Wagner N, Rieger M, Bedi A, Hout W (2017) Gender and policing norms: evidence from survey experiments among police officers in Uganda. J Afr Econ 26(4):492–515. https://doi.org/10.1093/jae/ejx014

Jurisprudential Inquiry into the Dialogic Imperative of Criminal Procedure

Purvi Pokhariyal and Deepa Dubey

Abstract Injustice is a complex and multifaceted issue that can manifest in various forms, including economic, social, and political injustices. These injustices are often perpetuated and reinforced by the dialectics of law and lack of dialogic criminal procedure. The law is a social construct that is in constant flux, reflecting the values and beliefs of society at large. This dialectical relationship is particularly evident in the criminal justice system, where the law regulates and controls individual behavior. However, the effectiveness of the law in achieving these goals is often called into question, particularly when it comes to the treatment of victims of crime.

This chapter aims to provide an in-depth analysis of the dialectics of law in the criminal justice system and how dialogic procedure can play a role in the pursuit of justice. The chapter begins by providing a kaleidoscopic perspective on access to justice and how justice can be pursued by legitimizing the dialogic procedure. The chapter further analyzes the impact of legal education and the role of jurists in mediating the dialectics of law in the criminal justice system by propagating dialogic procedures for all the stakeholders, such as the significance of "victim impact statements" (VIS) in the criminal justice delivery system, VIS envelops the complete distress faced by the victim due the occurrence of the crime, therapeutic jurisprudence, and communicative theory. This chapter explores and analyzes such a dialogic procedure that leads to better representation of the victims, promoting rehabilitative jurisprudence in India.

The central contention of the chapter delves into the dialogic criminal procedure that seeks to facilitate a more restorative than punitive approach by creating opportunities for dialogue and negotiation. Furthermore, the chapter examines the implications of the dialectics of law for the future of the criminal justice system. The chapter argues that a deeper understanding of the dialectics of law through legal education is essential for developing a more effective and equitable justice system,

P. Pokhariyal (✉) · D. Dubey
School of Law, Forensic Justice and Policy Studies, National Forensic Sciences University, Gandhinagar, Gujarat, India
e-mail: purvi.pokhariyal@nfsu.ac.in; deepa.dubey@nfsu.ac.in

© The Author(s), under exclusive license to Springer Nature Singapore Pte Ltd. 2026

G. S. Bajpai et al. (eds.), *Beyond the Gavel: A Paradigm Shift in Global Criminal Justice*, https://doi.org/10.1007/978-981-95-4487-5_5

and there is a need to address the structural and systemic issues that create disparities and inequalities in the criminal justice system.

Keywords Communicative theory • Dialogic asymmetry • Therapeutic jurisprudence • Victim impact statement *justice* • *Adversarialism*

1 Introduction

The inexorable quest for justice forms the bedrock of any legal system, striving to uphold equity, fairness, and justice. However, the traditional adversarial system often accords precedence to confrontation over effective communication, thus impeding the potential for a comprehensive dispensation of justice (Jorstad 1990). In response to this inherent limitation, an emergent cadre of legal scholars and practitioners vociferously espouse the adoption of dialogic criminal procedure, an overarching framework that extols the intrinsic potency of discourse, collaboration, and comprehension in the relentless pursuit of justice. Dialogic criminal procedure challenges the entrenched precept that justice is an outcome achieved solely through a win-lose approach. Rather, it embraces the transformative potential nestled within meaningful dialogue and harmonious cooperation among all stakeholders ensnared within the intricacies of the legal process (Alfieri 1987). By fashioning an inclusive platform conducive to systematic interchange, dialogic criminal procedure aspires to transcend the limitations inherent in adversarialism, fostering empathy and nurturing a more impartial, judicious legal system (Yeager 2004).

Supplementing the conceptual underpinnings of dialogic criminal procedure, the dialogue within law confers additional layers of nuance and profundity to this paradigm. It cogently recognizes the perpetual flux and dialectical nature of legal principles, values, and perspectives, all of which remain susceptible to ceaseless dialogue and debate (Henry 1985). By embracing the dialectic, dialogic criminal procedure engenders the harmonious synthesis of diverse viewpoints, engenders critical introspection, and concomitantly strives toward justice that remains exquisitely context-sensitive and agile in its responsiveness (Newton 2006). The ensuing discourse undertakes a comprehensive examination of the conceptual framework and manifold benefits that inhere within the dialogic criminal procedure, thereby illuminating its transformative potential in transcending the limitations of adversarialism. Furthermore, it shall meticulously scrutinize the pivotal role played by dialogue and collaboration in enhancing stakeholder satisfaction and fomenting effective rehabilitation. Additionally, the inclusion of pertinent case studies shall serve to elucidate the substantive impact and efficacy of dialogic approaches within diverse jurisdictions (Bottoms 2012).

Numerous jurists proffer invaluable insights into the contemporary dialogic criminal procedure, cogently delineating its role as a catalyst for legal metamorphosis, the ethical imperative of dialogue, and the concomitant significance of public trust and confidence within the justice system (Norrie 2011). Moreover, by delving into case studies from various jurisdictions, this chapter illustrates the tangible manifestations of successful dialogic practices, wherein victims are endowed with satisfaction, offenders are reintegrated into society, and communities are involved in meaningful engagement.

Nevertheless, as with any paradigm shift, dialogic criminal procedure confronts a plethora of challenges, ranging from institutional resistance and logistical impediments to the delicate balancing act of dialogue and procedural efficiency. Careful consideration of these obstacles remains imperative for the successful implementation of dialogic criminal procedures within the legal fabric. The imbibing of dialogic criminal procedure and the assimilation of the dialectic of law proffer a compelling trajectory toward a more equitable and just legal system. By prioritizing communication, collaboration, and comprehension, dialogic approaches enhance the quality of decision-making, augment stakeholder satisfaction, and efficaciously contribute toward the attainment of justice (Punishment, Retribution and Communication 2004). The chapter contributes to the ongoing discourse surrounding the dialogic criminal procedure, conclusively underscoring its potential to foster a more inclusive, enlightened, and equitable society. This chapter delves into the intricacies inherent within the complex concept of dialogic criminal procedure and the dialectic of law, thereby accentuating the paramount and pivotal role accorded to the vehicle of dialogue in the attainment of justice. The perspectives offered by few legal scholars, the deployment of global statistical data, and the judicious examination of relevant case studies underscore and substantiate the transformative impact that dialogic criminal procedure so resplendently engenders. Through a comprehensive analysis of the fundamental principles that undergird this paradigm and its manifold practical applications, this chapter seeks to underscore the profound value of dialogic procedure in the pursuit of justice.

2 The Dialectic of Law: An Understanding of the Role of Dialogue

The underpinning tenets of legal positivism, as conceptualized by H.L.A. Hart (Toh 2005), posit that the authority of law emanates from a system of rules determined by recognized sources of legal power (Finnis 2007). However, this positivist construct has encountered substantial criticisms, particularly from Ronald Dworkin, who propounds that the evaluation of law ought not to be limited to its formalistic characteristics, but must extend to encompass its moral and ethical dimensions (Adorno et al. 1976). Dworkin's incisive critique illuminates the inherent limitations of a purely positivist approach, thereby beckoning the exploration of a more nuanced examination of the role of dialogue within the contours of the legal system (Dworkin 1967).

Arising from the manifold deficiencies associated with legal positivism, Lon Fuller posits that law is not confined solely to a collection of rules, but rather assumes the character of an instrument of efficacious communication. Fuller cogently argues that legal rules ought to possess clarity, comprehensibility, and the ability to effectively guide human conduct (Fuller 1964). Moreover, he vehemently emphasizes the profound significance of law as a vehicle for nurturing the ethical imperatives that undergird a just society (Hart and Fuller 1965). In Fuller's exposition, a dialogue emerges as a pivotal catalyst, facilitating the effective communication of legal precepts and aligning them harmoniously with the values cherished by the community they purport to serve.

For example, in the context of criminal procedure, the implementation of dialogic principles can be seen in the use of restorative justice practices. These practices seek to foster dialogue and understanding between offenders, victims, and the affected community, providing an alternative approach to the traditional adversarial system (Umbreit et al. 2007). By encouraging open communication and accountability, restorative justice allows for the acknowledgment of harm, the opportunity for healing, and the potential for the reintegration of offenders into society (Wenzel et al. 2008).

Jürgen Habermas's seminal theory of communicative action proposes another lens reflecting upon the importance of dialogue in the justice delivery system (Habermas and Burgerm 1990). Habermas postulates that an ideal society is one wherein individuals engage in open, rational discourse within a public sphere, thereby encouraging the free exchange of ideas and opinions (Funk et al. 1986). This deliberative democracy dovetails with the profound conviction that dialogue is not only a prerequisite for reaching decisions that are equitable and just, but also for fostering societal cohesion and democratic governance.

The adversarial nature intrinsic to criminal proceedings, often predicated upon the prioritization of contention between opposing parties, tends to diminish the voices and perspectives of defendants, victims, and the broader community (Kirchengast 2013). Dialogic criminal procedure endeavors to rectify this inherent imbalance by affording a platform for inclusive communication.

Dialogue within the ambit of criminal procedure ensures that all stakeholders' interests and apprehensions are duly taken into cognizance, thereby facilitating a more holistic comprehension of the salient issues at hand. By embracing the sanctity of dialogue, the legal system transcends the facile dichotomy of winners and losers, thereby striving toward outcomes that are consonant with the precepts of equity, justice, and social concord (Pemberton and Reynaers 2011). Dialogic criminal procedure acutely recognizes the innate dignity and agency vested within every individual ensnared within the vicissitudes of the legal process, affording them ample opportunities to articulate their lived experiences, aspirations, and exigencies in a manner that befits their rightful place within the fabric of justice.

3 Kaleidoscopic Perspectives on Dialogic Criminal Procedure

i. The Salience of Communicative Equality Nicola Lacey underscores the overarching significance of communicative equality within the intricate fabric of dialogic criminal procedure. Lacey propounds that the mere semblance of dialogue is insufficient; rather, it is imperative to anchor the discourse in substantive equality (Lacey 2001). This entails the creation of an environment wherein the voices of marginalized and vulnerable individuals are not only accorded a perfunctory audience but are also bestowed with the due consideration they inherently deserve. By resolutely empowering these individuals through the amplification of dialogue, the legal apparatus redresses the pernicious power differentials that pervade the criminal justice environment, engendering a more equitable, compassionate, and inclusive adjudicatory process.

The establishment of Lok Adalats in India represents a significant stride toward achieving justice through communicative equality within the legal framework. In a manner reminiscent of scholarly emphasis on communicative equality within the complex fabric of criminal procedure, Lok Adalats prioritize substantive equality over superficial dialogue. The assertion that dialogue must be anchored in substantive equality resonates profoundly within the ethos of Lok Adalats, where the mere appearance of dialogue is deemed inadequate. Instead, Lok Adalats strive to create an environment where the voices of marginalized and vulnerable individuals are not only given a cursory audience but are also afforded the profound consideration they inherently merit. By diligently empowering these individuals through the amplification of dialogue, Lok Adalats play a pivotal role in rectifying the pervasive power imbalances that characterize the criminal justice landscape. This commitment to communicative equality engenders a more equitable, compassionate, and inclusive adjudicatory process. It is within this context that Lok Adalats emerge as a beacon of hope, offering an alternative avenue for justice that transcends traditional legal paradigms.

The success of Lok Adalats in promoting access to justice is underscored by empirical data reflecting their remarkable efficacy. Indeed, Lok Adalats have emerged as a formidable force in resolving disputes expeditiously, with over 50 lakh matters adjudicated in 2017 alone. This substantial caseload exemplifies the resounding success of Lok Adalats in addressing the pervasive backlog of cases that plagues the traditional judicial system. Furthermore, the efficiency of Lok Adalats is underscored by their ability to settle an impressive 4000 cases per day, thus alleviating the burden on conventional courts and facilitating the timely resolution of disputes (Pandey and Law 2023).

Central to the efficacy of Lok Adalats is their commitment to informal and amicable dispute resolution mechanisms. Unlike traditional court proceedings, Lok Adalats operate in a congenial atmosphere, where parties engage in dialogue facilitated by former judicial office-bearers or other knowledgeable individuals. This informal setting fosters open communication and encourages collaborative efforts toward resolution, thereby promoting a sense of fairness and equity among all parties involved. Moreover, Lok Adalats offer a financially accessible avenue for justice, as parties are not burdened with court costs or other expenses. This financial accessibility ensures that justice is not contingent upon one's socioeconomic status, thus upholding the principles of equality and fairness enshrined in the legal system (Ijlmh 2020).

Lok Adalats stand as a testament to the transformative power of communicative equality in promoting access to justice. Through their steadfast commitment to substantive equality and efficient dispute resolution mechanisms, Lok Adalats have emerged as a cornerstone of the legal system. By empowering marginalized voices and redressing power differentials, Lok Adalats foster a more equitable, compassionate, and inclusive adjudicatory process, thereby advancing the noble ideals of justice and fairness.

ii. Deliberating on Dialogic Asymmetry Richard L. Lippke dissects the conundrum of dialogic asymmetry that insidiously permeates the criminal procedure (Lippke 2013). Lippke astutely discerns that adversarialism, with its inherent proclivity for exacerbating power imbalances between the prosecution and the defense, leads to inequitable outcomes (Lippke 2009). To rectify this glaring infirmity, Lippke suggests the proposition of embracing dialogic methodologies that mitigate the effect of asymmetry. By nurturing an environment characterized by candid and constructive dialogue, wherein both parties can proffer their contentions, thereby ensuring a manifestly just, balanced, and egalitarian procedural trajectory.

Illustrating this theoretical framework, the adoption of mediation and arbitration as alternative dispute resolution mechanisms in criminal cases epitomizes the potential of embracing dialogic methodologies. These avenues facilitate dialogue between parties, striving to attain mutually acceptable resolutions outside the confines of traditional courtroom proceedings. For instance, mediation serves as a constructive avenue for addressing conflicts between victims and offenders, providing a structured platform for the expression of concerns and perspectives. Similarly, arbitration offers a forum for negotiation and compromise between defendants and prosecutors, fostering the exploration of tailored solutions reflective of the unique nuances of each case.

By engendering an ethos of dialogue and collaboration, mediation and arbitration serve as effective means to mitigate the inherent power imbalances entrenched within adversarial proceedings. They afford both adversaries an equitable opportunity to engage in the resolution process, thereby espousing principles of fairness and equity. Furthermore, these alternative dispute resolution modalities offer a pragmatic solution to alleviate the strain on conventional court systems by expediting the resolution of cases with efficiency and efficacy. Nonetheless, it is imperative to acknowledge the nuanced landscape surrounding these mechanisms. While mediation and arbitration hold promise in mitigating dialogic asymmetry, their efficacy may be circumscribed by the nature of the case and the willingness of parties to engage earnestly in the dialogue. Moreover, their applicability may vary across different contexts, particularly in cases involving grave offenses or substantial power differentials (Epps and Washington University in St. Louis 2016). Lippke's advocacy for embracing dialogic methodologies furnishes a cogent framework for redressing dialogic asymmetry within criminal procedure. By nurturing an environment characterized by robust and equitable dialogue, we chart a course toward a legal system that epitomizes principles of justice, fairness, and inclusivity.

iii. The Ineluctable Necessity of Communicative Accountability Antony Duff, expounds upon the inescapable and indispensable imperative of communicative accountability within the criminal procedure. Duff contends that dialogue serves as a potent instrument of control, holding legal authorities, and participants to the exacting standards of accountability for their actions and decisions. By subjecting decisions to reasoned scrutiny and incisive critique, dialogue begets an ethos of transparency and legitimacy that pervades the precincts of criminal justice. It bequeaths an opportunity for the restoration of ruptured relationships and the fortification of moral agency, enabling a fertile terrain wherein participants introspectively ruminate upon their actions and engage in constructive dialogue aimed at mending the wounds inflicted upon the fabric of society (Duff 2005). In practical terms, the concept of communicative accountability manifests in various aspects of the criminal procedure. For instance, during court proceedings, the adversarial process inherently involves dialogue between opposing parties, such as prosecutors and defense attorneys, as they present arguments, evidence, and counterarguments before a judge or jury. This dialogue not only serves to adjudicate legal disputes but also holds participants accountable for the integrity of their arguments and the accuracy of the information presented. Furthermore, communicative accountability extends beyond the courtroom to encompass interactions between law enforcement officers and members of the public. Police officers are increasingly equipped with body cameras and are encouraged to engage in dialogue with individuals during encounters, promoting transparency and accountability in law enforcement practices. By subjecting police actions to scrutiny and critique, dialogue facilitates the identification and remediation of instances of misconduct or abuse of power, thereby fostering trust and legitimacy in law enforcement agencies (Duff 2022).

Duff's emphasis on dialogue as a means of restoring ruptured relationships and fortifying moral agency underscores the transformative potential of communicative accountability. In cases where harm has been inflicted upon individuals or communities, dialogue provides a platform for acknowledging wrongdoing, offering apologies, and seeking restitution or reconciliation. By encouraging participants to introspectively ruminate upon their actions and engage in constructive dialogue aimed at mending societal wounds, communicative accountability fosters a sense of collective responsibility and promotes healing and restoration within the broader fabric of society.

Duff's perspective underscores the profound significance of dialogue as a cornerstone of accountability within the criminal justice system. By embracing communicative accountability, legal authorities, participants, and communities alike can work toward a more transparent, legitimate, and morally robust framework for adjudicating disputes and upholding the values of justice and equity.

4 The Promotion of Communication and Collaboration in Criminal Procedure

i. Pre-Trial Stage: Ensuring Infallible Communication The pre-trial stage constitutes a pivotal juncture wherein the imperatives of infallible communication assume paramount significance. The deployment of open discovery processes, mandating an exhaustive and comprehensive disclosure of evidence by both prosecution and defense, brings about the element of transparency and information exchange par excellence. Additionally, pre-trial conferences, underpinned by the bedrock principles of cooperation and dialogue, serve as a fertile terrain for multifaceted deliberations on case management, potential plea agreements, and the incisive identification of key issues. It is through the orchestration of such communicative modalities during this phase that the legal system bestows upon itself the capacity to enhance the efficacy, expeditiousness, and inherent fairness of subsequent proceedings.

ii. Trial Stage: Embracing Dialogue within the Courtroom The trial stage stands as the veritable centerpiece of the intricate fabric of criminal procedure, and it is within the precincts of the courtroom that the transformative power of dialogue assumes its full resonance in the quest for justice (Kirchengast 2010). Judicial case management, epitomized by proactive judicial oversight and unwavering engagement, serves as a hallowed conduit through which dialogue between all litigants assumes a character of constructiveness. By expansively elucidating the opportunities for cross-examination and affording the participants the requisite space for meaningful and substantive engagement between contending parties, the courtroom is, in essence, transmuted into an intellectually fecund and fertile domain wherein dialogue, in all its manifold manifestations, is judiciously woven into the very fabric of the proceedings (Lippke 2009). Within this paradigm, the presentation of evidence, the articulation of cogent legal arguments, and the very exploration of alternative resolutions are subsumed under the aegis of an emancipatory dialogue that begets a jurisprudential aspect that is both fair and just (Prentice 2009).

iii. Post-trial Stage: Sentencing and the Pursuit of Restorative Justice The post-trial stage, ensconced within its temporal confines, bestows an opportune moment to embrace dialogue as an indispensable tool to achieve restorative justice (Strang and Braithwaite 2017). The unfettered engagement in dialogue during the sentencing process confers upon the legal system a panoramic vista wherein the multifarious contours encompassing the offense, the intrinsic needs of the victim, and the latent potential for the rehabilitation of the accused are brought into sharp focus. It is within this cathartic crucible of dialogue that the veritable essence of restorative practices assumes its fullest efflorescence, as victim-offender dialogues and conferences, among other transformative modalities, unfurl a space wherein participants can candidly and openly engage in interlocution (Umbreit et al. 2007). Within this domain of emotive resonance and profound vulnerability, empathy burgeons, accountability emerges as a guide, and the indomitable possibility of healing for all stakeholders materializes (Wenzel et al. 2008), thus coalescing the intrinsic imperatives of justice with the salutary triumphs of dialogue.

5 Illuminating the Impact of Dialogic Criminal Procedure

The impact of dialogic criminal procedure finds empirical validation in the form of amplified defendant satisfaction, as substantiated by statistical evidence. A comprehensive study conducted by Robert M. Bloom laid bare the undeniable correlation between the provision of an environment conducive to meaningful dialogue and heightened levels of defendant satisfaction, transcending the narrow confines of outcome determinants. The discerning scrutiny of comparative analyses spanning diverse jurisdictions, resplendent with their multifarious legal regimes, has consistently furnished cogent and compelling evidence attesting to the inexorable nexus between the robust implementation of dialogic practices and the rise in defendant satisfaction.

The triumph of dialogic criminal procedure, when viewed through the prism of restorative justice programs, manifests in diminished conviction rates (Wenzel et al. 2008). Restorative justice, replete with its philosophical moorings in dialogue, reparation, and reintegration, has emerged as an indomitable force in curbing the deleterious cycle of conviction (McAlinden 2011). A case study rooted in the history of New Zealand's illustrious legal landscape unraveled a staggering conviction rate of a mere 14% among participants who actively engaged in Family Group Conferences, far outshining the national average of 41% (Moyle and Tauri 2016). These resplendent statistics, etched in the fabric of evidentiary rigor, irrefutably underline the transformative potency of dialogic modalities, engendering far-reaching societal dividends that resonate in the fabric of justice itself.

6 The Praxis of Dialogic Criminal Procedure in Context

The praxis of dialogic criminal procedure finds its quintessence within the purview of drug courts, where the therapeutic jurisprudence approach stands as a resplendent exemplar (Casey and Rottman 2000). These specialized courts, by their profound commitment to dialogue, unravel transformative potentialities. They transcend the traditional confines of punitive measures, instead embracing a comprehensive treatment and rehabilitation paradigm steeped in the tenets of dialogue, collaboration, and support (Rottman and Casey 1999). Within the hallowed halls of drug courts, individuals grappling with the perils of substance abuse are afforded a ground for dialogue, wherein the underlying causes of their afflictions are unveiled, examined, and addressed. By eschewing the orthodox predilection for incarceration and embracing the transformative potential of dialogue, drug courts kindle a glimmer of hope, ushering in enhanced outcomes in terms of recovery, community reintegration, and the triumph over the blight of addiction (Winick 2013).

The South African Truth and Reconciliation Commission (TRC) epitomizes an illustrious case study that underscores the profound impact of dialogic criminal procedure on a national canvas. In the wake of the apocalyptic legacy of apartheid, the TRC rose as a beacon of justice, unfurling the majestic tapestry of dialogue, healing, and reconciliation (Allan and Allan 2000). Within its chambers, victims and perpetrators, juxtaposed in their shared humanity, engaged in profound dialogue that transcended the traditional boundaries of justice (Chapman 2007). The TRC's arduous quest was fueled by an unquenchable thirst for truth, the cathartic power of dialogue, and the ceaseless yearning for a more inclusive and cohesive society. While the TRC was not immune to challenges and complexities, its enduring impact stands as a testament to the indomitable power of dialogue in surmounting deep-seated societal divisions, fostering national healing, and forging a path toward a more just and harmonious existence.

7 Challenges and Critiques of Dialogic Criminal Procedure

i. Vulnerabilities to Manipulation and Coercion One of the foremost challenges confronting the domain of dialogic criminal procedure resides in the inherent vulnerabilities to manipulation and coercion (Erez 1994). The sanctity of dialogue mandates the establishment of an environment that zealously safeguards the integrity and voluntariness of participants' contributions (Moynihan and Soss 2014). This necessitates an equitable distribution of power dynamics, the provision of requisite support structures, and the unwavering maintenance of procedural safeguards (Newton 2006). By adhering to these imperatives, the risks associated with manipulation and coercion can be assuaged, thereby preserving the principles of equity, fairness, and justice.

ii. Resource Constraints and Temporal Limitations The efficacious implementation of dialogic criminal procedure is irrevocably contingent upon the availability of adequate resources and temporal latitude, a facet that assumes paramount significance in the context of a justice system beleaguered by multifarious resource constraints (Pieczka 2011). The exigencies of effective communication necessitate the presence of trained personnel, commensurate infrastructure, and a resolute commitment to allocating the requisite temporal allotments for dialogue (Roberts and Erez 2004). In light of these challenges, a judicious calibration of priorities and resource allocation becomes imperative, ensuring the sustainable and efficacious operation of dialogic approaches within the broader justice framework.

iii. Striking a Delicate Balance Between Dialogue, Efficiency, and Finality The pursuit of justice necessitates the delicate harmonization of dialogue, efficiency, and finality. While the embrace of dialogue augments the quality of decision-making processes, it must not be permitted to unduly protract the legal trajectory (Norrie 2011), thereby impinging upon the just aspirations of victims or perpetuating the anguish and turmoil experienced by the accused (Lacey 2005). The attainment of equipoise between the imperative for dialogue and the expeditious disposition of matters calls for a nuanced and discerning approach, one that deftly orchestrates the application of dialogic principles in accordance with the contextual exigencies characterizing each distinct case (Tremblay 2005).

8 The Role of Legal Education in Promoting Dialogic Criminal Procedure

i. Integrating Dialogic Principles into Legal Curricula The transformative evolution of the criminal justice system necessitates a comprehensive approach that commences with the realm of legal education. Law schools assume a pivotal role in molding the future generation of legal professionals who will be instrumental in advancing dialogic criminal procedure. By seamlessly integrating dialogic principles into legal curricula, aspiring lawyers are imbued with the essential proficiencies in effective communication, active listening, and empathic engagement. Legal education ought to engender a critical examination of the prevailing adversarial system and encourage the exploration of alternative approaches that prioritize dialogue and collaborative endeavors.

ii. Clinical Legal Education Fostering Practical Engagement with Dialogic Approaches: Clinical legal education offers a fertile terrain for law students to actively immerse themselves in tangible legal issues and cultivate pragmatic skills. By assimilating dialogic criminal procedure within clinical programs, students are afforded the invaluable opportunity to personally witness the transformative potential of dialogue (Giddings 2013). Engaging in simulations, mediation sessions, and restorative justice programs, students gain firsthand familiarity with the intricacies and challenges associated with implementing dialogic practices (Giddings 2008). Clinical legal education emerges as a fertile crucible for nurturing a new cohort of lawyers armed with the acumen to adroitly champion the cause of dialogic criminal procedure.

iii. Continuing Legal Education: Ensuring Professional Development Continuing legal education programs play an indispensable role in fostering the professional development of practicing lawyers. These programs must encompass dialogic criminal procedure as a salient constituent, ensuring that legal practitioners remain apprised of the ever-evolving practices and philosophies. Workshops, seminars, and conferences devoted to dialogic approaches serve to deepen lawyers' comprehension of the pivotal significance of dialogue in the attainment of justice. By nurturing an ethos of ongoing learning and introspection, continuing legal education empowers practitioners to effectively embed dialogic principles within their daily legal practice.

iv. Legal Ethics and the Ethical Imperative of Dialogue Legal ethics serve as the bedrock upon which the legal profession firmly stands. Ethical standards must cogently reflect the intrinsic value of dialogue and collaboration in the relentless pursuit of justice (Weaver 1983). Codes of conduct ought to explicitly acknowledge the criticality of meaningful communication, respectful engagement, and the recognition of diverse perspectives. By infusing legal ethics with the ethical imperative of dialogue, the legal profession underscores its unwavering commitment to fostering a more just, equitable, and harmonious criminal justice system.

9 Implementing Dialogic Criminal Procedure: Overcoming Challenges and Building Consensus

i. Addressing Institutional Resistance and Cultural Barriers The successful implementation of dialogic criminal procedure necessitates a concerted effort to overcome institutional resistance and cultural barriers entrenched within the legal system. Conventional practices firmly rooted in adversarialism may staunchly oppose change, perceiving dialogue as a formidable challenge to established norms (Yeager 2004). To forge consensus, it becomes imperative to deploy educational initiatives, raise awareness through strategic campaigns, and initiate pilot projects that effectively demonstrate the advantages of dialogic approaches. By dispelling misconceptions and garnering support among legal professionals, policymakers, and the general public, the transformative potential of dialogic criminal procedure can be actualized (McCann 2006). Collaboration among diverse stakeholders, including judges, prosecutors, defense attorneys, and community representatives, remains pivotal to navigate these challenges and foster the development of a shared vision for a more inclusive and dialogic justice system.

ii. Providing Training and Resources for Effective Communication Effective communication stands as the cornerstone of dialogic criminal procedure. To ensure its successful integration, comprehensive training programs must be developed, tailored to cater to the needs of legal practitioners and actors within the justice system. These programs ought to emphasize the cultivation of active listening skills, proficient questioning techniques, empathy, and conflict-resolution strategies. Concurrently, the guidelines, toolkits, and exemplars of best practices can prove to be indispensable in supporting professionals in the seamless incorporation of dialogic principles into their daily practice.

iii. Evaluating and Adapting Dialogic Practices The efficacy and sustainability of dialogic practices hinge upon their continuous evaluation and adaptation. Establishing mechanisms for regular assessment, diligent monitoring, and constructive feedback becomes essential in identifying strengths, weaknesses, and areas warranting improvement. Insights gained from these evaluations hold the potential to inform policy changes, and procedural reforms, and refine the application of dialogic approaches. Embracing a culture of perpetual learning and adaptability ensures that dialogic criminal procedure remains agile in response to the evolving needs of the justice delivery system.

iv. Collaborating with Other Disciplines and Stakeholders Dialogic criminal procedure thrives within a multidisciplinary context, necessitating robust collaboration with various disciplines, including psychology, sociology, and restorative justice experts. Such interdisciplinary engagement offers invaluable insights that enrich the efficacy of dialogic practices. Simultaneously, actively involving community organizations, victim support groups, and marginalized communities serves to ensure the responsiveness and accountability of the justice system to diverse voices.

v. The Victim Impact Statement Victim voices through dialogue within the criminal procedure is the inclusion of victim impact statements. The victim impact statement allows victims to share the emotional, physical, and financial impact of the crime in their own words, directly addressing the court during sentencing or parole hearings. By integrating victim perspectives through dialogue, the legal system acknowledges the importance of victim participation and recognizes their right to be heard.

10 Conclusion

In conclusion, the implementation of dialogic criminal procedure holds tremendous potential for advancing the pursuit of justice. By prioritizing effective communication, fostering collaboration, and embracing diverse perspectives, the legal system can transcend the limitations of the adversarial model. The integration of dialogic principles into legal education, through curricula, clinical programs, and continuing education, equips legal professionals with the necessary skills and mindset to advocate for and apply dialogic approaches.

While challenges exist, such as institutional resistance and resource constraints, the benefits of dialogic criminal procedure are compelling. Increased defendant satisfaction, diminished conviction rates, and societal healing demonstrate the transformative impact of dialogic practices. By recognizing dialogue as an ethical imperative and integrating dialogic principles throughout the criminal justice system, we can take significant strides toward a more just, inclusive, and equitable pursuit of justice. The perspectives of jurists and case studies have underscored the importance of dialogic criminal procedure in promoting fairness, transparency, and meaningful participation. By addressing challenges, collaborating with other disciplines and stakeholders, and fostering a culture of continuous evaluation and adaptation, the legal system can harness the power of dialogue to create a more responsive and accountable justice system.

The adoption of dialogic criminal procedure represents a paradigm shift toward a justice system that values open communication, collaboration, and the recognition of diverse perspectives. By embracing dialogue as an ethical imperative and integrating dialogic principles into legal education, the legal profession can contribute to a more just and equitable society. While challenges exist, the transformative potential of dialogic approaches in enhancing stakeholder satisfaction, reducing conviction rates, and promoting societal healing cannot be understated. By working collectively to address challenges, provide adequate resources, and foster interdisciplinary collaboration, we can build a robust legal framework that prioritizes fairness, inclusivity, and the pursuit of justice for all.

References

Adorno TW, Adey G, Frisby D (1976) The positivist dispute in German sociology. Br J Sociol 27(4):509. https://doi.org/10.2307/590190

Alfieri AV (1987) The antinomies of poverty Law and a theory of dialogic empowerment. NYU Rev Law Soc Change 16:659–712. https://repository.law.miami.edu/cgi/viewcontent.cgi?article=1589&context=fac_articles

Allan A, Allan MM (2000) The south African truth and reconciliation commission as a therapeutic tool. Behav Sci Law 18(4):459–477

Bottoms A (2012) Beyond Procedural Justice: A dialogic approach to legitimacy in Criminal justice. https://dialnet.unirioja.es/servlet/articulo?codigo=3922505&gt

Casey P, Rottman DB (2000) Therapeutic jurisprudence in the courts. Behav Sci Law 18(4):445–457

Chapman AR (2007) Truth commissions and intergroup forgiveness: the case of the south African truth and reconciliation commission. Peace Conflict J Peace Psychol 13(1):51–69. https://doi.org/10.1037/h0094024

Duff A (2005) Punishment, communication and community. Debates Contemp Polit Philos:387

Duff RA (2022) Punishment as communication. https://ssrn.com/abstract=4171062

Dworkin R (1967) The model of rules. Univ Chicago Law Rev 35(1):14. https://doi.org/10.2307/1598947

Epps D Jr, Washington University in St. Louis (2016) Adversarial asymmetry in the criminal process. N Y Univ Law Rev 91:762–854. https://www.nyulawreview.org/wp-content/uploads/2018/08/NYULawReview-91-4-Epps_0.pdf

Erez E (1994) Victim participation in sentencing: and the debate goes on. Int Rev Victimol 3(1–2):17–32. https://doi.org/10.1177/026975809400300202

Finnis J (2007) On Hart's ways: law as reason and as fact. Am J Jurisprudence 52(1):25–53. https://doi.org/10.1093/ajj/52.1.25

Fuller LL (1964) The morality of law. Yale University Press.

Funk N, Habermas J, McCarthy T (1986) The theory of communicative action. Vol. 1: reason and the rationalization of society. Philos Rev 95(2):269. https://doi.org/10.2307/2185595

Giddings JM (2008) Contemplating the future of clinical legal education. Griffith Law Rev 17(1):1–26. https://doi.org/10.1080/10383441.2008.10854600

Giddings JM (2013) Promoting justice through clinical legal education. Soc Sci Res Netw. https://doi.org/10.2139/ssrn.2740164

Habermas J, Burgerm T (1990) The structural transformation of the public sphere: an inquiry into a category of bourgeois society. Choice Rev Online 27(07):27–4175. https://doi.org/10.5860/choice.27-4175

Hart HLA, Fuller LL (1965) The morality of law. Harv Law Rev 78(6):1281. https://doi.org/10.2307/1338941

Henry S (1985) Community justice, capitalist society, and human agency: the dialectics of collective Law in the cooperative. Law Soc Rev 19(2):303. https://doi.org/10.2307/3053458
Ijlmh (3 July 2020) Access to justice: "through Lok Adalat issues and challenges.". Int J Law Manag Humanities. https://ijlmh.com/access-to-justice-through-lok-adalat-issues-and-challenges/
Jorstad EE (1990) Litigation ethics: a Niebuhrian view of the adversarial legal system. Yale Law J 99(5):1089. https://doi.org/10.2307/796597
Kirchengast T (2010) The criminal trial in law and discourse. Springe Strang
Kirchengast T (2013) Victim lawyers, victim advocates, and the adversarial criminal trial. New Criminal Law Rev 16(4):568–594. https://doi.org/10.1525/nclr.2013.16.4.568
Lacey N (2001) In search of the responsible subject: history, philosophy and social sciences in criminal Law theory. Modern Law Rev 64(3):350–371. https://doi.org/10.1111/1468-2230.00325
Lacey N (2005) Punishment, communication and community. Routledge eBooks, pp 397–417. https://doi.org/10.4324/9780203986820-31
Lippke RL (2009) The case for reasoned criminal trial verdicts. Can J Law Jurisprudence 22(2):313–330. https://doi.org/10.1017/s0841820900004719
Lippke RL (2013) Adjudication error, finality, and asymmetry in the criminal law. Can J Law Jurisprudence 26(2):377–398. https://doi.org/10.1017/s0841820900006111
McAlinden A (2011) 'Transforming justice': challenges for restorative justice in an era of punishment-based corrections. Contemp Justice Rev 14(4):383–406. https://doi.org/10.1080/10282580.2011.616369
McCann MW (2006) Law and social movements: contemporary perspectives. Ann Rev Law Soc Sci 2(1):17–38. https://doi.org/10.1146/annurev.lawsocsci.2.081805.105917
Moyle P, Tauri J (2016) Māori, family group conferencing and the mystifications of restorative justice. Vict Offenders 11(1):87–106. https://doi.org/10.1080/15564886.2015.1135496
Moynihan DP, Soss J (2014) Policy feedback and the politics of administration. Public Adm Rev 74(3):320–332. https://doi.org/10.1111/puar.12200
Newton S (2006) The dialectics of law and development. Cambridge University Press eBooks, pp 174–202. https://doi.org/10.1017/cbo9780511754425.005
Norrie A (2011) Alan Brudner and the dialectics of criminal Law. New Criminal Law Rev. https://doi.org/10.1525/nclr.2011.14.3.449
Pandey R, Law L (9 June 2023) Live law. Live Law. https://www.livelaw.in/lawschool/articles/role-of-lok-adalats-in-promoting-access-to-justice-230348?infinitescroll=1
Pemberton A, Reynaers S (2011) The controversial nature of victim participation: therapeutic benefits in victim impact statements. Soc Sci Res Netw. https://doi.org/10.2139/ssrn.1745923
Pieczka M (2011) Public relations as dialogic expertise? J Commun Manag 15(2):108–124. https://doi.org/10.1108/13632541111126346
Prentice CM (2009) Relational dialectics among in-Laws. J Fam Commun 9(2):67–89. https://doi.org/10.1080/15267430802561667
Punishment, Retribution and Communication (From Punishment, Places and Perpetrators: Developments in Criminology and Criminal Justice Research, P 78–96, 2004, *Gerben Bruinsma, Henk Elffers, et al., eds. -- See NCJ-206450) | Office of Justice Programs* (no date) https://www.ojp.gov/ncjrs/virtual-library/abstracts/punishment-retribution-and-communication-punishment-places-and
Roberts JV, Erez E (2004) Communication in sentencing: exploring the expressive function of victim impact statements. Int Rev Victimol 10(3):223–244. https://doi.org/10.1177/026975800401000302
Rottman DB, Casey P (1999) Therapeutic jurisprudence and the emergence of problem-solving courts. PsycEXTRA Dataset. https://doi.org/10.1037/e564202006-002
Strang H, Braithwaite J (eds) (2017) Restorative justice: philosophy to practice. Routledge
Toh K (2005) Hart's EXPRESSIVISM and his BENTHAMITE project. Legal Theory 11(02). https://doi.org/10.1017/s1352325205050044
Tremblay L (2005) The legitimacy of judicial review: the limits of dialogue between courts and legislatures. Int J Constitutional Law 3(4):617–648. https://doi.org/10.1093/icon/moi042

Umbreit MS, Coates RB, Vos B (2007) Restorative justice dialogue: a multi-dimensional, evidence-based practice theory. Contemp Justice Rev 10(1):23–41. https://doi.org/10.1080/10282580601157521

Weaver M (1983) Clinical legal education—competing perspectives. Law Teacher 17(1):1–8. https://doi.org/10.1080/03069400.1983.9992587

Wenzel M et al (2008) Retributive and restorative justice. Law Hum Behav 32(5):375–389. https://doi.org/10.1007/s10979-007-9116-6

Winick BJ (2013) Problem solving courts: therapeutic jurisprudence in practice. Springer eBooks, pp 211–236. https://doi.org/10.1007/978-1-4614-7403-6_12

Yeager PC (2004) Law versus justice: from Adversarialism to communitarianism. Law Soc Inquiry-J Am Bar Found 29(4):891–915. https://doi.org/10.1111/j.1747-4469.2004.tb01079.x

Victim Impact Statements in the Indian Criminal Justice System

G. S. Bajpai and Prerna Deep

Abstract This chapter critically examines the multifaceted role and impact of victim impact statements in the criminal justice system. It focuses on insights from the jurisdictions of common law which are the United States, the United Kingdom, South Africa, and Canada. This study focuses on the impacts of victim impact statements on providing sentences, the psychological well-being of victims, various challenges associated with this context, and also the legal groundwork in that field. Victim impact statements have the capability to support the victims of crime by ensuring that their perspectives are taken into the judicial process. There are various challenges to victim impact statements in India because of the procedural, cultural, and legal dimensions present in the country. This chapter demonstrates the importance of a multifaceted approach that not only considers the perspective of the victims through victim impact statements but also gives importance to the complications of the adversarial system, in the purview of which, the rights of the victims have outshined the participation of victims. The objective of this chapter is to inculcate an impartial and supportive legal system that corresponds with international approaches that are embedded in the sociocultural context by promoting reforms in the judiciary and facilitating victim support mechanisms. This multidimensional approach towards victim impact statements aims to facilitate reforms from a procedural and legislative view that enhances and ensures that justice prevails with a victim-centric approach in the legal system of India. This nuanced understanding of victim impact statements seeks to catalyse legislative and procedural reforms that enhance the delivery of justice by ensuring a more victim-centric approach within the Indian legal framework.

Keywords Victim impact statements • Criminal justice • Judicial reforms • Victim participation • Victim rights

---

G. S. Bajpai (✉) · P. Deep
National Law University Delhi, Delhi, India
e-mail: prerna.deep@nludelhi.ac.in

© The Author(s), under exclusive license to Springer Nature Singapore Pte Ltd. 2026

G. S. Bajpai et al. (eds.), *Beyond the Gavel: A Paradigm Shift in Global Criminal Justice*, https://doi.org/10.1007/978-981-95-4487-5_6

1 Introduction

Victim impact statement (hereinafter referred to as 'VIS'), in simple terms, can be defined as a statement by the victim of a crime, wherein the crime victim either pens down or orally narrates their side of the story, elaborating on the physical, mental, emotional monetary, and/or sexual harm that occurred due to the criminal action or omission on the part of the perpetrator and/or offender (Prasanth 2023). The statement is also known as a victim statement or impact statement. Although referred to by different names in various jurisdictions, for the sake of clarity and consistency, this chapter will use the term VIS throughout the chapter. According to the Criminal Justice Department of the United States,

> Victim impact statements describe the emotional, physical, and financial impact you and others have suffered as a direct result of the crime. Victim impact statements can be either written or oral statements (Criminal Justice Division, the United States, Victim Impact Statements, 2020).

This statement serves as a way for the victim to be part of the criminal justice system, and it is often seen as a tool that influences decision-making of the justice system. This is a part of the ideology of restorative justice, where the questions are not about what laws were broken by whom and for what reason but rather on who has been hurt, what the needs of such an individual are, and who is obligated to fulfil those needs—restorative justice focuses on the needs of the victim rather than the rights that have been violated (Zehr 2002). The concept of VIS first emerged in the United States ('U.S.') in a notable case involving Charles Manson, an infamous cult leader and serial killer (Jenkins 2019). It was during the parole hearings of his followers, who were responsible for the brutal murder of actress Sharon Tate, that the potential of VIS became evident. With deep sorrow, the victim's mother conveyed the profound grief and pain her family endured, questioning the mercy shown to her daughter as she pleaded for her life. Her impactful words played a significant role in the decision-making process, as none of Manson's followers was released on parole:

> 'What mercy, sir, did you show my daughter when she was begging for her life?'... 'What mercy did you show my daughter when she said, "Give me two weeks to have my baby, then you can kill me?"' (Day 2016)

In Canada, the VIS outlined in the Canadian Victims Bill of Rights plays a distinct and crucial role in the criminal justice process, differentiating from the more general victim statement. This statement primarily informs the Correctional Services of Canada ('CSC') or the Parole Board of Canada ('PBC') about the crime's impact on the victim and their family, including emotional and physical repercussions, safety concerns, and any desired conditions for the offender's release pertaining to the victim's safety. These statements must be submitted before sentencing to potentially have a bearing on the outcome, unlike victim statements, which are directed to the CSC or PBC after sentencing (Government of Canada 2015a). As per the South African Law Commission, VIS is defined as a written expression by the victim or an authorised individual that details the impact of the offence, including physical, psychological, social, and financial consequences (South African Law Commission 2004). The Indian Criminal Justice System, which is an adversarial system of justice, focuses on the administration of justice for the deterrence of crimes, such that the accused's rights are protected, and the victims are provided with justice (UNODC 2018). The case of *Karan v. State NCT of Delhi* (2021) is a landmark judgement in the Indian jurisdiction with regard to VIS, where the court laid down guidelines for the Victim Compensation Scheme and mandated the District Legal Services Authority to prepare a 'Victim Impact Report' in consultation with the victim. The developments in the victim rights jurisprudence across jurisdictions highlights the ongoing struggle the criminal justice system is facing in giving adequate voice to victims and creating a legal framework that not only acknowledges but actively supports the rights and needs of victims.

2 Research Methodology

This chapter further delves into the importance and execution of victim impact statements in India by carrying out a comparative analysis of the implementation and impact that VIS has on other countries, with a deep-rooted culture pertaining to VIS in countries such as the United States, Canada, the United Kingdom, and South Africa. This chapter examines the implementation and impacts of VIS in the mentioned jurisdictions and it also digs deeper to identify the variations, challenges, concerns, and success rates pertaining to the evolving jurisprudence in present-day India. This study also emphasises the cases that illuminate demonstrations of the application of VIS in these countries and also in India to study the practical results and efficiency of the systems all over the world.

3 Comparative Perspectives

3.1 India

The evolution of victim rights in the Legal System of India has witnessed a drastic change in the overall judicial process, which shifted to a balanced and sympathetic system that took into consideration the voices of victims and their well-being (Nagpal and Rawandale 2023). Earlier, the legal system was based on an accused-centric approach, which transformed into a victim-centric approach as the judiciary started to address the hardships of victims and enhanced their empowerment through amendments and inclusions that showcase the evolving legislative goals and societal dynamics. The evolution is in accordance with the global developments worldwide and is also undertaken by India's social and economic dynamic. The evolution of victimology in the Jurisprudence of India over the years was marked by the facilitation and enhancement in recognising the rights of victims which were commenced by Justice Krishna Iyer's court order in the case of Rattan Singh (*Rattan Singh v. State of Punjab, 1979)* and Maru Ram (Maru Ram v. Union of India, 1981) which was a similar case. Both these cases sanctioned changes in the legislature for the inclusion of measures that address the distress of the victims of crime who were not given importance previously. This initiative was taken by the Supreme Court in the case of Dayal Singh (*Dayal Singh v. State of Uttaranchal, 2012*). This case urged that the criminal trials in the judiciary should be more focused on balancing the rights of the victims of crime and the accused so that there is fairness and justice in the system. Another relevant case law pertaining to these measures is the Balasaheb Rangnath Khade case (*Balasaheb Rangnath Khade v. the state of Maharashtra & Ors.*). This case ensured that the voices of victims are to be heard in the court without the permission of the court being required. This leads to the rights of individuals to appeal to a higher court if the victim perceives the order of the court as unjust or if the victim was not compensated sufficiently.

The VIS assessment was standardised in the case of *Karan v. State of Delhi* (2020). This case also necessitated the formation and submission of the victim impact report (VIR) during the phase of sentencing. This was aimed mainly to calculate the physical, economic, and emotional effects on the victims. This was instrumental in taking an appropriate decision concerning sentencing and compensation. The ambit of VIS was widened because the particulars of the crime against the victim were specified. This was again a valuable tool to assist the judge in making decisions for the restitution and appropriate penalties as per the harm caused to the victims. Moreover, the creation of procedures took place concerning the economic assessment of the offender in compensating the victim and the complete impact of the crime on the victim that includes both the aspects that are reparative and punitive. This provides a very comprehensive route to mitigate the predicament of the victim.

The progression towards Indian jurisprudence that embodies the method of victim-centric has been characterised by considerable judicial activism and compassionate legal interpretations. The role of the victims in the criminal justice system has been strengthened by the recent judgments that incorporated the very basis of VIS. This incorporation significantly marks the compensatory rights of victims and a fair trial. This switch not only aligns India with the essence of international rules but also ensures a road to recovery and upholds the principle of justice that includes the dignity of victims and addresses their complaints in a holistic way. This affirms the goal towards augmenting the rights of victims in the legal system and creating an environment that is fair and equitable.

3.2 The United States

The use of VIS in the United States was challenged in the landmark case of *Payne v. Tennessee* (1991). The case brought into question the 'admissibility of VIS', especially in the death penalty cases. The issue arose because the Eighth Amendment had previously prohibited the submission of such statements in a capital sentencing jury, as seen in *Booth v. Maryland* (1987) and *South Carolina v. Gathers* (1989). Ultimately, the Supreme Court ruled that informing the jury about harm caused by the accused is a crucial aspect of sentencing. This decision clarified and affirmed the continuation of VIS, marking a significant development in the legal validity of VIS. In another highly publicised case of *The People v. Turner* (2018), the victim's impact statements vividly detailed her assault and its profound aftermath on her life. The statements not only highlighted her trauma but also spurred societal actions in Ohio (Miller 2016). Women in Ohio protested in order to avoid such instances in the future so that other women of the state are protected from similar fates by creating awareness about the instance, thus underscoring the powerful role these statements tend to play beyond the courtroom (Barmann 2022).

The Crime Victims' Rights Act of 2004, implemented in the United States, further solidifies the right of victims to be reasonably heard in any public proceeding in the district court involving release, plea, sentencing, or any parole proceeding. This right, although specifically applicable to public proceedings, gives victims a voice in the criminal justice system. The senate's clear statement of intent regarding this right emphasises the fact that when a victim invokes this right during plea and sentencing proceedings, the victim should be allowed to 'provide comprehensive input on the character of the victim, the impact of the crime on the victim's family, the community, and the sentencing recommendations' (Doyle 2021). State-specific regulations reflect the evolving role of VIS. For instance, Missouri permits victims to submit written statements or speak in court during plea bargains if the victim is deceased or otherwise incapacitated (2013 Missouri Revised Statutes, n.d.). Similarly, Rhode Island ensures that victims have the opportunity to discuss the impact of the crime before a sentence is given and also during plea negotiations (Rhode Island General Laws, 2023). Thus, it is evident that over the years of socio-legal evolution, VIS has become an integral part of the US judicial process. In the US judicial process, the victims and their families are allowed to have a say in sentencing the offenders, and it is also ensured that their voices are heard, which reinforces the justice system's commitment to address the needs and rights of victims (Allen 1992). In the United States, as discussed earlier, judicial perspectives pertaining to VIS have undergone significant transformations that reflect the evolving recognition of victims' voices in the sentencing phase of capital trials. The landmark case of *Booth v. Maryland* (1987) represents a critical juncture in the judicial handling of VIS, where the U.S. Supreme Court scrutinised the constitutionality of a Maryland statute mandating the inclusion of victim impact statements in pre-sentence reports for capital cases. The court encountered a set of statements which described the victims as 'amazing people' who were 'butchered like animals', this reflects the family's view that the defendant was beyond rehabilitation. The Supreme Court's decision to uphold the Maryland Court of Appeals' affirmation of the death sentence while considering the straightforward and factual nature of the VIS, highlighted a cautious yet pivotal acknowledgement of the potential utility of VIS in the sentencing phase without constituting an arbitrary influence on the jury's decision-making.

However, the legal thought regarding VIS took a definitive turn with *Payne v. Tennessee* (1991). Herein, the Supreme Court effectively overturned its previous stance in *Booth*, concluding that the Eighth Amendment does not impose a per se prohibition against the capital sentencing jury's consideration of victim impact evidence that relates to the personal characteristics of the victim and the emotional impact of the crime on the victim's family. This decision acknowledged a broader scope for the inclusion of VIS, emphasising retribution as a legitimate sentencing goal and marking a significant shift towards recognising the emotional and personal dimensions of the crime's impact on the victim's family. The court's decision in Payne liberalised the use of VIS, granting states the discretion to permit such statements to influence the sentencing phases of capital trials. This marked a substantial shift from the more restrictive view seen in Booth, reflecting a judicial acknowledgement of the potential for VIS to contribute meaningfully to the justice process, despite the inherent risks. This reflects a broader judicial recognition of the need for the criminal justice system to address not only the legality but also the human impact of crimes, aligning the legal processes with societal values and the justice they strive to uphold (Cornille 1993).

3.3 Canada

The outcomes of the House of Commons Standing Committee on Justice and Human Rights 1998 report highlight the importance of VIS. Suggestions from this report led to numerous amendments in the CrPC in the year 1999 that improvised the rights of victims in order to promote their participation in the judicial process. The victims could read their statements in the courts and express their perspective on the crimes that took place only due to the amendments that were made by considering the suggestions of the Committee. This ensured the timely delivery of the perspectives of victims through VIS to the defence and the Crown. This development in the criminal justice system embarks on a shift towards empowering and protecting the victims. The impact of the House of Commons Standing Committee on Justice and Human Rights 1998 report was instrumental in further developing the role of VIS. Recommendations from this report led to significant amendments to the Criminal Code in 1999, enhancing victims' rights to enhance participation in the sentencing process. These amendments allowed the victims to read their statements aloud in court and ensured the timely delivery of VIS to the crown and defence post-conviction, marking a pivotal shift towards empowering victims within the legal process.

The Department of Justice Canada commenced in-depth research and consultations that included focus groups across various cities to listen to the perspectives of victims about their experiences with VIS. These perspectives demonstrated varied experiences and showed apprehension among victims pertaining to the impacts of VIS on the judicial process of providing sentences. This reveals that there are various discrepancies between the expectations of victims and the power of the judiciary, which strives to take into account numerous factors pertaining to the judicial process and the sentence decisions. The Canadian Resource Centre for Victims of Crime's analysis of the 'Victim Impact Statements in the Canadian Criminal Justice System' (Government of Canada 2015b) demonstrates the significance of VIS in empowering the victims with a voice with which they can reach out for help for the suffering of crimes that they have endured and the effect of these crimes on the victims. This shows that VIS is an important aspect of the Victim Rights Moment. It is recommended that the impact of crime should be taken into consideration in order to abstain from disputes about facts in the phase of trials in court. According to section 722 of the Criminal Code of Canada, it is important for the judges to keep into account the victim impact statement provided by the victims. It also details the process that needs to be followed to submit VIS at the proceedings of the judiciary, which also includes parole hearings in order to ensure that the perspectives and sufferings of victims are taken into account without compromising the fairness of the judiciary. VIS and the perspectives of victims are taken into consideration well in the Canadian Justice System.

Despite the significance and importance of VIS, they are not implemented uniformly across all the cases in Canada. They have been considered in fewer cases in the process of sentencing, which may be due to reasons such as personal decisions of the victim, administration difficulties, or less willingness to submit the victim impact statement. Due to these factors, the judiciary should act in order to maintain the integrity and effectiveness of the procedure of sentencing. The outcomes that were derived from D'Avignon's (2002) study demonstrate that the judges of Manitoba signify the importance of VIS, in which, according to 41% of judges, a VIS is frivolous in the cases of minors, which focused on the importance of VIS prevalently in the cases of heinous crimes such as violent or the crimes associated with property. This standpoint is furthermore supported by observations of the judiciary that the universal requirement of VIS has the possibility of overreaching legal resources without any significant benefits. Interestingly, it has been noted that a significant number of VIS include victims' recommendations for sentencing, a practice which is unexpected due to the common practice of editing out such recommendations by prosecutors. This indicates a potential area for improving the clarity and purpose of VIS to ensure that it meets its intended role without overstepping into the territory of judicial decision-making.

Despite its importance, VIS is underutilised. A small fraction of victims chose to engage with this process and even fewer present their statements orally, although those who do often report significant benefits. The effectiveness of VIS is limited by several challenges: Many victims are unaware about the fact that they can submit statements at the parole stage, and there are unrealistic expectations about the impact of these statements on sentencing outcomes. Additionally, victims often struggle with understanding the statement's purpose due to which they find the process complex. Support for victims is lacking, which complicates their ability to articulate their experiences effectively (Government of Canada, 2008). Furthermore, linguistic and literacy barriers, along with tight timelines for submission can prevent effective communication of their experiences. To ensure that the voices and perspectives of the victims are taken into consideration in a more effective manner, within the Judicial system of Canada, it is essential to promote awareness, support, and accessibility that can improve the incorporation of VIS into the judicial system.

The development of VIS in Canada reflects the relevant steps towards incorporating the voices and perspectives of the victim into the Judicial process, which aims to take into consideration the voices of the victims as well as the objectives of the judiciary. However, the effectiveness of VIS in influencing sentencing remains uncertain, pointing to ongoing challenges in bridging the gap between plausible benefits and practical implementation. Dufour et al.'s study on the relationship between victim impact statements and judicial decision making: An Archival Analysis of Sentencing Outcomes' (2023) signifies the impact of victim impact statements (VIS) on the process of sentencing in Canada from 2016 to 2018. The study delves into 1,332 sentencing rulings in accordance with VIS to reveal its impact on the decisions of the judiciary pertaining to incarceration, probation, ancillary orders, and eligibility for parole. Despite the importance of VIS in heinous crimes, the study also found that when the controlling was carried out for crime type, VIS had insignificant outcomes and impact on the impacts of sentencing. It was also revealed from the study that the oral communication of VIS resulted in longer sentences when compared to written submissions. The study also determines the limited and insignificant influence of VIS on the process of sentencing which contributes to the debate on the participation of the victims in the criminal proceedings and its efficiency in shaping decisions of the Judiciary.

3.4 South Africa

An enriching development has enshrined its way into the constitution of South Africa due to the incorporation of VIS in the legislation since 1994. This was the golden period for victims in which their rights got recognition and marked the political growth of South Africa. The constitution of South Africa also ensures that each individual in the country has the 'right to equal benefit' from the law which is a significant provision in the statutes of South Africa and extends to both, the offenders and the victims. However, commentators like Kgosimore argue that the constitution, alongside the Criminal Procedure Act tends to benefit offenders by addressing the rights of victims primarily in their capacity as witnesses rather than as victims in their own right (Brenda et al. 2010). This situation suggests an inherent conflict between the rights of victims and those of offenders, potentially undermining the victims' ability to seek redress and acknowledgement within the justice system. As per the South African Law Commission, VIS is defined as a written expression by the victim or an authorised individual that details the impact of the offence, including physical, psychological, social, and financial consequences. Originally intended to inform the court of the subjective experience of harm suffered by the victim, VIS serves multiple functions—(a) It highlights the circumstances surrounding the crime and its execution, (b) outlines the identity and character of the victim, and (c) describes the effect of the crime on the victim and their family. This provides the courts with a comprehensive understanding of the crime's impact beyond the legal facts, offering a more holistic view of the consequences borne by the victim.

Despite the established framework for VIS, there are critical voices concerning their implementation and effectiveness. The critique primarily focuses on the potential marginalisation of victims due to the legal emphasis on their roles as witnesses. It suggests a need for a more explicit delineation of victims' rights in the legal framework to prevent their overshadowing by the rights of the accused. Singh's analysis on 'Victimization and Victim Impact Statements: An Analysis of the Consequences on Victims of Crime and the Aims of the South African Victim Charter' delves into the impacts of victimisation and the role of victim impact statements (VIS) in South Africa, aligning with the national victim charter (Singh, 2014). It discusses the immediate and long-term effects of crime on victims, including physical, psychological, and emotional aspects, and distinguishes between primary victimisation (the direct impact of the crime) and secondary victimisation (inadequate societal responses). The study underscores the importance of VIS in giving victims a voice during sentencing and conveying the broader consequences of crime to courts, but it notes mixed outcomes in the effectiveness of VIS. Singh calls for informed policies and systemic improvements to better address victim needs, advancing discussions on victim rights and restorative justice in South Africa and beyond (Singh, 2014).

3.5 United Kingdom: The Victim's Personal Statement

In England and Wales, the Victim Personal Statement (hereinafter referred to as 'VPS') was introduced via the Victim's Charter of 1996, offering victims a broader platform to express the impact of a crime at various stages of the criminal justice process (O'Connell 2012). Unlike the VIS, which is primarily used during sentencing, the VPS can influence decisions on prosecution, bail, and even address concerns about a victim's security, highlighting issues related to race, culture, and disability (Moynihan 2015). Despite its comprehensive scope, the VPS scheme has not had a significant impact, largely due to a lack of public awareness and insufficient obligations on police, prosecutors, and other justice professionals (except legal professionals) to inform victims about the VPS scheme (Roberts and Manikis 2012).

According to the Victims Code of 2020, Right 7, victims are entitled to make a personal statement in their own words, describing how the crime has affected them physically, emotionally, financially, or otherwise (Making a Victim Personal Statement 2021). This statement is considered by judges or magistrates in sentencing and also aids the social services in providing the necessary support to the victim. Judges or magistrates are expected to take these statements into account unless there is a compelling reason not to. In cases where the victim has passed away or is a minor, a close bereaved relative, parent, or guardian can make the statement. The process is facilitated by police authorities or a Witness Care Officer, who acts as the victim's primary contact. If the defendant pleads guilty or is found guilty, VPS can be read aloud in court, in whole or in part, at the discretion of the judge or magistrate. It is crucial that this statement is submitted before the hearing begins, which cannot be altered once submitted. If additional significant details need to be included later, the victim must file a new statement. This system as a whole ensures that the voices of victims are heard and considered in the judicial process, emphasising the addressing of the personal perspective of criminal acts beyond the legal proceedings. VIS has been executed all over the UK, but its implementation varies across the different jurisdictions of the UK, and different approaches have been undertaken by these jurisdictions in order to embed VIS in the Judicial process, which is impacted by various historical, legal, and procedural nuances.

3.5.1 Northern Ireland

In Northern Ireland, the relevance of the VIS procures a unique position in the context of the UK. Northern Ireland does not have a statutory basis for the incorporation of VIS, unlike the other jurisdictions that facilitate its incorporation, leading to a culture that is more improvised and less formal in nature. Since June 2006, only 435 cases have been recorded that sustained the use of VIS in the judicial proceedings, demonstrating a significantly low uptake. This minimal use is primarily undertaken in cases that involve sexual offences or heinous crimes, signifying a narrower scope of practical application towards heinous offences.

In Northern Ireland, the nature of VIS is non-statutory, which means that its implementation is not uniform across the whole criminal justice process. The Department of Justice has addressed this shortcoming, and for now, it is striving to find ways in order to strengthen the effectiveness and efficacy of VIS. Nonetheless, despite these efforts, this improvised application has been criticised for the potential undermining of the uniform application and fairness in the criminal justice system. This inconsistent application can lead to discrepancies in how the voices of victims are heard and incorporated into the judicial proceedings. which depends upon a specific category of crime and the prudence of the respective legal entities who are legally involved in the process.

Northern Ireland's approach to VIS is less effective when compared to other jurisdictions' legislative measures that expressly support and facilitate the incorporation of VIS into legal proceedings. For example, in regions like Canada, the law has made it important for the courts to take into consideration whether the victim has been given the privilege to make a VIS, which provides a more structured and accountable structure where the voices of the victims are also taken into consideration. In contrast, the approach in Northern Ireland remains has discrepancies and demonstrates a significantly variable application, which impacts uniformity in VIS implementation and also the perceived and legitimate value of these statements pertaining to the process of criminal justice and its administration.

The position of VIS in Northern Ireland demonstrates the relevance of both the challenges and the opportunities for promoting the role of victims within the process of sentencing. Further, it is crucial to keep in mind that the reforms address the procedural shortcomings as well as impact how victims are perceived and treated within the criminal justice system. Solidifying the concept of VIS with the help of the legislature and its application practically across the country could significantly enhance the process of attaining justice within the system, making it more incorporative towards the rights of the victims as well as their needs.

3.5.2 England and Wales

The use and operation of VIS is called VPS in England and Wales. This has emerged to provide a greater room for the victims in the Indian Criminal Justice System. In contrast to other jurisdictions, the VPS system in England is governed through non-legislative methods like practices of judicial directions and the guidance of crown prosecution services.

VPS is crucial in helping the victims to express the impact of the crime committed on them and offers their input at varied stages of the Criminal system, particularly at the stage of bail and sentencing. In some of the jurisdictions, like England, the victims are allowed to orally communicate their statements in court. However, the VPS must be submitted in writing, and the victims are prohibited from reading their statements in court. The prohibition restricts emotional communication by the victim which might influence the judges/jury. A critical review written by Freya Rock named 'Victim Personal Statements: A Review of Recent Research and Developments' criticises the use of VPS introduced in England and Wales in 2001. The review demonstrates that even though there is legislative support, the VPS still faces hindrances in influencing judicial decisions. It further shows that the objective of VPS is to make an informed decision while understanding the VIS. However, its impact is restricted due to inconsistent usage and ambiguity in its purpose. Rock suggests future research should explore reasons for low VPS utilisation and advocate for reforms to better integrate VPS into sentencing processes, highlighting the ongoing need for evaluation and adjustment to serve victims effectively (Rock 2024).

There have been efforts to broaden the scope of offences that can include a VPS, reflecting a growing recognition of the diverse impacts of different types of crimes on victims. Efforts have been made to widen the ambit of crimes that could encompass VPS. This effort clearly demonstrates that there are varied impacts of crimes on different individuals. This development manifests a transition towards recognition of the repercussions of crime beyond those readily visible and conventionally acknowledged. It is often argued that VPS stands at a cross between traditional judicial practice and the participation of victims in the judicial system. Critics contend that the ongoing scheme suppresses the voice of the victim, especially in the trial, the role of victims has become invisible, and the entire dispute is showcased between the state and the respondent. VPS is a component of a larger initiative that emphasises that the roles of victims from mere witnesses that need to be switched to direct participants in the judicial process, reflecting their personal and emotional stakes.

In contrast to the United States, where the VIS system directly impacts the sentencing result, the VPS system in England and Wales places more weight on the impact of crime instead of influencing the sentencing result. Such type of administration in the criminal justice system reflects its alignment with the adversarial system. Therefore, the evolving nature of VIS in England and Wales reflects that there is a need to incorporate victim perspectives.

3.5.3 Scotland

The emergence of VIS in Scotland is quite unique. Scotland is very subtly incorporating the VIS system into their judicial system, which illuminates it on balancing the adversarial system and victim-centric approaches of the criminal justice system. The structure of VIS was set up in 2009 in England. This allowed the victims to write their statement and submit it to the court. This step, to a great extent recognised the rights of the victims. However, the VIS system was restricted to 'higher tariff' offences meaning that it was applicable only when the gravity of the offence was high. Before the formal adoption of VIS in Scotland, the victims were unaware of this provision. In other jurisdictions, like the US and New Zealand, the VIS system recommends sentencing. However, in Scotland, the impact of crime is more prioritised and there is no recommendation provided for sentencing. The system prevents the integration of information including any suggestion concerning the sentence or narration of crime. This is again, in alignment with the broader system of the UK, where the victim's voice is balanced with the impartiality and fairness of the Judicial system.

The strategy of the UK pertaining to VIS reflects a very careful incorporation of victims' feedback. Although the statement of the victim is acknowledged, especially when it comes to the impact of crime, there is still a caution to balance the right of the accused within the adversarial system. This reflects the current dispute concerning the position of the victim in the criminal justice system that has traditionally witnessed any event as a point of contention between the victim and the accused.

The incorporation of a victim-centric approach can be seen across various jurisdictions, with some hindrance. The legislative structure in Canada is considered to be very progressive since it takes into account the participation of victims in the criminal justice system. This stands in contravention of the UK method and nascent victimological practices of South Africa. Although the criticisms have prevailed, there is a worldwide phenomenon to incorporate the voices of these victims. The international switch to a victim-centric approach not only concedes the impact of crime but is also instrumental in shaping the entire criminal justice system. The VIS system needs to be carefully implemented owing to diversity in legal, social, and cultural contexts. The article by Sam Garkawe, named 'Victim Impact Statements and Sentencing', responds to the impact of VIS on sentencing in the context of the

Common Law System. The article proposes that the suffering of the victims needs to be directly connected to the actions of the offender. According to the article, accuracy should be augmented to prevent any kind of prejudice in VIS, and in order to achieve this, a framework of strict guidelines needs to be constructed. It is said in the article that VIS is necessary in order to enhance the victims' participation in the Judicial system, and to incorporate the articulation of their emotions, which helps them in their recovery. Sam Garakawe supports the balanced approach, which depicts that objective and subjective assessment of both the offenders and the victims' needs to be done (Garkawe 2007). The primary goal of the legal system is fairness, justice, and resources. Results of judicial decisions and victim satisfaction need to be taken into consideration while taking into account the primary requirements. The subtle integration of VIS reflects that there is a modification in the existing system in order to meet the social and legal expectations. This again demonstrates the shift towards a victim-centric approach. The international viewpoint also underscores the necessity to continuously refine the terms of VIS, so that the requirements of victims and the principle of justice are upheld.

4 Legal and Ethical Implications

The primary focus of the Indian adversarial system is deterrence and preventing the accused from inflicting harm on the innocents. However, the victims in India still face a lot of issues and often go through stigmatisation and secondary victimisation, as was observed in the case of Mallikarjun. Although in a number of cases the victims' rights have often been given recognition, as in the case of the Bhopal Gas Tragedy. India still has a long way to go. This section of the article will examine the ethical and practical challenges in the implementation of VIS in India. This involves aspects, like the likelihood of unfairness in sentencing, and disappointment among victims because of the concern that VIS might unjustly impact court decisions.

Incorporating victim impact statements (VIS) into the system could face hindrances due to existing systemic and procedural shortcomings. The current approach of the judiciary towards victim rights needs to be improved in order to prevent worsening of the vulnerabilities of the disadvantaged communities like Dalits, Muslims, and Tribal groups (Jadhav and Khalkho 2020). Without protections in place, implementing the VIS programme might lead to punishments for these communities, ultimately undermining fairness. Victims sharing their impact statements could experience trauma if they lack support systems. In high-profile cases, media attention has the potential to increase pressure on the judiciary, influencing decisions and casting doubts on the courts' integrity and credibility. The subjective nature of VIS might also introduce bias into judicial rulings, along with sentimental testimonies, possibly affecting the judges' impartiality, leading to inconsistent sentencing. However, Davis and Smith's study 'The Effects of Victim Impact Statements on Sentencing Decisions: A Test in an Urban Setting' (1994) and Roberts' study 'Listening to the Crime Victim: Evaluating Victim Input at Sentencing and Parole'

(2009) reveal the limited influence of victim impact statements (VIS) on sentencing decisions did not demonstrate any significant effect on how the harm inflicted upon victims was taken into consideration or resulted in punitive sentencing (Davis and Smith 1994a). Both studies acknowledge potential benefits for victims, such as increased involvement and emotional closure of the victims, though it should be noted that these statements do not necessarily lead to harsher penalties. Roberts also emphasises the need for a balanced approach that respects both victim rights and justice principles (Roberts 2009). In 'Impact of Victim Impact Statements on Legal Decisions in Criminal Proceedings: A Systematic Review of the Literature Across Jurisdictions and Decision Types', mixed results were found on the impact of VIS, calling for more diverse research to understand its broader implications (Kunst et al. 2020). Meanwhile, Edna Erez and Linda Rogers' study 'Victim Impact Statements and Sentencing Outcomes and Processes: The Perspectives of Legal Professionals' highlights a resistance within the legal community towards incorporating victim input into sentencing decisions, indicating a gap between empowering victims theoretically and their limited influence in the practical world (Erez and Rogers 1999). Additionally, in 'The Use of Victim Impact Statements in Sentencing for Sexual Offences: Stories of Strength' by Davies & Bartels, the minimal actual influence of VIS on sentencing is explored despite their intended function to give victims a voice, advocating for clearer sentencing policies and a more victim-centred approach to enhance VIS's therapeutic potential for victims of sexual offences (Erez and Rogers 1999).

The procedural framework in India currently limits victims' participation, treating them as mere witnesses. This limitation is exacerbated by the absence of concrete sentencing guidelines, granting judges broad discretion in determining penalties. Such discretion, combined with emotionally charged statements, could worsen disparities in sentencing for similar offences. Addressing these concerns necessitates the careful consideration of VIS's role in the justice system, including guidelines for the use of VIS, training for legal practitioners, and the measures to support victims while protecting the rights of the accused.

Specific issues pertaining to VIS in India include the lack of procedural structure, starting from the often-ignored filing and registration of an FIR under section 154 of the CrPC (Ohri 2021). With 50 million cases pending (Yasir and Scholiers 2024), the courts are overburdened, and the incorporation of VIS in the system can further complicate case management. VIS might also serve as a mere procedural end rather than providing therapeutic benefits, due to the system's emphasis on deterring crime and punishing the guilty, not on emotional support. Therefore, the victims should limit their statements to facts, detracting from the essence of VIS (Ghosh 2022).

Moreover, VIS can create unrealistic expectations among victims about the outcomes of their statements, leading to potential hostility towards the system among these victims when their expectations are unmet (Singh 2022). VIS can lead to bias in the judicial decision-making, leading to subjective rulings, rather than objective ones. The influence of the public, media, and stakeholders could further disrupt judicial processes, particularly problematic given the existing backlog of cases (Edna Erez 1991). Lastly, marginalised communities might suffer due to the implementation of VIS without appropriate safeguards being constructed. (Prema et al. 2021) This is because of the fact that these communities are already vulnerable to discrimination and exploitation (DHNS 2023). The field test analysed the impact of VIS on the sentiments of the victims of crime pertaining to their involvement and their overall satisfaction, which was found to have no significant impact on their condition. While VIS offers a straightforward way to involve victims, it does not necessarily increase efficiency and victim's satisfaction within the judicial process (Davis and Smith 1994b).

While the introduction of VIS in India marks a shift towards a more victim-centred approach in legal proceedings, it also involves an important aspect, which is navigating a landscape marked by unique challenges. The effective integration of victim impact statements (VIS) necessitates reforms and meticulous planning of the implementation procedure in the judiciary to guarantee that victims receive support without undermining the integrity and credibility of the justice system.

5 Exploring the Viability of Victim Impact Statements in the Indian Legal Context

This part explores the real-world aspects and obstacles of incorporating VIS into the judicial system. It also suggests advice for introducing VIS in order to ensure that they are appropriate, just, and respectful to the victims' rights, while upholding the judicial principles.

5.1 Balancing Rights: Addressing Victim Marginalisation in India's Adversarial System

The rights of the accused have often been traditionally prioritised in the adversarial system of India, but this is always at the expense of the victims' rights. This non-equilibrium has reduced the credibility of the Indian Judicial system. This imbalance in rights has created a perception among the victims that they are in a better position if they remain silent, instead of fighting for justice (Raghavan 2020). The operation of VIS is at the core to recognise the harm and loss suffered by the victims. VIS often functions as a therapeutic jurisprudence, and it defines the right of victims in addressing the tangible and intangible impact of the crimes on the lives of victims. From a penological perspective, VIS illuminates the direct effects of crime on victims, which can inform strategies for rehabilitation, restoration, and deterrence of offenders (Prasanth 2023). By providing detailed insights pertaining to the disrupted lives of victims caused by victimisation, VIS can facilitate a ground-breaking shift towards restoration for both victims and offenders and enhance societal awareness of the consequences of criminal acts. In 'Victim Participation in

Criminal Justice: A Quantitative Systematic and Critical Literature Review', Holder and Englezos analyse 58 studies from 2002 to 2021, primarily from common law jurisdictions, to examine victim participation in criminal justice systems (Holder and Englezos 2023). They have strongly criticised the existing research for its vague definitions of 'participation' and varied implications for the justice outcomes. A review of victims' participation in the criminal justice system finds that victim participation is mainly carried out at trial, and the review further highlights that there is a need for future research on the clear-cut operationalisation of VIS. Although the objective of victim participation is to empower them, it frequently falls short underscoring the psychological impact on victims and its impact on the result of judicial decisions (Holder and Englezos 2023).

5.2 Strategies for Effective Integration of VIS in the Indian Judicial System

For the successful incorporation of VIS into the Indian Judicial System, one needs to weigh the entire situation and analyse its merits and demerits. This encompasses the implementation of procedures for submission and evaluation of VIS to check that they remain suitable in the Indian Judicial System. Crystal clear instructions should be made so that the admissibility of any content in the VIS can be judged. Moreover, the legal basis of all the facts needs to be constantly analysed. This will ensure that the entire system is bias-free and undue influence on the judicial decisions can be prevented. Furthermore, training programmes for judges are also crucial so that they can objectively interpret the VIS without being biased. These programmes need to effectively make a clear distinction between emotional elements and the factual impact of crime so that a consistent and fair judicial procedure is carried out. Also, victim support services should be established as it is crucial to support the victims emotionally, in order to prevent re-traumatisation of victims and maintain their dignity in the judicial system. An innovative approach might involve creating a separate body tasked with the preliminary assessment of VIS. This body can review statements before they reach the court, ensuring compliance with guidelines and safeguarding the trial's fairness. Nagpal and Rawandale's study (2023) traces the evolution of victim's rights under Indian law, drawing comparative insights from the United States. It highlights legislative changes influenced by social movements, especially those advocating for women's rights and victim justice. The paper outlines the development of victim rights in India, starting from primarily compensation-focused recognition to expanded rights including participation in criminal processes and victim compensation schemes, particularly post the Malimath Committee Report and judicial decisions. Contrasting with the United States formalisation of victims' rights through the Crime Victims' Rights Act 2004, the study notes that while both countries have seen similar social pressures driving victims' rights, the United States has implemented more concrete legislative protections. Critically, the study critiques the limitation in the practical empowerment of victims within India's judicial process despite legal provisions and calls for stronger enforcement and clearer definitions of victim's rights. It emphasises the ongoing need for the development and enforcement of victim's rights in both countries to ensure fairer and more effective justice systems.

5.3 Promising Benefits of Implementing VIS in India

When thoughtfully implemented, VIS can significantly enhance the efficacy and fairness of the Indian criminal justice system. The effective establishment and implementation of VIS has the potential to augment the efficiency and fairness of the Indian Criminal System. If the victims are allowed to articulate their statements, then it is going to foster a more comprehensive understanding of the repercussions of criminal behaviour among the authorities. This leads to suitable sentencing decisions. Moreover, this understanding can lead to restorative justice, where the needs of the victim and the suffering that the victim has endured can be better integrated into the judicial system, which will increase the contentment of victims and the credibility of the criminal justice system. Besides the formalisation of VIS into the judicial system, it can lead it to a more equilibrium position where the rights and the requirements of the victims are taken into account along with the rights of the accused. The 168 VIS given during Larry Nassar's sentencing: a case involving widespread sexual abuse of young athletes is comprehensively analysed in Cassell and Erez's study called 'How Victim Impact Statements Promote Justice: Evidence from the Content of Statements Delivered in Larry Nassar's Sentencing' (2023). The research in this study uses quantitative and qualitative methods and underscores the effect of VIS, motivation, and the content of VIS in those cases where the sentencing was already determined. It also highlights that offering details to the court, giving advantages to the victims, and providing education to the public at large. In opposition to the earlier studies, this study shows that VIS does not, in any way, compromise the severity of the punishment or promote prejudices; instead, it fosters fairness and maintains judicial impartiality. This study argues that the introduction of VIS might have a certain positive impact on the Indian Judicial System, as it promotes victims' participation, provides emotional support to the victims and leads to awareness in the community concerning the impact of crime. The study also points out that further empirical research needs to be conducted to comprehend the long-term impact of VIS on victims' psychology and implications on the criminal justice system. Thus, concluding that VIS is crucial for not only individuals but also for augmenting the fairness, equilibria concerning the rights of victims and accused, an empathetic attitude towards the criminal justice system, and credibility of the same.

6 Conclusion

The examination of VIS in the context of the Indian Criminal Justice System demonstrates that there is a need to incorporate a victim-centred approach in the judicial process. VIS has varying definitions in various economies, cultures, and societal frameworks. It is found that in some jurisdictions, VIS impacts the sentencing, while in other jurisdictions, VIS primarily helps the victims to articulate their needs, preventing further re-traumatisation of the victims and aiding them in their healing process. This article highlights that structured reforms need to be done, such as training the judges, establishing victim services to support them, the submission process of VIS needs to be standardised, and a preliminary review mechanism of VIS should be incorporated. These reforms promote emotional support to the victim and try to balance the sentencing by allowing the judges to make informed decisions. This chapter's discussion highlights the potential of VIS to be implemented at any stage of the criminal justice system, enhancing sentencing practices to better fulfil victims' rights.

However, the effective implementation of VIS in India faces substantial challenges, necessitating more than just the integration of this tool into the current system. Given India's diverse cultural environment and the existing judicial backlog, compounded by casteist and religious turmoil, there is a pressing need for increased awareness and a more supportive ideology towards victims interacting with judicial entities (Gupta 2024). As noted in the Malimath Report, the Indian system is heavily loaded in favour of the accused, often leaving the victim merely as a witness without the right to participate actively in the judicial process (Government of India, Ministry of Home Affairs 2003). To conclude, it is emphasised that the inclusion of VIS might seem like a promising step, since it promotes inclusive and empathetic legal systems. However, the accomplishment of the same depends upon thoughtfulness and culturally sensitive implementation. This takes into account the requirements of the victims and the necessities of achieving justice. This is not only a legislative change but also a fundamental movement in the culture of India's legal system towards a victim-centric approach. India can leverage the full potential of VIS to improve the effectiveness, equity, and compassion of its criminal justice system, and increase public trust and satisfaction by using this methodical and considerate approach.

Statutes

2013 Missouri Revised Statutes:: TITLE XXXVIII CRIMES AND PUNISHMENT; PEACE OFFICERS AND PUBLIC DEFENDERS:: Chapter 557 General Sentencing Provisions. (2013). Justia Law. Retrieved 2024, from https://law.justia.com/codes/missouri/2013/title-xxxviii/chapter-557/

2023 Rhode Island General Laws:: Title 12 - Criminal Procedure :: Chapter 12-28 - Victim's Rights :: Section 12-28-4. - Right to address court prior to sentencing.

(2023). Justia Law. Retrieved 2024, from https://law.justia.com/codes/rhode-island/title-12/chapter-12-28/section-12-28-4/#:~:text=(a)%20Prior%20to%20the%20imposition

Cases

Balasaheb Rangnath Khade v The State Of Maharashtra & Ors, (Supreme Court of India 2012).
Booth v. Maryland, (U.S. Supreme Court June 15, 1987). https://supreme.justia.com/cases/federal/us/482/496/t
Dayal Singh v. State of Uttaranchal, (Supreme Court of India 2012).
Karan v. State NCT of Delhi, (Delhi High Court 2021). https://indiankanoon.org/doc/73331712/
Lalita Kumari v. Government of U.P. & Ors., (Indian Supreme Court 2014). https://main.sci.gov.in/pdf/aorexam/leading_cases/31.pdf
Maru Ram v. Union of India, (Supreme Court of India 1981).
Mallikarjun Kodagali (Dead) v. The State of Karnataka, (Indian Supreme Court 2018). https://indiankanoon.org/doc/111899692/#:~:text=It%20was%20held%20that%20the,with%20the%20right%20to%20appeal.
Mallikarjun Kodagali v State of Karnataka, (Supreme Court of India 2019).
Payne v. Tennessee, (U.S. Supreme Court 1991). https://supreme.justia.com/cases/federal/us/501/808/
Puran v Rambilas, (Supreme Court of India 2001).
Rattan Singh v. State of Punjab, (Supreme Court of India 1979).
Rattiram v State of Madhya Pradesh, (Supreme Court of India 2012).
Sakshi v Union of India, (Supreme Court of India 2004).
Satya Pal Singh v State of Madhya Pradesh (Supreme Court of India 2015).
South Carolina v. Gathers, (U.S. Supreme Court June 12, 1989). https://supreme.justia.com/cases/federal/us/490/805//
The People v. Brock Allen Turner, (Court of Appeal of The State of California 2018). https://casetext.com/case/people-v-turner-973
Vishaka v. State of Rajasthan, (Indian Supreme Court 1997). https://indiankanoon.org/doc/1031794/

References

Books

Zehr H (2002) The little book of restorative justice. Good Books

Journals

Allen D (1992) Payne v. Tennessee: victim impact statement's role in capital murder sentencing. Univ Dayton Law Rev
Brenda, Ann, Beukman (2010) Victim impact statements and the role of the South African criminologist. US-China Law Rev 7(3):47–53
Cornille SA (1993) Retribution's harm component and the victim impact statement: finding a workable model. Univ Dayton Law Rev 18(2) https://ecommons.udayton.edu/udlr/vol18/iss2/4
Davis RC, Smith BE (1994a) The effects of victim impact statements on sentencing decisions: a test in an urban setting. Just Quart 11(3):453–469. https://doi.org/10.1080/07418829400092351
Davis RC, Smith BE (1994b) Victim impact statements and victim satisfaction: an unfulfilled promise? J Crim Just 22(1):1–12. https://doi.org/10.1016/0047-2352(94)90044-2
Dufour GK, Ternes M, Stinson V (2023) The relationship between victim impact statements and judicial decision making: an archival analysis of sentencing outcomes. Law and Human Behav 47(4):484–498. https://doi.org/10.1037/lhb0000535
Edna Erez (1991) Victim impact statements trends and issues in criminal justice system. 33. https://www.aic.gov.au/publications/tandi/tandi33
Erez E, Rogers L (1999) Victim impact statements and sentencing outcomes: The perspectives of legal professionals. *British Journal of Criminology, 39*(2), 216–239.
Garkawe SB (2007) Victim impact statements and sentencing. Monash Univ Law Rev 33(1) https://researchportal.scu.edu.au/esploro/outputs/991012822284602368
Gupta, S.(2024) Victim impact statement: relevance in the Indian criminal justice system
Holder RL, Englezos E (2023) Victim participation in criminal justice: a quantitative systematic and critical literature review. Int Rev Victimol 30(1):026975802311512. https://doi.org/10.1177/02697580231151207
Kunst M, de Groot G, Meester J, van Doorn J (2020) The impact of victim impact statements on legal decisions in criminal proceedings: a systematic review of the literature across jurisdictions and decision types. Aggression Viol Behav 56:101512. https://doi.org/10.1016/j.avb.2020.101512
Moynihan S (2015) The Voiceless Victim: a critical analysis of the impact of enhanced victim participation in the criminal justice process. IALS Student Law Rev 3(1). https://doi.org/10.14296/islr.v3i1.2247
Nagpal M, Rawandale CJ (2023) Tracing journey of crime victim's position under Indian law with evolutionary insights from the United States' federal code on victims' rights. Cogent Arts Human 10(2). https://doi.org/10.1080/23311983.2023.2286071
Prema E, Sundar VS, Rajavenkatesan PRL (2021, November 23) Access to justice for marginalized Dalit people in India: analyzing the challenges in attaining the sustainable development goals. Atlantis Press. https://doi.org/10.2991/assehr.k.211112.056
Roberts JV (2009) Listening to the crime victim: evaluating victim input at sentencing and parole. Crime Just 38(1):347–412. https://doi.org/10.1086/599203
Roberts JV, Manikis M (2012) Victim personal statements in England and Wales: latest (and last) trends from the witness and victim experience survey. Criminol Crim Just 13(3):245–261. https://doi.org/10.1177/1748895812452281
Rock F (2024) Victim personal statements [Review of Victim Personal Statements]. University of Cambridge. https://www.sentencingacademy.org.uk/wp-content/uploads/2024/02/Victim-Personal-Statements-A-Review-of-Recent-Research-and-Developments.pdf
Singh AS (2022) Procedural limitations of victim impact statement in India: a critical analysis. J Victimol Victim Just 251660692211171. https://doi.org/10.1177/25166069221117186

Reports

Doyle C (2021) Crime Victims' Rights Act: A Summary and Legal Analysis of 18 U.S.C. § 3771 [Review of Crime Victims' Rights Act: A Summary and Legal Analysis of 18 U.S.C. § 3771]. Congressional Research Service. https://sgp.fas.org/crs/misc/RL33679.pdf

Government of Canada, D. of J (2008, April 18). Victims of Crime - Research Digest. Www.justice.gc.ca. https://www.justice.gc.ca/eng/rp-pr/cj-jp/victim/rr07_vic4/p1.html#ftn6

Government of India, Ministry of Home Affairs. (2003). Committee on Reforms of Criminal Justice System. https://www.mha.gov.in/sites/default/files/criminal_justice_system.pdf (Government of India, Ministry of Home Affairs, 2003)

O'Connell F (2012) Victim Impact Statements (NIAR 952-11). Northern Ireland Assembly

Online Sources

Barmann J (2022, August 22) Stanford Rapist Brock Turner Goes Viral Again Via "Whisper Network" In Ohio. SFist - San Francisco News, Restaurants, Events, & Sports. https://sfist.com/2022/08/22/stanford-rapist-brock-turner-goes-viral-again-on-tiktok-in-ohio/

Day M (2016, June 10) The origin of victim impact statements has its roots in the Charles Manson case. Timeline. https://medium.com/timeline/the-powerful-origin-story-of-victim-impact-statements-696073817e0a

DHNS (2023, November 26) When state doesn't intervene, marginalised get dominated: CJI Chandrachud. Deccan Herald. https://www.deccanherald.com/india/when-state-doesn-t-intervene-marginalised-get-dominated-cji-2785190

Ghosh A (2022, March 4) Unravelling the Question of Victim Impact Statements at Sentencing. P39A Criminal Law Blog. https://p39ablog.com/2022/03/unravelling-the-question-of-victim-impact-statements-at-sentencing/

Government of Canada, D. of J (2015a, July 20) Victim Impact Statement. Www.justice.gc.ca. https://www.justice.gc.ca/eng/cj-jp/victims-victimes/factsheets-fiches/victim-victime.html#:~:text=A%20victim%20impact%20statement%20is

Government of Canada, D. of J (2015b, July 23) Victim impact statement - Canadian Victims Bill of Rights. Www.justice.gc.ca. https://www.justice.gc.ca/eng/cj-jp/victims-victimes/sentencing-peine/vis-dv.html

Jadhav D, Khalkho S (2020) Safeguards for Marginalised a Must if India Wants to Adopt "Victim Impact Statement." The Wire. https://thewire.in/law/criminal-law-reform-victim-impact-statement

Jenkins JP (2019) Charles Manson | Biography, Murders, & Facts. In Encyclopaedia Britannica. https://www.britannica.com/biography/Charles-Manson

Making a Victim Personal Statement. (2021). https://assets.publishing.service.gov.uk/media/5a7cd21040f0b6629523c02e/victims-vps-guidance.pdf

Miller C (2016) Stanford Victim Letter Impact Statement from Brock Turner's Victim [Review of Stanford Victim Letter Impact Statement from Brock Turner's Victim]. Stanford. https://s3.documentcloud.org/documents/2852615/Stanford-Victim-Letter-Impact-Statement-From.pdf

Ohri R (2021, July 15) Court slams Delhi Police for not filing FIR of riot victim. The Economic Times.https://economictimes.indiatimes.com/news/india/court-slams-delhi-police-for-not-filing-fir-of-riot-victim/articleshow/84420764.cms?from=mdr

Prasanth P (2023, October 21) The importance of victim impact statements in criminal law. Bar and Bench - Indian Legal News. https://www.barandbench.com/columns/victim-impact-statement

Raghavan A (2020, October 7) Restoring Public Trust in the Indian Judiciary Calls for More Scrutiny, Not Less. The Wire. https://thewire.in/law/restoring-public-trust-in-the-indian-judiciary-calls-for-more-scrutiny-not-

UNODC (2018, May) Organized Crime Module 9 Key Issues: Adversarial versus Inquisitorial Legal Systems. Unodc.org. https://www.unodc.org/e4j/en/organized-crime/module-9/key-issues/adversarial-vs-inquisitorial-legal-systems.html

Yasir S, Scholiers E (2024, January 13) "A Lifelong Nightmare": seeking justice in India's overwhelmed courts. The New York Times. https://www.nytimes.com/2024/01/13/world/asia/india-judicial-backlog.html

The Need for Participatory Action Research as Victim Assistance Methodology for Vulnerable Towards Sexual Exploitation

Vipin Vijay Nair

Abstract This chapter investigates the importance of applying participatory action research (PAR) to assist victims, especially those who are marginalized. This analysis mainly focuses on victim support systems with a critical evaluation of how efficient these systems are in India. It investigates key aspects like victim advocacy, legal aid, and community programmes aimed at helping people affected by crime. The aim is to contribute to the ongoing discourse about the enhancement and expansion of victim support services. This chapter seeks to offer comprehensive assistance to victims, thereby empowering them in their journey towards recovery through PAR; it will present findings from rehabilitation and protective homes in India. In this regard, it encourages active participation from the affected parties to collectively address their issues and concerns. To create a more inclusive and effective support system that promotes greater resilience and well-being among vulnerable populations, PAR must be embedded into victim assistance initiatives.

Keywords Participatory action research • Victim assistance • Vulnerable victim • Coping mechanism • Sexual exploitation • Rehabilitation

1 Introduction

Poverty, mental health issues, and other forms of vulnerability often intersect, creating complex challenges for individuals and communities. Participatory action research (PAR) has been seen as a new way to meet the needs of vulnerable populations and enable them to play an active role in both the research and solution

V. V. Nair (✉)
Jindal Institute of Behavioural Sciences, O.P. Jindal Global University, Sonipat, India
e-mail: vvnair@jgu.edu.in

© The Author(s), under exclusive license to Springer Nature Singapore Pte Ltd. 2026

G. S. Bajpai et al. (eds.), *Beyond the Gavel: A Paradigm Shift in Global Criminal Justice*, https://doi.org/10.1007/978-981-95-4487-5_7

development processes. It is important that various indicators associated with weak towards exploitation are known so as to apply participatory action research in its research methodology.

1.1 Victims of Commercial Sexual Exploitation in India

The definition of trafficking in India is covered under Indian Penal Code, 1860. It is defined as transportation, transfer, harbouring, recruitment, or receipt of any individual for any sort of exploitation. In addition to Indian Penal Code, there are various other laws that regulate trafficking for various purposes. For example, Immoral Traffic (Prevention) Act, 1986, deals with trafficking and sexual exploitation. Similarly, the Child Labour Regulation Act, 1986, and the Bonded Labour Regulation, 1986, deal with exploitation through bonded labour. Each of these laws operates independently through various enforcement mechanisms and prescribes specific punishment and sentencing for respective offences. The vulnerability of an individual due to age, physical and mental condition, geographical location, caste, culture, or being susceptible to commercial sexual exploitation due to various other external factors. These individuals, with the possibility of sexual exploitation under various laws mentioned before, are addressed as vulnerable to commercial sexual exploitation.

The Ministry of Women and Child Development recently introduced the Trafficking of Persons (Prevention, Protection and Rehabilitation) Bill in July 2018. The bill proposed a law to investigate all types of trafficking and involve the rescue, protection, and rehabilitation of trafficked victims. The bill was envisioned to create various investigation and rehabilitation authorities in different districts, states, and at the national level. It also specifies the introduction of various anti-trafficking units to rescue victims and investigate cases of trafficking. The introduced bill adds to the existing list of legislation available against the prevention of trafficking, like immoral traffic prevention act, 1986. Both the legislation shares certain similarities, like the creation of rehabilitation and protection homes, rescue of traffic victims, especially victims of commercial sexual exploitation and creating awareness towards trafficking. The bill also introduced certain exclusive provisions like confidentiality of witnesses, victims, and complaints. It envisioned time-bound trials and timely repatriation and reintegration of victim to society. The bill tabled in Lok Sabha was subsequently passed in 2018, which lapsed before the 2019 Rajya Sabha session. The bill is yet to be reintroduced in parliament to be officially cleared and enacted as an act (Gandhi 2018).

The National Crime Records Bureau, in its Crime in India Report 2018, reflected a continuous increase in the number of cases of human trafficking from 918 (2016), 1127 (2017) to 1313 (2018). The report also highlighted cases of trafficking and sexual exploitation. Under various special and local laws. The Immoral Traffic (Prevention) Act reflected a decline in the number of cases reported from 2337 (2016), 2127 (2017) to 1882 (2018). The crime in India report shows 38,503 victims of human Trafficking between 2011 and 2019 (NCRB 2019). Various reports show that during 2011–2019, only 107 victims of trafficking could file an application for compensation in various district and state authorities. Only 85 among them were found eligible for compensation, and 77 among them received compensation. The reason for non-registration of complaints by victims of commercial sexual exploitation were pointed out towards lack of evidence and proof of exploitation. The victims of commercial sexual exploitation face discrimination and derogatory remarks from various legal and police professionals while seeking compensation (Khan 2020).

1.2 Assistance Towards Women Victims of Exploitation in India

Hammond and McGlone (2014) pointed out that the needs of victims of commercial sexual exploitation change from time to time. It differs from the time they enter commercial sexual exploitation as a trafficked victim to the time they are reintegrated back into society. Macy and Johns (2011) and Muraya and Fry (2016) have considered need-based assistance into four categories, namely emergency needs, short-term assistance, intermediate assistance, and long-term assistance. Emergency needs involve first-hand response to any traumatic incident through legal, medical, or psychological assistance. Short term needs include necessities involving food, shelter, clothing, and any aspect of psychological, legal, medical assistance. Ongoing or intermediate needs include continuous medical care, psychological counselling, vocational training, and legal help. Victims of commercial sexual exploitation require long-term assistance that creates opportunities towards efficient rehabilitation and reintegration. These assistances involve life skill training, vocational training, employment opportunity, housing facilities, and financial assistance.

A holistic assistance programme from beginning to end caters to provide a smooth transition for the victim from trauma to reintegration towards society (Surtees 2008). Assistance towards women victims of exploitation or categorize into government-sponsored assistance and nongovernmental initiatives.

1.3 Government-Sponsored Assistance

The Ministry of Women and Child Development has notified several central-sponsored schemes for the empowerment of women in the entire country; few of the schemes can be noted as below:

Swadhar Greh started in 1969 by the Government of India provides temporary shelters to women through various support services and empowerment of the women victims. The objective of Swadhar Greh included assistance towards the primary needs of food, shelter, medical treatment, and counselling to regain emotional support and start life with dignity. Beneficiaries of Swadhar Greh include any woman victim of violence without discrimination on the basis of caste, religion, and socioeconomic status. The inclusion criteria of beneficiaries involve women who were deserted, victims of natural disasters, women prisoners released from jail without any family support, domestic violence victims, and victims of trafficking. The victims of trafficking are first considered under the Ujjawala Scheme towards the protection and rehabilitation of victims of commercial sexual exploitation. Swadhar Greh act as a temporary shelter to reduce distress by providing various support services like legal aid, medical facility, vocational training, and counselling (Scheme 1969).

One Stop Centre is constituted from the Nirbhaya fund that focus of empowerment of women facing violence in private or public spaces. One stop centre acts as a single point of assistance for any incident of violence, including rape, acid attack, domestic violence, and any other act of violence. One stop centre sponsored by the Ministry of Women and Child Development provides various forms of assistance, including medical, legal, psychological, and other temporary assistance required to reduce the traumatic experience of the victim. These forms of assistance involve professionals from varied industries with years of experience in handling victims of violence.

1.4 Nongovernmental Initiatives

The majority of the assistance in India provided to victims of exploitation is rendered by nongovernmental initiatives. These nongovernmental organizations are supported through sponsors, donations, or any financial assistance provided by the state government. Many nongovernmental organizations have been working in different states for decades, accommodating the needs of victims of commercial sexual exploitation (especially victims of trafficking) and assisting the local police personnel through raids, insider information, and support services. These organizations also provide various vocational and educational training to the rescued victims of commercial sexual exploitation, such as stitching, embroidery, computer courses, handmade jewellery, cloth making, and vocations.

1.5 Rehabilitation of Victims of Commercial Sexual Exploitation in India

Best practice guidelines for rehabilitation suggest empowerment as a key element to meet short-term, ongoing, or long-term needs of victims of commercial sexual exploitation (Macy and Johns 2011; Muraya and Fry 2016). The main goal of rehabilitation is to empower victims to take control of their lives and to be self-reliant

(Aron et al. 2006; Caliber 2007). Kvinnoforum (2003) defined 'empowerment as a process of facilitation by trafficking victims to be an agent controlling their own life'. Kabeer (1999) defined empowerment as 'the process to provide ability to those victims devoid from making strategic choices for their life'. Kabeer's definition involves three major elements of rehabilitation: resources, agency, and achievement. The element of resource refers to any materialistic or human resource needs, which would be required by the victims of commercial sexual exploitation to improve their lives. The agency element of empowerment provides the victims with authority and opportunity in deciding their way ahead and achieving their life goals. This element initiates better decision-making capabilities. The final element of empowerment, as suggested by Kabeer, discusses the achievement of the victim. This element refers to different outcome envision through the process of empowerment and rehabilitation.

1.6 Ujjawalla Scheme

A comprehensive scheme for the prevention of trafficking and rescue, rehabilitation, and reintegration of victims of trafficking for commercial sexual exploitation was initiated by the Ministry of Women and Child Development, Government of India, in 2007. The objective of the scheme involved the prevention of trafficking of women and children for commercial sexual exploitation, by involving the community and various stakeholders through awareness campaigns, workshops, and other such events. This scheme also provided immediate and long-term assistance through necessities like food, shelter, clothing, medical, legal, and counselling assistance. The beneficiaries of the scheme included:

(a) Women and children vulnerable to trafficking for commercial sexual exploitation;
(b) Women and children who are victims of trafficking for commercial sexual exploitation.

This scheme involved various agencies, ranging from the central government, state government, and women's organizations. Local bodies, private trusts, voluntary organizations, and nongovernmental organizations are coming together to deal with the issue of trafficking. The components of the scheme included prevention, rescue rehabilitation, reintegration, and repatriation. The prevention element of the scheme included the formation of various community vigilance groups for sensitization workshops, awareness campaigns, and various events in advocating the issue of trafficking. The element of rescue under the scheme involved information gathering through the network of police, NGOs, women's groups, community groups, and other organization working on the ground. The element of rehabilitation included setting up of rehabilitation and protective Homes (UJJAWALA Home), which provided basic amenities, medical care, legal aid, and counselling facilities for the victims of commercial sexual exploitation. These rehabilitation and protective homes also included various vocational and educational training for the beneficiary. The reintegration element of the scheme involved setting up a halfway home and restoration with the family members. The final element of the scheme involved repatriation, especially in terms of cross-border reintegration by setting up transit centres and covering various expenditures involved in the entire process of preparation (Ministry of Women and Child Development, Government of India,, and UN Office on Drug and Crime 2008).

2 Literature Review

The active involvement of vulnerable and marginalized groups in research and policy development is crucial, as it ensures that the resulting initiatives are directly responsive to their unique experiences, needs, and priorities (Dalcin and Pinheiro 2023). Participatory research increases the influence of those who would have little say in research, also promoting meaningful engagement, diverse perspectives and improvement in the quality of research (Asaba and Suarez-Balcazar 2018). Participatory approaches can lead to more equitable and impactful solutions if they are grounded in the voices and lived experiences of these underrepresented communities that address the root causes of their challenges.

For example, a project on poverty in Niagara Falls, Canada, was conducted using a participatory approach that invited a group of women living in poverty to speak about issues around well-being, stress when living in poverty and social assistance (Collins 2005). The researchers gained vital insights into the experiences of those affected, from which better informed, empathetic aid programmes may be developed.

Similarly, a participatory action research study carried out in India's Sundarban area aimed at preventing self-harm and suicide through pesticide among low-income groups (Chowdhury et al. 2013). Throughout the course of this project, it actively included every member of the local community, thereby leading to the development of intervention measures suitable for this culture, hence saving it from suicidal tendencies due to pesticide consumption. By doing so, this enhanced programme's success chances in addressing complex population health problems in such vulnerable communities.

Also, rural areas with high levels of health disparities have been addressed by using participatory action research approaches. For instance, the Indian Family Stories Project used an approach based on participatory action research to collaborate with community members so as to come up with culturally suitable healthcare ideas that matched their requirements and settings (Garwick and Auger 2003). This collaborative approach enabled community members themselves to be absorbed as participants, hence ensuring tailored interventions were put into place targeting unique experiences that they face each day.

These instances demonstrate how important it is to utilize participatory action research techniques for understanding vulnerable populations' needs. For instance, involving community members throughout all stages of research, starting from identifying priorities to designing and implementing impactful solutions would be a more sustainable approach that has some meaning for those people served (Ozer and Douglas 2017). Community-based participatory research is an effective method in addressing complex health and social problems at the local level because it creates active partnerships between researchers and community members, leading to targeted interventions that will be easily adopted by the communities (Carter et al. 2019).

However, though participatory research is highly promising, there are major obstacles that need careful handling. Some of these include long-term engagement of researchers and funding bodies, as well as grappling with complex power relations often obtaining in vulnerable communities (Collins 2005). In this regard, researchers have to become facilitators who encourage trust building and collective ownership of the outcomes of such activities through a shared decision-making process. Thus, researchers need to assume a position of humility, accepting their own limitations in terms of expertise and appreciating how much community-based knowledge, otherwise known as different perspectives, contribute towards successful achievement of research goals. Overcoming these challenges is crucial to ensuring that participatory research truly empowers vulnerable populations and leads to the development of meaningful, impactful solutions.

However, despite these challenges, participatory action research has its gains. In this way, its benefits are obvious and can be seen throughout multiple themes in health, such as narrowing disparities in health care distribution, improving service accessibility for all people and promoting a fairer outcome for the most disadvantaged members of society. Humble researchers are required in effective participatory research who know that their areas of expertise are confined and who respect the high value of worlds that they are not familiar with. Researchers need to embrace a collective approach that enables vulnerable populations to influence policies and strategies affecting their lives directly for more effective interventions. This link between scholars and societies creates a basis for iterative cycles of learning and action, which ultimately empower people who are most affected by specific challenges to become active contributors in finding solutions (George et al. 2018).

Protection of trafficked persons necessitates keeping them safe from the harmful influence of their traffickers and their agents, even if these agents purport to act under the aegis of the law. Frequently dost lawyers get signed vakalatnamas from trafficked individuals and claim to represent them. On a simple interview with trafficked persons, it is evident that they do not have the money to pay such lawyers, nor do they know of their identity. These lawyers are part of criminal networks who instruct them on how to safeguard the network, not its victims (Mendonca 2014). Courts should ensure that different advocate represents the accused so as to save against these lawyers to protect the trafficked person. An individual victim may be linked to a reliable NGO if she so desires, which would offer her assistance, advice and training on various skills. The city-based NGOs and destination areas shelter homes can then work together with community-based organizations in source areas for this purpose on victims of trafficking. A supportive community is where a survivor recovers best in life. In fact, state agencies can employ programmes like the

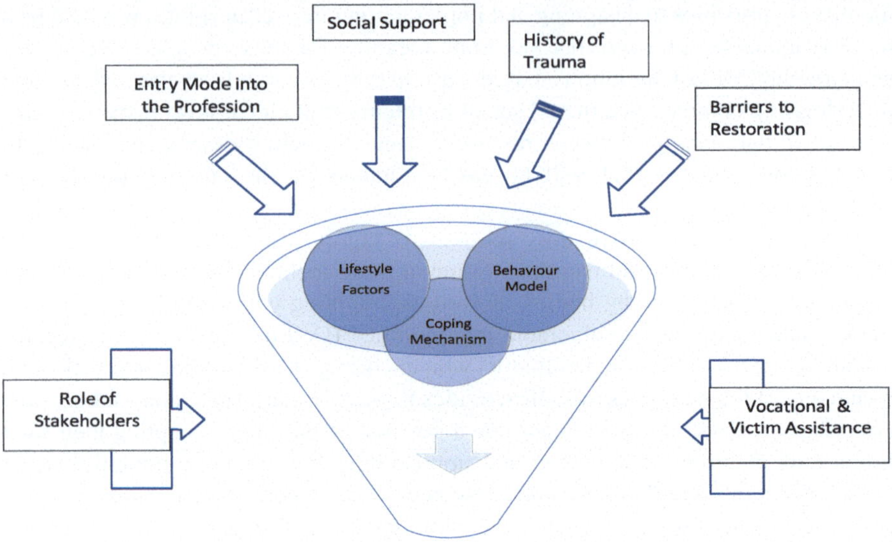

Fig. 1 Theoretical synthesis framework for effective rehabilitation of vulnerable victims

Ujjwala programme, which can create some schemes for survivors' adequate support. Trafficking is everyone's fundamental right in India state agencies have thus far failed millions of Indians, allowing criminal networks to inflict unimaginable abuse upon them all. To correct this mistake, state governments can assist trafficked survivors by implementing Ujjwala schemes.

The theoretical synthesis framework for effective rehabilitation of vulnerable victims integrates various critical elements to provide a holistic approach to victim rehabilitation. At its core, the framework emphasizes the interplay between lifestyle factors, coping mechanisms, and behavioural models, highlighting how these aspects collectively impact the victim's recovery process. External factors such as the role of stakeholders, including community and support services, are crucial for providing comprehensive care and support systems. Additionally, vocational and victim assistance programmes are essential for facilitating long-term recovery and reintegration into society. By addressing both the internal and external influences on victim rehabilitation, this framework aims to offer a well-rounded strategy for effectively supporting vulnerable victims (Nair et al. 2021c) (Fig. 1).

3 Methodology: Participatory Action Research

Participatory action research is a subgroup of action research that explores understanding and improves the world through various actions, bringing changes within society (Gillis and Jackson 2002). The origin of participatory action research is traced back to the works of Kurt Lewin on group action and relations (Lewin 1946). Participatory action research differs from conventional research in three ways.

Firstly, PAR focuses on research that initiates action, which is pursued in a reflective way. Participants collect and analyse different data and foresee the action that is required to be pursued. The subsequent action is then further researched to depict correlation with the earlier data collection, aims and objective to conclude future course of action. Secondly, participatory action research places a major emphasis on the power dynamics by sharing the power between the researcher and the participant. This process is conducted by fading the line between the researcher and the researched. The participant is not just considered as a respondent but the one who plays a crucial role as a partner to the entire research process, including involving suggestions towards the research question, data collection, analysis, and contributing towards the further course of action deciphered from the research finding (Baum et al. 2006). Wadsworth (1998) foresees participatory action research as a new paradigm towards science that differs from the old scientific paradigm. The positive science believes in a single reality that need independent variable to be observed and measured under control environment. It involves a process with various variables manipulated to determine causes and effects relationship. In contrast, participatory action research observers are believed to have a significant impact towards the phenomenon that they are observing and bring inquiry towards various values that influence the entire study. Lastly, participatory action research contradicts the approach of the removal of data and information from its context. Moreover, it advocates the involvement of participants in the process entirely. The degree of involvement differs in terms of the contribution and willingness of the people to be involved in the research (Baum et al. 2006). The choice of participatory action research, complimented with the three factors highlighting the difference from the traditional research, aligns with the research gap, suggesting the importance of including victims of commercial sexual exploitation as active participants.

3.1 Participation

Participation is considered one of the crucial elements within participatory action research. Participation differs from involvement, where participation reflects active engagement at every process, and involvement indicates the presence of the respondent in the process. Being an active part of the process, participation provides respondents with the opportunity to the respondent to contribute their opinions, which would influence the research outcomes.

3.2 Empowerment

Power dynamics is a key underlying concept of participatory action research. Participatory action research focuses on empowering involved respondence Labonte (1990) conceptualized empowering as working on the power dynamics between two individuals to reduce any power difference or inequality occurring due to a lack of resources. Foucault's (1980) stance is key towards participatory action research focused on reflecting power because of the interaction between different institutions, individuals, and various sources of knowledge. The entire participatory action research movement challenged the structure of control and surveillance, which continued with the traditional research (Foucault 1980). When researchers tend to control research objectives and aims, they establish their influence and dominance within the study. Participatory action research avoids the power paradigm between the researcher and the researched. Various developments in participatory action research has provided dedicated participation opportunities to researched and the researcher to improve the structure of research by working as an alliance.

3.3 Lived Experience

Participatory action research contradicts the view of Husserl, who suggests that the real property of any element accounts for those that can be measured, quantified, or counted. Husserl also highlighted that the scientific world is an extraction from the living world, the world that we always experience. The scientific world is methodical and well-coordinated, unlike the uncertainty, non-systematic, and indistinct world on the other side. Contrary to the set phenomenon, participatory action research draws its influence from various phenomenologists, extending the importance of experiences. They argue that humans cannot be described in isolation without the experiences that they share; similarly, how an experience cannot be described in isolation without the individual who is experiencing the phenomenon. Moreover, it suggests that experiences guide individuals in uniting the subject and the object into a whole (Crotty 1998).

3.4 Critical Reflection

Crotty (1998) claims that as interpretivists lays dedicated importance towards accounts of individual experiences into the research, over the opinion of critical theorists that highlights lived experiences as a response towards that tradition, culture, and environment. Critical theorist refers to critical reflection as the social paradigm to initiate action for change and question various norms and rules within the study. Freire stated that 'reflection without action is mere verbalism or an easy-going revolution, and action without reflection is sheer activism or just action for display'. On the same lines, participatory action research foresees the togetherness of action and reflection. When action and reflection are accommodated at the same time, it complements and supports each other.

3.5 *Characteristics of Participatory Action Research*

The procedure of participatory action research can be understood through the seven principles that highlight the characteristics of its research design (Stringer 1999). The primary principle resonates that the issue starts within the network and can be described, discussed, and understood by the network only. The network in the research can be described as the community members who would be part of the study. Furthermore, the conclusive objective of participatory action research explores the extremity of the social reality and enhancement of the lives of the community members, including the network individuals who are respondents of the research. Thirdly, participatory action research includes complete cooperation of the network at all phases of the research process. Fourth principle includes the scope of the network, including the vulnerable, the abused, victimized group in the research. The fifth principle of the research process is to illuminate community members through the process of research for independent and individual improvement. Participatory action research extends its horizon for being more than a scientific method and explores various procedures with the community members to provide a legitimate investigation towards the social reality. Ultimately, participatory action research enables the researcher to be a dedicated participant, active member in the network and encourages cooperation from the network rather than separation from the community.

3.5.1 Association

Participatory action research involves collaboration between the community members and the researcher. This collaboration begins from the problem statement till the implementation and execution of the resulting outcome within the action research (Whyte et al. 1991).

3.5.2 Inclusivity of Local Knowledge

Participatory action research involves members of the community in the research process. It is believed that participants are aware and knowledgeable of their problems and issues to be included in the research process. Moreover, involvement of local community members within the research enhances their role and participation within the study.

3.5.3 Diversity

Participatory action research utilizes diverse models of research. It establishes the incorporation of various theories, models, and assessment patterns towards varied issues. It also highlights that issues may pertain to various geographical locations, communities, cultural, economic, and political dimensions.

3.5.4 Dedication Towards Cause

Participatory action research focuses on individual cases within the community. It directs towards the creation of various models and theoretical premises according to specific cases and initiates action towards it.

3.5.5 Evolving Process

Participatory action research utilizes an evolving research paradigm. It evolves at every stage of research, starting from research questions to the implementation of research outcome in collaboration with the community members. This emergent research process contributes towards a participatory approach within the study and utilizes suggestions, recommendations, and voices from the community itself.

3.5.6 Bridge Between Scientific Evidence and Social Research

The entire research process involves the active participation of researchers and the research belonging to the community. As most of the participation in the research involves community members, they provide active insight through experiences reflecting their social reality, aligned with the scientific vigour and contribution expressed by the researcher towards the study. This collaboration between the researcher and the researcher bridges the gap between scientific analysis and social research over a specific issue.

3.6 Methodological Rationale

The study complements the methodological gap, aims of the study, and objective of the research. It includes community members, as an active part of the entire research. Participatory action research as a research design complements the role of respondents within the study through their opinions and experience sharing over various issues. Participatory action research formulates the entire blueprint of the research, keeping in mind the beliefs, values, culture, and environment of the researched. The concept of inclusivity is a key within participatory action research. Participatory action research provides various advantages over other research designs within the said study, and a few of them are narrated below:

3.6.1 Participation

The collaboration of the community member and the researcher plays a vital role in participatory action research. Considering the methodological gap, it is vital to utilize a research design which dilutes the domination and agency principle associated with the research and respondents. The element of participation provides a holistic outlook while pursuing action-oriented research. The participation of vulnerable group, i.e. victims and vulnerable to commercial sexual exploitation, initiates active response across the process of research.

3.6.2 Empowerment

The participatory action research focuses on empowerment of the abused and victimized members of the community. The study focuses on a critical and marginalized population awaiting resolution and action against their issues. Participatory action research provides a platform to these critical population to voice their problems and contribute towards exploring various solutions. The involvement of vulnerable group, i.e. victims and vulnerable to commercial sexual exploitation, provides voice to express their problems and issues.

3.6.3 Lived Experience

The researcher in participatory action research involves himself with the day today activity of the community members, which provides a comprehensive and active experience sharing platform. The regular interaction between the researcher and research guides the study towards its result outcomes in collaboration with the members of the community. The experience shared by the vulnerable group, i.e. victims and vulnerable to commercial sexual exploitation, provides real-life information on the issue.

3.6.4 Critical Reflection

The entire study utilizing participatory action research reflects the true issues and problems faced by the community members and illuminates the need for action-oriented research. The study focuses on factual and genuine representation of the issues faced by the respondent within the community and reflecting it through various scientific evidence in accordance with the researcher's expertise.

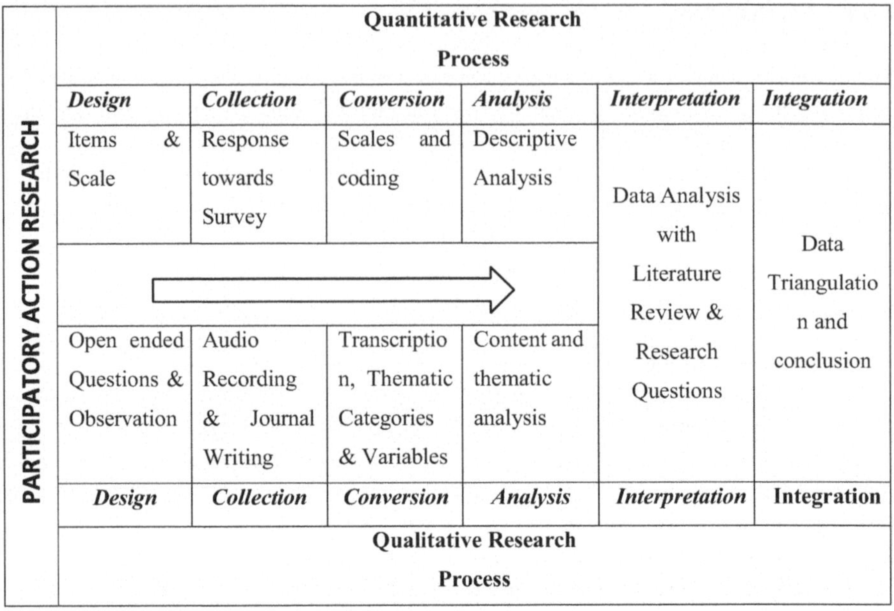

Fig. 2 Step-by-step participatory action research process

3.7 *Effective Participatory Action Research Procedure*

Nair et al. (2021c) proposed Step by Step Participatory Action Research (PAR) Process is a collaborative and iterative methodology designed to engage stakeholders actively in the research process to address real-world problems. This process begins with identifying the issue of concern, followed by engaging stakeholders to co-create research questions and objectives. To ensure that every voice is listened to and respected, the collection of information is done in a participatory manner. For example, on data analysis, it has been held collectively as a way of allowing different ideas to form the basis for any findings. The next action involves coming up with action plans based on this analysis, which are then implemented and monitored together with all stakeholders involved. The cycle ends with an evaluation of what has been achieved and sharing the learning leading to another round of reflection and action. This approach makes sure that research is anchored in community needs, thus resulting in feasible and lasting solutions (Fig. 2).

4 Methodological Analysis

The results from Nair et al. (2021a) for quantitative methods (Stress Coping Behaviour Scale and Systematic Observation) and Nair et al. (2021b) for qualitative methods (Conversational interviews and Observation method) emphasizes the importance of participatory action research and can be summarized through the following case study representation from various participants of the rehabilitation and protective homes in India.

4.1 North Zone

My journey at the rehabilitation and protective (R&P) home has been very fruitful. I did not imagine that I would like it here and would make so many new friends. I still remember the first time; I was brought here by a police officer. He was not very cordial and was rushing all the administrative responsibilities. The centre coordinator was very helpful and made sure that I felt comfortable at this new place. My experience of the outside world has been very tormenting because of all the traumatic incidents. There were times when I thought about taking my life away. The time spent at the rehabilitation and protective (R&P) home has given me hope. I feel a sense of positivity to survive in the outside world. I still have certain bad habits that I am unable to dissuade from my lifestyle. There are certain urges that make me vulnerable and anxious towards drugs and alcohol. The rehabilitation and protective (R&P) home ensures that we follow a fixed timetable in performing all the duties as assigned to you. There have been frequent visits by counsellors, and we have also been taken to the General Hospital nearby. I, myself, have learnt the skill of embroidery. I believe that I can use this later in my life. The friends that I have made here are very helpful, and I feel a sense of belonging with them. I have heard centre coordinator talking to other staff members about the financial crunch. I do believe that there can be various improvements in the centre, but I am happy that I am out of my past life, and I can aspire to start a new one soon.

4.2 West Zone

I feel like home is being part of this rehabilitation and protective (R&P) home. The centre coordinator has been friendly and helpful over my time here. I have made many friends, whom I consult in case of any problem. I have also learned how to tackle my own problem with the help of a counsellor, my friends, and the centre coordinator. Starting days at this rehabilitation and protective (R&P) home was very difficult, and I had to consult the counsellor frequently for assistance. I was living in a neighbourhood where there were incidents of sexual exploitation, but I was lucky that I was saved by a local NGO and was brought here. I have learned several skills, including painting, diya making, jewellery making, and I am about to complete a computer education course. The centre is filled with a lot of girls. Among those, there are a few who are my friends, and I can discuss anything with them. There are some other girls who live on a different floor and do not interact much with me. There are some elderly women with whom I am not that comfortable, but I tried to be with my friends. In case of any difficulty, I will talk to the centre coordinator. We also get time to play, meditate, watch TV, and do yoga. The centre timetable helps me to be on time and do my work on time. I hope that the training given here will be helpful to get a job and to be able to make money when I go outside. I hope that with this initiative and many girls being rehabilitated, the perpetrators will be arrested, and there will be a time when no girls will be brought here for safety.

4.3 South Zone

The rehabilitation and protective (R&P) home provides us with a sense of security and belongingness. It has initiated dedication, discipline, a hardworking nature, passion, and a humble nature within me. The centre does not give me a sense of being a rehabilitation and protective (R&P) home. We have a dedicated space for prayer, and we have regular prayers happening every week. We also have religious heads coming to guide us towards a better future. We have been fortunate to learn new technology, different educational skill sets, and several vocational training programmes. I have felt more confident and positive over time by interacting with other beneficiaries. I am now able to solve my problems and help others in solving their problems. We usually do not go out, but any essential commodities reach to the centre very quickly. We are in a very good location with the hospital and various other shops nearby. We go to the hospital for a regular check-up and there has also been a counsellor visiting our centre regularly. The centre mostly has young females who have similar experiences to mine. I tried to console them and motivate them to think about a better life from now on. I started learning to cook and enjoy doing it. I spend my time reading books and interacting with my friends. The centre coordinator is very calm and patient with all of us. In times of festivals, we get sweets and gifts from the centre coordinator and people visiting the centre. The centre also offers various other services, other than the rehabilitation and protective (R&P) home, to offer to sponsors and donors. We are lucky, at times, to receive recreational provision and amenities from visiting donors and sponsors. I am very happy with my stay here, and I hope to get back to society and be successful. I hope that I do not fall into the hands of the traffickers and hope the centre coordinator will help me to get settled in life and be away from the bad world.

5 Conclusion

The adoption of participatory action research as a methodology for victim assistance and support services can be a powerful tool in addressing the complex needs of vulnerable populations. By actively involving these individuals in the research and program development, service providers can create more effective, empathetic, and sustainable interventions that truly address the root causes of their challenges and empower them to be active participants in their own well-being.

In conclusion, it is evident that there is a need for participatory action research as a methodology for victim assistance. By enabling vulnerable people and communities to become active participants in research and decision-making processes, the method can help to create more equitable and efficient support structures, thereby improving the lives of those who are grappling with multifarious problems. Nair et al. (2021c) proposed a model for rehabilitation emphasizes an inclusive model with the inclusion of stakeholders affecting rehabilitation for victims and vulnerable to commercial sexual exploitation. The model is derived from the theoretical synthesis as mentioned in Fig. 1. The model includes contributions from health care workers, law enforcement professionals, mental health professionals, and social workers. The current model of rehabilitation under the Ujjawala Scheme, 2015 dictates in writing as per the legislature to provide medical aid, psychological assistance, legal aid, and any other assistance. The scheme lacks in highlighting the role of stakeholders in various phases of rehabilitation (Fig. 3).

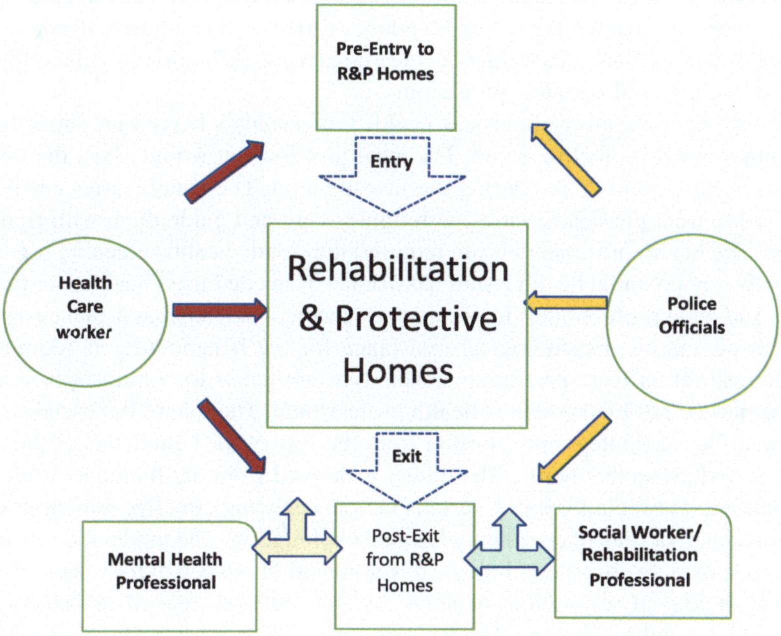

Fig. 3 Inclusive model of rehabilitation for victims and vulnerable to commercial sexual exploitation

The health care worker and law enforcement official play a crucial role pre-entry into the rehabilitation and protective (R&P) home. The official should be sensitive and provide all relevant information to the beneficiary for their knowledge. A sensitization workshop should be provided to all front-line workers combating commercial sexual exploitation. The officials should be trained and mentored to avoid misuse of their power or any laws and legislation against the vulnerable or a victim of commercial sexual exploitation. The process should be made smooth and hassle-free for the beneficiary, and proper paperwork should be completed before assigning a designated official towards specific beneficiary. It should be noted that the allocated health care worker and law official should take proper follow-up with the beneficiary till proper rehabilitation. The entire process would include pre-entry formalities, regular visit at rehabilitation and protective (R&P) home and ensuring proper restoration of the beneficiary post exit from the Ujjawala home. The role of a mental health professional can be included pre-entry to the Ujjawala home, but is crucial on the first day at the rehabilitation and protective (R&P) home. Every Ujjawala home should have a permanent staff member designated as counsellor and a social worker, respectively. The responsibility of counsellor or mental health professional would be to ensure complete psychological restoration of the beneficiary and assess the capability of effective reintegration towards the society. The appointed social worker should work closely with the beneficiary to formulate an effective reintegration strategy and establish a safe transition from the rehabilitation and protective (R&P) home to society. Both the counsellor and social worker should ensure regular follow-up of the beneficiary post exit from the rehabilitation and protective (R&P) home to ensure holistic restoration of the beneficiary. This model extends the victim-centric approach reflected by Mendonca (2014) and emphasize the dedicated functionality of various stakeholders in the effective rehabilitation of vulnerable and victim of commercial sexual exploitation.

The role of law enforcement and health professionals begins pre-entry to the rehabilitation and protective home. The legal professional would assist the beneficiary with pre-screening and during the investigation. The beneficiaries need to be sensitized to treat the beneficiaries with utmost care and guide them with rights of victims. The health professionals are required to provide health screening pre-entry to identify any potential health issues. Assistance is needed from health care professionals and legal professionals to provide any medical and legal assistance required by the beneficiaries. Psychological assistance for the beneficiaries is required to provide restoration from past trauma. The assistant needs to continue post exit in case the need is felt by the mental health professional. The role of the social worker guide in effective reintegration starting from the stay of the beneficiary at the rehabilitation and protective home. The model is derived from the findings of the conversation interview, emphasizing various factors deterring effective reintegration of vulnerable and victims of commercial sexual exploitation. The model focuses on all the themes, namely absence of holistic development of the beneficiary, lack of complete psychological restoration, negative societal outlook, fear of traffickers, and misuse of laws and regulations. The inclusive model highlights the focus on relevant stakeholders and their dedicated efforts across the process of rehabilitation to counter the deterrents to effective reintegration.

The future scope emphasizes over exploration of further research, eliminating various limitations persistent in the present study. The future research should focus on the inclusion of most of the rehabilitation and protective (R&P) homes across India with a proportionate sample of both vulnerable and victims of commercial sexual exploitation, with representation of all states. The future research would envision funding from various ministries and departments of various state governments to ensure accessibility to every rehabilitation and protective (R&P) home, irrespective of their geographical location. The current study lays the foundation of utilization of participatory action research to understand and explore issues associated with various vulnerable sections of society. The current study also expands the research in exploring the longitudinal impact of various vocational training, recreational activity, psychological assistance, and other assistance towards beneficiaries at rehabilitation and protective (R&P) homes. This would guide in understanding the role of specific victim assistance programmes in the effective rehabilitation of vulnerable and victims of commercial sexual exploitation.

References

Aron L, Zweig J, Newmark L (2006) Comprehensive services for survivors of human trafficking: findings from clients in three communities. Urban Institute, Justice Policy Center. Retrieved from, https://www.urban.org/sites/default/files/publication/43051/411507-Comprehensive-Services-for-Survivors-of-Human-Trafficking.PDF

Asaba E, Suarez-Balcazar Y (2018, September 3) Participatory research: A promising approach to promote meaningful engagement. Informa 25(5):309–312. https://doi.org/10.1080/11038128.2018.1541224

Baum F, MacDougall C, Smith D (2006) Participatory action research. J Epidemiol Commun Health 60(10):854

Caliber (2007) Evaluations of comprehensive services for survivors of human trafficking: Key comprehensive services for survivors of human trafficking: findings from clients in three communities findings and lessons learned. U.S. Department of Justice

Carter WM, Morse WC, Brock RW, Struempler B (2019, August 29) Improving physical activity and outdoor recreation in rural Alabama through community coalitions. Centers for Disease Control and Prevention, 16. https://doi.org/10.5888/pcd16.190062

Chowdhury AN, Banerjee S, Brahma A, Biswas MK (2013, April 23) Participatory research for preventing pesticide-related DSH and Suicide in Sundarban, India: a brief report. Hindawi Publishing Corporation, pp 1–10. https://doi.org/10.1155/2013/427417

Collins SB (2005, March 1) An understanding of poverty from those who are poor. SAGE Publishing 3(1):9–31. https://doi.org/10.1177/1476750305047983

Crotty M (1998) The foundations of social research: meaning and perspective in the research process. Sage

Dalcin CB, & Pinheiro AKB (2023 January 24) The challenge of healthcare for vulnerable and marginalized populations. Universidade Federal do Ceará 24, e83107–e83107. https://doi.org/10.15253/2175-6783.20232483107

Foucault M (1980) Power/knowledge: selected interviews and other writings, 1972–1977. Vintage

Gandhi M (2018) I sincerely apologise for using the term 'other ones' during the debate on the Trafficking of Persons (Prevention, Protection and Rehabilitation) Bill, 2018, in Lok Sabha. I did not 'snigger', I was embarrassed at my own lack of knowledge. People 4(21)

Garwick A, Auger S (2003, December 1) Participatory action research: the Indian Family Stories Project. Elsevier BV 51(6):261–266. https://doi.org/10.1016/j.outlook.2003.09.006

George A, LeFevre A, Schleiff M, Mancuso A, Sacks E, Sarriot E (2018) Hubris, humility and humanity: expanding evidence approaches for improving and sustaining community health programmes. BMJ 3(3):e000811–e000811. https://doi.org/10.1136/bmjgh-2018-000811

Gillis A, Jackson W (2002) Research methods for nurses: methods and interpretation. F.A. Davis Company, Philadelphia

Hammond GC, McGlone M (2014) Entry, progression, exit, and service provision for survivors of sex trafficking: implications for effective interventions. Glob Soc Welf 1(4):157–168. https://doi.org/10.1007/s40609-014-0010-0

Kabeer N (1999) Resources, agency, achievements: reflections on the measurement of women's empowerment. Dev Change 30(3):435–464. https://doi.org/10.1111/1467-7660.00125

Khan F (2020, February 18) India had 38,503 victims of trafficking in 2011–19. Only 77 have got compensation. The Print. Retrieved from https://theprint.in/india/india-had- 38503-victims-of-trafficking-in-2011-19-only-77-have-got-compensation/365761/

Kvinnoforum S (2003) European good practice on recovery, return and integration of trafficked persons. Kvinnoforum

Labonte R (1990) Empowerment: notes on professional and community dimensions. Can Rev Soc Policy 26:1–12

Lewin K (1946) Action research and minority problems. J Soc Iss 2(4):34–46

Macy RJ, Johns N (2011) Aftercare services for international sex trafficking survivors: informing US service and program development in an emerging practice area. Trauma Viol Abuse 12(2):87–98

Mendonca M (2014) Survivor-Centric Approach towards Crimes of Commercial Sexual Exploitation. Journal of the national human rights commission.

Ministry of Women and Child Development, Government of India & UN Office on Drug and Crime (2008) India country report: To prevent and combat trafficking and commercial sexual exploitation of children and women. Retrieved from http://www.childtrafficking.com/Docs/mwcd_08_india_report_1009.pdf

Muraya D, Fry D (2016) Aftercare services for child victims of sex trafficking: a systematic review of policy and practice. Trauma Viol Abuse 17(2):204–220. https://doi.org/10.1177/1524838015584356

Nair VV, Sahni SP, Andzenge DD (2021a) An explorative study of coping mechanisms towards vulnerability and victimization within commercial sexual exploitation in India. Int J Public Sociol Sociotherapy (IJPSS) 1(2):51–61. https://doi.org/10.4018/IJPSS.2021070104

Nair VV, Sahni SP, Andzenge DDT (2021b) Experiences of survivors of commercial sexual exploitation availing rehabilitation at R&P homes in India. Tort J 31(1):64–75. https://doi.org/10.7146/torture.v31i1.121473

Nair VV, Sahni SP, Andzenge DD (2021c) Exploring coping mechanism of vulnerable & victims of commercial sexual exploitation: a participatory action research in rehabilitation & protective homes in India [Doctoral Dissertation]. O.P. Jindal Global University

NCRB, N. (2019) Crime in India: 2018 Statistics

Ozer EJ, Lavi I, Douglas L, Wolf JP (2017) Protective factors for youth exposed to violence in their communities: A review of family, school, and community moderators. *Journal of Clinical Child & Adolescent Psychology, 46*(3), 353–378.

Scheme SG (1969) National Portal of India

Stringer ET (1999) Action research, 2nd edn. Sage, Thousand Oaks, CA

Surtees R (2008) Re/integration of trafficked persons: handling "difficult" cases. NEXUS Institute

Wadsworth Y (1998) What is participatory action research? action research international, paper 2. J Public Health 15:52–60

Whyte WF, Greenwood DJ, Lazes P (1991) Participatory action research: through practice to science in social research. Participatory Action Research, 19–55

Criminal Law: Navigating the Jurisprudential Landscape

Increasing Interdisciplinary Influences on the Indian Criminal Justice: With a Focus on Criminal Justice and Forensic Science Interface

B. B. Pande

Abstract The modernization of criminal justice is the outcome of multiple influences coming from sister disciplines like criminology, victimology, and forensic science. The colonial criminal justice did not require much legitimization from other social sciences, because it drew all its power from the imperial supremacy. However, in the 1950s, which also marks the end of the colonial rule, two developments had started impinging upon the criminal justice: First, the United Nations' rise on the scene that had infused scientific and modern thinking in crime prevention and treatment matters. Second, the subjection of the criminal justice and its processes to the constitutional and human rights touchstone, which demanded compliance with fairness and justice standards. While the first development was responsible for imparting new legitimacy to the criminology and forensic science ideas and methods, the second development ensured the fairness of the criminal justice outcomes. With the post-1950s resurgence of scientific criminology and forensic science in the Universities in the North and the South, the traditional basis for the legitimization of the criminal justice experienced change. However, the change emanating in the area of forensic science became more profound, because of its better sync with the science and technology orientation. This is the main reason for certain significant recent legislative initiatives culminating in the enactment of the BNSS and the BSA 2023. Furthermore, there is yet another development that is likely to alter the chemistry of the interface itself, which, in the context of the British Criminal Justice has been described by Lucia Zedner as 'From Criminal Justice to Security Society' discussed here in Part VI. A similar 'alternate rationalization of crime and re-orientation of criminal justice to pre-crime stages' appears to be gaining popularity in India as well. Thus, the normative legitimization and infusion of forensic science, on the one hand, and its extensions to new pre-crime stages, on the other, are likely to alter the balance of the criminal justice and forensic science interface in the future.

B. B. Pande (✉)
Delhi University, New Delhi, India

National Human Right Commission, New Delhi, India

Indian Society of Criminology, New Delhi, India

© The Author(s), under exclusive license to Springer Nature Singapore Pte Ltd. 2026

G. S. Bajpai et al. (eds.), *Beyond the Gavel: A Paradigm Shift in Global Criminal Justice*, https://doi.org/10.1007/978-981-95-4487-5_8

Keywords Modernization of criminal justice · Interdisciplinary influences · Constitution and human rights touchstone · Forensic science interface · Alternate rationalization of crime and criminal justice · Incorporation of science and technology orientation to new procedures and evidence laws

1 Introduction

With the growing appreciation for the interdisciplinary influences in the field of Criminal Justice, today there is a stronger urge to join hands and share knowledge amongst the scholars of criminology, forensic science, and the law. It is manifested in the trend of holding interdisciplinary congregations nicknamed as 'Criminology Conclaves', which is evidenced in the happening of three such conclaves in the last 6 months. (The First Conclave was organized at the NFSU, Delhi Campus, on 31 August and 1 September 2023; the Second by the NLUD, on 'Shaping the Discourse and Scholarship in Criminology', on 23 December 2023; and the Third by the NUJS, Kolkata, on 20–22 March 2024.) While the first two conclaves were dominated by the experts drawn from the criminology and law streams, the Third reversed the order by charting the 'Trends in Forensics, Law and Criminology', with a dominant involvement and participation of the Forensic Science experts.[1] The Third Conclave was designedly aimed at the integration of the three knowledge streams with a view to empowering the Criminal Justice System for the Viksit Bharat Odyssey.[2]

Since our focus here is on the interface between the criminal justice and forensic science, we discuss the issues relating to the conceptual understanding and the definitional boundaries of the key elements, namely the 'Criminal Justice', and the 'Forensic Science'. Assuming that, because of a longer evolution and greater legislative and judicial action on the front, the term 'Criminal Justice' has become

[1] The organizers of the 'Third Conclave' as a part of the 'International Conference on Trends in Forensics, Law and Criminology: Empowering Criminal Justice in the twenty-first Century and Beyond" at the National University of Juridical Sciences, Kolkata, on 20–22 March 2024 have reported that the conference evoked the participation from the inland and foreign scholars numbering to 235. Of the total number of participants, 153 were drawn from the forensic science (including medical forensics) stream, 45 from the law stream and 33 from the criminology stream. The breakup of the resource persons totalling to 43 in number, 35 were from the forensic science, nine from the law and five from the criminology disciplines.

[2] My responsibility to present a valedictory address to the Third Conclave required me to explore the interdisciplinary linkages, particularly between criminology and forensic science, which proved more difficult than expected, because most of the established textbooks on criminology or forensic sciences, either relied upon the legacy of the foreign authorities or ignored the Indian historical context as inconsequential. However, my search for the interdisciplinary linkage was largely rewarded by getting access to Professor K. Chockalingam's masterly article: 'The Emergence and the History of Criminology: A Global and Indian Perspective' published in the special edition 2023 of the *Indian Journal of Criminology*, at pp. 23–40, which shall be discussed in detail in the later part.

more or less settled and requires much less deliberation in comparison with forensic science. Therefore, it is logical to shift the focus to the ways and purposes for the understanding and the precision with which the term 'forensic science' is understood and defined. Hitherto, the term 'forensic science' and the knowledge stream associated with it have been understood narrowly and unilaterally by linking it to a criminal case for the proof of a 'fact in issue' as per the Evidence Act, which in the commonly used parlance, can be described as the 'forensic evidence science'. However, in the contemporary context there is increasing deployment of science and technology for surveillance, external and internal security, biometric data, deployment of AI and multiple modes of digitalization, etc.; the term forensic science is used broadly and explained by an umbrella term 'forensic security science'. Both the narrow and the broad conceptualization of 'forensic science' may have some similarities, but their purposes are markedly different because the first aims to provide the best and the most scientific evidence to prove a 'crime', while the second relates to providing exploratory evidence for the 'pre-crime' stages. Thus, the aforesaid three considerations tend to coalesce in the phenomenon of interface that may be decoded best by attempting to explore a phase-wise evolution of this ever-changing phenomenon.

2 The British Colonial Criminal Justice System

Ever since the English people set foot into India, first, as traders and, later, as sovereign power, the British Criminal Justice made inroads into the Indian society, by replacing the prevalent Hindu and Islamic criminal law systems. The East India Company started with trading activities in the three Presidency towns of Madras, Bombay, and Calcutta, but soon secured administrative powers to settle disputes of civil and criminal nature between the company and the people in the Presidencies and their suburbs. The first instalment of the British Criminal Justice came in the form of Company Regulations that were issued by the Governor Generals, from time to time. With the assumption of sovereignty in 1858, the British Criminal Justice received official recognition, manifesting in the enactment of the comprehensive substantive and procedural law Codes and Acts such as the Indian Penal Code, 1860 the Criminal Procedure Code, 1861 (as amended in 1882 and 1898) the Indian Police Act, 1864 and the Indian Evidence Act, 1872. The aforesaid Criminal Justice laws aimed at imposing hitherto unknown crime concepts that were enforced by a coercive criminal justice machinery, which operated more for the legitimization of the ruling class power. According to Barry Wright, the colonial rule in India posed twin challenges of reconciliation between liberties and state power, thus: 'These reflected unresolved tensions between the rule of law and liberties on the one hand, the requirements of sovereignty and state power on the other'.[3] Another scholar N. Hussain has appreciated the nature of the colonial Criminal Justice, thus: 'The ideological justification for the British presence in India drew heavily on a much-vaunted tradition of ancient British liberty and lawfulness… Government by rules became the basis for the conceptualization of the "moral legitimacy" of British colonial rule'.[4]

As against Barry Wright and N. Hussain's view of the criminal justice from above, Ranabir Samaddar takes a critical view of the colonial foundations of the rule of law from below: First, by relying upon the legalistic framework for identifying a criminal and Second, by developing criminal responsibility and punishment around expressly laid down rules of evidence. For the identification of the "Criminal", the Penal Code and the other criminal legislations provided the basic framework that had to be made known and acceptable amidst the native society. According to Samaddar: 'Criminal legislation had to operate simultaneously in two different registers: on the one hand, it had to argue that criminality was occurring in distinct cultural milieus of society and in communities (thus, the idea of criminal tribes, for instance); on the other, the trial and punishment process was to be public, non-communitarian legal and scientific. Thus, the questions such as who comprised a criminal, how criminal elements enmeshed with the public, what methods were illegal, and so on, were issues that defined the power of sovereign authority, marking at the same time, everyday government ability of rule that needed to cope with crimes unsettling the society'.[5] In the same context Samaddar opines 'Detecting the crime and criminal was important because the technology of detection was a miniature way of knowing the "true" bodies of individuals or groups, as if that could lead to the unravelling of the mystery of the "true" mind of the criminal individual or the group—What kinds of bodies harboured what kind of minds and what kinds of minds called for what kind of bodily practices. If such practices were made visible, described and represented, the process of judgment was necessarily rendered public'.[6] The rationale of the total process is explained this way: 'Reason would from now on dictate new forms and process of punishment, still closely centering on the body but making the inspection, diagnosis, judgment and punishment a matter

[3] Barry Wright (2011) "Macaulay's Indian Penal Court: Historical context and organizing principles", in Weng-Cheong Chan et al. (eds.) Codification, Macaulay and the Indian Penal Code – The Legacies and Modern Challenges of Criminal Law Reform, Ashgate Publishing Ltd., 2011, at p. 26

[4] N Hussain, The Jurisprudence of Emergency: Colonialism and the Rule of Law, University of Michigan Press, 2003, quoted by Barry Wright, supra, at p. 27 f.n. 31

[5] Ranabir Samaddar, Crime, Passion and Detachment: Colonialism and the Rule of Law in Kalpana Kannabiran et al. (eds), Challenging The Rule(s) of Law (2008), Sage India, at p. 357

[6] bid. at pp. 357–58

of rational process. Together, the Indian Penal Code (IPC), the Indian Criminal Procedure Act, and the Indian Evidence Act were inextricably linked to the colonial strategy of power of rule, namely, imposing responsibility, making responsibilities public, disciplining the irresponsible and then punishing them'.[7]

However, the processes of searching for the 'crime' and locating the 'criminal' hinged on the state furnishing evidence as per the written text of evidence law. Since the evidence law itself was based on reason, as per Samaddar 'On the basis of the reason, a new forms of power grew, namely, judicial power... Not only was physical conquest the basis of the ascendance of reason, but reason depended on close physical scrutiny of various kind. In this way, the Evidence Act remains the great instance of the physicality of Indian politics'.[8] Since the aim of colonial power was to remove the subjectivities of the native society that were prevalent in the Indian society, there was a search for a legal science of evidence that could generate knowledge about facts, relevance and proof. It was realized early enough that the scientific and objective evidence needed could only be met by the deployment of suitable technologies for the identification of the clan or group of the accused and his personal predilections.

2.1 *Early Forensic Science Sprouting in the British India*

In order to ensure the objectivity of the evidence, with a view to offsetting the subjectivities of the accused and the criminal justice officials, the colonial administration relied upon the then prevailing techniques such as: (a) Anthropometric measurement and (b) Finger printing and photography. The anthropometric measurement worked well in the initial stages, when the administration focused on the communities and caste groups that could be better known through the anthropological and anthropometric methods. Criminality, then, was seen as a trait of the group or the community and the Criminal Tribes Act, 1871, is a product of this kind of approach. But because of the criminal liability being individual-centric very soon the anthropometric technique came under disuse. The Inspector General of Police for the Lower Provinces of Bengal, Mr Edward Henry, in his Report to the Government of Bengal in 1896, found enough evidence to establish that fingerprints were a less expensive and surer means of confirming the identity of any given person. As a consequence, the Government of India, by a resolution in 1897, adopted the system of fingerprinting throughout India. Following this, in 1899, the first National Fingerprint Bureau, perhaps one of the first in the world, was set up at Calcutta.[9] The technique of fingerprinting and its success encouraged the colonial administration to repose greater faith in science and technology-based evidence

[7] Id. at pp. 358–59

[8] Ibid. at p. 356

[9] Ibid

collection techniques and go ahead with the development of photography with a view to building a typology of criminals for the purposes of establishing a system of surveillance under the Governor Generalship of Lord Canning. But because of the 1857–58 Rebellion, the photographic exercise on typology of the Indians under the title *The People of India* had to be shelved, and the official project of the state was placed under the Political and Secret Department.

Thus, forensic science that began as a tool of criminal justice to impart objectivity to evidence later turned into a means of surveillance over the Indian people, which could be more appropriately described as forensic security science in the making.

3 Developing Linkages Between Criminology and Forensic Science

It is coincidental that by the time the colonial rule was coming to an end, the United Nations had started taking a keen interest in crime and its scientific understanding. With this end in view, the First United Nations Congress on the Prevention of Crimes and Treatment of Offenders was held in 1955, and the UNESCO Report 1957 laid emphasis on the teaching of Criminology and Criminal Justice Administration at the College and University levels the world over, for which they had arrived at a consensus at a Symposium in London in 1955. Professor K. Chockalingam in the recently published comprehensive article 'Emergence and History of Criminology: A Global and Indian Perspective'[10] has opened up many trails of inquiry, such as the genesis and growth of the discipline of Criminology in India, linkages between criminology and sister disciplines, the role of the Indian Society of Criminology in nurturing the professionals drawn from the diverse allied streams, etc. The article has assiduously traced the record of the linkage between criminology and forensic science in the Departments of the Universities of the North and the South. The article mainly focuses on the post-1950s resurgence of scientific Criminology, which is explained by, first, the focus on the Department of Criminology at Sagar University, Madhya Pradesh, in 1959, followed by the later developments in the Universities of the South, particularly the Madras University and the Madras Medical College. Professor Chockalingam's account of the combined criminology and forensic science course, starting with a 1 year part time Diploma Course at the Madras Medical College in 1961 and later turning into a 2 year full time master's degree course in 1965, at the same location is insightful. The growing popularity of the combined criminology and forensic science can be on account of the excellence of the course planning and also because of the growing

[10] Chockalingam K, The Emergence and the History of Criminology: A Global and Indian Perspective, Special Edition 2023, Indian Journal of Criminology, National Law University, Delhi, pp. 23–40

attraction towards science and technology for explaining crimes. Equally insightful and interesting is how the 1967 batch of the master's degree course students' initiative, to set up a Criminology and Forensic Science Study Circle that ultimately culminated in the founding of the Indian Society of Criminology in 1970, which was attached to the Department of Psychology at the Madras University. This is also evidence of the close linkage between the discipline of criminology and forensic science. The linkage not only forged deep academic bondage but also led to an understanding between the criminology and forensic science, teachers and students, and the police and forensic science professionals. Thereafter, in 1974 an M.A. Criminology and Forensic Science Course was started at the Department of Psychology, Madras University, which came under an independent Department of Criminology under the Madras University in 1983. The article has traced the growth of criminology in the north and the west, particularly the Tata Institute at Bombay, which has followed a different path of criminological inquiries, with which we are not concerned here. Our inquiry here centres around the interdisciplinary linkages, particularly between criminology and forensic science.[11]

However, after the creation of the Department of Criminology at Madras University in 1983, the subject of criminology experienced significant expansion by developing linkages with the other social sciences, law, and the criminal justice administration. At times, these expansions in the field of criminology were at the cost of the forensic science linkage, which was to some extent made up by the common platform of the Indian Society of Criminology, that had by then developed a few good traditions like providing opportunities for airing their common concerns and professional anxieties, as well as for seeking recognition for the good work in the discharge of their professional responsibilities. Despite the palliatives provided by the common forum of ISC regional meets and Annual Conferences, the disciplines of criminology and forensic science continued to grow in their grooves and drift apart in the course of their disciplinary journeys.

4 Independent Growth of the Forensic Science

Hitherto, forensic science has grown, either under the shadow of the criminal justice, as 'forensic evidence science' or under the shadow of criminology, as a science to establish the causes of crime, in the tradition of biological determinism, psychological determinism, sociological determinism, or economic determinism. But the year 2019 can be identified as the watershed year from the point of view of the reforms in the Criminal Justice System, particularly the forensic science, pursuant to a decisive shift in the thinking of the dominant right-wing political outfit. The key components of such a shift are: First, a compelling desire to shed the colonial legacy by upholding the spirit of national pride, Second, a strong need to connect the

[11] Id. at pp. 29-33

Criminal Justice System to the prevailing majoritarian mood and aspirations, and Third, to impart scientific and technological orientation to the archaic Criminal Justice System. Decoding the aforesaid three components further, particularly in the context of forensic science knowledge, the rulers had realized quite well that the 'Colonial Criminal Justice sought forensic science services for securing "power" through legitimacy, but the democratic Constitution – centric criminal justice had to remain in search of credibility in the eyes of the citizen'. Furthermore, 'the scientific proof and explanation of crime and criminality has a greater appeal in the eyes of all the stakeholders'. Finally, in order to become appropriate Criminal Justice System of the Vikasit Bharat that could compete with the best in the world, the processes must place greater reliance on speed, fairness and determinism'. With these ends in view the science and technology input has been greatly enhanced in the post 2019 period, which can be witnessed in the following notable developments in the forensic science domains.

4.1 Forensic Science Knowledge Augmentation with the Proliferation of the New Forensic Science Courses

The forensic science knowledge and awareness have remained low, because earlier, forensic science was understood and applied as a 'talisman', to be used in the interest of the holders of power in select cases. Therefore, the post-2019 started its justice reform shift by creating objective and scientific education about the concept of universal forensic science for all. This vital task of the forensic science knowledge augmentation is assigned primarily to the National Forensic Science University, Gandhinagar (Gujarat), which is accorded a National University and Institute of National Importance status in 2020, along with the six adjunct campuses and two academies by now. The Gandhinagar NFSU runs Eight Schools that offer 46 courses in forensic science and allied subjects and serves as the nodal institution for coordinating studies in forensic science throughout the country. In addition to the network created by the NFSU institutions, forensic science knowledge is disseminated by the Directorate of Forensic Science Services, New Delhi, and the Central Forensic Science Laboratory, Pune. This vast network of institutions remains actively engaged in imparting courses on DNA forensics, cyber security, ballistics, questioned documents, narcotics, forensic psychology, food technology, multimedia forensics, forensic accounting and fraud investigation, digital forensics, and futuristic defence studies.[12]

[12] (2018) 10 SCC 1

4.2 Creation of the Forensic Science Normative Framework

In order to impart a forensic science orientation to the Criminal Justice System and the agencies responsible for its operation, it was realized that, for bringing about a lasting change, the normative system would require substantial changes, particularly in the procedural and evidentiary domains. The government had by then considered it appropriate to begin the normative restructuring by introducing the Criminal Procedure (Identification) Bill in the parliament in early 2020. The identification bill aimed at conferring powers on the enforcement agencies to take measurements of the criminals and prospective criminals as per the provisions of the Criminal Procedure (Identification) Act, 2022. The Identification Act, 2022, as per Section 2(b), authorizes a wide range of 'measurements' such as 'finger impressions', 'palm impressions', 'foot impressions', 'photographs', 'iris and retina scan', 'physical and biological samples and their analysis', 'behavioural attributes including signatures', 'hand writing or any other examination'. Similarly, the act under Section 3 defines the three categories of persons in a loose and inclusive manner, by going much beyond the 'convicts' whose measurements were authorized by the Identification of Prisoners Act, 1920, that stands repealed by Section 10 of the act. The two new categories whose measurements are authorized by the sub clauses (b) and (c) of Section 3, are person who are ordered to give surety for good behaviour under Section 117 or are facing proceedings under Sections 107 to 110 of the Cr.P.C. or any person who is arrested in connection with an offence under any law or detained under any preventive detention law. Thus, the persons enumerated in sub clauses (b) and (c) are non-convicts or may be acquitted in the end, but their measurements may be collected and preserved in terms of Section 4(1)(b) at the National Crime Records Bureau. As per Section 4(2) the measurement records shall be retained in digital or electronic form for a period of 75 years, but in cases of final acquittal or discharge, the concerned person may seek that the records be destroyed. The Identification Act, 2022 not only expands the forensic science boundaries to the new and sophisticated kinds of measurements, but extends it much beyond the domains of the crimes in pre-trial and trial stages, also to the pre-crime stages where the person is facing security or good behaviour proceedings or is just an arrestee or detenue who may be shortly acquitted.

The Identification Act, 2022, is like a precursor to the comprehensive infusion of the forensic science component that is followed in the Bharatiya Nagrik Suraksha Sanhita 2023 and the Bharatiya Saksha Adhiniyam 2023. The BNSS norms relating to Forensic Science are spread over the pre-trial and trial stages and are aimed at imparting (a) expedition to criminal proceedings and (b) enhancement of their credibility with the use of forensic evidence. The first aim of the expedition is provided for by Section 65 (use of science in summons procedure), Section 105 (search and seizure through scientific means), Section 193(3)(a) (all communications between police and magistracy to be electronic), Sections 210, 215, 265, 308, and 330 introduced to speed up the criminal proceedings. Unlike the first aim, the aim of enhancing the credibility of criminal proceedings by relying upon the forensic science evidence is the underlying philosophy of Section 176(3),which provides the procedure for investigation in respect to all cognizable offences punishable with imprisonment of 7 years or more, the officer in charge, from the date of the notification, shall cause the forensic expert to visit the crime scene to collect forensic evidence and cause the videography of the process in mobile or other electronic device. Provided, where the forensic facility is not available, the state may avail the facility from the other state. The provision is unique and may lead to expeditious and scientific disposition in criminal cases. It would have been a welcome move if such a progressive measure could be extended to below 7 year imprisonment offences, that constitutes of the bulk of criminal offences in India today.

Coming to the Bhartiya Saksha Adhiniyam (BSA) 2023, the forensic science evidence from any source has now been accorded emphatic recognition under Section 2(d), defining 'document' that includes electronic and digital records. Similarly, under Section 2(e) 'evidence' is defined to include under (ii) electronic or digital records, which can be called as documentary evidence. Further elaboration of documentary evidence is evident in Section 57 Explanations 4, 5, 6, and 7 that accords a primary evidence status to all the electronic and digital records in different stages of generation. In order to dispel any doubt about the admissibility and credibility of electronic and digital record special provisions under Sections 61 to 63 have been created. Furthermore, to impart special status and credibility to electronic and digital evidence, special rules of presumptions under Section 81 (Presumption as to Gazettes in electronic or digital records), Section 85 (Presumption as to electronic agreements), Section 87 (Presumption as to Electronic Signature Certificates), and Section 93 (Presumption as to 5-year-old electronic records).

Though the BSA has created new provisions for recognizing electronic and digital evidence by according them their due status, the new Saksha Adhiniyam has missed out on paying much attention to the sources from which the electronic and digital evidence is generated. The new Section 39 is framed mostly on the lines of Section 45 of the old act, which is mainly concerned with the relevance of the third-party (expert) evidence. That appears to be the reason for Section 39 repeating the earlier section except for the addition of words 'or any other field' in Section 39(1) and the addition of sub clause (ii) to make the opinion in any electronic or digital form before the court a relevant fact as expert evidence. The BSA has neither provided any definition of a 'forensic expert' nor laid down any criterion for higher credibility for forensic expert evidence. This appears to be a contradiction in respect to what is professed and what is normatively provided.

5 The Broadening Horizons of Criminal Justice and Forensic Science

A notable feature of the postcolonial development, both on the criminal justice and the forensic science fronts has been, their all-round expansion that can be described as 'boarding of the horizons'.

5.1 *The Expanding Domains of the Criminal Justice*

Though the Article 372 of the Constitution of India, nicknamed as the 'adaptation clause', did provide a new lease of life to the colonial penal laws that continue to rule us, in a way, till 1 July 2024. But on account of the constitutional rights network and the human rights regime, the hegemony of the colonial penal laws in course of time got considerably diluted. The constitution and human rights had a decisive influence on the legislative reforms, both in the amendments to the provisions of the existing penal statutes and in the enactment of new penal laws. Equally significant has been the route of the judicial reforms, coming from the apex court rulings, which have interpreted the constitutional rights and the statutory measures in the light of the changed social and political context, on the one hand, and augmentation of the ambit of the old rights by creating new remedies and generating reliefs, on the other. Hereafter, we discuss a few notable judicial reform rulings, thus:

5.1.1 Rulings Resetting the Boundaries of Offences on the Basis of the Constitutional Touchstone

In the Independent Thought vs. Union of India[13] a Child Right NGO had challenged Section 375 Exception 2 of the Penal Code that exempted the husband for nonconsensual sexual intercourse with wife above the age of 15 from the offence of rape on the grounds that it accords marital exemption for 'child' rape for wife between 15 years and 18 years. The Two Judge Bench of the Supreme Court held that the Exception 2 is unconstitutional, so for any prosecution for the intercourse with a 'child wife' is concerned, the Court devised a reading down technique, limiting it to 'sexual intercourse with a wife above 18 years of age'.

The second ruling on this line is the Five Judge Bench in Navtej Johar and others vs. Union of India[14] that resolved the issue raised by a clutch of 48 petitions filed by several groups of the LGBT community affected by the reversal of the NAZ foundation vs. NCT of Delhi by the Two Judge Bench of the Supreme Court. The challenge before the court centred round the wide, indiscriminate nature of criminalization arising on account of Section 377 of the Penal code that applied to every kind of homosexual relationship. The Five Judge Bench ruling unanimously struck down the criminalization of homosexual relationships between consenting, adult partners in privacy, thereby restricting the ambit of a long-accepted colonial law that worked on the basis of an unscientific bias against a large section of marginalized population.

The third ruling in this line is Joseph Shine vs. UOI,[15] where the Five Judge Bench was required to test the constitutionality of Section 497 or the offence of adultery under the Penal Code. Though the petition had sought uniformity in the

[13] (2017) 10 SCC 800

[14] (2018) 10 SCC 1

[15] Supreme Court of India (2019a) 3 scc 39

adultery offence by questioning the female partner's exemption from liability, the bench unanimously ruled that the very act of criminalization of adulterous relationship was itself unconstitutional, because Section 497 postulates a notion of marriage which subverts equality between the spouses.

5.1.2 The Constitutional Rarefication of the Death Penalty

Though the Supreme Court continues to uphold the constitutional validity of the death penalty right through the first challenge in Jagmohan Singh vs. Union of India ((1971) 1 SCC 20), Full Bench Bachan Singh vs. UOI ((1980) 2 SCC 684) and the bench decision in Triveniben vs. UOI ((1989) 1SCC 678), but in every case of constitutional challenge, the court has been tightening the noose against death penalty sentencing. The Bachan Singh majority ruling of Justice Sarkaria is known for upholding the constitutionality of the death penalty but subjecting its applicability only to 'rarest of rare cases' and this 'rarest of rare case' test is to be arrived after balancing the 'aggravating circumstances' with the 'mitigating circumstances'. The creative potential of the Bachan Singh ruling was later on relied upon by the Supreme Court in Santosh Kumar Bariar ((2009) 2 SCC (cri) 1150) and now *In re: Framing the Guidelines Regarding the Potential Mitigating Circumstances to be Considered While Imposing Death Sentence* (A Three Judge Bench Reference 19 September 2022)[16]. This reference decision of Justice Ravinder Bhatt (concurred by Chief Justice U.U. Lalit and Justice Sudhanshu Dhulia) has focused on the issue of the nature of compliance with the requirements of Section 235(2) of the Cr. P.C. by the trial courts in death penalty cases.

5.1.3 Fair Trial Based on 'Flawed' Forensic Testimony Earns Anokhilal Acquittal After Thirteen Years in the 'Death Row'

Anokhilal case is a classic example of how a fair trial guarantee works in the criminal justice system and can yield to an accused being convicted and sentenced to death in 2013, acquittal after 13 years. Initially in February 2013, Anokhilal, a poor villager in Khandwa, M.P., was prosecuted for rape, murder, and aggravated POCSO offences and put on trial that was completed in less than a month. After conviction, the accused was sentenced to death. The M.P. High Court confirmed the death sentence in the next three months. In the appeal before the Supreme Court, the Three Judge Bench in Anokhilal vs. state of M.P,[17] after a detailed deliberation on the issue of compliance with the fair trial requirements, ordered a de novo trial in the case. In

[16] (2019) 20 SCC 196

[17] Id

the retrial hearing before the special Judge POSCO Act, Khandwa,[18] a team of four Project 39A of the National Law University Delhi, lawyers had represented Anokhilal. The advocacy was centred around the inadequacy of evidence to support the prosecution's case based on the 'last seen with the victim' evidence and the flaws in the forensic evidence. The Special Judge in Para 173(d) has pointed out, "DNA of another man has been found in the vaginal slides and the anal slides of the deceased, which conclusively proves that the crime of rape was not committed by the accused Anokhilal". Again, in para 176, the judge reiterates that 'the above report has been prepared by scientists based on machines, which is completely absolute evidence. The likelihood of such evidence favouring either the prosecution or defence is zero... Therefore, contrary to all the evidence in the case, the accused in entitled to get the benefit of DNA report of PP-58 which establishes the involvement of any person other than the accused in the crime of rape'.[19] Thus, Anokhilal gets acquittal, for all the offences for which he was charged, on 19.03.2024. He walks back as a free man, now aged 34 years, after over 13 years of initial arrest, trial, conviction, and death row detention, because the flaws in the forensic testimony proved fatal to the POCSO Act trial.

6 The Alternate Rationalization of Crime, Reorientation of Criminal Justice and Shift of Focus to Pre-Crime Stages: Their Impact on the Criminal Justice and Forensic Science

Here, the focus shifts to the new and innovative ways of conceptualizing crimes, techniques of their identification, and measures of controlling them, which in turn gets reflected into the altered notions of the criminal justice and the forensic science.

The theme of alternate rationalization of crime, reorientation of criminal justice and shift to pre-crime stages in the English Criminal Justice System has been examined by Lucia Zedner in chapter 8 titled 'From Criminal Justice to Security Society', in her masterly treatise on Criminal Justice (Oxford Univ. Press, 2004).[20] The chapter is prefaced by an imaginary conversation about a 'pre-crime', society where people are arrested before they break any law. This is in anticipation of their breaking the law in future. The supporter of pre-crime system boasts: 'Happily they don't because we get them first before they can commit an act of violence. So the commission of crime itself is absolute metaphysics. We claim they are culpable...' 'In our society we have no major crimes'... 'but we do have a detention camp full of

[18] Zedner, Lucia, From Criminal Justice to Security Society, Ch. 8, Criminal Justice, Oxford University Press, 2004, pp. 283–311

[19] Id. at pp. 284–287

[20] Id. at pp. 284–287

would be criminals' (Part of P.K. Dick's Minority Report, London: Gollancz 2002 at pp 2–3).[21]

Lucia Zedner's ideas on the alternative thinking about criminal justice are structured around the three notions, namely (a) Reconception of crime on the basis of the rational choice theory that perceives 'crime' not as a pathological or poorly socialized person's act, but an act indulged for utility maximization. Thus, crimes are no longer seen as threats to the moral order that need punishment, but imposition of calculable cost. The orientation around calculable cost of crime entails a shift from retrospective crime concern for punishment to prospective concern with future offences. Such economic analysis de-dramatizes crime and presents it as an ordinary activity to which individuals are exposed in everyday life. (b) Changes in the orientation of criminal justice, which takes the focus away from the sovereign's right to punish, replacing it with the sovereign's promise to secure protection. This reverses the orientation of criminal justice from the classical backward looking to a prospective protection-oriented processing. In the altered criminal justice, the policing has to assume a preventive, deterrent, and innovative position. Thus, in such a dispensation: 'the shift towards prevention, surveillance and security has been the subject of considerable criminological attention.'[22] As per Lucia Zedner there is a growing divide between the 'Old Penology' and the 'New Penology'. The 'New Penology' is emerging: 'it is actuarial. It is concerned with the techniques for identifying, classifying and managing groups assorted by levels of dangerousness'. The focus is on targeting suspect populations and making actuarial assessments of their likelihood of offending in particular circumstances or when exposed to certain kinds of opportunity.[23] (c) From 'post-crime' criminal justice to 'pre-crime' society, shifts the focus to prospective concern for risks as yet unrealized. 'This will entail a move in substantive focus from workings of criminal process, trial and punishment, and towards the physical environment and opportunity structures in which crime is committed.'[24] The pre-crime strategies would largely depends upon situational crime prevention that would require the criminal justice agents to move outside the criminal process like the new technologies of control and prevention that includes environmental design, street architecture and planning of urban spaces. All the pre-crime actors are supposed to share and take away the exclusive right and power from the state and locate it in the community or the corporate entity. Already, a strong pro-market lobby has come to support private provisioning of the security.[25] In her succinct conclusion to the growing reality of movement towards 'security society', away from the 'punishment state', the author sums up, thus: 'The expansion of security industry has enlarged not diminished the penal state. And though

[21] Id. at p. 289

[22] Id. at p. 289

[23] Id. at pp. 288–296

[24] Id. at p. 297

[25] Id. at pp. 296–304

security is posited as a universal good, its pursuit tends to exclude those deemed as risks, erodes civil liberties, and corrodes trust, the very cement of civil society'.[26]

6.1 Extending the Boundaries of the Indian Criminal Justice and Forensic Science to the 'Pre-crime' Stages

Even the English Criminal Justice System, which has a much longer history of evolution, is facing the accusations of over-criminalization and expanding the ambit of criminalization by the devices such as 'hybrid criminalization' in the writings of scholars such as Andrew Ashworth[27] and others. Therefore, there should be little surprise if the Indian Criminal Justice, in the process of shedding the colonial criminal justice legacy, undertakes to readjust and reconfigurate the boundaries of the 'crime' and 'criminal justice' by enacting penal statutes with a view to streamlining its security. Since our purpose here is limited to tracking the widening and shifting trajectory of criminal justice as well as forensic science, our focus would be on the penal statutes that have a tendency to either push the boundaries of the offence to the 'pre-crime' stages or to the forensic evidence that lies outside their known spheres of traditional criminal justice.

Before a behaviour is formally designated as 'crime' by the legislature, it may remain in the 'name and shame' or 'name calling' stages. 'Urban naxals', 'land jihadi', 'love jihadi', and 'desh-drohi', etc. are the commonly used labels belonging to this genus. But for how long and for what purpose a 'flawed behaviour' remains in 'name calling' stage is a part of the deviance policy, though it does have significant bearing on the regulation and control of the behaviour. It may be interesting to learn quite a few lessons from how the out of the box imagination of the label 'love jihad' has had wide-ranging ramifications. First, it became the rallying point for the enactment of several state anti-conversion laws, under which forcible religious conversion for the purpose of marriage is made a serious crime, apart from declaring the interfaith marriage 'null and void'.[28] Second, 'Love Jihad' also becomes a hot cinematic theme, which can be cashed on the box office by making a full-length film: *The Kerala Story*, depicting the trickery and fraud involved in a majority of interfaith marriages in the Kerala State. Third, the 'love jihad' folklore itself becomes a powerful divisive device that can influence the mindset at all levels of society. A recent study conducted by the *Indian Express* (18 April 2024) relating to the differential responses of the Allahabad High Court Benches, in respect to the police protections extended to the interfaith married couples, is very revealing. Out

---

[26] Id. at p. 305

[27] Ashworth, Andrew, "Is the Criminal Law a Lost Cause?" (2000) 116(2) LQR

[28] Under the U.P. Prohibition of Unlawful Conversion of Religion Act, 2021, between Jan. 1, 2021, and April 30, 2023, 427 conversion-related cases were reported in Uttar Pradesh, leading to the arrest of 833 persons. The Hindu, 18.04.2024

of the 15 orders passed on the petitions from the interfaith live-in couples for the police protection filed before the six benches, in 12, the High Court Benches denied to order protection, only in three the protection by the police was ordered.[29] Such a divided view of things that concern the constitutionally guaranteed freedoms and choices does not auger well for the interfaith married couples and for the democracy.

The same kind of 'pushing the boundaries effect' may be created for criminal justice and forensic science by the promulgation of an order by a District Magistrate/ Executive Magistrate under Section 144 Cr.P.C. (now Section 163 BNSS). The order is a part of public order policing, which may last up to a period of 2 months, subject to its extension up to 6 months. An interesting study relating to the deployment of Section 144 in Delhi conducted by a team of four lawyers appropriately titled as 'When Law Creates Crimes'[30] has revealed the wide ranging implication of the naive-looking Section 144, for the criminal justice and forensic science. The study focused on the post-COVID 1 year under Section 144 orders in the NCR, Delhi. The study is based on RTI responses to 6100 orders, of which 5400 were inspected with respect to the reasons of their issual, which were classified into four categories: The first category of 25% Section 144 orders were issued to private establishments directing them to install CCTV cameras at different sensitive points with a view to establishing a parallel surveillance system. In the second category of 43% of orders under Section 144 were issued to regulate business and services through a range of directions for compulsory registration and recording of documents about tenants, labourers/servants/employees, before providing a job or accommodation. The purpose of these orders/directions is to treat the entire service class population as potential criminals who require constant monitoring and surveillance.[31] The third category of orders was limited to public order threats such as unlawful assemblies and activities that threatened the interest of the society in a special way, like flying kites with 'special manjhas' or 'bursting crackers'. In the fourth residuary category fall self-effacing activities like hookah bars or harmful addictions that work against the interest of society in the long run. This short study on Section 144 orders targets a wide section of the Delhi population, particularly the marginalized sections, in the pre-crime zones. Similar push into pre-crime zone may arise on account of many other loosely worded laws that leaves wide discretion in the hands of the enforcement agencies.

[29] IndianExpress, 18.04.2024 Can UP interfaith live-in couples get police protection? Yes, no, maybe

[30] Vrinda Bhandari, Abhinav Sekhri, Natasha Maheshwari and Madhav Aggarwal, When Law Creates Crimes", Times of India city edn, 24.03.2023

[31] Id

7 Futuristic Projections of the Criminal Justice and Forensic Science Debates

From the point of view of the criminal justice and forensic science interface, the post 1 July 2024 era is likely to be an era of far-reaching happenings and new possibilities. This is mainly because of three reasons, namely: First, never before, the criminal procedure and criminal evidence law have been subjected to such a comprehensive normative change, Second, never before the science, technology and electronics components have been deployed for imparting such a change in the orientation of this criminal processes and, Third, never before, such unanimity and political will has been witnessed to bring about changes in the Criminal Justice System. But all these quick and far-reaching changes need to reach to the ground levels, where the investigation, prosecution and trial relating to criminal cases are conducted by the specific agencies that are likely to get additionally burdened with the forensic evidence tasks? Why has there not been any thinking about a directorate of forensic services? What specific roles would be performed by the 'forensic experts', who still remain statutorily underrecognized? Even more problematic would be the extension of the forensic science to the pre-crime stages deliberated in the part VI earlier. Such extensions of the forensic science tend to push the debate to the 'forensic security science' domains, that has a tendency to provide a paradigm shift to the criminal justice rule of law itself. Even in the advanced Western countries, the scholars are grappling with the problem of 'Too Much Security Challenge'[32] and the 'AI challenge'. Lucia Zedner has examined the 'too much security' issue or is 'security' an unqualified good? in the light of six paradoxes, namely: 'security pursues risk reduction but presumes the persistence of crime; that the expansion of security has enlarged not diminished penal state; that security promises reassurance but in fact increases anxiety; that security is posited as universal good but presumes social exclusion; that security promises freedom but erodes civil liberties; and finally that security is posited as public good but its pursuit is inimical to good society'.[33] The lesson we need to take from Lucia Zedner's view on security is like the other means of crime control; 'security' also requires testing in the light of special justifications that require subjection to the rule of law. Both the 'security' or 'AI challenges' designed and approved by the advanced Western society standards would need to pass the Indian Constitution and Human Rights threshold, because ultimately the criminal justice and the forensic science is meant to render justice to the Indian citizen, on the Indian terrain.

---

[32] Zender L (2003) Too Much Security? Int J Social Law 31:155-184

[33] Id

References

A Three-Judge Bench Reference dated September 19, 2022

Ashworth A (2000) Is the criminal law a lost cause? Law Quart Rev 116(2)

Barry Wright (2011) Macaulay's Indian penal code: historical context and organizing principles. In: Weng-Cheong C et al (eds) Codification, Macaulay and the Indian Penal Code – the legacies and modern challenges of criminal law reform. Ashgate Publishing Ltd, p 26

Bhandari V, Sekhri A, Maheshwari N, Aggarwal M (2023) When law creates crimes. Times of India, City Edition, April 24

Chockalingam K (2023) The emergence and the history of criminology: a global and Indian perspective. Indian J Criminol, Special Edition 2023, 23–40. National Law University Delhi

Hussain N (2003) The Jurisprudence of emergency: colonialism and the rule of law. University of Michigan Press

Indian Express (2024) Can U.P. Inter-Faith Live-in couples get police protection? Yes, no, maybe. Indian Express, April 18, 2024

Pokhariyal P.. (n.d) Forensic Science Knowledge Update (Internal academic report. National Forensic Sciences University, Gandhinagar)

Samaddar R (2008) Crimes, passion and detachment: colonial foundations of rule of law. In: Kannabiran K et al (eds) Challenging the rule(s) of law. Sage, India, pp 356–371

Supreme Court of India (2017) 10 SCC 800

Supreme Court of India (2018) 10 SCC 1

Supreme Court of India (2019a) 3 SCC 39

Supreme Court of India (2019b) 20 SCC 196

Zedner L (2004) From criminal justice to security society. Chapter 8 in Criminal Justice. Oxford University Press, pp 283–311

Examining Victims' Rights in China From the Perspective of the United Nations Declaration on the Basic Principles of Justice for Victims of Crime and Abuse of Power

Jing Cao, Jan Van Dijk, and Marc Groenhuijsen

Abstract This article presents an evaluation of China's alignment with the 1985 United Nations *Declaration on the Basic Principles of Justice for Victims of Crime and Abuse of Power*, a seminal document in the advancement of victims' rights globally. Through a multidimensional approach encompassing legal research, semi-structured interviews with criminal justice officials and other stakeholders, and a large-scale survey of Beijing residents on their experiences with crime and the police, this study assesses the development and current state of victims' rights in China against the Declaration's benchmarks. Our analysis reveals that since the adoption of the new Criminal Procedure Law in 1996, China has made considerable progress in codifying victims' rights. However, challenges persist, particularly in ensuring compassionate treatment, adequate state compensation, and adequate social support for victims. Although legal frameworks and practices show a convergence towards UN standards, particularly in facilitating victim participation and improving information dissemination, the effectiveness of communication and actual enforcement of participatory rights in trials need enhancement. Furthermore, while specialized considerations for vulnerable groups exist, general satisfaction with police performance is low, indicating deficiencies in victim reception and protection measures. The provision of legal assistance to victims has seen improvements, but the overall availability of state compensation and specialized support services remains insufficient. Our findings highlight the ongoing nature of efforts

J. Cao (✉)
Department of Foreign Languages, Southwest University of Political Science and Law, Chongqing, China

J. Van Dijk
Leiden University and Tilburg University, Tilburg, The Netherlands
e-mail: JDijk@nscr.nl

M. Groenhuijsen
Tilburg University, Tilburg, The Netherlands
e-mail: M.S.Groenhuijsen@tilburguniversity.edu

© The Author(s), under exclusive license to Springer Nature Singapore Pte Ltd. 2026

G. S. Bajpai et al. (eds.), *Beyond the Gavel: A Paradigm Shift in Global Criminal Justice*, https://doi.org/10.1007/978-981-95-4487-5_9

required to fully realize the Declaration's objectives in China, pointing towards areas in urgent need of attention to ensure justice for crime victims.

Keywords China • Victims' rights • ICVS • United Nations

1 Introduction

This year, Professor. Dr K. Chockalingam will reach the respectable age of 80 years. We are happy that the editors of this volume, professors Bajpai, Shekhar and Priyamvada, have decided to issue a Festschrift in his honour on this special occasion. Even though a similar volume was published only 4 years ago (Shekhar and Sahni 2020), there are many reasons to once more pay tribute to the immense achievements of Prof Chockalingam in the field of victimology. We feel privileged to have an opportunity to contribute to this endeavour. In choosing our topic, we took a close look at the life and writings of Prof Chockalingam. It is obvious that he has always been a pioneer in promoting victims' rights. Since China borders India, and is—like India—one of the most populous countries in the world, it looks like a fair idea to assume that he will be interested in recent developments within this jurisdiction. And we have never forgotten that Professor. Chockalingam himself did play a role in paving the road for the adoption of the 1985 UN Declaration. He participated in the UN Interregional Meeting of Eminent Persons in New Delhi in 1985, and he took part in the Seventh United Nations Crime Congress in Milan (Italy) later that same year, a meeting which has subsequently been labelled as the 'proverbial labour room for the 1985 UN Declaration'. In writing this chapter on the impact of the Declaration in China, we congratulate Prof Chockalingam not only on his 80th birthday, but also on his impressive career in India as well as elsewhere on the globe.

At this juncture, victim-related studies in China are still limited in both quantity and scope. A review of the currently available research literature shows that publications on crime victims are confined to the disciplines of criminology and criminal law. The main issue in this literature is how the commission of crimes can be prevented through interventions in the behaviour of potential victims (Cao 2024). These studies stand in the international tradition of victimological studies from the 1950s and 1960s on the interactions between offenders and victims, the possible role reversals between them, and the co-responsibility of victims for the crimes committed against them (Von Hentig 1948; Wolfgang 1957; Fattah 1971).

After the emergence of the so-called Chinese crime victims' movement[1] around 2006, the focus of Chinese publications on victims gradually shifted from 'victim precipitation' to the establishment of state relief systems and other services for

[1]The mass killing case that happened in a Chinese temple on 14 July 2006 raised the awareness of different segments of Chinese society of the necessity to improve the standing of victims within the framework of criminal law procedure. This case further triggered a national campaign to establish a national relief system for victims of violent crime. Consequently, numerous scholars recognize the 'Temple Killing' case as a pivotal turning point marking the birth of the Chinese crime victims' rights movement.

victims of crime (Tian 2008). In this respect Chinese victimology has, as happened elsewhere already in the 1980s, belatedly become more truly victim-centred. However, comprehensive studies on the rights of victims of crime in criminal procedure and their practical implementation or on the nature and impact of victimization by crime, remained scarce (Zhao and Xu 2015; Jiang and Chen 2012).

From a historical perspective, the rights of both defendants and crime victims in the criminal justice system were very limited during the first three decades of the People's Republic of China, established in 1949 (Liu 2005; Zhao 2010). Although limited on both sides, they could be said to be in a state of equilibrium. However, between 1966 and 1976, the 10-year-long Cultural Revolution (*wen ge*)[2] devastated the legal foundations of Chinese society. The subsequent 'crackdown on crime policy' (*yan da*)[3] of 1983, designed to better protect the public from the impact of serious crime, further undermined a rights-based Chinese criminal justice system (Trevaskes 2010). The rights of both defendants and victims were made totally subordinate to the agenda of the tough-on-crime policies.

Towards the end of the twentieth century, Chinese politicians and scholars felt that the criminal policies of the state relied too much on punishment as the primary, and often sole function of criminal justice, and that this focus had led to many miscarriages of justice and abuses of the rights of suspects/defendants (Trevaskes 2007). In response to this criticism, strengthening the protection of the rights of suspects/defendants was adopted as the principal aim of penal reform in China (Tsin 2009). Unfortunately, this key priority has, for a long time, eclipsed the equally pressing need to strengthen the rights of victims of crime too.

Rights for victims of crime have, for a long time, been overlooked not only in China but in many other parts of the world as well. It was only in the late 1970s, early 1980s that some scholars and activists in western industrialized countries, such as the United States, Australia, England and Wales, and the Netherlands, introduced and advocated for a so-called victims' or victims' rights movement (Friedman 1985; Joutsen 1987; Van Dijk 1988, 1999; Young and Stein 2004; Wemmers 2010). Since then, victim-friendly initiatives such as the establishment of state compensation schemes, rape crisis centres and shelter homes, as well as general victim support schemes, have been adopted in jurisdictions in North America, Europe and elsewhere in the world. Parallel to this, the position of the victim in criminal procedure has been incrementally strengthened in many jurisdictions. These actions and

---

[2]The Cultural Revolution, known in Chinese as 'Wén Gé', officially titled the Great Proletarian Cultural Revolution, was a sociopolitical movement in China that lasted from 1966 to 1976. Initiated by Mao Zedong, then Chairman of the Chinese Communist Party (CCP), its stated goal was to preserve Chinese Communism by purging remnants of capitalist and traditional elements from Chinese society and to impose Maoist orthodoxy within the CCP. The movement resulted in widespread upheaval, characterized by political zealotry, factional struggles, and the upending of cultural institutions. Intellectuals and historical artifacts suffered particularly harsh treatment.

[3]Yan Da is a short term for 'taking severe and speedy action against serious illegal and criminal activities'. This policy programme was first introduced by the former chairman of the Central Commission of the PRC, Deng Xiaoping, in order to remedy the chaotic public safety situation resulting from the Cultural Revolution. It has been reconfirmed in 2004, 2010, and 2014.

practices have eventually led to a worldwide consensus that 'crime does harm victims, not just the state' and that therefore the rights of and support for victims should be regarded as a new key concern for criminal justice systems (Groenhuijsen 1999; Brienen and Hoegen 2000; Waller 2010).

On 29 November 1985, governments from all over the world unanimously adopted the *Declaration of Basic Principles of Justice for Victims of Crime and Abuse of Power* at the United Nations General Assembly. With this declaration, now commonly referred to as the Magna Carta for Crime Victims, all UN Member States, including China, one of the five permanent members of the United Nations Security Council, have committed themselves to make all necessary efforts to better cater to the needs of victims of crime.

Over the past 30 years, reforms of national laws to better comply with international legal instruments on victims' rights, such as the UN Declaration have proliferated in many western industrialized countries in Europe, North America, and Australia, as well as in some Asian countries, including Japan and South Korea (Chan 2007; Groenhuijsen and Letschert 2012). Nevertheless, at this juncture, most governments are still struggling to honour their pledge of almost forty years ago.

In light of the aforementioned observations, the present contribution aims to offer a preliminary examination of the current state of affairs concerning rights for victims of crime in China. This study intends to fill the research gaps concerning victims' rights in China by assessing the legal position of victims of crime in China in reference to internationally accepted standards for victims' rights, notably those of the 1985 UN Declaration.

2 Methodology

We have examined the compliance of the current laws and practices of the rights of victims of crime in China with the global standards incorporated in the said Declaration. As a normative benchmark for our assessment, we employed the eleven articles of the declaration detailing the key principles of justice for victims, grouped under four headings: *Information and Participation, Treatment and Protection, Reparation and Compensation,* and *Legal Assistance and Social Support.*

The seminal study of victims' rights in Europe conducted by Brienen and Hoegen (2000) offered critical insights into how the domestic laws of the twenty-two Member States of the Council of Europe at the time relate to the 1985/11 Recommendation of the Council of Ministers on the position of the victim in criminal procedure.[4] Content-wise, the said recommendation is a mirror image of the 1985 UN Declaration. Unquestionably, this comparative study provides a robust

[4]The Council of Europe is an international organization promoting human rights in Europe, founded in 1949, currently encompassing 46 Member States.

model for a systematic analysis of China's domestic law from an international perspective. However, the approach of Brienen & Hoegen had its limitations. Although it aimed to look at both formal and practical implementation of the recommendations (law in the books vs. law in action), many of its country studies contained few empirical data relating to the actual implementation of victims' rights. Moreover, the study presented no results from national surveys in the various countries on the extent and nature of victimization, the responses of actual victims to their victimization or their experiences with the police.

To determine the level of compliance with the benchmark, we extended the methodology of the study of Brienen and Hoegen with the conduct of semi-structured interviews with a broad sample of relevant officials and with the analysis of official statistical data on the implementation of key victims' rights, where available. Second, a major part of our study is the presentation and analysis of the results of an internationally standardized victimization survey executed among a representative sample of the general population of Beijing. This survey, akin to other victimization surveys, performs two essential functions. Firstly, it quantifies the actual extent and impact of criminal victimization in China and, secondly, it monitors the responses of victims to their victimization and possible encounters with the police.

By integrating these legal and empirical perspectives, an in-depth and nuanced understanding of the current status of victims' rights in China has hopefully been attained.

The study on the legal situation consists of a comprehensive literature review, as well as an examination of the degree of alignment between rights for victims of crime in the corpus of Chinese law and the international standards set out by the UN Declaration. The initial research involved a systematic literature review of Chinese legal texts pertaining to the rights afforded to victims of crime. Existing legislation and regulations concerning the subject of 'victims of crime in China' were systematically reviewed by utilizing the largest electronic legal database in China, PKULAW. The keywords used in searching this database were the two official legal terms for 'victim' in the Chinese language (*bei hai ren* and *shou hai ren*). After screening out undesirable search results, such as irrelevant and/or outdated legal articles, the remaining material was analysed in reference to the eleven main principles outlined in the 1985 UN Declaration. This legal desk research on the historical and present legislation in China on victims' rights extended to national laws, bylaws, guidelines, provisions, and so-called joint Opinions of organs of the Communist Party, Ministries, and the People's Supreme Court.

For practical reasons, the interviews with stakeholders were carried out in the city of Chongqing where the first author of this chapter is based. The questionnaire designed for the interviews with stakeholders was structured along the main content of the UN Declaration. It consists of a list of questions concerning the roles of different authorities pertaining to the four key themes covered by the Declaration: information and participation, treatment and protection, reparation and restoration, legal assistance, and social support. Data collected from these interviews, coupled with the available official statistics on victims' rights, were employed to investigate the practical implementation of the relevant legal provisions in China and to determine how the Chinese criminal justice system empirically relates to the principles of justice contained in the UN Declaration. Although it must be acknowledged that direct inputs from victims were not incorporated in this part of the study, the selected interviewees—police chiefs, public prosecutors, criminal court judges, staff members of the Women's Union, attorneys, and academics—play crucial roles in the application and enforcement of victim's rights. Therefore, their perceptions of what happens in practice can offer important insights into the actual state of victim's rights in one of the largest cities of China.

Supplementing these interviews, a large-scale population survey on victimization experiences was conducted in 2014 among a net sample of 2000 randomly selected inhabitants of Beijing, the capital city of China. Respondents were interviewed about their personal experiences with victimization by crime over the past five years, and identified victims were subsequently asked about their experiences with the police and victim support. The interviews were conducted using the technique of Computer Assisted Telephone Interviewing (CATI). In the course of the study, a pilot was done in Beijing among a net sample of 1000 respondents with Computer Assisted Web-based Interviewing (CAWI). The results on victimization differed from those of the CATI interviews and raised methodological issues similar to those of pilots with CAWI versions of the ICVS previously conducted in Europe (Van Dijk et al. 2010). It was decided not to incorporate the results of this pilot in the final presentation of results because of doubts concerning their validity and reliability.

Notably, since the survey is a repeat of the International Crime Victims Survey (ICVS), conducted in over 80 countries across the world, the results can be analysed from an international and comparative perspective (Van Dijk, 2016). As the same survey has, under the supervision of the United Nations Interregional Criminal Justice Research Institute (UNICRI), been carried out in Beijing before in 1994, the results also shed light on changes in victimization and interactions with police over the past thirty years in Beijing. This part of the study will illuminate where China stands on the global victimological map in terms of victimization and victims' responses.

3 Universally Accepted Principles of Justice for Victims of Crime

Victims of crime used to be described as the 'Cinderellas of the criminal justice system' (Schafer 1960),[5] or the 'non-person in the eyes of the professional participants' (Shapland 1983). Today, such criticisms are somewhat obsolete as countries

[5]The epic fairy tale character of Cinderella has been used as a metaphor quite a few times in our field. The Indian hero in victimology, judge Krishna Iyer, once wrote: 'Criminology is a Cinderella among social sciences and Victimology is a Cinderella of Criminology'.

around the world have made sincere efforts to 'rebalance' criminal justice systems through reforms in favour of victims of crime (Groenhuijsen 2005; Davies 2015). Regardless of the differences between adversarial, inquisitorial, or mixed systems, governments across the world have actively sought to enhance the legal status of victims and, in parallel, improve social services for victims of crime (Mawby 2007; Zedner and Hoyle 2007; Walklate 2007). Scholars describing the history of the victims' rights movement point to the unanimous acceptance of the *Declaration of Basic Principles of Justice for Victims of Crime and Abuse of Power* by the General Assembly of the United Nations in 1985 as its greatest achievement (Groenhuijsen 2005). As a follow-up, the United Nations Office on Drugs and Crime (UNODC) has published, in collaboration with the Ministry of Justice of the Netherlands and the Department of Justice of the United States, a *Handbook on Justice for Victims on the use and application of the Declaration* and a *Guide for Policymakers* (UNODC 1999).

The declaration was the outcome of a lengthy process involving group discussions, lobbying, and numerous adjustments and compromises. A contentious issue was whether the obligations of States regarding victims of crime should also apply to victims of 'Abuse of Power', such as torture, systemic pollution, corruption, and exploitation (Bassiouni 2006). In the end, both categories of victims were incorporated in the proposed declaration, though the contents regarding victims of abuse of power were significantly curtailed.[6] As noted above, on 29 November 1985, the declaration was adopted by the UN General Assembly in New York as an annex to resolution 40/34 (UN Audiovisual Library of International Law).

In the same year, another international legal document, the *Recommendation on the Position of the Victims in the Framework of Criminal Law, and Procedure*, was adopted by the Council of Ministers of the Council of Europe.[7] It shared the ambition of urging the international community to enhance the legal status of the victim. The contents of these two documents overlap to a large extent, except for one substantive difference: the category of 'victims of abuse of power' is included in the declaration in a separate section, but is not addressed at all in the recommendation. Also, the recommendation, unlike the Declaration does not have specific provisions on participation in the trial, the right to victim support and the right to state compensation.[8] Both documents have in common that they are not legally binding but belong to the category of 'soft law.'

Inspired by the UN Declaration as well as the said recommendation, more detailed international legal instruments with similar content have been established,

[6] The rights of victims of abuse of power would later become the subject of a separate international legal instrument, adopted in 2005 by the United Nations General Assembly, the 'Basic Principles and Guidelines on the Right to a Remedy and Reparation for Victims of Gross Violations of International Human Rights Law and Serious Violations of International Humanitarian Law'.

[7] The recommendation was issued by the Council of Europe on June 29, 1985.

[8] The latter omission can be explained by the fact that the Council of Europe had adopted a dedicated Convention on that topic two years previously: European Convention on the Compensation of Victims of Violent Crimes, Strasbourg, 24.XI.1983 (CETS 116).

for instance the legally binding 2001 *European Union Framework Decision on the Standing of Victims in Criminal Proceedings*, later transposed in the *2012 Victims Directive* and the 2005 *United Nations Guidelines on Justice in Matters Involving Child Victims and Witnesses of Crime* (Waller 2010).

After 1985, spurred on by the momentum generated by the adoption of UN Declaration, many countries around the world have carried out criminal justice reforms, which aimed at improving victim's procedural status and strengthening the enforcement of victim's rights. Many countries also introduced a comprehensive system for the protection of and assistance and support for crime victims through legislation and policy-setting. The adoption of this large array of international and national legal instruments concerning the rights of victims of crime suggests full agreement among governments that these rights must be incorporated in domestic legislation and honoured in practice. However, as Groenhuijsen pointed out, '*the fact that the major protocols are to a large extent identical does not necessarily reflect a genuine international consensus. People who have actually negotiated these protocols stated that quite often it is only a small group of intellectuals or moral entrepreneurs who have succeeded in persuading the international institutions to adopt new and aspirational standards, without them really understanding the implications of doing so*'. (Groenhuijsen 2005)

Therefore, it is important to always keep in mind that despite a seemingly universal agreement regarding the validity of these standards for victims of crimes, this by itself does not ensure incorporation in domestic law, let alone full compliance in practice. In fact, several international studies have, as outlined above, concluded that none of even the most developed countries has as yet fully implemented the standards set out in these documents (Waller 2010; Brienen and Hoegen 2000; Groenhuijsen 2014; Van Dijk and Groenhuijsen 2018). Despite various efforts taken by the United Nations to guide and encourage Member States to achieve its minimum standards for victims' rights, international evaluations have repeatedly shown that up till now the implementation of the Declaration can only be described as 'unsatisfactory' in both the developing and developed world (Groenhuijsen 2014).

As observed by Brienen and Hoegen (2000) in their model study on the implementation of the *Council of Europe Recommendation 1985/11*, international legal standards such as the recommendations must be applicable to a variety of different national legal systems and must therefore, of necessity, be formulated in relatively abstract language. Considering the membership of the United Nations spanning the world, this is even more the case with resolutions of the General Assembly setting legal standards, such as the UN Victims' Rights Declaration. In this regard, it is important to stress that the declaration itself speaks of basic principles of justice rather than minimum standards as is the case in some other UN legal instruments, such as, for example, the one on the treatment of prisoners from 1954. The open, nonbinding character of the principles of justice for victims is especially evident in the language of articles on compensation. According to Article 11 governments must 'review their practices, regulations, and laws to consider restitution as an available sentencing option in criminal cases'. This article falls far short of the imperative statement that governments should make offender compensation a sentencing

Table 1 The basic victims' rights of the 1985 UN Victims Declaration broken down into four categories

Category	Basic rights of victims of crime
Information and participation	Art.5: Right to be informed about rights to seek redress; and 6(a): right to information on the proceedings **(Information on proceedings)** Art.6(b): Right to present views to the judicial authorities **(Presentation of views)** Art.7: Right to be offered the opportunity to participate in informal dispute resolution, including mediation **(Informal dispute resolution)**
Treatment and protection	Art. 4: Be treated with compassion and respect **(Compassion and respect)** Art.6(d): Right to protection against retaliation/intimidation **(Protection against retaliation and intimidation)** Art.6(d): Right to see their privacy/identity protected **(Protection of privacy/identity)**
Reparation and compensation	Art.8-9: Right to receive restitution from the offender **(Compensation from offender)** Art.12: Right to receive compensation from the state in cases of violent crime **(Compensation from state)**
Legal assistance and social support	Art.6(c): Entitlement to proper legal assistance throughout the legal process **(Legal aid)** Art.14-17: Right to receive social support/assistance **(Social assistance)**

option. According to Article 12, governments should 'endeavour' to provide compensation to victims of violent crime, and the establishment of national funds for this purpose 'should be encouraged'. This kind of language offers no precise guidance on what specific reforms are required in domestic legislation and criminal policy.

Nevertheless, from the 1985 UN Declaration's articles concerning rights for crime victims, eleven clear-cut principles of justice have been distilled (Van Dijk and Goodey 2004; Van Dijk 2005). These can be grouped under four headings concerning respectively 'Information and participation', 'Fair treatment and protection', 'Reparation and compensation', and 'Legal assistance and Social Support' (see Table 1). These eleven principles will serve as our conceptual framework (our 'searchlight') for the analysis and assessment of Chinese victims' law.

4 The Prevalence of Crime Victimization in China

According to the Chinese Law Yearbook, the average number of criminal cases recorded by the police between the years 2010 and 2021 is 6.06 million (see Table 2). Among them, crimes with direct personal victims such as homicide, assault, robbery, rape, trafficking in women and children, theft, and fraud accounted for about 85%. This means that, on average, some 5 million inhabitants of China per year are victimized in China by crimes recorded by the police.

Table 2 Statistics on criminal cases recorded by the public security organs of China

Year[a]	No. of recorded cases[b]	Rates of cleared up cases (%)[c]
2010	5.96 million	39.03
2011	6.00 million	38.51
2012	6.55 million	42.86
2013	6.59 million	40.13
2014	6.54 million	36.93
2015	7.17 million	31.27
2016	6.42 million	33.24
2017	5.48 million	38.03
2018	5.07 million	37.92
2019	4.86 million	39.30
2020	4.78 million	38.61
2021	5.03 million	39.17

[a]Data retrieved from the 2011 to 2022 Chinese Law Year Books
[b]Types of crimes included in this data are homicide, assault, robbery, rape, trafficking of women and children, theft (burglary and theft of motor vehicle), property fraud, and others (less than 0.05%)
[c]Calculated on the basis of official data

Of these police-recorded crimes, 37.9% were cleared up (see Table 2). These official data reveal that there were, on average, almost 3 million criminal cases recorded by the police that ended up without criminal suspects. Correspondingly, 3 million crime victims and their families will not have been able to gain justice and vindication in the judicial process (Cao 2024).

According to the above presented figures, there has been an annual increase of recorded crime between 2010 and 2015. Thereafter, the numbers have consistently and significantly fallen. Still, the total number of personal victims of crime in China per year can be estimated at 4 million per year.

Considering that the number of crimes recorded by the police does not include the unreported or undiscovered crimes, the actual number of victims of crime in China is likely to be much higher than what the official statistics suggest. Although there is no accurate data regarding the actual number of crime victims in China, it is reasonable to assume that there is a large number of victims who are hiding beneath the dark figure of crime and that the rights and interests of those 'invisible' victims are not in any way protected through an official channel (He and Marshall 1997).

In addition to these official crime statistics, which in China are mainly collected by the national police department, there is another, internationally recognized instrument to measure the levels and trends of crime victimization in a country. The International Crime Victims Survey (ICVS), currently in its sixth round,[9] has been deployed in over 85 countries worldwide since 1987 and serves as the leading

[9]To date, there have been six sweeps of the ICVS (1989, 1992, 1996, 2000, 2005, and 2010 onwards) that have examined over 400,000 respondents throughout the world. For updates, see Ghauharali et al. (2011), and van Dijk et al. (2021).

Table 3 Rates of victimization in urban areas by five types of crime, by world region/city and year

World regions/cities (year)	Car theft	Burglary	Robbery	Personal theft	Assault/threat
Africa (2000/10)	1.5	8.0	4.0	11.6	5.2
Asia (2000/5)	0.2	4.8	0.8	8.1	2.6
Caribbean (2014/5)	1.9	4.1	2.7	4.8	6.9
Eastern Europe (2000/2)	0.8	4.4	1.8	8.2	2.9
Latin America (2000/9)	1.4	5.9	7.8	11.0	4.7
United States (2005/New York)	1.6	1.9	2.3	7.7	5.1
Western Europe (2005/2010)	1.2	2.3	1.4	5.4	4.1
Kyrgyz Rep. (2015/Bishkek)	0.8	5.1	2.0	11.1	1.7
Kazakhstan (2017/Astana)	0.4	2.0	0.7	4.3	4.7
China (2014/ Beijing)	0.5	2.2	0.4	9.3	2.0
World average (2000)	1.2	4.5	3.0	8.1	4.5

Source: Van Dijk 2008; Cao 2024. See also www. icvs-crime.eu

instrument for examining true victimization rates on a global scale. This standardized instrument measures experiences of crime independently of police records and serves the purpose of collecting comprehensive crime data so that problem areas and vulnerable groups can be identified and compared internationally. It examines experiences of victimization, experiences with the police of reporting victims and attitudes towards domestic criminal justice practices, as well as feelings of security amongst representative samples usually ranging between 2000 and 3000 participants per country.

The results of our victimization survey in Beijing show that one out of every three residents (33.2%) has been a victim of at least one of the 14 crimes listed in the ICVS questionnaire within the 12 months preceding the survey. The results of the two surveys conducted in Beijing in 1994 and 2014 indicate that from an international comparative perspective China/Beijing has changed from a low crime location across the board to one with a moderately high level of property crime and a persistently low level of violent crime, both of robberies and threat/assault and sexual violence.

Despite the fact that from an international perspective, the overall victimization rates in Beijing 2014 were only slightly higher than the average rates of cities situated in developed countries and much lower than those in many developing countries (see Table 3), the absolute number of persons falling victim to crimes in a year in China is huge. In the upcoming discussions on victims' responses, it will be revealed that only roughly one in five of all crimes experienced are reported to the police in Beijing (see Table 4). Considering that in 2014 the police recorded around 5 million crimes affecting persons,[10] the total number of criminal victimizations in

[10]According to the data published by the National Bureau of Statistics, in 2014, the number of criminal cases registered by police was 6,539,692; among which crimes with direct victims such as homicide, assault with injury, robbery, rape, trafficking in women and children, theft and fraud account for about 85%.

Table 4 International comparison of reporting rates (latest results from the ICVS database since 2010)

		Car theft	Theft from/ out of a car	Burglary	Theft of personal property	Robbery	Sexual offences (women)	Assault and threat of violence
Reported to the police	Year	%	%	%	%	%	%	%
Average		72	53	66	38	43	11	32
Kazakhstan	2018	68	32	53	26	38	12	17
Kyrgyzstan	2015	60	35	51	24	41	32	20
Georgia	2020	36	22	42	29	16	9	39
China	2014	70	49	54	24	37	4	34
Japan	2019	87	58	55	40	42	14	42
Germany	2010	76	79	86	43	36	5	24
Netherlands	2010	95	79	92	54	52	22	33
Sweden	2010	93	79	77	52	49	3	35
Switzerland	2014	75	69	82		45	10	22
United Kingdom	2010	87	68	88	59	62	13	37

that year can be estimated as at least 25 million.[11] For a country as large as China, whose population counts for 18% of the entire world population (UN, 2017), the provision of better rights and services for victims is obviously of great humanitarian and political relevance.

5 Concurrence of Chinese Victims' Rights in Law and Practice with the UN Declaration

5.1 Information and Participation

5.1.1 Information for Victims

The right of reporting victims to be informed about the outcome of criminal investigations and/or case filing by the police lacks a clear legal basis and is, unsurprisingly, found wanting in practice too. On the positive side, victims are usually informed by the police about their role in the proceedings, including their right to file an incidental civil action through the receipt of a written notice. However,

[11] This calculation assumes that the reporting rates in Beijing represent the national rate and that the types of crime included in the questionnaire cover the bulk of crimes recorded by the police. The estimate will be deflated because, as is known from surveys in other countries, a proportion of crimes reported to the police are not duly recorded and entered into the statistics of recorded crime.

Table 5 Reported crimes in Beijing in 1994 and 2014 (percentage of crimes experienced reported to the police)

Variable	2014 (%)	1994 (%)
Household crime		
Theft of car	70.0	100.0
Theft from car	49.1	27.6
Theft of motorcycle	40.9	60.0
Theft of bicycle	19.3	45.3
Burglary (with entry)	54.1	56.7
Personal crime		
Robbery	37.0	37.1
Personal theft	24.0	19.1
Sexual incident	3.2	7.6
Assault/threat	33.7	36.3

respondents expressed doubt about the effectiveness of a written notice as the mode of communicating with victims. Although it is supposed to be undersigned by the victim upon receipt, there is no assurance that victims will fully understand its contents.

The findings of the victimization survey reveal that the rates of Chinese victims who report their victimization to the police lie somewhat below the international mean (see Table 4) and have not improved since 1994 (see Table 5).

A possible explanation for the comparatively low reporting rates for burglary is the drop in the proportion of households insured against losses from burglaries and, therefore, in the proportion of households required to report to the police to claim insurance. In Beijing, the coverage by insurance has decreased to below 10% in 2014. However, reporting rates for robbery, a type of crime where insurance is less pertinent, also tend to be somewhat lower in Beijing than on average. By way of comparison, ICVS-based surveys in Tamil Nadu, India, from 2002, showed equally low reporting rates for burglary (52%) and for robbery (42%) (Chockalingam 2003).

The percentage of reporting victims of five types of crime who expressed satisfaction with their treatment by the police lies at 21%, far below the international mean of 50% in 2005 (see Table 6). The satisfaction rates of burglary and robbery victims in India in 2002 were significantly higher (respectively 46% and 48%) than in China (Chockalingam 2003).

Victim satisfaction shows no improvement in Beijing since 2004. Recent improvements in the treatment of victims by the police have apparently not yet led to higher levels of satisfaction in 2014 than 10 years ago. Since low victim satisfaction rates are strongly correlated with low readiness to report crimes to the police, these results suggest that reporting rates are unlikely to rise in China without significant further improvements in the reception and treatment of victims by the police.

Key decisions in the prosecutorial stage of the proceedings, such as no prosecution decisions are normally duly communicated to the victims. Prosecutors also inform victims about their right to seek redress from the offender in the criminal proceedings (incidental civil action). Courts commonly inform victims of the date and place of the trial of the defendant in their case, and about the verdict, although

Table 6 Victim satisfaction with police by type of crime in China and elsewhere (%)

Type of crime	China 2014	Worldwide 2005
Theft from a car	19.0	52
Burglary with entry	13.6	52
Robbery	42.1	49
Sexual incident	50.0	55
Assault/threat	30.0	52
Average five crimes together	20.7	53

according to some respondents, this practice is often limited to victims who act as plaintiffs in a civil action.

Although heavy caseloads of officials may hinder full implementation of the information rights of victims, Chinese legal practice in this domain seems by and large to be in sync with the UN principle of justice concerning the right to information about the proceedings.

5.1.2 Victim Participation

A keystone of the participatory rights mentioned in the UN Declaration is the right 'to present views' to the judicial authorities. This right was introduced in China as part of the new Criminal Procedural Law (CPL) of 1996, and has been strengthened thereafter in the revisions of 2012 and 2018. In addition, prosecutors are duty-bound to hear the views of the victim and insert a written report about these views in the case file. In court, the victim and/or his attorney not only have the right to express views about the crime but can also put questions to the defendant. The victim is also allowed to make a statement in person about the impact of his/her victimization. Another pertinent form of possible participation is that victims have the formal right to ask prosecutors to appeal a court judgement in the first instance.

In China, as elsewhere, fast-track procedures have recently been introduced in criminal proceedings, potentially jeopardizing the implementation of victims' rights. In order to avoid this, special procedural rules have been introduced to ensure that in the fast-track processing of cases, the rights of victims in seeking compensation from the offender are respected.

In spite of these improvements in the law, the extent to which the participatory rights of the victims in the trial are actually exercised by victims in practice remains limited. The reason for this is that in China, few victims are requested to attend the trial in person, or will do so on their own initiative.

According to the 1979 CPL, victims have the right to appeal against parts of the judgments regarding their incidental civil actions before a higher court. In the 1996, CPL victims were additionally awarded the right to petition higher level prosecutors to appeal against the criminal part of the verdict in the first instance, such as an acquittal.

Chinese law also offers victims the procedural option of initiating private prosecutions when prosecutors have dropped their cases. In recent years, private prosecution cases have made up 2% of all cases. According to stakeholders, the use of this option is often unsuccessful due to the incapacity of the victims to collect the necessary evidence by themselves and as a result of insufficient support from the police or courts in this endeavour. It must be noted, though, that similar findings about the limited effectiveness of the instrument of private prosecution have been recorded in many other jurisdictions (Brienen and Hoegen 2000).

The UN Declaration mentions informal dispute resolution/mediation under the heading of participation. Mediation between offenders and victims has traditionally been part of the Chinese criminal justice system. Under the current law, it is an option in the investigation stage for crimes punishable by less than 3 years imprisonment. Mediation can also be initiated by the court in a later stage of the proceedings (CPL, 2012, Article 101). According to Art. 288 of the CPL of 2018, if the defendant has shown genuine remorse and obtained the forgiveness from the victim after paying compensation and/or offering an apology to the victim, the parties may reach a settlement. In cases where a settlement has been reached, the People's procuratorate can decide not to prosecute, or the court may impose a more lenient punishment.

Although according to some stakeholders, police staff and prosecutors are insufficiently equipped for the task of facilitating mediation, and the operational implementation of mediation/reconciliation is therefore far from perfect, legislation as well as practice seem in line with the UN Declaration's principle that victims ought to be offered this opportunity in appropriate cases.

Although information and participation of victims leave room for improvement, Chinese law and practices in these areas seem, in conjunction with a free legal aid programme (to be discussed below), to be roughly in line with the relevant standards of the UN Declaration.

5.2 *Treatment and Protection*

As stated in the *Handbook on Justice for Victims* (UNODC 1999), the right 'to be treated with compassion and respect' is of crucial importance for a proper, nontraumatizing treatment of victims by the authorities. In China, to our knowledge, no legal provision has been adopted explicitly reflecting this quintessential victim's right. While special provisions seek to assure that vulnerable victims such as minors and female victims are treated with due consideration, a general provision concerning the need to treat all victims with compassion and respect is missing. The absence of formal legislation does not necessarily imply that police practices are necessarily deficient in this respect. Our interviews with stakeholders did not suggest that reporting victims are often treated inconsiderately or without respect. Moreover, although the victimization survey indicated that only one in five victims was satisfied with the treatment received from the police—a satisfaction rate that is comparatively low on an international scale (see Table 6)—there were very few reports of abusive or inconsiderate behaviour as a reason for their dissatisfaction (see Table 7).

This is in contrast with findings from ICVS-based surveys in some Latin American countries, where such negative experiences have been frequently reported by reporting victims (Van Dijk 2008). It appears that in everyday police practice in Beijing, the principle that victims should be treated with consideration and respect is reasonably well observed.

As mentioned above, the low level of satisfaction of victims with their treatment by the police suggests that victim reception leaves room for improvement. By addressing these issues, policymakers can work towards improving the overall treatment by the authorities of citizens who do report crimes and thereby towards a reduction of the 'dark numbers of crime' and improved crime control.

5.2.1 Protection

Since the adoption of the Law against Domestic Violence of 1998, special protection measures such as restraining orders for perpetrators of domestic violence are widely applied to safeguard the safety of victims of domestic violence. However, the general provisions on the protection of the safety of victims are limited to the most threatening types of crime, and even in those instances, they are rarely implemented in practice, according to the officials interviewed. Contrary to what is common in most other large countries, no infrastructure is in place in China to offer adequate protection for victims/witnesses in organized crime cases.

Protection of victims emerges as one of the areas where improvements could be introduced to better suit the basic principles of justice of the UN Declaration. International good practices for this can be found in the UN Handbook for Victim Justice (UNODC 1999), and its follow-up for child victims (UNODC 2009).

Our overall assessment of the implementation in China of the treatment and protection provisions of the Declaration is mixed.

5.3 Reparation and Compensation

The third category of principles relates to the right to restitution (compensation from the offender) and to financial aid/compensation/relief from the state in cases of violent crime.

According to Chinese legal doctrine, the most important way to protect the civil rights and interests of victims is considered to be the filing of an incidental civil action reclaiming the material damage caused by the criminal (Chen and Chai 2012). The administration of criminal law is meant to have a deterrent impact and prevent crimes through the threat of punishment. Since incidental civil actions enhance the deterrent value by adding the obligation to pay compensation, they serve the functions of criminal justice. Civil liability in criminal cases also serves the aim of restorative justice, by making up the losses of victims through private compensation and thereby repairing damaged social relations between offender and victim and within the community at large.

As mentioned above, the Chinese CPL contains an equivalent of the provision in Napoleonic, continental law of the *partie civile*,[12] namely, the option for victims to attach an incidental civil action for damages to the criminal procedure. This legal provision, already present in the1979 CPL under article 53, was changed under the 1996 CPL into article 77. The 2012 amendments extended the possibilities for seizure and freezing of assets on behalf of the victim as 'civil party' (Art. 100). According to Article 101 of the *Criminal Procedure Law (2018)*, if the victim suffers material losses due to the infringement of criminal acts on his/her personal rights or property, he/she has the right to file an 'incidental' civil action to the People's court during the criminal proceedings and hence become the civil plaintiff in the criminal case. It is meant to offer the victim an easy and cost-effective alternative to filing a civil action in a civil court.

The Interpretation by the Supreme People's Court Regarding the Application of the Criminal Procedure Law of the People's Republic of China (2021) details the scope of the possible outcomes of incidental civil actions. Article 192 stipulates that compensation for violations of the victim's personal rights covers reasonable expenses for treatment and rehabilitation, such as medical, nursing and transportation expenses, as well as missed income due to work disability. If the victim is permanently disabled, compensation shall also be paid for the expenses of living aids and other related costs. If the victim dies from his injuries, the funeral expenses and other expenses of his dependents shall also be compensated. However, loss of income and compensation for emotional distress of dependents are not covered according to this article.

In addition, Para. 2 of Art. 175 of the said interpretation specifically states that a People's court shall generally not accept an incidental civil action filed to claim

Table 7 Reasons for dissatisfaction with treatment by police by reporting victims in Beijing

Reasons for dissatisfaction	%
Didn't do enough	18.7
Were not interested	19.2
Didn't find or apprehend offender	19.8
Didn't recover my property	26.9
Didn't keep me properly informed	7.7
Didn't treat me correctly or were impolite	2.2
Were slow to arrive	1.1
Other reasons	4.4
Don't know	0.0

[12] In Germanic law, similar provisions are known as '*Adhaesionsverfahren*'.

compensation for mental injury. The practice of excluding immaterial damages from the scope of incidental civil compensation has been widely critiqued by Chinese legal experts and even by some criminal justice officials.

According to national statistics, incidental civil actions are filed in around 7% of all criminal cases (this amounts to over three million actions per year). From a comparative, international perspective, this is a relatively high rate (Brienen and Hoegen 2000). Less favourable is that these numbers are trending downwards in recent years, and that, according to a local study in Beijing, only between 6 and 13% of the verdicts are ever enforced. Respondents have pointed out that newly introduced rules concerning the scope of compensation and the maximum sums awarded have made the incidental civil action less attractive for victims. Obviously, the rather low enforcement rate will also discourage many victims from filing an incidental civil action.

From an international perspective, Chinese law on seeking compensation from the offender in the criminal proceedings seem to meet the standard of the UN Declaration. However, as in many other countries, enforcement of the verdicts remains unsatisfactory. Many studies about different jurisdictions have led to the same conclusion. Apparently, the only solution for this problem is to make the state responsible for collecting the compensation order from the offender, as is the case in the United Kingdom and the Netherlands.

To date, China has not introduced a national law on compensation from state funds for victims of violent crime for material and/or immaterial damages, although in recent years proposals to that end have repeatedly been made. In 2009, a commission of the Communist Party's Central Committee, the Minister of Justice and the Supreme Court jointly issued an Opinion on Relief for Crime Victims, which envisages nationwide schemes for relief/compensation from local governments for victims of violent crime. Although this opinion is now more than a decade old, actual follow-up seems to have been taken by only a handful of municipalities.

The end-conclusion on state compensation is that although the provision of state compensation to victims of violent crime is recognized as a victims' right in the said Opinion, its implementation falls far short of the global standard set by the United Nations. Follow-up legislation on this issue seems therefore urgently called for.

5.4 *Legal Assistance and Social Support*

The 1996 CPL determines the right of victims to ask an attorney to participate in legal proceedings on their behalf. The new CPL grants the victim's attorneys the same set of procedural rights as those of the defendant. The 2012 amendments to the CPL have further strengthened the rights of the victim's attorney: the attorney now has the right to apply for withdrawal of the judge (Art. 28), and apply for reconsideration of judicial decisions (Art. 218). The attorney also has the right to be served with the written judgment at the same time as the victim (Art. 196). Finally, the attorney has been given the right to file a petition to the public prosecutor at the same level or the next higher level if he/she believes any criminal justice authority has impeded the exercise of his/her procedural rights (Art. 47).

Perhaps most pertinent, relevant Opinions from the communist party and government have in 2009 resulted in the introduction of a nationwide free legal aid programme covering victims of crime, especially victims of domestic violence. Consequently, the number of free legal aid provided to victims in criminal cases has gone up.

5.4.1 Victim Support

At present, there exists no law or national programme for the provision of counselling or social support to crime victims, other than services such as shelter homes in a limited number of municipalities provided in the framework of the Anti-Domestic Violence Law of 1998 by local coalitions of NGO's focusing on women's rights. There exists as yet no national association for victim support services similar to those in many other nations.

The victimization survey revealed that the majority of Chinese victims of serious crimes received support from known persons such as relatives (32%), friends (34%), and neighbours (9%); whereas 12% received support from the police. All other agencies/organizations constituted only 17%. These results are very similar to those from the Beijing survey conducted 20 years ago. This indicates, first, that the rapid transformations of Chinese society have not fundamentally eroded informal social support networks in the spirit of *guanxi*.[13] In fact, the supporting role of friends in adversity seems to have become even more important. Second, the results confirm the virtual absence of special victim support organizations in Beijing in 2014 (only 5% of victims received such assistance). The 2004/5 ICVS sweep showed, on average, 9% of victims of serious crimes in Western countries (burglary, robbery, sexual incidents, and threats/assaults) had received victim support from such organizations globally (e.g., 17% in England/Wales and 14% in the Netherlands). The reception by victims of special support in Beijing is rare by comparison. Particularly noteworthy is that only 2% of (female) victims of sexual offences had received any of such specialized help in Beijing.

As discussed, in Beijing/China, 5% received specialized help, and 56% of victims of serious crimes would have welcomed receiving such specialized victim support services (see Table 8). The need for such help is the most common among victims of sexual offences (67%). These results point to a considerable gap between the interest of crime victims in receiving special support and the actual supply of such services.

[13] *Guanxi*, meaning 'networks/connections', is arguably a key feature of Chinese society in contrast to the tradition of individualism in the West. *Guanxi* is the wide-spread promotion of close interpersonal ties, encouraging strong relationships and personal stakes in both family and the community against the background of Confucianism.

To sum up our findings, while legal assistance in China for victims has been improved, the provision of support services for victims of crimes in China falls far short of the aspirational perspective of the UN Declaration.

6 Conclusion

Some findings of the ICVS provide insights in the way a country's victims' rights implementation is experienced by the victims themselves. The findings of the victimization survey in Beijing reveal that the rates of victims who report their various types of victimization to the police lie somewhat below the international mean as measured by the ICVS in other countries, and have not improved since 1994.

The percentages of reporting victims of five types of crime who expressed satisfaction with their treatment by the police was 21%. This satisfaction rate lies far below the international mean (50%), including that in neighbouring India. The rate shows no improvement since 1994 either. Apparently, recent improvements in the treatment of victims by the police had not yet led to higher levels of victim satisfaction in 2014. Since low satisfaction rates are strongly correlated with low reporting, these results suggest that reporting rates in China are unlikely to go up without significant further improvements in victim reception by the police. International 'best practices' of such improved reception can be found in the United Nations' *Handbook on Justice for Victims* published by UNODC. Experimental studies have shown that training of police detectives in victim-friendly interview procedures can significantly improve victim satisfaction and thereby increase their willingness to report future victimizations (UNODC 1999; Skogan 2005, 2014).

The victimization survey conducted in 2014 in Beijing confirmed that very few victims of crime are offered specialized support. The same survey reveals that there is a great unmet demand for such services among victims of serious crime. Most tellingly, a majority of female victims of violence indicated they would have appreciated such support. These results point to a huge gap between the supply and demand of such services.

The survey results indicate shortcomings in the implementation of current victim laws and policies in at least two respects: (1) the overall treatment by the police of citizens reporting crimes to them; and (2) the provision of specialized help to victims of serious crimes, including female victims of domestic violence or sexual offences.

An obvious policy implication coming out of the survey is that the Chinese police ought to be trained in handling the reports of crime victims in a more victim-friendly way.

Since the adoption of the UN Victims Declaration in 1985, many countries have strived to bring their national laws and practices concerning victims' rights up to the global inspirational standards set by the Declaration. China, where victims' rights were relatively poorly developed at the time of adoption of the Declaration, has, over the past 2 decades, made considerable progress with the introduction and

Table 8 Percentages of assistance received and welcomed by victims of serious crimes in Beijing in 2014 and 1994

Variable	2014	1994
Received assistance from		
Relatives	31.9	33.9
Friends	33.5	15.4
Neighbours	8.8	12.3
Police	11.5	11.5
Social welfare agency	2.2	1.0
Religious organization	2.7	0.1
Specialized agency	5.5	0.1
Others	3.8	2.2
Would specialized help for victims have been welcome?		
Yes	56.0	63.0
No	26.8	11.4
Don't know	17.2	25.6

implementation of essential victims' rights. In the domain of procedural rights in the criminal proceedings, grouped under the headings of information and participation, legal assistance, and compensation from the offender, China's victims' rights seem now at par with UN standards and international practices. This seems to be less the case with the rights of victims to be treated with compassion and respect, the right to receive financial compensation from the state and the right to receive specialized support or counselling. In the latter areas, the Chinese authorities have taken several initiatives, notably concerning victims of domestic violence, but seem to be struggling for financial reasons to introduce nationwide comprehensive programmes catering to all categories of victims of crime.

International comparisons of the implementation of victims' rights are difficult to make due to a lack of comprehensive socio-legal assessments similar to the present one from other countries. The limited available evidence suggests that even in the European Union, which in 2012 issued a legally binding Directive on victims' rights, almost all countries fail to fully implement some or many of the essential victims' rights (Groenhuijsen and Pemberton 2009; Van Dijk and Groenhuijsen 2018). This seems, as in China, especially the case with rights concerning the provision of state compensation and specialized assistance.

In China, as in many other countries, implementation of the UN Declaration is a work in progress. We hope that the results of our studies will help to put the efforts of the central and local government in China to empower and support victims of crime in line with the Declaration into a higher gear. If this could be achieved, the millions of victims of crime per year in China would finally get the fair deal they deserve.

References

Bassiouni MC (2006) International recognition of victims' rights. Hum Rights Law Rev 6(2):203–279

Brienen MEI, Hoegen EH (2000) Victims of crime in 22 European criminal justice systems. Wolf Legal Publishers (PhD Tilburg University), Nijmegen

Cao J (2024) Taking stock of victim's rights in China: An analysis of the Chinese criminal justice system from the perspective of the United Nations Victims' Rights Declaration of 1985. Tilburg University (diss), Tilburg

Chan W-C (ed) (2007) Support for victims of crime in Asia. Routledge

Chen H (2012) Xingshi Beihairen Quanli Baozhang Yanjiu [Research on the protection of the rights of crime victims]. Intellectual Property Publishing House. (not retrievable from Google[14])

Chen W, Chai Y (2012) Xingshi fudai minshi susong zhidu de xinfazhan [The new development of incidental civil action]. ECUPL Journal, No.5. (not retrievable from Google)

Chockalingam K (2003) Victimization by crime in four large cities in southern India. In: Forum on crime and society, Vol. 3. United Nations, New York, pp 117–127

Davies P (2015) Victims: continuing to carry the burden of justice. British Society of Criminology Newsletter, No. 76

Fattah EA (1971) Is the victim guilty: the role of the victim in murder incident to Robbery. Presses de L'Université de Montreal, Montreal

Ghauharali RRR, Kamperman AM, van de Mheen D (2011) Prior Victimization, Region, and Neighborhood Effects on Fear of Crime in Mumbai, India. Asian Journal of Criminology, 6, 141–159.

Friedman LC (1985) The crime victim movement at its first decade. Public Adm Rev 45:790–794. Special Issue: Law and Public Affairs

Groenhuijsen M, Letschert R (eds) (2012) International victim's rights instruments. Wolf Legal Publishers

Groenhuijsen M, Pemberton A (2009) The EU framework decision for victims of crime. Eur J Crime Crim Law Crim Just 17:43–59

Groenhuijsen MS (1999) Victims' rights in the criminal justice system: a call for more comprehensive implementation theory. In: van Dijk JJM, van Kaam RGH, Wemmers J (eds) Caring for crime victims: selected proceedings of the Ninth International Symposium on Victimology, Amsterdam, August 25–29, 1997. Criminal Justice Press, Monsey NY, pp 85–115

Groenhuijsen MS (2005) International protocols on victims' rights and some reflections on significant recent developments in victimology. In: Snyman R, Davis L (eds) Victimology in South Africa. Van Schaik Publishers, pp 333–351

Groenhuijsen MS (2014) The development of international policy in relation to victims of crime. Int Rev Victimol 20(1):31–48

He N, Marshall I (1997) Social production of crime data: a critical examination of Chinese crime statistics. Int Crim Just Rev 7:46–64

Joutsen M (1987) The role of the victim in European criminal justice systems: a cross national study of the role of the victim. Helsinki Institute for Crime Prevention and Control

Liu JH (2005) Dui xingshi beihairen susong diwei de zairenshi [Reunderstanding the litigation status of crime victims]. J Soc Sci 2:59–63. (not retrievable from Google)

[14] Although the referenced literature is not available through Google, it can be accessed through the China National Knowledge Infrastructure (CNKI). CNKI, as the world's largest and continuously updated Chinese academic literature database, encompasses a wide range of resources including academic journals, master and doctoral dissertations, conference papers, newspapers, yearbooks, patents, standards from China and abroad, scientific and technological achievements, economic statistics data, reference works, and images, as well as selected foreign language resources such as those from Springer.

Mawby R (2007) Public sector services and the victim of crime. In: Walklate S (ed) Handbook of victims and victimology. Chapter 8. Willan Publishing, Cullompton
Schafer S (1960) Restitution to victims of crime. Stevens and Sons, London
Shapland J (1983) Victim-witness services and the needs of the victim. Victimology 8(1–2):233–237
Shekhar B, Sahni SP (eds) (2020) A global perspective of victimology and criminology: yesterday, today and tomorrow: Festschrift for Prof. Dr. K. Chockalingam 50 years of teaching in the field of victimology. Bloomsbury Publishing
Skogan WG (2005) Citizen satisfaction with police encounters. Police Q 8(3):298–321
Skogan WG (2014) Using community surveys to study policing. In: Reisig MD, Kane RJ (eds) The Oxford handbook of police and policing. Oxford University Press, Oxford, pp 449–470
Tian S (2008) Fan Zui Bei Hai Ren De Quan Li Yu Jiu Ji [Right and relieves of crime victims]. Law Press, China. (not retrievable from Google)
Trevaskes S (2007) Severe and swift justice in China. Br J Criminol 47(1):23–41
Trevaskes S (2010) Policing serious crime in China: from strike hard to 'kill fewer', vol 35, Routledge
Tsin M (2009) Overlapping histories: writing prison and penal practices in late imperial and early republican China. J World Hist 20(1):69–97
UN Office on Drugs and Crime (UNODC) (1999) Handbook on justice for victims: on the use and application of the Declaration of Basic Principles of Justice for Victims of Crime and Abuse of Power. Retrieved from https://digitallibrary.un.org/record/414602
UN Office on Drugs and Crime (UNODC) (2009) Training Programme on the Treatment of Child Victims and Child Witnesses of Crime for Prosecutors and Judges. Retrieved from https://www.unodc.org/documents/justice-and-prison-reform/Training_Programme_on_the_Treatment_of_Child_Victims_and_Child_Witnesses_of_Crime_-_Prosecutors_anf_Judges.pdf
United Nations, Department of Economic and Social Affairs, Population Division (2017) World Population Prospects: The 2017 Revision, Key Findings and Advance Tables. ESA/P/WP/248
Van Dijk J (1988) Ideological trends within the victims' movements: an international perspective. In: Maguire M, Pointing J (eds) Victims of crime: a new deal? Open University Press, Milton Keynes, pp 115–126
Van Dijk J (1999) Criminal victimization and victim empowerment in an international perspective. In: van Dijk JJM, van Kaam RGH, Wemmers J (eds) Caring for crime victims: Selected proceedings of the Ninth International Symposium on Victimology, Amsterdam, August 25–29, 1997. Criminal Justice Press, Monsey NY, pp 15–39
Van Dijk J (2005) Benchmarking legislation on crime victims: the UN Victims Declaration of 1985. In: Vetere E, Pedro D (eds) Victims of crime and abuse of power: Festschrift in honour of Irene Melup. United Nations, Vienna
Van Dijk J (2008) The world of crime: Breaking the silence on problems of security, justice and development across the world. SAGE Publications CA
Van Dijk J (2016) Illuminating the dark numbers of crime: victimization surveys and beyond. Criminology in Europe/ Newsletter of the European Society of Criminology
Van Dijk J, Goodey J (2004) Benchmarking legislation on crime victims: the UN victims' declaration of 1985. In: Opferhilfe in der Schweiz: Erfahrungen und Perspektiven. Haupt, pp 202–208
Van Dijk J, Groenhuijsen M (2018) A glass half full, or half empty? On the implementation of the EU's Victims Directive regarding police reception and specialized support. In: Walklate S (ed) Handbook of victims and victimology, 2nd edn. Routledge, pp 275–292
Van Dijk J, Mayhew P, van Kesteren J, Aebi M, Linde A (2010) Final report on the study on crime victimisation. INTERVICT, Tilburg University, Tilburg
van Dijk, J., Nieuwbeerta, P., & Joudo Larsen, J. (2021). Global Crime Patterns: An Analysis of Survey Data from 166 Countries Around the World, 2006–2019. Journal of Quantitative Criminology.
Von Hentig H (1948) The criminal and his victim. Yale University Press, New Haven
Walklate S (2007) Imagining the victim of crime. Open University Press/ McGraw-Hill, Mainhead
Waller I (2010) Rights for victims of crime: rebalancing justice. Rowman & Littlefield Publishers

Wemmers JA (2010) A short history of victimology. Victimology, Victim Assistance and Criminal Justice: Perspectives Shared by International Experts at the Inter-University Centre of Dubrovnik

Wolfgang MF (1957) Victim precipitated criminal homicide. J Crim Law Criminol 48:1

Young M, Stein J (2004) The history of the crime victims' movement in the United States. US Department of Justice, Office of Justice Programs, Office for Victims of Crime, Washington, DC

Zedner L, Hoyle C (2007) Victims, victimization, and criminal justice. In: Maguire M, Morgan R, Reiner R (eds) The Oxford handbook of criminology, 4th edn. Oxford University Press, Oxford

Zhao GL, Xu R (2015) Zhongguo xingshi beihairen guojia jiuzhu de xianzhuang, tuwei yu lifa jiangou [Current situation, breakthrough, and legislative construction of state aid for criminal victims in China]. Journal of Fujian Normal University (Philosophy and Social Sciences Edition) 1:1–9+166. (not retrievable from Google)

Zhao J (2010) Xingshi beihairen de susong quanli yu fanzuiguan zhi guanxi yanjiu – yi jingyanxing kuaxueke fanshi wei zhongxin [Research on the relationship between criminal victim's litigation rights and their views on crime -- based on the empirical interdisciplinary paradigm]. Law Rev, 2, pp. 132–140. https://doi.org/10.13415/j.cnki.fxpl.2010.02.018. (not retrievable from Google)

Organized Crime *Sans Frontière*: The Case of Maritime Piracy in East Africa

Sarah Agnela Simons

Abstract Professor Chockalingam's inspiration and knowledge footprints transcend land and sea geographical borders in time and space. This chapter is a salute for one of the world's most eminent pioneer Victimologists of our times on his 80th birthday by using this chapter to disseminate some unpublished findings from the author's 2018 Master of Philosophy (MPhil thesis) entitled *Analysis of Maritime Piracy in Eastern Africa between 2000 and 2010 and its impact on Seafarers Occupational Risk Perception*. The research report documents an academic empirical research endeavor undertaken between 2011 and 2018 at Cardiff University's Seafarers International Research Centre www.sirc.ac.uk sponsored by The Nippon Foundation www.www.nippon-foundation.or.jp. The study analyzed how the maritime piracy along the East African coast influenced perceptions of the maritime work environment by forty-four ship crew interviewed at a leisure center for off-duty crew in a port in the United Kingdom.

Maritime Piracy is a global phenomenon with constantly shifting hotspots. This chapter seeks to explain how piracy crisis along the East African coast between 2005 and 2015 exposed the dichotomy and tension between the thriving global shipping industry and failed economy of Somalia operating parallel to each other in the same geographic area.

Keywords Ship crew · Maritime piracy · Seafarers · Somalia · Shipping industry

1 Introduction

This chapter is a contribution to a festschrift in honor of Professor Chockalingam on the occasion of his 80th birthday entitled: *BEYOND THE GAVEL: A Paradigm Shift in Global Criminal Justice*. It is submitted under Section 1.2: *Criminology:*

S. A. Simons (✉)
Department of Sociology, Faculty of Social Sciences, Ahmadu Bello University, Kaduna State, Nigeria

© The Author(s), under exclusive license to Springer Nature Singapore Pte Ltd. 2026

G. S. Bajpai et al. (eds.), *Beyond the Gavel: A Paradigm Shift in Global Criminal Justice*, https://doi.org/10.1007/978-981-95-4487-5_10

Unveiling the Dynamics of Deviance, under the subtheme *Impact of Globalization on Criminal Behavior.* The author seeks to explain how the initially localized criminal behavior of Somali pirates in East Africa resulting in part, from decades of lawlessness and disintegration of law and order in Somalia, had wider repercussions on global shipping that required a global counter-piracy legal and operational response to diffuse the crisis. To achieve this noble objective, the discussion focuses on the following two factors of relevance to the theme of this book: Firstly, how friction between two significantly different and parallel economies operating in the same geographic space can give rise to manifestation of criminal behavior. Secondly, how the impact of unchecked localized lawlessness and land-based criminality in weak states can transcend geographic land borders and spill over into the adjacent maritime environment with global repercussions. Such a trend could give rise to challenges in demarcating jurisdiction among countries with failed legal and criminal justice systems.

2 Globalized Context of Criminal Behavior

Globalization as a modern social phenomenon has increased opportunities for interaction of individuals, organizations, and systems across national borders, different geographic regions of the world, and continents. The resulting borderless (*sans frontière*) social context has transformed the world into a global village wherein both positive and negative outcomes are experienced and transmitted. Benefits include multi- and cross-cultural exchange, information sharing on biodiversity, enhanced information-sharing across the world wide web, quick dissemination of news on events, etc. On the contrary, the borderless nature of the global economy creates a conducive environment for interaction among individual criminals, collaboration between criminal groups, adoption of criminal behavior, and assimilation of criminal elements participating in multiple organized crimes online and in person. The author shares research findings that demonstrate how the global shipping industry became vulnerable to local criminal behavior of Somali pirates and international illegal fishing companies operating within this globalized maritime context. To unpack and clearly explain the various aspects of the multifaceted and complex maritime piracy phenomenon in the Eastern and Horn of Africa, the chapter first presents a brief introduction of the different stakeholders who comprise the global maritime industry and who were identified during the research. Secondly, the piracy facilitators are listed alongside their criminal behavior and illegal activities that sustained the gradual transformation of maritime piracy into an international organized crime.

Various watercraft ply Indian Ocean, often operating in maritime corridors adjacent to lawless hinterland such as the failed states of Somalia and Yemen. These two countries have witnessed prolonged conflict and rely on humanitarian assistance due to lack of legitimate sources of livelihood. This contrast demonstrates how globalized networks could influence crime by attracting attention as moving targets for criminals. When ship voyages include transiting busy maritime corridors adjacent to weak states, the multiple maritime industry stakeholders and the contributions of "piracy diaspora" clandestine activities can create tension that exacerbates the vulnerability of seafaring professionals and seafarer-sending communities worldwide. This complicated social dynamic was illuminated by the kidnap-for-ransom mode of piracy that was witnessed in the Eastern Africa and Horn of Africa region. The absence of a functional Coast Guard in Somalia and lack of a regional maritime security strategy created a legal vacuum and conducive environment for the borderless predatory behavior of pirates to evolve from isolated incidents in Somalia national waters into an international organized criminal enterprise in international waters (Simons 2018) in Eastern Africa and the wider Gulf of Aden coastline.

A discussion of some problematic features observed by the author during the study highlight the nexus between a globalized shipping industry in the maritime environment, and the origin, development, and escalation in criminal behavior as occurring within the same geographic area. The emergence of maritime piracy and its worsening into a crisis of global concern along the East African coast and expansive north west Indian Ocean from 2005 is explained to highlight how both legitimate international shipping activities and illegal international fishing activities in the global maritime environment contributed differently to the emergence and escalation in piracy.

Subsequently, maritime piracy evolved as a modern organized criminal enterprise, in which pirates' *modus operandi* kept changing and a Somali "piracy diaspora" emerged as facilitators of this criminal network. The web of activities included money laundering of ransom proceeds of piracy crime. Credible intelligence reports during the research period pointed to a piracy ransom money trail that transcended national borders into the foreign exchange flows of suspected laundered piracy ransom proceeds, sustaining real estate development, and a mushrooming of forex bureaus in some countries in the region (World Bank 2013). Piracy in East Africa is portrayed as a problematic situation that presented multiple opportunities for national, regional, and international collaboration among various stakeholders. Concerted antipiracy interventions brought criminal behavior under control.

From about 2005 to 2013, attacks on ships along the busy East African coast and Gulf of Aden shipping corridor became a major concern to multiple stakeholders worldwide due to an increase in kidnap-for-ransom pirate attacks on ships. Although seafarers were the primary target of pirates, the research concluded that multinational profile of professional and nonprofessional stakeholders whose livelihood is linked to the global shipping industry worldwide were affected by ripple effects arising from the illegal boarding of ships, abduction, and holding hostage for ransom of ship crew in East Africa. For the benefit of readers with no prior exposure of the maritime sector, the chapter presents an initial description of a typical pirate attack, the network of piracy facilitators ("piracy diaspora") that emerged as beneficiaries of the piracy crisis, and the multifaceted and multinational nature of the maritime security dilemma in the piracy "high-risk area" of East Africa during the research period. This chapter seeks to explain the impact of globalization of the shipping industry on criminal behavior in the failed state of Somalia. To do so, the chapter starts by describing the different stakeholders who combine to perform different roles in the modern global maritime industry. Such a description is intended to highlight the vulnerability of the parallel thriving globalized shipping industry (maritime environment) that stands in sharp contrast to criminal behavior incubating for decades in the failed economy in Somalia (hinterland). In this regard, the three primary facts regarding multinational dimensions of ships in the international fleet include national profile of ship crew targeted by pirates, ship ownership, and ship registration ("flag").

In the modern global shipping industry, the ship owner, crew members, and passengers (where applicable) often comprise of different nationalities. The owner may be domiciled in a different country from that in which the ship company is registered. Furthermore, the crew working on board ships at any given time may have been recruited by (manning/crewing) agencies in different countries. Additionally, the company or client(s) whose cargo is being transported by the ship could all be based in different countries. Therefore, in the unfortunate event that a ship falls into the hands of pirates and crew and/or passengers are taken hostages, notifying all the stakeholders and raising the ransom became an operation of global dimension. A simple mapping of maritime sector stakeholders illustrates how localized pirate criminal behavior had the potential for inflicting harm on communities worldwide by spreading ripple effects of pirate attacks across multiple geographic zones (Simons 2020).

The decade-long maritime security crisis along the coast of East Africa and in the wide Gulf of Aden area developed into maritime security phenomenon that came to be known as "Somali Piracy." Three interrelated aspects are explained to illustrate how in creating a more interconnected world, globalization also created a conducive environment for the transboundary spread of criminal behavior from land-based communities to seafarers' mobile professional work environment. Such a discussion seeks to illuminate the (erstwhile hidden) vulnerability of global networks and how in targeting ship crew, pirates operating in one region of the world (East Africa) were able to spread the fear of victimization from the Somalia piracy hotspot" to communities from which seafarers hail worldwide.

3 Pivotal Role of International Shipping Industry

Throughout human history, various watercrafts have provided a means of transport for passengers and of goods. In the twenty-first century globalized political economy, the international shipping industry plays a crucial role in linking worldwide supply chains by ferrying about 90% of global trade. Thus, the shipping industry has been described as the "lifeblood of the global economy" (International Chamber of Shipping 2024). Modern technologically advanced ships are built to ensure safe navigation, passenger safety, comfort and mechanized and efficient handling of liquid, solid, and gaseous cargo sourced globally and its delivery to destinations worldwide. Ships have become the preferred mode transportation for different types of goods, and are preferred for delivering large quantities of goods in solid, liquid, and gaseous form as it is cheaper to transport in bulk by sea (Fernley's Review, 2010).

A wide variety of vessels ply the seas either as stationery structures or as mobile floating or submarine built environments. Stationary/floating structures include oil rigs and research vessels. While mobile vessels include submarines, cruise ships, oil tankers, container ships, refrigerated ships, roll-on-roll off (ro ro), navy ships, aircraft carriers, ferries, car carriers, bulk carriers, yachts, and liquid food tankers, among others. The discussion in this chapter reveals some vulnerabilities of the global political economy wherein the global shipping industry plays a crucial role in linking interconnected worldwide production, supply chains and markets. The explanation is framed within geopolitical realities of Somalia in the 2005 to 2015 timeframe, whereby decades of lawlessness on land in a failed state that had been largely ignored by the international community spilled over into the maritime environment manifesting itself through unchecked pirate attacks.

This land to sea multi-jurisdiction spread of criminality disrespecting physical borders exposed two vulnerabilities: firstly, of the thriving shipping industry; and secondly, of the global political economy heavily dependent on supply chains interconnected by an international shipping industry whose voyages operate adjacent to failed/weak states. Therefore, as ransom premiums increased, hostage periods increased and the number of ships and crew detained threatened to disrupt global shipping supply chains. A culture of lawlessness normalized piracy criminal behavior in Somalia, which is a failed state with the longest sea coastline in Africa. Located adjacent to a busy shipping corridor in East Africa, it soon became the top maritime piracy "hotspot" worldwide during the research period.

Fish remains a major source of protein, a family craft and major source of livelihood for indigenous fishing communities who have inhabited the coast of Somalia for many centuries. The piracy crisis in East Africa exposed the tension that can exist between two parallel economies operating within the same maritime-hinterland geographical space. The maritime economy dimension of the piracy crisis is represented by the contrasting fortunes of the thriving international shipping industry operating along the East African coast, parallel to a small scale Somali indigenous fishing industry represented by local fishermen and other largely-destitute residents in the failed state of Somalia. These two realities operated side by side for centuries until maritime piracy emerged as a topical issue.

4 Conceptualizing Modern Maritime Piracy

International Maritime Organization (IMO) is the specialized agency of the United National Organization charged with responsibility for maritime safety and pollution from ships. IMO mandate includes developing and maintaining the regulatory framework for shipping, maritime safety, environmental concerns, and legal-technical cooperation. Its work is implemented through promotion of international treaties by the 167 member states. The main international regulations include United

Nations Convention on Law of Sea (UNCLOS), International Convention for Safety of Life at Sea, and International Convention on Maritime Search and Rescue.

The two main definitions of Maritime Piracy are derived from UNCLOS, adopted in Resolution A.1025 (26) on 2 December 2009 by the 26th Assembly Session of the International Maritime Organization (IMO). It defines maritime piracy as "*Any illegal acts of violence or detention, or any act of depredation, committed by individuals, for private ends against a private ship or aircraft*" (Van Dyke 1985).

In its counter-piracy activities, the International Maritime Bureau (IMB) applies this UNCLOS definition of maritime piracy in its interpretation of maritime piracy activities to include criminal intent. IMB in its reports regards piracy as "*(the) Act of boarding any vessel with intent to commit theft or any other crime, and with an intent or capacity to use force in furtherance of that act*" (IMB Report 2012).

5 Piracy Crisis in Eastern Africa

The re-emergence of modern-day maritime piracy in the expansive and busy Eastern Africa and the northwest Indian Ocean area also referred to as the Gulf of Aden has been attributed to a combination of on-land factors as well as off-shore factors. Each of the two factors will be explained to reflect some of the main perspectives from which the piracy crisis was viewed. The on-land factors include such the cumulative effect of decades of lack of rule of law on land in Somalia. Following the fall of the Somali President Said Barre, Somalia disintegrated into decades of interclan clashes, leading to a breakdown in the rule of law and failure of state machinery, resulting in widespread lawlessness and massive emigration of Somali refugees into neighboring countries and overseas.

Prolonged clan-based infighting in Somalia and the breakdown of national governing systems left the national territorial waters unprotected without a custodian of the country's maritime environment and resources. Fishing has been an indigenous socioeconomic activity in Somalia from time immemorial. Local Somali fishermen use small scale dragnets for fishing. The horn of Africa region experiences cycles of severe famine. Thus, fish has provided a reliable source of protein and income from time immemorial. Prolonged interclan clashes and political instability left the protection of the coast and water resources to disgruntled local Somali fishermen wary of the possibility of depletion of local fish stock by foreign ships. Early reports on causes of piracy in East Africa stated that a few isolated incidents of illegal boarding of ships foreign by artisan fishermen targeted large fishing ships engaged in International Illegal, Unlicensed, and Unregulated Overfishing. Documented sources accessed by the author indicated that these early ship boarding incidents by angry fishermen were preceded by formal complaints by delegations of Somali officials to the respective United Nations agencies about the encroachment into Somalia national and international waters by large, more technologically advanced fishing trawlers, offshore fish laundering, and dumping of toxic waste in Somali coast. Fishing vessels from Korea, Japan, Norway, Italy, and other developed maritime nations were identified as culprits of International Illegal, Unlicensed, and Unregulated Overfishing in Somalia (Clark 2009).

In these early isolated incidents, the illegal boarding of the foreign culprit ships by local artisan fishermen was aimed at demonstrating their displeasure at the illegal overfishing fishing activities and depletion of fish stock in Somali territorial waters (Couper et al. 2015). This view was also corroborated by reports of international news media who conducted face-to-face interviews with local Somali fishermen at the height of the crisis. One report stated that a Bosaso fisherman, Mohamed Adan Ahmed, in an interview with *Aljazeera* stated that illegal, unlicensed, and unregulated fishing by big foreign fishing ships forced then to turn to piracy ten years ago in order to recoup their losses. *"We got fed up and took guns to the sea"* (Source: *Aljazeera,* 6 October 2015).

Pirate attacks on ships along the East African coast were orchestrated by individuals and groups who contributed the human and no-human requirements. The land-based piracy infrastructure was provided by owners of speedboats, gun owners, and agents who recruited brave youth possessing speedboat-maneuvering skills. The fearless and "ready for hire" pirates embarked on ship-hijacking missions, while their logistics were facilitated with speed boats to chase slow-moving ships, guns with rocket-propelled grenades used to threaten into submission ship crew who defied orders to stop the ship midstream.

During research fieldwork, the author pieced together the chronology of pirate attacks describing how after boarding and taking command of the ship, pirates would ask for the ship Captain to identify himself, then order him to turn off the ship location identifier equipment, and contact the ship owner to begin ransom negotiations. Other piracy facilitators included multilingual ransom negotiators who mediated between the ship owner and pirates in ransom negotiations, but remained largely anonymous to the public and only known to the pirates. During ransom negotiations, ship crew were held hostage either on the ship or at secret locations on land. The welfare of hostages was maintained by the supply of goods and services. These included food, water, translation, and medical services provided by land-based facilitators (Simons 2018).

From around 2005, the illegal boarding of fishing ships escalated into indiscriminate pirate attacks on all types of ships plying the East Africa-Guld of Aden route, detention of ships and ship crew (seafarers) in kidnap-for-ransom mode of piracy. A worsening situation was characterized by increase in ransom premiums demanded by pirates for hostage release, a sharp rise in the number of attempted and successful illegal boarding of ships, prolonged hostage period, and introduction of torture of hostages to force ship companies to hasten ransom payments. During the research period, more reports on piracy began emerging in open sources, indicating that seafaring professionals threatened to boycott voyages that included the East African "high-risk area" in order to reduce the risk of falling into the hands of pirates. It was also reported that some companies offered crew a kind of 'risk allowance' when their ship transited through East Africa. These factors combined to raise global concern among the shipping fraternity about the potential risk of harm that piracy posed to ship crew and effect of interruption of delivery of goods in global supply chains by the shipping industry, brought on by a prolonged piracy crisis.

In response to the worsening piracy situation, humanitarian, legislative, and operational maritime security aspects in the wider North West Indian Ocean were addressed through concerted, successful multiagency and multinational efforts. As the piracy crisis worsened, pirate criminal behavior kept changing. For instance, it was reported that they adopted different modes of operation to include the use of hijacked ships as motherships to attack other unsuspecting vessels; exchanging hostages with land-based criminals for weapons; and expansion of area of pirate attacks further afield eastwards and southwards (BBC 2010).

6 Maritime Piracy "Diaspora": Organized Joint Criminal Enterprise

From 2005 onward, the piracy situation escalated as the number and frequency of pirate attacks increased and pirates demanded higher ransom premiums. The worsening situation was attributed to the large sums of foreign currency cash payments made by owners of illegal fishing vessels to the local fishermen in order to secure the release of culprit ships detained by local traditional guardians of the fishing communities. As word spread in Somalia about the ransom windfall occasioned by availability of such lucrative and easy ways of obtaining large quantities of foreign cash, this attracted the attention of individuals of different age groups, social status in Somalia to offer a variety of services required for the success of the maritime piracy business model (World Bank 2013).

The growing success rate of this clandestine joint enterprise triggered and fuelled a piracy frenzy in Somalia and the wider Horn of Africa region. The number of failed as well as successful attempts by pirates increased. In addition, pirate attacks were no longer limited to illegal fishing vessels, but widened to include different types of cargo ships, cruise ships, private yachts and even humanitarian ships bringing relief food supplies to Somalia. Majority of pirate suspects intercepted and apprehended by anti- piracy security personnel were Somali youth (UNODC 2009). Engagement in piracy activities could have provided Somali youth emboldened by decades of clan fighting amidst breakdown in the rule of law, with an opportunity to become seaborne 'gangs for hire', to make a living making from piracy activities piracy. Juvenile criminology research evidence abounds tracing the onset of truancy and criminality to childhood experiences.

7 Piracy "Diaspora" Multiplicity of Criminal Behaviors

With time, a kind of "pirate diaspora" emerged bringing together maritime piracy facilitators as comprising of individuals with skills for effecting the different roles required for effective implementation of the maritime piracy business model. From piracy reports, the author deduced that facilitators included (a) those who hired out speedboats to pursue slow-moving ships, (b) those who availed firearms along with rocket-propelled grenades for firing at ships, forcing them to slow down or stop, (c) fearless agile youth adept at using firearms, boarding ships using crude rope ladders, and who could speak enough English to command the ship crew to surrender, identify the ship captain from among the crew on board so as to order him to commandeer the ship off course to anchorage along the coast within Somalia national waters, and (d) land-based facilitators also referred to as "on-shore infrastructure" consisting of providers of hospitality (food, water, medical attention), language translators in telephone ransom negotiations between ship owner and pirates and communication for ransom air drop onto the ship deck before crew and ship were released (World Bank 2013).

All categories of facilitators appear to have been attracted to the clandestine enterprise in response to a combination of "pull factors" including but not limited to the following three: (i) an increase in public awareness in Somalia of the lucrative untapped potential that could be reaped in targeting multinational, unarmed crew who could be kidnapped for ransom, (ii) the increase in the pirate attack success rate, and (iii) lack of a maritime security guardian to establish deterrence measures along the 3,025 kilometer long Somalia coastline, which is the longest national coastline in Africa (*The Nairobi Convention* 2000). Thus, decades of lawlessness and disorder in failed state of Somalia spilled over into the adjacent busy international shipping lane. Thus, the lawlessness was no longer confined to land and escalated to borderless mayhem.

8 Multilevel Impact of Piracy and Global Response

Due to the pivotal role of shipping industry in global political economy, any issue hampering the smooth movement of ships, if unchecked, could affect global supply chains. As piracy evolved into an organized criminal enterprise with global ramification, concerns about the toll that piracy was having on the shipping industry arose from multiple factors including commercial interests and the impact on ship crew who were the actual primary targets of pirates (Oceans Beyond Piracy 2013). Voyage disruptions resulted from the increase in number of ships and seafarers detained, delays in delivery of cargo resulting in supply chain disruptions, and hiking in ransom premiums resulting in longer hostage periods (Simons 2018). Concerns for the well-being of detained crew and effect of constant worries on family members who were concerned for the safety and well-being of their loved ones led to the establishment of a Maritime Piracy Humanitarian Response Program (MPHRP 2013).

The author's study involved interviewing a heterogeneous sample of forty four ship crew. Research findings revealed that concerns about piracy outweighed other occupational hazards. This was the uniform feedback of all respondents whether or not they had worked on ships that transited along East African coast. They had heard of the brutality with which pirates treated abducted crew, the effect of the hostage experience on crew, and how families of abducted crew struggled to make ends meet while their breadwinners were held hostage. Knowing that ship crew were the primary targets in the kidnap for ransom mode of piracy in East Africa, all this information made crew fear falling victim to pirates. This fear remained a nagging thought and occupational risk on the agenda of crew stories shared on board ships worldwide. The sample of respondents interviewed said that they felt like potential victims, since pirates targeted ship crew to kidnap them and hold them hostage until huge and increasing ransom amounts were paid to secure their release. Piracy was referred to as the "P" word for seafarers and they were actively discouraged from discussing piracy stories for fear of spreading fear among their peers. During the crisis, ships acted as mobile maritime piracy fear amplifying centers on a global scale. Fear of maritime piracy victimization became a reality among the global seafaring professionals.

Collection and dissemination of maritime piracy statistics remain the responsibility of International Maritime Bureau (IMB) through its Piracy Reporting Centre (PRC) in Kuala Lumpur and London-based International Maritime Organization (IMO). IMB is the focal point for combating all types of maritime crime and malpractice, gathers information from various investigative sources and reports, and provides its members with timely advice through a variety of communication avenues, while the PRC provides a 24-hour point of contact for ships to report when hijacked, attacked, or robbed and serves as an in-house piracy self-reporting mechanism for IMB, as well as a centralized global repository for ships to report suspicious incidents and pirate attacks. PRC provides an awareness-raising function to all ships and to International Maritime Organization on emerging piracy threats, specific incidents and attacks, emerging trends posing a threat to maritime security and locations of high-risk areas.

Regular PRC evidence informed reports highlighted the shipping community to increased pirate attacks on ships along the coast of East Africa and in the Gulf of Aden. This became a major concern to the global shipping industry and seafarer sending communities. Modern seafarers are migrant workers, whose careers are developed within an evolving global, mobile, and maritime work environment that has been reputed to have a high mortality and mobility rate (Sampson 2003). As the number of detained ships increased, this disrupted the global supply chain and caused a delay in the delivery of goods. To compound the problem, reports of threats by ship crew to boycott contracts that included voyages through the busy Horn of Africa shipping corridor raised alarms of the cumulative toll of piracy on the global economy.

9 Counter-Piracy Global Responses

An assessment of piracy literature by the author prior to the research period revealed diverse perspectives on causative factors contributed to the emergence of modern piracy along the coast of East Africa. These included the presence of multiple weak and failed states, chronic poverty, growth of piracy as an opportunity for quick financial gain, lack of institutional mechanisms to police the coast of East Africa, etc. These factors in themselves had the potential for creating a conducive environment for piracy to thrive (Simons 2018). Some reports identified the Eastern Africa maritime environment as an offshore victim of inland distortions in security management and enforcement agencies in Somalia including police, army, and navy (Hastings 2009; Murphy 2008; Ong-Webb 2007). Before the maritime piracy situation was brought under control, the crisis along the coast of East Africa was characterized by frequent attacks on ships, increasingly higher ransom premium demands, longer hostage periods during which voyages by ships loaded with cargo were interrupted and delayed delivery of goods delayed.

In a nutshell, these negative outcomes following illegal boarding of ships over time pointed to a worsening piracy situation in which localized pirate criminal behavior impacted heavily on the global economy.

As piracy criminal activities increased in intensity, the notoriety of the piracy epicenter along the coast of East Africa quickly earned it the label of the "piracy global hotspot." In addition, the location of this maritime security risk within a busy shipping corridor of the Suez Canal connecting global markets meant that the maritime security situation had to be brought under control to avoid further adverse ripple effects to the global economy. Pirate attacks were impacting the global community at different levels. At a shipping industry level, piracy increased the cost of insurance premiums, with ship owners having to pay a US $3 million Kidnap and Ransom (K&R) fee for a single trip through Gulf of Aden. Payment of ransom demanded turned piracy into a very lucrative business in which ship's crew were regarded and treated by pirates as commodities (Beynon and Nichols 2006). The precarious regional maritime insecurity situation arising from unchecked criminal behavior of pirates called for a significant counter-piracy response. Compounding the location, the wide extent of the north west Indian Ocean affected by the predatory pirate activities required significant resources and a multipronged counter-piracy intervention to diffuse the maritime piracy phenomenon in East Africa.

Although a discussion of all the counter-piracy measures is beyond the scope of this chapter, some commendable counter-piracy efforts warrant mentioning as commendable examples of Good Practice initiatives. Noteworthy are activities that targeted pirate criminal behavior at international legal, strategic and operational levels through pre-emptive and reactionary interventions. These facilitated filling legal loopholes at global, regional, and national levels. For instance, International Maritime Organization (IMO) initiated adoption of a multicountry counter-piracy strategy collaboration between the United States (US) and the maritime industry actors. This aimed at preventing pirate attacks and other criminal acts of violence against U.S. vessels, persons, and interests. In 2007, U.S. President signed a comprehensive and sweeping policy governing diplomatic and legal action to fight piracy, and emphasized collaborative strategies by states and other maritime sector stakeholders.

In addition, on 5 October 2008, United Nations Security Council adopted Resolution 1838[50] that sanctioned use of counter-piracy military force to protect ships from pirates in East Africa. This UN resolution, in effect, authorized "hot pursuit" operations inside Somalia's territorial waters to prevent pirates from diverting hijacked vessels into national waters operating as a safe haven for pirates.

Other commendable counter-piracy steps included United Nations Security Council resolutions 1816, 1846, and 1851 passed in 2008, that provided an international legal umbrella authorizing cooperating states and other Eastern Africa antipiracy patrols and interdictions "*to pursue and capture pirates in Somali waters with stipulation that consent must first be received from Transitional Federal Government of Somalia and that UN Secretary General must be notified*" (Middleton 2009, p. 3).

Recognizing challenges that piracy posed to Transitional Government of Somalia and regional partners who lacked effective counter-piracy capacity, an interagency *Countering Piracy off Horn of Africa: Partnership and Action Plan* was developed in December 2008 to prevent, disrupt, and prosecute piracy off the Horn of Africa. This regional collaboration strategy was designed in collaboration with international and industry partners to assist in creating and implementing suitable bilateral law enforcement and judicial capacity-building activities among Eastern Africa regional states.

International efforts to deal with piracy included a multinational collaborative initiative code-named *Operation Atalanta* that combined deployment along coast of East Africa of a multinational European Naval force (EU NAVFOR Source), with support from NATO countries (EU NAVFOR 2010). *Operation Atalanta* brought together skilled military personnel from a number of NATO countries to provide air and sea surveillance of the expansive north west Indian ocean area. The proactive and reactive actions included accompanying ship convoys and rapid response to distress calls by vessels under pirate attack. The strategic and operational interventions facilitated both prevention and counter-piracy activities.

At a national level, assistance in the re-establishment, training, and equipping of Somalia Coast Guard further strengthened the capacity of national law enforcement infrastructure and personnel. These are a sample of efforts to strengthen maritime legal capabilities at national, regional, and global level while encouraging counter-piracy collaboration. Thus, a global response implemented succeeded in countering local national "piracy diaspora" criminal behavior. Eventually, this combination of strategic and operational efforts yielded positive results through concerted efforts by diverse stakeholders and filled the legal, law enforcement, and tactical vacuum to put in check localized criminal behavior in East Africa.

10 Conclusion

The discussion in this chapter sought to explain the origin of the decade-long piracy crisis along the East African coast that started around 2005, how on-land criminality and breakdown of rule of law escalated into the adjacent maritime environment where it manifested as a maritime piracy crisis, and how international collaborative efforts brought it under control. Three of the views regarding piracy causative factors that have been stated include (i) pervading lawlessness that bred and normalized criminality in the weak/failed state of Somalia, (ii) lack of a suitable guardian to enforce institutional maritime security mechanisms necessary to police the long coastline of Somalia, (iii) lack of legitimate means of livelihood, and (iv) availability of multiple easy targets in the form of slow-moving ships plying along the coast of East Africa. One could also argue that the inherent nature of the maritime environment would make it practically impossible to demarcate Somali territorial waters from international waters. It remained unclear whether the pirates had any idea of the boundaries between national and international waters.

On land in the failed state of Somalia, general desperation among the local populace arising from toll of cycles of drought, severe famine, chronic poverty were major contributing factors that could be framed within criminology theory. However, that task was beyond the scope of this chapter. The study reiterated the common view in other piracy reports that concluded that idea of piracy ransom payments may have provided local Somali population with opportunities for quick financial gain. During the years of prolonged piracy crisis, the cumulative criminal behavior of pirates affected the globalized political economy that was already heavily dependent on the international shipping industry.

The emergence of maritime piracy criminal behavior on land in the Horn of Africa is framed and linked within the escalation into widespread criminality at sea as a widening circle of criminal behavior on land. In the on-land and off shore nexus of pirates' criminal trajectory, piracy appears to have become normalized among pragmatic-minded "piracy diaspora" who provided the on-shore infrastructure that sustained the decade-long piracy crisis. Thus, it can be inferred that lawlessness on land in Somalia largely ignored by the international community had exposed the vulnerability of a thriving global political economy heavily dependent on supply chains interconnected by an international shipping industry operating adjacent to failed/weak states. In this regard, the profile of maritime piracy network of facilitators highlights the need for global crime prevention programs to incorporate interventions that address the root causes of local criminality. The study recommended a closer observation and analysis of potential risks that failed/weak states pose to the global political economy especially in volatile areas of fragile peace and security (Simons 2018).

The discussion has also demonstrated the seamless progression from nationwide juvenile criminality in Somalia amidst a climate of lawlessness, to the manifestations of criminal pirate behavior and emergence of organized criminal networks all within the same space (Somalia). This on-land criminality and at-sea criminality of international fishers illustrates the co-occurrence of multiple crimes in the same geographical region of East Africa. The combination of foreign illegal fishing, illegal boarding of foreign fishing boats by local artisan fishermen to express their disapproval, payment, and receiving of informal payments of large amounts of cash in foreign currency to secure release of foreign vessels encouraged more attacks on ships. Thus, illegal overfishing and unbridled retaliatory action by some individuals from among the local Somali fishing community provided a "criminal incubation" point for the emergence of a "piracy diaspora." They in turn developed maritime piracy as a joint enterprise with a business model that saw piracy quickly evolve into an international organized criminal enterprise. In this way, the chapter has discussed the maritime piracy crisis in East Africa to showcase the complicated nexus between criminal behavior at a local level and possible links to transnational organized criminal networks associated with money laundering.

An additional perspective discussed in this chapter is the fact that globalization provides the opportunity for the global community to support weak/failed states to check criminal behavior. Global problems are best tackled with global action. Strategic counter-piracy measures to address a rising threat of piracy in East Africa required designing and operationalization of international and regional multinational collaborative agreements. Based on UN resolutions, IMO spearheaded amendments of relevant international legislative and regulatory instruments to provide a suitable framework for international anti-piracy collaborative efforts, especially those in East Africa. These efforts filled legal vacuums in Eastern Africa maritime security through adoption of Djibouti Code of Conduct, a multinational collaborative information and situational awareness sharing agreement that came into force on the 29 January 2009. This enabled collaboration among twenty-one countries located adjacent to Indian Ocean to enhance the region's counter-piracy capabilities as an on-going effort.

As drafting of this chapter was concluded, recent intelligence reports raised fresh concerns regarding recent pirate activities in the Gulf of Aden as a possible pointer to an unstable maritime security status of the previous global piracy hotspot. Noteworthy is the hijacking of the merchant vessel RUEN on 14 December 2023, its commandeering to Puntland, then further deployment by pirates as a mothership to launch attacks. The 13 March 2014 and hijacking of bulk carrier ABDULLLAH, coupled with attacks by Houthis on merchant ships transiting the Red Sea, are raising concern about the possibility of a resurgence of piracy threat in the Gulf of Aden (Borer, 24 March 2024).

This chapter concludes by rationalizing maritime security as an area of international cooperation whereby thinking globally and acting locally could pre-empt, prevent the spread of criminality, while countering and weakening the stranglehold of organized criminal networks that often exploit legal vacuums in weak/failed states. Shared learning forums bringing together judicial and law enforcement personnel from different countries in a given region are instrumental in countering piracy criminal behavior in a globalized world economy. In this regard, the author recommends a similar approach as was adopted in 2008 co-creation of the *Regional Action Plan to Prevent and Counter Human Trafficking in East Africa* by judicial and law enforcement representatives drawn from the thirteen East African countries. This collaborative endeavour supported by UNODC and Interpol Sub-Regional Bureau (SRB) for Eastern Africa generated a landmark Action Plan approved by the East African Police Chiefs Cooperation Organization (EAPCCO) in 2008. The planestablished a collaborative mechanism to guide multi-jurisdiction pathways to counter the organized crime of human trafficking in Eastern Africa region.

The mode of operation and profile of maritime piracy facilitators in East Africa provided an illustration of the danger of focusing on fighting international organized crimes without addressing the root causes of local criminality. As our world becomes more interconnected, it is imperative that the impact of globalization on criminal behaviors continue to be the focus of continuous inquiry among multicountry researchers, especially, those from the global south. In a globalized world whose complexities transcend geographic boundaries, this festschrift has provided an opportunity to share evidence of how less visible, largely ignored, and unreached communities, like Somalia, can quickly evolve into transnational organized criminal networks.

On a final note, the chapter recommends continuous and closer scrutiny of potential risks that failed/weak states pose to the global political economy in volatile areas of fragile peace and security. Strengthening of the capacity of weak/failed states to prevent development of criminal behavior and counter law breaking with rehabilitation, rather than retribution mechanisms, may be a more sustainable crime prevention strategy in our diverse and interconnected global village.

References

Aljazeera Illegal overfishing and the return of Somalia's pirates. A report by Jessica Hatcher. Published On 6 Oct 2015. Accessed on 10 September 2024 at: https://www.aljazeera.com/features/2015/10/6/illegal-overfishing-and-the-return-of-somalias-pirates

BBC News (2010) Kenya ends trials of Somali pirates in its courts. A BBC news brief updated at 14:27 GMT, Thursday, 1 April 2010 15:27 UK accessed at http://news.bbc.co.uk/2/hi/africa/8599347.stm on 11.09.2024

Beynon and Nichols (Eds.), (2006) Patterns of Work in the Post-Fordist Era: Fordism and Post-Fordism, 2 Vols. Cheltenham: Edward Elgar.

Borer L (24 March 2024) Increasing pirate attacks in Gulf of Aden and the Indian Ocean: from fishing conflicts to the RUEN case in Risk Intelligence A/S accessed online at www.riskintelligence.eu on 5th October 2024

Clark (2009) "Maritime Piracy: Nature, Impact and Legal Frameworks for Prosecution" in International Journal of Criminal Justice Sciences vol.4 Issue 1 January – June 2009.

Couper A, Smith H, Ciceri B (2015) Fishers and Plunderers: theft, slavery and violence at sea. Pluto Press. ISBN: 9780745335926 eBook ISBN: 9781783713363

European Union Naval Force Somalia (EU NAVFOR) (2010) EU NAVFOR-Atalanta Area of Operation Extended - Operation Atalanta. A Press release by EU NAVFOR Operation Headquarters, Middlesex on 09/22/10. Accessed online at http://www.eunavfor.eu/2010/09/eunavfor-atalanta-area-of-operation-extended/ on 05/10/10

Fernley's Review (2010) Key Facts on World Seaborne Trade between 1969 and 2010 retrieved at: http://www.marisec.org/shippingfacts/worldtrade/volume-world-trade-sea.php on 19.05.2018

Hastings J (2009) Geographies of state failure and sophistication in maritime piracy hijackings. Polit Geogr 28(4):213–223

International Maritime Bureau (IMB) (June 2012) Human cost of Somali Piracy: deaths of hostages held by Somali pirates 'increasing'. An IMB Maritime Report, Piracy Reporting Centre, Kuala Lumpur: June 2012

Maritime Piracy Humanitarian Response Program (MPHRP) (2013). www.mphrp.com

Middleton R (2009) Pirates and how to deal with them. Chatham House Publication, London. Accessed online at http://www.chathamhouse.org.uk/files/13845_220409pirates_law.pdf on 05.10.2010

Murphy MN (2008) Piracy and the exploitation of sanctuary. In: Norwitz JH (ed) Armed groups: studies in national security, counterterrorism and counterinsurgency. Newport, R. I. U.S. Naval War College

Oceans beyond Piracy (2013) The Human Cost of Piracy 2012. A Working Paper for the One Earth Future Foundation: Colorado. Accessed at http://oceansbeyondpiracy.org/sites/default/files/hcop2012forweb.pdf on July 20, 2013

Ong-Webb G (2007) Piracy in Maritime Asia: current trends. In: Lehr P (ed) Violence at Sea: piracy in the age of global terrorism. Routledge, New York

Sampson (2003) Transnational Drifters or Hyperspace Dwellers: An Exploration of the Lives of Filipino Seafarers Aboard and Ashore in Journal of Ethnic and Racial Studies 26(2), pp. 253–277.

Simons (2018) Analysis of Maritime Piracy in Eastern Africa between 2000 and 2010 and its impact on Seafarers Occupational Risk Perception. A Master of Philosophy thesis submitted to Faculty of Social Sciences, Cardiff University, Wales, United Kingdom, 2018. Accessible at: http://orca.cf.ac.uk/112454/1/0938502%20Sarah%20Simons%20MPhil%20Thesis%2C%20FINAL.pdf.

Simons S (2020) Maritime piracy victimization of seafarers and their families. In: Joseph J, Jergenson S (eds) An international perspective on contemporary developments in victimology. Springer, Cham. https://doi.org/10.1007/978-3-030-41622-5_9

The Nairobi Convention (2000). https://nairobiconvention.org/

United Nations Office of Drugs and Crime (UNODC) (2009) Counter Piracy Programme. Regional Programme Promoting the Rule of Law and Human Security in Eastern Africa. www.unodc.org

Van Dyke JM (1985) United Nations Convention on the Law of The Sea 1982: a commentary volume 1. In: Nordquist MH (ed) Center for Ocean Law and Policy, University of Virginia. Martinus Nijhoff Publishers, Dordrecht, pp 241–242

World Bank (2013) The Pirates of Somalia: Ending the Threat, Rebuilding a Nation. © Washington, DC. http://hdl.handle.net/10986/16518 License: CC BY-NC-ND 3.0 IGO. Retrieved at: https://documents1.worldbank.org/curated/en/840211468188347064/pdf/76713-v2-Box393223B-PUBLIC-pirates-of-somalia-executive-summary-web.pdf on 12.09.2024

Frozen in Time: Why India Needs a Cold Case Center

Beulah Shekhar and Rithin Joseph

Abstract Cold cases are unresolved criminal investigations that remain unsolved over time and present several challenges that necessitate a systematic approach to resolution. Drawing from current investigative methods and worldwide best practices, this chapter examines India's pressing need for a cold case center. This chapter highlights the difficulties in conducting investigations and the possibility of contemporary forensic and technology techniques to resolve a number of prominent cold cases in India, including the Aarushi Talwar case, the Amar Singh Chamkila murder, the Beerman killings, and the Stoneman murders.

This chapter employs a qualitative research design, specifically using content analysis of secondary data, to explore the need for and structure of a dedicated cold case center in India, emphasizing the benefits such as enhanced investigative efficiency, ensured justice for victims and their families, and restored public confidence in the criminal justice system. The need for a specialized unit is highlighted by the present shortcomings in the Indian law enforcement system, which include a lack of funding, antiquated technology, and administrative difficulties. The investigation shows that new leads and insights into cold cases can be obtained through the use of sophisticated forensic techniques, data analytics, and digital forensics. The success stories of cold case units in countries like the United States, South Korea, and Australia, where persistent and updated investigative methods have led to breakthroughs in long-unsolved crimes, serve as a compelling model for India.

A detailed methodology for establishing a cold case center is presented, with its various objectives, including the integration of cutting-edge forensic science, increased interagency cooperation, and dedicated resources to address the backlog

B. Shekhar (✉)
Department of Criminology & Forensic Science, Parul University, Vadodara, Gujarat, India
e-mail: drbeulahshekhar@gmail.com

R. Joseph (✉)
School of Behavioural Forensics, National Forensic Sciences University, Delhi, India
e-mail: rithin.joseph@nfsu.ac.in

© The Author(s), under exclusive license to Springer Nature Singapore Pte Ltd. 2026

G. S. Bajpai et al. (eds.), *Beyond the Gavel: A Paradigm Shift in Global Criminal Justice*, https://doi.org/10.1007/978-981-95-4487-5_11

of unsolved crimes. This chapter proves how establishing a permanent cold case center would enhance the efficiency of investigations, ensure justice for victims and their families, and restore public confidence in the criminal justice system. In order to resolve the backlog of unsolved crimes in India, this chapter promotes the combination of state-of-the-art forensic science, enhanced interagency cooperation, and specialized resources. The results demonstrate the importance of a cold case center in the administration of justice as well as the wider ramifications for the criminal justice system.

Keywords Cold cases • Forensic science • Criminal investigations • India • Law enforcement • Justice • Technological advancements • Unsolved crimes • Investigative techniques • Public confidence

1 Introduction[1]

Justice delayed is justice denied.—William E. Gladstone

Cold cases are criminal investigations that have not been solved within a certain period and remain unresolved despite the exhaustion of all available investigative leads. These cases can involve various crimes, including homicides, sexual assaults, and missing persons. The definition of a cold case varies among different agencies. According to the National Institute of Justice (NIJ), a cold case is "any case whose probative investigative leads have been exhausted" (2008). This means that even an unresolved case involving unclaimed human remains that are only a few months old may be deemed "cold" if no additional leads for investigation can be found. According to Lee (2023), cold cases are those in which preliminary investigations have failed, frequently as a result of insufficient evidence or the destruction of investigation documents and are later revisited using new scientific techniques or after discovering new evidence. Fraser (2016) defines cold cases as those which involves re-evaluating unsolved cases using original witness statements and new forensic evidence, often with a fresh investigative perspective.

The major significance of cold cases lies in the prolonged absence of justice for victims and their families, the continuous threat posed by perpetrators who remain free, and the societal impact of unsolved crimes that undermine public confidence in the criminal justice system. Some cases like the Zodiac Killer, Jack the Ripper, and the Stoneman murders are a few classic examples.

In a paper by Lee (2023), he explains how the landscape of violent crime has evolved in complexity and sophistication, paralleling advancements in science and

[1] This chapter references laws in effect at the time the cases occurred such as the Indian Penal Code (IPC), Criminal Procedure Code (CrPC), and the Indian Evidence Act (IEA), but not the new laws such as Bharatiya Nyaya Sanhita, Bharatiya Nagarik Suraksha Sanhita, and Bharatiya Sakshya Act that have since replaced them.

technology. Investigative agencies, including the police, have adopted various technical theories and investigative techniques to uncover truths and apprehend criminals. However, cold cases—particularly those over a decade old—present significant challenges, such as evidence preservation and the loss of investigation records. Additionally, cases previously halted due to expired statutes of limitations are now resurfacing as critical issues.

To address this, police departments in various countries, like the USA, UK, South Korea, Australia, etc., have established cold case units at local agencies, utilizing scientific investigation methods to achieve notable successes. For example, the Seoul Metropolitan Police Agency solved the Guro Pub murder in South Korea using advanced forensic techniques and persistent investigative work. Similarly, the Daejeon Metropolitan Police Agency managed to solve the Daejeon bank robbery by revisiting old evidence and applying modern forensic science. These efforts highlight the effectiveness of cold case units in solving previously unsolved crimes through meticulous and updated investigative approaches. Despite these advancements, the current temporary nature of these units highlights the need for a permanent, stable, and dedicated organizational structure. Systemic issues, including limited interagency cooperation, restricted information sharing, and the perception of investigations as performative, further impede progress. Additionally, the expertise required for thorough investigations is often lacking due to constrained resources.

There are many obstacles and restrictions in the field of cold case investigations in India. Cold case resolution is frequently hampered by law enforcement agencies' lack of resources (Sekhri 2020), outdated technology (Charan and Manikyam 2023), and administrative roadblocks especially bureaucratic delays, which impede the resolution of cold cases. Additionally, a poor clearing rate and an increasing backlog of unsolved crimes are also caused by the absence of defined procedures and specialized teams to handle these cases methodically. Furthermore, in the Indian system, the idea of cold cases is not well-known or accepted.

The reliance on traditional investigative methods, without integrating modern forensic and technological advancements, further complicates efforts to solve cold cases. Despite some progress in the adoption of DNA technology and forensic databases, the implementation remains sporadic and inconsistent across different jurisdictions in India. The absence of a centralized system to manage and review cold cases exacerbates the issue, leading to a fragmented and inefficient approach to solving these crimes (National Institute of Justice).

To improve cold case investigations, there is a need to consider the practices of developed countries, such as introducing specialized investigators, establishing permanent dedicated teams, and implementing professional investigator certification systems. These measures could enhance cooperation and optimize crime analysis systems. This study proposes focusing on key violent crime cases, aiming to apply high-level investigative efforts consistently until resolution, thereby ensuring a more efficient and effective approach to solving cold cases.

2 Need of the Study

The urgent requirement for policy change is crucial in today's context. Establishing a dedicated Cold Case Center in India, supported by the latest forensic technologies and research-driven practices, can significantly enhance the country's criminal justice system. Policies should be looked at on allocating resources and funding for the Cold Case Center, training law enforcement personnel in advanced forensic techniques, encouraging interagency collaboration and information sharing, and developing protocols for the systematic review and reopening of cold cases. By advocating for these changes, we can unlock the potential to solve even the most challenging cases, providing justice for victims and their families, and reinforcing public trust in the criminal justice system.

To effectively address cold cases, it is essential to draw on best practices from around the globe. Successful cold case units in countries like the United States, Canada, and the United Kingdom have implemented comprehensive approaches that integrate advanced forensic technologies, dedicated resources, and multidisciplinary collaboration. These units have demonstrated the value of continuous training, leveraging cutting-edge technologies to uncover new leads and solve previously intractable cases.

By adopting a similar framework and fostering an environment that encourages innovation and collaboration, we can significantly develop a proposal to create an effective cold case center in India.

3 Methodology

3.1 Objectives

1. Analyzing the need to establish a cold case center in India.
2. Formulating hypothetical solutions to cold cases in India based on today's technological advancements.
3. Analyzing the best practices around the globe.
4. Proposing a structure for the establishment of a cold case center in India.

3.2 Research Design

This study employs a qualitative research design, specifically using content analysis of secondary data, to explore the need for and structure of a dedicated cold case center in India. The research is empirical in nature, as it involves the systematic analysis of existing data sources to draw conclusions.

3.3 Data Collection

3.3.1 Secondary Data

The study relies on a wide range of secondary sources, including academic papers, government reports, and case studies from law enforcement agencies. The data selected pertains to cold case investigations, highlighting best practices, challenges, and successful models from various countries including the USA, UK, South Korea, and Australia.

3.4 Data Analysis

3.4.1 Content Analysis

The collected data was systematically reviewed and coded to identify key themes and patterns related to the challenges and successful strategies in cold case investigations. Common themes include the role of forensic science, interagency cooperation, resource allocation, and legislative support.

4 Need for Establishing a Center for Cold Case Investigations: Insights from Researches Around the Globe

A dedicated center would bring together experts in forensic science, criminal investigation, and judicial proceedings. These professionals can focus exclusively on cold cases, ensuring that they receive the attention and resources needed for thorough investigation. This specialized approach increases the likelihood of solving complex cases that have remained "cold" for years. Modern forensic techniques, such as DNA profiling, genetic genealogy, and advanced fingerprint analysis, have revolutionized the investigation of cold cases.

A dedicated center can ensure the systematic application of these technologies, enhancing the ability to identify perpetrators and exonerate innocent individuals. For instance, advancements in DNA technology have been pivotal in solving numerous cold cases globally, by analyzing evidence previously deemed unsuitable for testing (Iowa State University News 2023; Mulawka 2014). Hence, there is an urgent need for the utilization of forensic technologies and the involvement of forensic experts in tackling and resolving cold cases.

Chapman et al. (2019) made an effort to comprehend the necessity of forensic specialists in handling cold cases in Western Australia. The authors reviewed the existing literature to gain understanding of the purported composition of cold case teams in order to bolster the suggested methodology. The authors also examined several commissioned reports aimed at enhancing forensic services and cold case reviews. The results showed that there is no evidence of improved collaboration with scientists and outside specialists in published literature, despite a plethora of studies and suggestions to that effect. By communicating and working together, police investigators and forensic scientists can improve case priority, lessen prejudices, and use cutting-edge scientific techniques to improve the efficiency of cold case investigations. Additionally, academic institutions can offer valuable resources, such as student interns and researchers, to support police departments with limited resources.

Despite the widely recognized and urgent need for the integration of forensic technologies and expertise in resolving cold cases, significant action or initiatives by agencies or the government remain lacking. However, it is important to acknowledge positive steps being taken, such as the recent approval of the "National Forensic Infrastructure Enhancement Scheme" (N.F.I.E.S.) by the Indian government. This initiative, with a budget of Rs. 2254.43 crore, aims to enhance forensic infrastructure, including campuses and laboratories. This development marks a significant step, because it also plays a vital role in countering various crimes, cold cases included, through investing in universities that specialize in forensics, criminology, and criminalistics.

A study by Stupperich et al. (2017) in Germany proved that student intern resources are highly beneficial while looking at expanding new ideas such as a cold case center; hence, investing in universities that specialize in criminalistics and forensics is a productive initiative. Since 2014, students from the Police Academy of Lower Saxony collaborated with local police departments and district attorneys to analyze cold cases. The students reviewed numerous cases, resulting in the closure of many, while identifying new connections and suggesting forensic re-analysis for some. Early results of the program indicate that, although the students' analyses do not hold the status of evidence, they provided new leads in every case that were valuable for professional detectives.

Another initiative that would enhance the functionality of a cold case center would be establishing a central repository for cold cases. Improved coordination and information exchange between law enforcement agencies can be facilitated by this data repository. Several databases can be integrated using this centralized method, which facilitates pattern recognition, case linking, and lead generation. Effective database management can turn cold cases into hot cases by providing valuable investigative leads and helping save time and resources needed to solve them (National Institute of Justice). Chapman et al. (2019) stated that cold case review teams would function better with the integration of forensic scientists into them and maintaining a central repository can improve the quality of forensic analysis and case review processes. This collaboration can lead to better evidence handling and case solvability (Chapman et al. 2019).

A dedicated center can also advocate for necessary policy and legal reforms to support cold case investigations. This includes expanding DNA databases, standardizing protocols for evidence preservation, and promoting legislative changes to extend the statute of limitations for serious crimes. Such reforms are essential to create a conducive environment for solving cold cases and preventing future crimes

(Iowa State University News) (RAND). The following findings from a study by Davis et al. (2015) further supported this. With only 20% of agencies having a procedure for starting cold case investigations, 10% having specialized cold case investigators, and 7% having a formal cold case unit, the majority of agencies don't perform much cold case work. Funding for cold cases is shaky; grants or additional monies provide for the majority of funding, with line items in the budget covering 20% of cold case activity. About one out of every five cold case inquiries are resolved, which is a low success rate. Access to investigative databases and the amount of funds were agency factors linked to greater clearance rates.

Solving cold cases can significantly impact public perception of the criminal justice system. When old cases are resolved, it demonstrates a commitment to justice and accountability, thereby restoring public trust (Bettles et al. 2022). Moreover, providing closure to victims and their families has profound social and psychological benefits, reinforcing the importance of addressing cold cases as a priority. A study testing the same effect was done by Davis et al. (2014). This study examined the factors influencing the solvability of cold cases by analyzing 189 cases, both solved and unsolved, in Washington, D.C. The results underscored the significance of obtaining new information from witnesses and the application of investigative techniques. Successfully resolving cold cases can bolster public confidence in the justice.

5 Reflections on Cold Cases in India

India's cold cases provide a fascinating glimpse into the evolving landscape of criminal investigations. Analyzing a few of these cases in the context of the investigative methods used then and what is trending now can offer insights into how modern techniques could potentially solve them.

1. The Aarushi Talwar Case (2008)

The murder of 14-year-old Aarushi Talwar and her domestic help, Hemraj, in Noida is one of India's most high-profile and controversial cases. Multiple investigations and convictions have taken place; yet, the case remains fraught with unanswered questions and inconsistencies.

Methods Used Then:

- Initial Investigation: The local police's initial efforts were plagued by procedural errors, contamination of the crime scene, and general forensic negligence.
- CBI Involvement: The case was later escalated to the Central Bureau of Investigation (CBI), which employed DNA testing, narco-analysis, and polygraph tests to gather evidence.
- Technology and Limitations: The investigation was hindered by limited use of advanced forensic technology, relying heavily on witness statements and circumstantial evidence.

Trending Methods Now:

- Advanced DNA Profiling: Current forensic science includes next-generation sequencing and enhanced DNA recovery techniques that can analyze even degraded samples effectively.
- Digital Forensics: Modern investigations leverage digital footprints, analyzing data from mobile devices, computers, and online activities to uncover crucial evidence.
- Behavioral Analysis: Contemporary methods also utilize psychological profiling to understand the motives and mental states of suspects better.

Hypothetical Outcome Using New Methods:

- If revisited with today's forensic advancements, the Aarushi Talwar case might see significant breakthroughs. Advanced DNA profiling could uncover new biological evidence that might exonerate or implicate suspects. Digital forensics could reveal previously overlooked communications or other digital evidence. Behavioral analysis could offer deeper insights into the psychological dimensions of the suspects, potentially clarifying inconsistencies and leading to resolutions that were not possible before.

2. The Scarlett Keeling Case (2008) (see footnote 1)

The murder of a young British girl on Goa's Anjuna Beach, initially dismissed as an accidental drowning, was later revealed to be a case of drug-induced rape and murder. Despite the revelations, the case remains unsolved, with the accused never being convicted.

Methods Used Then:

- Initial Investigation: Initially deemed an accidental drowning by local police, the case lacked a thorough initial investigation.
- Re-investigation: Public and media outcry led to a more detailed inquiry that uncovered evidence of rape and murder, utilizing basic forensic and toxicology tests.

Trending Methods Now:

- Toxicology Advancements: Current toxicology techniques can detect substances at much lower concentrations, potentially offering new insights into the drugs involved.
- Enhanced Forensic Imaging: 3D imaging and photogrammetry could reconstruct the crime scene with high accuracy, providing new perspectives on the events.
- Geolocation Analysis: Analysis of data from mobile devices can precisely track the victim's and suspects' movements.

Hypothetical Outcome Using New Methods:

- Applying these advanced methods could lead to a clearer understanding of the timeline and events surrounding Scarlett's death. Sophisticated toxicology could identify specific substances, enhanced imaging could reveal overlooked evidence at the scene, and geolocation analysis could provide crucial information on suspect whereabouts, potentially leading to breakthroughs in the case.

3. The Stoneman Killings (1985)

   Methods Used Then:

- Traditional Policing: Depended heavily on eyewitnesses, patrols, and standard detective tactics.
- Forensic Limitations: Forensic capabilities were minimal, largely relying on basic physical evidence such as footprints.

- Trending Methods Now:

  - Predictive Policing: Algorithms analyze historical crime data to predict and prevent future incidents. Geographic profiling and AI-driven systems like CNN can process large datasets, including surveillance footage, to identify patterns and anomalies. The use of "grey box" AI, which combines human expertise with AI algorithms, is particularly valuable in enhancing the accuracy of predictive policing models.
  - Enhanced Surveillance: AI-enhanced CCTV footage is used to identify behavioral patterns and potential suspects.
  - DNA Technology: Advanced techniques enable the recovery and analysis of trace amounts of DNA from crime scenes.

Hypothetical Outcome Using New/Latest Tech Methods:

  - Predictive policing could have pinpointed likely locations for subsequent attacks, potentially preventing them. Enhanced surveillance might have improved tracking of suspect movements. Modern DNA technology might have identified the perpetrator from minuscule biological traces left at the crime scenes, previously beyond detection capabilities.

4. The Monkey Man Case (2001)

In 2001, Delhi experienced a series of mysterious incidents involving sightings of a monkey-like creature, which sparked widespread panic and confusion.

Despite numerous reports and extensive media coverage, the case remains unsolved, with some attributing it to mass hysteria.

Initial Reactions:

- Public and Media Response (see footnote 1): Widespread reports from residents of Delhi described encounters with a "monkey-like" entity, causing a surge in public anxiety and extensive media coverage.

  Investigative Challenges:

- Lack of Physical Evidence: Despite numerous eyewitness accounts, no concrete evidence was gathered to substantiate the presence of any creature.
- Psychological Factors: Some experts considered the possibility of mass hysteria, where collective fear amplified the myth without a real threat.

Modern Analytical Approaches:

- Behavioral Science: Techniques like crowd psychology could analyze how urban legends like the Monkey Man gain traction and affect community behavior.
- Digital Media Analysis: Examining the role of media in propagating fear and folklore could provide insights into the dynamics of such cases.

Hypothetical Application of Modern Methods:

- Applying behavioral science could help understand the psychological underpinnings of how such incidents lead to widespread panic. Digital media analysis could track the spread and evolution of the Monkey Man narrative, potentially identifying factors that fueled the hysteria. These approaches might offer a clearer picture of the incident's impact rather than its factual basis.

5. The Amar Singh Chamkila Murder (1988):

The murder of famous Punjabi singer Amar Singh Chamkila and his wife by a gang of motorcyclists remains unsolved. No arrests have ever been made, and the motive behind the killings is still unclear. No arrests have been made, and the motivations behind the murder are still not understood, complicating the resolution of the case.

Potential Modern Investigative Approaches:

- Digital Forensics and Social Network Analysis: Examining any digital footprints or communications that could be linked to suspects or motives.
- Enhanced Ballistic and Forensic Analysis: Revisiting the forensic evidence with modern technology could provide new insights, potentially identifying the weapons used and linking them to other crimes or suspects.

Hypothetical Application of Contemporary Methods:

- Application of advanced ballistic analysis might help trace the murder weapons and connect them to other criminal activities, potentially leading to suspects. Social network analysis could unveil connections between the suspects and broader criminal networks, offering new leads in the long-unsolved case.

6. The Beerman Killings (2006–2007):

A series of seven murders in Mumbai, all involving a beer bottle left next to the victim, remains unsolved. The investigation was marred by allegations of police corruption and a lack of substantial evidence.

Initial Investigation Challenges:

- Evidence Collection: The key piece of evidence in each murder was a beer bottle left by the victim, but no conclusive forensic links were established
- Corruption Allegations: The investigation was complicated by claims of police corruption, which undermined the integrity and progress of the case.

Modern Investigative Techniques:

- Enhanced Forensic Analysis: Techniques such as fingerprint lifting from the beer bottles and DNA analysis of any residual contents could be more thoroughly applied.
- Data Analytics: Analyzing patterns of the killings and the locations using advanced crime mapping tools.

Hypothetical Application of Modern Methods:

- With today's forensic advancements, a re-examination of the beer bottles might reveal fingerprints or DNA traces that were previously undetected. Data analytics could offer new insights into the geographical patterns and timing of the killings, potentially identifying a suspect or a motive behind the patterned placement of the beer bottles.

Other cold cases include:

7. The Chennai Triple Murder (2008):

This case involves the brutal murder of a septuagenarian couple and their maid, who were found dead in their home with multiple stab injuries. The investigation has been marked by inconsistencies and a lack of evidence, leaving the true identity of the killer unknown.

8. The Rizwanur Rahman Murder (2007):

The death of computer graphics trainer Rizwanur Rahman near railway tracks was initially ruled as an accident. However, suspicions of foul play emerged due to his secret interreligious marriage, and many believe it was either murder or a suicide driven by societal pressure.

9. The Lal Bahadur Shastri Death (1966):

The sudden death of Mr. Lal Bahadur Shastri, India's second Prime Minister, has remained shrouded in mystery. Officially attributed to a heart attack, many believe there were more sinister circumstances involved, and the case remains unsolved.

10. The Vyapam Scam (Mid-1990s):

The Vyavsayik Pariksha Mandal scam involved a large number of fraudulent medical and engineering admissions in Madhya Pradesh, leading to the deaths of over 40 people connected to the scam. The investigation is ongoing, with many questions still unanswered.

These cases highlight the complexity and often the lack of resolution in India's cold cases, leaving many questions unanswered and the public seeking justice. Establishing a dedicated cold case center would be instrumental in addressing these challenges, providing the necessary resources and expertise to bring closure to these and other unsolved cases.

The field of forensic science has seen significant advancements in recent years, offering new opportunities to solve cold cases that have long remained unresolved. Technologies such as advanced DNA analysis, forensic mapping, and digital forensics have revolutionized how evidence is collected, analyzed, and interpreted. These developments present a compelling case for revisiting and reopening cold cases using the latest forensic techniques, suggesting that the potential for solving these cases is now greater than ever. Advanced DNA analysis, for instance, includes next-generation sequencing (NGS), which permits far more nuanced and detailed analysis of genetic material, even from degraded or minimal samples. DNA phenotyping can predict physical characteristics and ancestry from DNA samples, helping to create composite sketches of unknown suspects when traditional identification methods fail. Forensic mapping and geographic profiling, through technologies like crime scene reconstruction and geographic information systems (GIS), provide high-accuracy recreations of crime scenes and analyze the locations of crimes to predict the likely residence or base of operations of serial offenders.

Additionally, digital forensics, which encompasses modern tools for data recovery from damaged or encrypted devices and social media analysis, enables investigators to gather critical information about suspects' behavior, connections, and movements. Given these technological advancements, revisiting cold cases with today's forensic tools can potentially yield significant breakthroughs. Many cold cases initially lacked the forensic capabilities now available, which could provide new leads and evidence to bring justice to unresolved crimes.

6 Best Practices Around the Globe

Internationally, numerous cold case centers have established best practices to address the complexities of unsolved crimes. These centers, located in various countries, adopt diverse strategies to enhance the effectiveness of cold case investigations.

6.1 United States

1. Cold Case Foundation

In November 2011, Yellowstone County Sheriff Mike Linder conceived an idea to revive a series of dormant cold homicide cases. Linder believed these cases deserved renewed attention and hypothesized that even a small law enforcement agency could muster the manpower and resources to reopen and re-investigate solvable cases. The challenge was to achieve this without increasing the payroll and while enabling his Detective Division to manage its regular caseload simultaneously. This led to the development of The Cold Case Foundation. This foundation emphasizes continuous education through specialized courses and workshops that focus on various aspects of investigations, such as deception detection through handwriting analysis and advanced crime scene reconstruction techniques. These training sessions equip law enforcement professionals and practitioners with the skills necessary to handle intricate cold cases effectively.

The foundation lays down 5 steps to create a cold case unit in any department based on their experience:

6.1.1 Assess and Analyze

Sheriff Mike Linder of Yellowstone County sought to revive dormant cold homicide cases by leveraging existing resources. He tasked his command staff with identifying someone within the organization who had the time and expertise to review unsolved cases and explore how to establish a cold case unit (CCU). A recently retired Reserve Deputy, formerly a media manager, accepted the challenge. From December 2011 to April 2012, this deputy reviewed all unsolved homicides dating back to 1973, classifying each case by its solvability. He also sought guidance from other agencies with established cold case units to learn about structuring, staffing, and integrating the unit with existing detectives and command staff.

6.1.2 Policies and Procedures

Based on his research, the Reserve Deputy helped develop an organizational Chain of Command and a CCU Policy and Procedure manual, ensuring compliance with departmental policies and state law. The CCU Coordinator and volunteers reported directly to the Captain of Detectives, and the unit was housed within the Sheriff's Office Detective Division. Spare interview rooms were repurposed as CCU offices, with local businesses donating computers and office supplies. The department contacted 25 retired investigators with backgrounds in various law enforcement and legal fields, securing their participation.

6.1.3 Human Capital

A retired Crime Analyst and volunteers from the local Crime Prevention Center joined the effort. Fourteen out of the 25 contacted individuals volunteered to assist the CCU. The Reserve Deputy, who had conducted the initial case review and organizational setup, was appointed as the CCU Coordinator, responsible for working with volunteers and interfacing with detectives and command staff.

6.1.4 Public Awareness

The Yellowstone County Sheriff's Office formally established its cold case unit in April 2012. Cold Case Reports and Public Service Announcements that were aired on local media channels helped the campaign garner community support, which led to donations from individuals and organizations. A specific Cold Case website was made, and basic case information was posted on Facebook. On a few chosen examples, five half-hour videos were created and posted in YouTube with links to the website. For detectives' convenience, all cold cases were digitally scanned into Rack2file, rearranged into a more readable format, and entered into VICAP and other databases.

6.1.5 Investigate

Each volunteer investigator was designated as a Special Service Officer and paired with two detectives to review a case. Training for case reviewers and detectives was enhanced through sessions led by former heads of the Wyoming State Crime Lab and Wyoming DCI, focusing on DNA and evidence evaluation techniques. Reviewers were encouraged to approach each case with fresh eyes, identifying gaps and leads missed in the original investigations. Lists of potential witnesses and Persons of Interest still in the area were compiled for interviews. All evidence was re-evaluated for DNA testing using new forensic techniques.

6.1.6 Next Steps

After the Special Service Officers' reviews, detectives continued to pursue leads and incorporate the latest criminal investigation technologies. DNA samples were collected from individuals involved in the original investigations. The CCU's efforts have persisted without additional manpower, thanks to the dedicated volunteers, continuing the quest to solve these cold cases.

2. Federal Bureau of Investigation's Next Generation Identification (NGI) Biometric System

The Next-Generation Identification (NGI) biometric technology from the Federal Bureau of Investigation is another development that has improved the field of print identification. NGI is being used by the Latent Evidence Unit of the Oklahoma State Bureau of Investigation (OSBI) to help solve "Cold Cases." Even though the OSBI cold case project has been effective, it can be difficult to stay up with current casework while analyzing old evidence and case files. However, the success that has been attained shows that the acknowledgment and use of such potent technology is justified (Stokes 2019).

3. National Policing Institute

The National Policing Institute takes a multifaceted approach to addressing cold cases and enhancing police operations, heavily emphasizing the integration of modern technology and data-driven strategies. Their approach involves a blend of traditional policing practices augmented by new technologies like DNA profiling, digital forensics, and advanced data analytics. One significant element is the emphasis on building "digital trust" through ethical use of technology. This involves creating a framework that ensures data integrity, security, and controlled usage, which is vital for maintaining public trust in how law enforcement handles sensitive information and employs new technologies. This framework aims to mitigate risks associated with digital tools and ensure their responsible use in police operations.

Another important component of their plan is the switch to the National Incident-Based Reporting System (NIBRS). More thorough crime data is provided by this method, which can enhance the caliber of information accessible for resolving crimes, even cold cases. The information gathered under NIBRS includes thorough incident reports, which are essential for reexamining unresolved situations using fresh viewpoints and instruments.

Moreover, the institute advocates for continuous training and partnerships between researchers and practitioners to foster better practices in investigations. This includes enhancing the skills of law enforcement personnel through educational programs that focus on the latest investigative techniques and technologies. In addition to solving cold cases, this all-encompassing strategy seeks to improve law enforcement agencies' overall capacity to handle present and upcoming police difficulties.

4. National Institute of Justice (NIJ) Cold Case Investigation Working Group

The NIJ emphasizes the establishment of dedicated cold case units within law enforcement agencies. These units should be operationally separate and professionally managed, with experienced investigators assigned exclusively to cold case investigations. The NIJ's recommendations highlight the necessity of access to DNA databases and innovative forensic tools, as well as systematic assessments of cold case inventories to prioritize and tackle the most solvable cases. Cold case statistics reveal a grim scenario, with an estimated 242,000 unresolved homicides in the United States from 1980 to 2016. Currently, about 40% of homicides remain unsolved and the clearance rate has declined significantly from 78.3% in 1975 to 59.4% in 2016. This decline seems set to continue, with less than half of violent crimes being resolved annually. However, advancements in forensic technology provide new opportunities to tackle these unsolved cases. The National Institute of Justice (NIJ) has developed a best-practices guide to aid law enforcement in addressing these cold cases, offering 23 recommendations categorized into planning, designing, implementing, operating, and supporting cold case units. These recommendations stress the importance of specialized, well-equipped units focused on cold cases to improve clearance rates and address the backlog of unsolved crimes.

5. University of Central Oklahoma's Forensic Science Institute

The goal of this project is to collaborate with law enforcement organizations to maximize academic resources. The partnership entails applying cutting-edge forensic methods, conducting case file reviews, and creating best practice standards for cold case programs in a university setting using resources from the university. In addition to helping with case resolution, this gives forensic science students hands-on experience. Keatley and Clarke's (2019) research examines the effectiveness of a particular tool known as the Timeline Toolkit. The study presents a toolkit of temporal and dynamic analysis techniques that can be used to solve cold situations.

Numerous instances have successfully used these techniques, demonstrating the need for methodical, systematic procedures in cold case investigations.

The Timeline Toolkit is a comprehensive collection of methodologies tailored to support the investigation of cold cases by analyzing the temporal progression of behaviors and events. This toolkit encompasses techniques designed for both detailed, event-specific analyses and broader, life-history analyses. Key components of the toolkit include the following:

Temporal Analyses: Focused on comprehending the sequence and timing of events or behaviors, these methods offer valuable insights into cold cases with limited traditional evidence.

Parsing and Categorizing: Initially, episodes are deconstructed into discrete parts, such as behaviors (e.g., moving a body) or events (e.g., graduating school). These parts are then categorized to develop a detailed "dictionary" of actions, facilitating the comparison and analysis of cases.

Application Examples: The toolkit's efficacy is underscored by its successful application in various cold cases, often leading to the reopening of investigations by offering fresh perspectives. Noteworthy methods include crime script analysis and behavior sequence analysis, recognized for their efficacy in this context.

Academic Collaboration: Aiming to bridge the gap between academic research and practical detective work, the toolkit advocates for collaborative efforts to enhance investigative techniques. While these methods are not a panacea, they can significantly bolster investigative endeavors.

ReBSA Network: The Researchers in Behaviour Sequence Analysis (ReBSA) network plays a pivotal role in supporting the development and application of these methodologies. It fosters international collaboration among specialists in temporal analyses, furthering the toolkit's impact and reach.

6.2 United Kingdom

In the UK, several universities and institutions have established dedicated centers for investigating cold cases, focusing on integrating academic research with practical law enforcement techniques.

1. University of Winchester has created a cold case unit that involves students from forensic investigation programs. These students work under the guidance of international experts and academic staff to revisit and solve historical unsolved crimes. This program not only enhances the educational experience by applying theoretical knowledge to real-world scenarios but also supports law enforcement agencies with fresh perspectives on old cases.
2. University of South Wales participates in cold case reviews through its Centre for Criminology. This initiative reflects a broader trend within UK policing to

re-examine unsolved cases, particularly murders and stranger rapes, using advanced forensic science.

The focus often lies on reanalyzing DNA evidence, which can link old cases to offenders listed in national DNA databases. This approach has significantly increased the resolution of cold cases over the years.

6.3 Australia

In Australia, cold case investigations are actively pursued by various police departments, each employing updated forensic technologies and methodologies to tackle longstanding unsolved crimes.

1. Victoria Police maintains a dedicated Cold Case Team within its Homicide Squad, which handles over 200 unresolved cases. This team emphasizes the importance of community assistance in solving these cases, underlining that new information can lead to breakthroughs in cold cases. They advocate for public involvement, suggesting that even small tips can be the missing link in their investigations.
2. Western Australia: The WA Police Force has embraced modern DNA technologies and genetic genealogy to advance their investigations. Their approach is detailed through their public outreach via the "Cold Case Western Australia" podcast, which shares insights into ongoing cold case investigations. This initiative not only helps in gathering new information from the public but also keeps the community engaged and informed about the efforts being made to solve cold cases.

6.4 Others

Several countries besides the USA, UK, and Australia are also engaged in significant cold case initiatives, harnessing modern forensic science and collaborative strategies:

Canada: Canada has implemented numerous cold case units across its provinces, utilizing advances in DNA technology and other forensic methods to revisit unresolved crimes. The Royal Canadian Mounted Police (RCMP) and local police services actively review cold cases, encouraging public input and employing sophisticated investigative techniques.

Germany: Germany has made notable advances in cold case investigations, particularly through cooperation between state-level police forces and the Federal Criminal Police Office (BKA). They focus on integrating forensic analysis, particularly DNA technology, to revisit cases that have remained unsolved for decades.

Netherlands: The Dutch police operate specialized cold case teams that focus on serious crimes, including murders and sexual offenses that have not been solved. These teams utilize a wide array of modern forensic techniques, and they also actively engage the public through various media to generate new leads.

South Africa: In South Africa, the cold case unit operates under the South African Police Service, reexamining unsolved cases using new technology and methodologies. This unit has been pivotal in reopening numerous cases, aided by improvements in forensic capabilities.

These countries demonstrate an international effort toward solving cold cases, emphasizing the global nature of forensic advancements and the shared goal of achieving justice for victims and their families.

7 Current Practices and Challenges in India

Cold case investigations in India are characterized by a lack of uniformity and standardized procedures across various states and law enforcement agencies. Typically, these cases are handled by the same units responsible for current investigations, leading to a dilution of focus and resources. Unlike some Western countries that have dedicated cold case units, Indian police forces often do not have specialized teams or clear protocols specifically for cold cases (Iowa State University News 2023).

Investigation is a crucial and fundamental aspect of the criminal justice system. Effective and timely investigations are essential. In India, inefficiencies, lack of transparency, and delays in investigations often result in the innocent suffering, while culprits benefit through bail or acquittal. The police frequently fail to use scientific methods for evidence collection. Typically, they do not accurately record witness statements, instead writing their own versions (as per Section 161 of the Cr.P.C.). When investigators cannot find sufficient genuine evidence, they may resort to fabricating evidence. Investigating officers often do not adhere to the legislative provisions of the Cr.P.C., nor do they respect legal procedures, sometimes employing barbaric and torturous methods to extract information from suspects and, in many cases, from innocent individuals. The Code of Criminal Procedure (Cr.P.C.), enacted in 1973 and effective from April 1, 1974, is the primary legislation governing the procedural administration of substantive criminal law in India. It outlines the framework for crime investigation, suspect apprehension, and evidence collection, determining the guilt or innocence of the accused, and deciding the punishment for the guilty (Yadav 2013).

To ensure justice and uphold the integrity of the criminal justice system, it is imperative to address these investigative shortcomings and adopt more scientific and transparent methods. This could lead to less cold cases being generated and also if a case does become "cold," investigating it would be easier if the proper procedure, technological advancements, and legal proceedings are followed.

The current practices largely rely on conventional investigative methods, with occasional use of modern forensic techniques. However, the implementation of advanced forensic technology is inconsistent and often dependent on the availability of resources and expertise in specific regions. For instance, while some metropolitan areas may have access to DNA testing and forensic labs, many rural and smaller urban areas lack these facilities, resulting in significant disparities in the handling and resolution of cold cases.

8 Future Challenges for Investigators

One of the most significant challenges in cold case investigations is the chronic shortage of resources. Police departments are often underfunded and understaffed, making it difficult to allocate sufficient personnel and financial resources to revisit old cases.

This lack of resources hampers the ability to conduct thorough and time-intensive investigations required for cold cases. While forensic science has advanced significantly, its application in cold case investigations in India remains limited. Many regions lack access to modern forensic labs and equipment, and there is often a shortage of trained forensic experts. This limitation is compounded by issues such as the degradation of physical evidence over time, which further complicates the analysis and use of forensic techniques in cold case investigations (National Institute of Justice).

Bureaucratic inertia and the absence of standardized protocols for handling cold cases present another major challenge. Without clear guidelines and dedicated teams, cold cases are often deprioritized in favor of current investigations. Additionally, the lack of a centralized database for cold cases hinders the efficient sharing of information and collaboration across different law enforcement agencies (Iowa State University News 2022) (National Institute of Justice). The integration of technology in investigative processes is crucial for the effective resolution of cold cases. However, many police departments in India still rely on outdated systems and manual record-keeping, which impede the ability to systematically review and analyze old cases. The lack of access to comprehensive databases and advanced software tools for data analysis further exacerbates this issue (National Institute of Justice).

9 Proposed Center Structure and Operations

The proposed Cold Case Center will be strategically designed to leverage its status as a frontliner in forensic sciences in India. It will operate ensuring that it has the necessary governmental support and integration with national law enforcement policies. The center will be headed by a Director, who will be a seasoned professional with extensive experience in forensic science and criminal investigations. The Director will report to a governing board comprising representatives from various universities, ministries, senior law enforcement officials, and forensic experts.

9.1 Departments and Divisions

Investigative Division: This division will consist of experienced detectives and forensic analysts who will re-examine cold cases using advanced techniques and technologies.

Forensic Technology Division: Equipped with state-of-the-art forensic tools, this division will focus on DNA analysis, digital forensics, and other advanced methodologies.

Research and Development Division: This division will collaborate with academic institutions and research bodies to innovate and refine forensic techniques.

Training and Capacity-Building Division: This division will develop training programs for law enforcement agencies, ensuring they are equipped with the latest skills and knowledge.

9.2 Advisory and Support Units

Legal Advisory Unit: To provide legal support and ensure compliance with legal standards.

Victim and Witness Support Unit: To offer counseling and support to victims and witnesses involved in cold cases.

Public Relations Unit: To handle media relations and community engagement.

9.3 Description of the Center's Investigative Tools and Techniques

The Cold Case Center will employ a variety of advanced investigative tools and techniques to solve cold cases:

DNA Profiling and Genetic Genealogy: Utilizing next-generation DNA sequencing and genetic genealogy databases to identify suspects and victims.

Digital Forensics: Analyzing digital footprints, including social media activity, mobile phone records, and internet usage, to uncover new leads.

Forensic Databases: Integrating with national and international forensic databases to cross-reference evidence and identify patterns across jurisdictions.

Crime Scene Reconstruction: Using 3D modeling and other advanced technologies to reconstruct crime scenes and provide new insights.

Behavioral Analysis: Employing behavioral science techniques to profile suspects and understand criminal patterns.

These are a few of the many tools and techniques that could be implemented by the cold case center when in action.

9.4 Discussion on the Center's Role in Training and Capacity Building for Law Enforcement Agencies

The Cold Case Center will play a pivotal role in enhancing the capabilities of law enforcement agencies across India through comprehensive training and capacity-building initiatives:

9.4.1 Training Programs

Forensic Science Training: Courses on advanced forensic techniques such as DNA analysis, digital forensics, and crime scene investigation.

Cold Case Methodology: Specialized training on the unique aspects of cold case investigations, including handling of historical evidence and leveraging modern technologies.

Legal and Ethical Training: Ensuring that investigators are well-versed in the legal and ethical considerations of cold case investigations.

Workshops and Seminars: Regular workshops and seminars featuring experts from around the world to discuss the latest advancements and best practices in cold case investigations.

Collaborative Projects: Initiating joint projects with law enforcement agencies to apply new techniques and technologies in real-world scenarios, providing hands-on experience.

Resource Development: Creating manuals, guidelines, and online resources to support continuous learning and reference for law enforcement officers.

9.5 Implementation Plan

The successful establishment of a cold case center in India requires a detailed and strategic implementation plan, coupled with ample funding strategy. Below is an outline of how this could be achieved.

9.5.1 Defining Goals and Objectives

The primary goal of the cold case center would be to systematically address and resolve unsolved criminal cases through the application of advanced forensic techniques and collaborative investigative efforts. The center aims to enhance the efficiency and effectiveness of cold case investigations, thereby improving justice delivery in India.

9.5.2 Conducting Research

Conducting preliminary research to understand the specific needs and challenges in cold case investigations within the Indian context is crucial. This involves collecting data on the number of unresolved cases, the resources currently available, and the forensic capabilities of existing institutions.

9.5.3 Mapping Out Risks

Identifying potential risks, such as funding shortfalls, legal hurdles, or resistance from existing law enforcement bodies, and developing mitigation strategies. This could involve creating a risk register and conducting a SWOT analysis to ensure a comprehensive risk management approach.

9.5.4 Scheduling Milestones

Establishing a clear timeline with specific milestones will be essential. Key milestones could include securing initial funding, establishing partnerships, hiring staff, and launching pilot investigations. Utilizing tools like Gantt charts can help to visualize the timeline and ensure all stakeholders are aligned on project progress.

9.5.5 Assigning Responsibilities

Clear assignment of roles and responsibilities is necessary for the smooth functioning of the center. This includes defining the roles of forensic experts, law enforcement officers, administrative staff, and external collaborators such as academic researchers and technology providers.

9.5.6 Training and Capacity Building

Implementing a comprehensive training program for all personnel involved in cold case investigations: This could include specialized training in forensic science, evidence handling, advanced investigative techniques, and the use of new technologies. Partnerships with institutions like the National Forensic Sciences University (NFSU) can play a pivotal role in this aspect.

10 Additional Strategies and Recommendations for Improving Cold Case Investigations Collaboration Between Law Enforcement and Academia

Establishing partnerships with academic institutions can provide fresh perspectives and additional resources for cold case investigations. Universities can assist with forensic analysis, data review, and applying the latest research methodologies to unresolved cases. Such collaborations can also foster the development of best practices and training programs for both students and law enforcement professionals. There have been studies that have stated the advantages of such collaborations such as the German study earlier mentioned. Another such study is the study conducted by Fox et al. (2020). The purpose of the study was to outline the specific details and lessons learned during a cold case collaborative effort, which granted graduate students and a professor from the University of South Florida the opportunity to assist Pasco Sheriff's Office in the investigation of a cold case homicide. This collaboration helped in discovering certain leads in cold cases that were otherwise deemed shut.

10.1 Utilization of Advanced Forensic Technologies

Incorporating various advanced forensic technologies is crucial for solving cold cases. Continuous investment in and access to these technologies are essential for enhancing the capabilities of cold case units. Incorporating forensic scientists into cold case review teams can be a critical factor for success. Enhanced collaboration between investigators and forensic scientists can mitigate biases and better equip investigations with advanced scientific solutions (Chapman et al. 2019). Digital forensic investigations, especially multimedia forensics, can significantly improve examination efficiency. Using variable scale case-based reasoning methods helps locate evidence during the forensic process (Wang and Gao 2021). Similarly, reconstructing scenarios helps convert cold case information into actionable intelligence. This methodology has been beneficial in prioritizing cases and applying new and existing investigation methods effectively (Epskamp-Dudink and Winter 2020).

10.2 Effective Communication and Public Engagement

Engaging the public through media and community outreach can generate new leads and witness testimonies. Publicizing cold cases and encouraging community involvement can lead to the discovery of crucial information that might have been overlooked initially. Effective communication strategies include using social media, press releases, and public service announcements to keep cold cases in the public eye. Implementing these best practices and strategies can significantly improve cold case clearance rates and provide closure to victims' families.

By adopting a comprehensive approach that combines advanced technologies, academic collaboration, and public engagement, cold case investigations can become more efficient and successful.

These are just a few of the many strategies that could enhance the functionality of cold case centers if developed in India. However, this study also has some limitations that need to be addressed.

10.3 Limitations

This study primarily relied on secondary data sources, such as government reports, academic papers, and forensic analysis reports. While this approach provided a comprehensive understanding of the existing literature and practices in cold case investigations, it also posed certain limitations. Firstly, the absence of primary data collection, such as interviews with stakeholders including law enforcement officers, forensic experts, and legal professionals, limited the ability to capture firsthand insights into the challenges and suggestions for improving cold case investigations. Additionally, secondary data might not always reflect the most current practices or emerging trends in the field, potentially affecting the study's relevance. Another limitation is the potential for bias in the sources of secondary data, as reports and case studies may present information from specific perspectives. Lastly, the study's findings may not be fully generalizable to all contexts, particularly in regions with different legal and investigative frameworks. Future research should consider incorporating primary data collection methods to address these limitations and provide a more nuanced understanding of the complexities involved in cold case investigations.

10.4 Suggestions for Future Research

To address the limitations identified in this study, future research should incorporate primary data collection methods, such as interviews or surveys with key stakeholders involved in cold case investigations. This would provide valuable firsthand insights into the practical challenges faced by investigators and forensic experts, as well as their suggestions for improving the process. Additionally, longitudinal studies could be conducted to track the evolution of cold case practices and the impact of new technologies over time. Expanding the scope of research to include comparative analyses of different legal and investigative frameworks across various regions would also enhance the generalizability of the findings. Finally, integrating interdisciplinary perspectives from criminology, forensic science, and legal studies could provide a more holistic view of the factors influencing the success of cold case investigations.

11 Conclusion

The establishment of a dedicated cold case center in India is not merely a recommendation but a necessity. Unsolved crimes represent a significant gap in the justice system, leaving victims and their families without closure and allowing perpetrators to remain unpunished. A dedicated center would leverage advanced forensic technologies, foster collaboration between law enforcement and academia, and implement international best practices.

This center would address the current deficiencies in cold case investigations, enhancing the capabilities of investigators and ensuring that justice is served.

The systematic study and re-investigation of unresolved cases utilizing the most recent forensic techniques, such as DNA analysis and digital forensics, is only one of the many advantages that a cold case center would offer. The center would greatly boost cold case clearing rates by incorporating these cutting-edge methods, which would rebuild public confidence in the criminal justice system. Additionally, by providing training and capacity building, the center would guarantee that law enforcement personnel nationwide will be endowed with the abilities and know-how required to manage intricate investigations, promoting an environment of innovation and constant progress.

The backing and dedication of stakeholders and legislators are essential to the success of such an endeavor. In order to create and maintain the center, they must allocate the required funds and resources and acknowledge the significance of tackling the backlog of cold cases. This entails funding, legislative backing, and the development of cooperative frameworks involving a range of industries, including the corporate sector, academia, and the global forensic community.

References

Bettels K, Grimstead D, Allsop C, Chaussée A, Bolton-King RS, Colls CS et al (2022) Finding the missing and unknown: novel educational approaches to warming up cold cases. Sci Just 62(6):749–757

Chapman B, Keatley D, Oatley G, Coumbaros J, Maker G (2019) A review and recommendations for the integration of forensic expertise within police cold case reviews. J Crim Psychol 10:79–91. https://doi.org/10.1108/jcp-09-2019-0038

Charan J, Manikyam K (2023) Forensic science and its limitations in rape and murder cases in India. J Forensic Sci Med 9:91–97. https://doi.org/10.4103/jfsm.jfsm_98_21

Davis R, Jensen C, Burgette L, Burnett K (2014) Working smarter on cold cases: identifying factors associated with successful cold case investigations. J Forensic Sci 59. https://doi.org/10.1111/1556-4029.12384

Davis R, Jensen C, Kuykendall L, Gallagher K (2015) Policies and practices in cold cases: an exploratory study. Policing-Int J Police Strateg Manag 38:610–630. https://doi.org/10.1108/PIJPSM-10-2014-0107

Epskamp-Dudink, C., & Winter, J. M. (2020). Benefits of scenario reconstruction in cold case investigations. Journal of Criminal Psychology, 10(2), 65 to 78. https://doi.org/10.1108/JCP-09-2019-0035

Fox B, Miley L, Allen S, Boness J, Dodge C, Khachatryan N, Lyle M, McKinley S, Peake J, Rozo M (2020) Law enforcement and academics working together on cold case investigations: lessons learned and paths forward. J Crim Psychol 10:93–111. https://doi.org/10.1108/jcp-09-2019-0040

Fraser J (2016) Cold-case review: UK experience. 576–580. https://doi.org/10.1016/B978-0-12-800034-2.00080-X

Lee E (2023) A study on the effective investigation method of cold case. Korean Association of Criminal Psychology. https://doi.org/10.25277/kcpr.2023.19.2.111

Mulawka M (2014) Cold case unidentified postmortem fingerprint records. https://doi.org/10.1016/B978-0-323-26617-8.00009-0

Sekhri A (2020) Mobile phones and criminal investigations in India. https://doi.org/10.2139/ssrn.3590996

Stokes J (2019) Technical note: next generation identification - A powerful tool in cold case investigations. Forensic Sci Int 299:74–79. https://doi.org/10.1016/j.forsciint.2019.03.033

Stupperich A, Bettels K, Marquardt A (2017) Cold case investigation in educational settings in Germany. Forensic Sci Policy Manag: Int J 8:38–46. https://doi.org/10.1080/19409044.2017.1343409

Yadav R (2013) Investigation and criminal administration justice in India: a study of legislative and judicial trends. https://doi.org/10.2139/SSRN.2214493

Wang, A., & Gao, X. (2021). A variable scale case-based reasoning method for evidence location in digital forensics. Future Generation Computer Systems, 122, 209 to 219. https://doi.org/10.1016/j.future.2021.03.019

Victimology: Illuminating the Voices of the Silenced

Crime Victim's Access to Justice: Bridging the Gap—Independent Legal Representation

Michael O'Connell

Abstract This chapter examines crime victims' access to justice, tracing its historical foundations, contemporary barriers, and the evolving role of independent legal representation. Beginning with early legal codes, Magna Carta, and the Universal Declaration of Human Rights, it situates victims' rights within broader struggles for equality and dignity. Despite international instruments such as the UN Declaration of Basic Principles of Justice for Victims of Crime (1985) and the Rome Statute, victims in many jurisdictions remain marginalised, often relegated to the role of witnesses in adversarial systems. The chapter identifies key barriers—including legal complexity, fear of retaliation, emotional trauma, and prohibitive costs—that hinder victims' meaningful participation. It argues that independent legal representation is a critical remedy, enabling victims to exercise procedural rights, amplify their voices, and ensure fairness in criminal proceedings. Comparative analysis highlights diverse approaches: inquisitorial systems in Germany and France, hybrid models in Sweden and Belgium, reforms in India and Japan, and adversarial adaptations in the USA, UK, Australia, and Ireland. Evidence from pilot programmes and judicial rulings demonstrates that victim representation can reduce secondary trauma, enhance confidence, and improve substantive justice outcomes without undermining defendants' rights. The chapter concludes that independent legal representation is not a luxury but a necessity, integral to balancing the triangulation of interests between the state, the accused, and victims. By embedding victims' voices within criminal justice processes, societies can move towards systems that are more inclusive, compassionate, and procedurally fair, thereby bridging the persistent gap in victims' access to justice.

Keywords Victims · Access to justice · Barriers to justice · Victims' rights · Legal representation

---

M. O'Connell (✉)
Honorary Visiting JIBS Fellow, Jindal Institute of Behavioural Sciences, O.P. Jindal Global University, Sonipat, India

© The Author(s), under exclusive license to Springer Nature Singapore Pte Ltd. 2026

G. S. Bajpai et al. (eds.), *Beyond the Gavel: A Paradigm Shift in Global Criminal Justice*, https://doi.org/10.1007/978-981-95-4487-5_12

1 Introduction

In any society, the well-being of its citizens depends not only on preventing crime, but also on ensuring that those who become victims of crime receive justice. Victims play a pivotal role in the criminal justice system, yet their rights and participation are often overshadowed by the focus on the accused and legal procedures. Hence, victims face significant challenges in accessing justice despite the attention they deserve and are entitled to.

This chapter explores the concept of access to justice, the foundations of crime victims' right to access justice, and the barriers victims encounter in pursuing it. This chapter also explores the significance of independent legal representation for victims during criminal proceedings, and it concludes that providing independent legal representation is one of the most effective ways to empower victims, so that they can choose whether, when, and how to exercise their rights. Moreover, independent legal representation improves victims' access to justice.

In addition, this chapter is dedicated to Professor Dr Chockalingham who, for decades, has written and lectured on crime victims' rights in international law and domestic law in India. Given his strong, long-term advocacy for crime victims' rights, the chapter includes a section on crime victims' participatory rights in India.

2 Access to Justice

Lord Diplock in *Bremer Vulkan Schiffbau und Maschinenfabrik v South India Shipping Corporation Ltd* [1981] AC 909 at 977, stated that a justice system 'can only command the respect of a society's members if they trust that it is an impartial, equal, transparent and principled system that gives effect to the rule of law'. Access to justice is a fundamental principle of the rule of law that calls for the implementation of "legal guarantees of formal equality before the law" (Derrington 2018). It also calls for the elimination of barriers in justice systems that impede access to justice. However, reforms must be fair and just because to do otherwise challenges the concept of justice itself.

Access to justice is impossible in a criminal justice system that is 'intentionally designed for provoking symptoms of traumatic stress' (Herman 1997; see also Cousins 2020). It is impossible when people (especially marginalised groups, such as crime victims) lack confidence in, or even fear, the system, or cannot access it. Often people lack knowledge about their rights, role, and responsibility, and (except those accused of committing crime) they do not have a lawyer to assist them. Access to justice is enhanced when there are appropriate legal protections and legal aid (Mullen 2016).

For victims, access to justice means something different for different people (McDonald 2021). For some, it could simply be able to report a crime to police; being able to access information; or being able to access support services. For some, it could also mean being able to participate in decisions that affect them or being able to participate in a process to address the harm caused by the offender. However, for some victims—and therefore the focus of this chapter—having independent legal representation is a fundamental element.

Access to justice provides for rights that they can claim, and if claimed should be fulfilled on equal terms. Furthermore, there should be effective remedies to uphold his or her rights and advance his or her legally recognised interests. Conversely, in the absence of access to justice, crime victims are unable to have their voice heard, exercise their rights, or hold decision-makers accountable. Hence, access to justice is about amplifying victims' voices, such as guaranteeing them legal representation, fulfilling their rights, and holding others accountable for violations of these rights, as well as providing for remedies through 'institutions of justice' (United Nations Development Programme 2004, 2005). Before examining the barriers to access to justice, it is important to understand the foundations of the concept from the victims' perspective.

3 Understanding the Foundations for Crime Victims' Right To Access to Justice

Humans have been subject of laws since the emergence of society. For example the Babylonian *Code of Hammurabi* (i.e. a collection of 282 rules and the *Pentateuch* of the Jewish Old Testament (i.e. the first five books including law bequeathed by God) were proclaimed thousands of years ago, and the Roman *Corpus Iuris Civilis* (i.e. collections of laws and legal interpretations) was proclaimed about 1500 years ago. The authors of these early laws understood that, to make "justice visible" (UShistory.org 2024), they needed a universal set of laws for all under their control. The laws provided means to settle disputes as well as showed some compassion for victims and, despite inherent bias and discrimination, variously obliged the wrong doer to restore the wronged. Similarly, 1200 years ago, Aethelbert's Anglo-Saxon law, which placed an emphasis on preserving the peace, provided for wrong-doers and the wronged to negotiate monetary payments rather than resort to feuding. Some commentators claim these early laws prevailed in a 'golden age' for victims of crime, because victims played a direct role in determining the punishment for wrongs perpetrated against them or their property (Schafer 1967).

Magna Carta, which is over eight hundred years old (UK Parliament 2024), is one of the, if not the, most famous documents in British legal history. In approximately 3500 medieval Latin words on a single page, it sets out 'the foundation of the freedom of the individual against arbitrary authority of the despot'. Though the 'great charter' was revised and reissued several times, and much of its content today of little relevance, it still resonates with many. The original text had sections on law and legal procedure that were intended to guarantee inexpensive and open access to justice. Importantly, Magna Carta specified that all free 'men' should have access to justice.

In the seventeenth century, Sir Edward Coke reinvigorated interest in Magna Carta's constitutional significance. Coke saw the charter as laying the foundations of then modern British law and the basis of the 'rule of law'. He and others, such as John Wilkes, championed Magna Carta as comprising a set of principles associated with liberty, freedom, and resistance to oppression by the state and to corruption.

There have been efforts also to add human rights to the conceptions of Magna Carta. It condemns abuse of power and stipulates that there should be remedies for the abrogation of basic rights. Magna Carta might therefore be considered the first charter on victims' rights.

The *Universal Declaration of Human Rights*, endorsed by the international community in 1948, proclaims unalienable rights and freedoms of every individual across the globe. Although the Declaration does not mention crime victims specifically, it comprises several rights that can be seen from the victim's perspective (Wemmers 2013). Articles 1–2 set out the concepts of dignity, liberty, and equality. Articles 3–5 proclaim additional rights, such as the right to life and the right to security of the person, and articles 6–11 provide for the legality of human rights and remedies when these rights are violated.

In the 1980s, proponents for international law on crime victims' rights argued that affording rights to victims was a desirable means of improving their position in the administration of justice. Rights were necessary to ensure victims were treated with respect and dignity (Fenwork 1997). In 1985, the United Nations General Assembly agreed and endorsed the *Declaration of Basic Principles of Justice for Victims of Crime and Abuse of Power*, which emphasises the rights of crime victims. It states that victims should be treated with compassion and respect for their dignity, which is vital to prevent secondary victimisation. Furthermore, victims are entitled to access mechanisms of justice and prompt redress as provided by national legislation (Article 4 & 6). The declaration recognises that victims should have access to justice. For this purpose, amongst other entitlements, victims should participate in legal proceedings and present their views at appropriate stages (Article 6). This procedural right seeks to mitigate the decision-making power of the state by allowing the private interests of victims to influence the criminal justice process. Hence, this procedural right places victims in a stronger position—pathing the way for victims to be at least a genuine participant and give effect to the legal triangulation of interests. In addition, victims should be provided proper assistance throughout the legal process, which could be legal representation (see, e.g., the UN Principles and Guidelines on Access to Legal Aid in Criminal Justice Systems (2013)).

4 Other International Laws

Victims' right to access to justice is also replicated in other international laws. For example, Part VIII, article 12 of the *Basic Principles and Guidelines on the Right to a Remedy and Reparation for Victims of Gross Violations of International Human Rights Law and Serious Violations of International Humanitarian Law* (2006).

These principles are, proffered Cherif Bassiouni (2006, p. 205), "an international bill of rights of victims'. Parallel to this significant advancement is the development of the International Criminal Court.

Victims' procedural rights are a notable feature of the *Rome Statute* (see, e.g., articles 68) and the *Rules of Procedure and Evidence* (see, e.g., rule 89) that govern the International Criminal Court. These rights, however, do not go as far as those provided for in the Extraordinary Chambers in the Court of Cambodia (see rule 23 of the *Internal Rules* (2011)). In the former, victims are participants, whereas in the latter, they are a party to the proceedings. Notwithstanding, victims have faced hurdles in both legal entities (McAsey 2011).

Other international victims' rights law, such as the *Declaration on the Protection of All Persons from Enforced Disappearance* (1992) and the *International Convention for the Protection of All Persons from Enforced Disappearance* (2006), and the Convention against Transnational Organized Crime (2000) and its Protocols, recognise victims' right to justice. More recently, article 24 of the model legislative provisions to support the needs and protect the rights of victims of terrorism provides for victims' access to justice.

Likewise, the United Nations Sustainable Development Goals (https://sdgs.un.org/goals/goal16), Goal 16 focusses on promoting peace, justice, and strong institutions. Ensuring access to justice for victims aligns with this goal[3].

5 Barriers to and Measures to Enhance Access to Justice

Contrary to the expansion of victims' rights in international and domestic laws, adversarial criminal justice systems typically continue to view victims as witnesses to a crime against the state, thus excluding them from the criminal justice process, except when they are needed to testify. This is a major source of dissatisfaction for victims who seek validation in the criminal justice system (Wemmers 2013).

The barriers to victims' access to justice are many and varied. They include

Legal Complexity:

- Legal processes can be daunting for victims. Understanding legal jargon, procedures, and evidentiary matters poses challenges. Hence, simplifying legal language and providing clear information can empower victims. Additionally, educating victims about their rights, legal processes, and available resources, which could be done by workshops, pamphlets, and online user-friendly platforms for legal information and services (see, e.g., the US Office for Victims of Crime web-based resources, free online training and technical assistance, and an international directory of services; the Australia-based With You We Can website; Commissioner for Victims' Rights South Australia website).

Fear and Intimidation:

- Victims may fear retaliation or intimidation from perpetrators or their associates, which can be alleviated by protective measures, such as restraining orders and

safe spaces (e.g. remote witness rooms for giving testimony). Virtual court hearings can reduce the risks victims fear and improve accessibility.
- Some victims fear dealing with the police. In some places in the USA, trained social workers have been embedded in police stations as an alternative to particularly women and children (such as those from patriarchal cultures) dealing with uniformed police officers. This has proven useful in alleviating victims' fears about 'the police' and enhancing female victims' experiences when reporting crimes. (Lord 2015)

Emotional Trauma:

- Victims often suffer emotional distress, affecting their ability to engage in legal processes (Laxminarayan 2014), so trauma-informed support services are vital. In India, for example, authorities have applied a women-centred viewpoint to re-engineer the policing of victims of gender-based violence and introduced Women's Police Stations. In so doing, the police have tackled the masculinised symbols, norms, and values that have dominated formal and informal structures in policing. Research in India (Jassal 2020; Amaral et al. 2021), Argentina (Carrington et al. 2020a, b), and Brazil (Carrington et al. 2020b; Ostermann 2003) indicates that Women's Police Stations improve and increase access to justice and are a positive development in the prevention of gender violence.
- The focus on improving responses to victims is not confined to the police. Victim support services have been professionalised in many countries. These support services are staffed with trained professionals, who are accessible for emotional support, counselling, and guidance throughout legal proceedings, and if victims need.

Of relevance to this chapter, are the failure to treat victims as genuine participants in criminal proceedings; and the omission of independent legal representation for victims. Furthermore, and where there is provision for independent legal counsel, the prohibitive expense, which begs for accessible legal aid services. In some countries, lawyers offer pro bono services to victims and there are legal clinics (e.g. USA) and partnerships with law schools (e.g. National Law University, Dwarka, Delhi, India, to which Professor K. Chockalingham contributed). The remainder of this chapter is dedicated to independent legal representation for crime victims who choose to report offences.

6 Victims' Right To Independent Legal Representation

In most criminal justice systems, crime victims play a critical role beyond being mere witnesses. Their experiences, emotions, and perspectives are essential for understanding the impact of the offence. One crucial aspect of victim participation is their right to be heard during key stages of the process, such as bail hearings, charge (plea) decisions, and sentencing. There are various arguments for and against victims having independent legal representation to advance their participatory rights.

Providing legal representation, for example, is said to ensure that victims have a level playing field. Accused persons have legal counsel to protect their rights, so victims should also have access to legal support. Conversely, some fear that victim lawyers may become emotionally invested in their client-victim's interests, which potentially could affect their objectivity, and bias could impact the overall fairness of the trial. In adversarial criminal justice systems, criminal trials primarily focus on the accused's rights and the state's case against them. In this context, over several centuries, victims' role and responsibilities have evolved to be primarily witnesses, not parties to the proceedings. Some argue that this traditional role should be maintained.

Notwithstanding the opposition to victims having independent legal representation, balancing victims' rights with practical considerations is essential. Whilst legal representation can empower victims, it must be implemented thoughtfully to ensure fairness, efficiency, and the overall integrity of the criminal justice system, and as this chapter reveals, this is not only possible but also happening.

6.1 International Criminal Justice Systems

As mentioned above, the *Rome Statute* (1998) and the *Rules and Procedures* (2002) governing the International Criminal Court provide for victim participation at all stages of the proceedings, which, according to case law, should be determined case-by-case. Although the Rome Statute provides for the protection and consideration of the victim, it is the Rules and Procedures that provide for victim participation in person or via legal counsel (Dagras 2021).

The purpose of the victim participation via independent legal representation at the Extraordinary Chambers in the Court of Cambodia is to support the prosecution during the criminal proceedings, and to seek collective and moral reparations. The proceedings were to 'be fair and adversarial and preserve a balance between the rights of the parties [which included victims]' (Internal Rule 21(1)(a)). The participation of the victims at the Extraordinary Chamber served an important function "in terms of assisting in unearthing the truth" (Khan and Rudy 2010)—for all.

6.2 Inquisitorial Criminal Justice Systems

Articles 13 and 14 of the revised EU Victims' Rights Directive (European Parliament 2026) preserve the original 2012 victim's right to formal legal assistance (see European Union Victims' Rights Directive 2012/29/EU), but it is only applicable where they have legal status as a party to the criminal proceedings. Article 57 of the Council of Europe Convention on preventing and combating violence against women and domestic also states that victims have the right to legal assistance and free legal aid under conditions provided by the respective domestic law. As well, the Council of Europe Convention on the Protection of Children against Sexual Exploitation and Sexual Abuse states that child victims are entitled to access legal assistance, including where they have status in criminal proceedings. These provisions correspond with European criminal justice systems that have traditionally granted victims substantial access to the mechanisms of justice. Although at least two countries—Germany and France—have maintained in the main inquisitorial systems, most countries have shifted to hybrid systems that blend inquisitorial and adversarial approaches.

German law affords victims the status of 'secondary (or accessory) prosecutor' (Kury and Kilchling 2011). Victims, therefore, have similar trial participatory rights as other legal counsel, including access to evidentiary documentation, the ability to make submissions, the right to cross-examine the accused, and the entitlement to make a closing argument (Pizzi and Perron 1996; Braun 2014; Kirchengast 2017). They can also make a claim for restitution (Kirchengast 2017).

In France, the Code of Criminal Procedure requires a 'judicial authority [ensure] that victims are informed and that their rights are respected throughout the criminal process'. It also authorises victims 'under the conditions' in the Code to initiate a prosecution, including having the accused summonsed. Victims have the right to be assisted by an 'advocate' (not necessarily legal counsel) during criminal proceedings. The advocate is entitled to have access to evidentiary documents and can make submissions. These procedural rights, however, are more extensive if the victim has applied for *partie civile* status. The *partie civile* has standing as a party before the court who is able to present evidence, being able to challenge court decisions, and to tender information to the court about their injuries and/or losses resulting from the crime (Hodgson 2005; Kirchengast 2017; see also *Perez v France*).

6.3 Hybrid Criminal Justice Systems

Belgium law affords victims similar status and rights (Symons 2014). Finland, Italy, Luxembourg, Portugal, and Spain also provide extensive independent legal presentation for victims (Symons 2014). Victims' representatives can access evidence, make submissions, in some circumstances examine witnesses (including cross-examining the accused), apply for restitution, and comment on sentence (Bacik et al. 1998; Symons 2014).

The Swedish criminal justice system blends an adversarial approach with an inquisitorial approach. The law distinguishes three types of victims. The 'aggrieved person' who seeks formal standing becomes an 'aggrieved party' and may apply to the court to become an 'auxiliary prosecutor'. An aggrieved party may make submissions and question witnesses. If the state prosecutor declines to prosecute, the aggrieved party may commence a private prosecution with the assistance of private counsel. The *Code of Judicial Procedure* also provides for publicly funded advisor, who may be legal counsel. The trial features elements of the inquisitorial and adversarial systems, but the engagement of victims is rooted in the traditions of the inquisitorial system.

Reforms have also been made in Austria. Like 'common law – adversarial' English criminal justice, the victim was 're-directed' from criminal to civil procedure. Reform, however, re-introduced the victim as a 'participant' in criminal proceedings. Since 2006, persons who are victims of violence (including serious threat), victims of sexual assault, stalking victims and family members (parents, spouses, domestic partners, children, grandchildren, siblings) of a person killed as the result of an offence, as well as other kin (nieces/nephews, cousins) who witnessed the offence, are eligible to claim assistance in court proceedings (*Code of Criminal Procedure*). In addition to psychological assistance, these victims can ask for 'legal assistance' (i.e. legal advice and representation in court by lawyers). The legal assistance supports, advises, and substitutes for the victim who may participate 'actively' in investigations and criminal proceedings. In some circumstances, if the prosecutor 'drops the case', the victim has the right to apply to continue with the prosecution as a subsidiary prosecutor, as well as the right to appeal passages in 'court verdicts' that refer to him/her. Irrespective of the outcome of the criminal proceedings, for victims' legal assistance, is usually free of charge.

In the Netherlands, victims of a serious criminal offence and their next of kin have the right to be treated with respect, to be given the assistance of an interpreter and/or lawyer. In certain cases, victims of serious offences can also exercise the right to address the court. (*Victims' Status (Legal Proceedings) Act*)

In Ireland, the *Criminal Justice (Victims of Crime) Act* 2017 puts the European laws regarding victims' rights into Irish law. The Irish Legal Aid Board provides legal aid (i.e. representation in court) to victims in certain cases of sexual assault. Legal advice is available to a victim in a prosecution of such cases who want advice about the matter, and this assistance is free. Legal aid is also available to a victim of certain sex offences[1] where his or her prior sexual history is being raised by the accused, or his or her defence counsel. This assistance is also free.

6.4 Adversarial Criminal Justice Systems

Victims' interests have not been historically prioritised in adversarial criminal justice systems. As Doak (2005) expounds,

> Although many victims may feel as though they are 'owed' a right to exercise a voice in decision-making processes, such as prosecution, reparation and sentencing, the criminal justice system places such rights or interests in a firmly subservient position to the collective interests of society in prosecuting the crime and imposing a denunciatory punishment (Doak 2005, pp. 299–300)

[1] Rape, aggravated sexual assault, aiding, abetting, counselling, and procuring aggravated sexual assault, incitement to aggravated sexual assault, or conspiring to commit any of the foregoing offence.

Doak's explanation is echoed by Gillen (2018),

> The main principled argument against according [victims] the rights to independent legal representation during the criminal trial is that it is difficult to see how such a scheme can fit easily into the adversarial system in which, in a criminal trial, there are only two parties: the prosecution representing the public interest in the name of the Crown on whose behalf the proceedings are brought, and the accused (Gillen 2018, p. 126).

Almost a decade before the Gillen Review, the Stern Review (2010) urged further exploration of the potential benefits of independent legal representation to support victims during the trial process. Aptly, the Stern Review commented, 'it seemed to us that the contribution they made to the victim's experience was an important one.' (Stern 2010, p. 98)

Despite a raft of law reform, policy measures and procedural changes intended to improve the experience of victims and integrate their interests in recent years, victims still are dismayed when they discover that the prosecutor does not represent them (Hunter et al. 2013). The Commissioner for Victims and Witnesses in England and Wales reported that victims were outraged that were mere witnesses in their own case and that, in contrast to the accused person, they did not have their own legal representation (Payne 2009).

Lord Styne in *Attorney General's Reference* (No. 3 of 1999) HL 14 December 2000 recognised that a modern criminal justice system should balance the accused's interests, the state's interests, and the victims' interests. She described this as a triangulation of interests. She did not go as far as to hold that victims should be entitled to independent legal representation. Doak (2008, p. 147), however, suggests that while 'a victims' right to counsel would sit very uncomfortably within the adversarial framework, it may, conceivably, not be so incompatible that it may not function at all'. Likewise, Killean (2021, p. 1) argues that the 'adversarial process does not pose an insurmountable barrier to legal representation', which, as this chapter shows, is not unprecedented (see also Pizzi 1999).

6.5 United States – Federal

The US Federal *Crime Victims' Rights Act* 2004 provides ten rights afforded to victims of federal crimes, including the right to be heard during a criminal court proceeding involving release (e.g. bail), plea (e.g. charge bargain), sentencing, or parole application (section 3771). A victim, therefore, appears to have a right to be heard before a decision affecting their rights is made (i.e. the right to be consulted, or hearing rule) and the reciprocal obligation to consult before deciding about the outcome, such as a plea bargain (i.e. the no bias rule). This duty to accord procedural fairness requires the decision-maker (e.g. the prosecutor) to give a victim a reasonable opportunity to comment in the circumstances, which might not require a formal hearing of the kind that occurs in a court; however, a court can hear an application for relief when a victim complains they have not been accorded procedural fairness.

This right is not an infringement on the state's 'independent prosecutorial discretion' (see in re *Dean*, 527 F.3d 391 (5th Cir. 2008). Furthermore, victims of certain offences (i.e. violence, including sexual assault) have a right to make an 'impact statement' at sentencing. Additionally, these rights can be enforced by independent legal representation via a motion of relief or *writ of mandamus*. Thus, counsel for victims can be critical to the enforcement of victims' rights (National Crime Victim Law Institute 2023a)—in particular, to ensure procedural fairness.

In 2006, in *Kenna v. U.S. District Court for C.D. Cal.*, the United States Federal Court in the Ninth Circuit, recognised '[t]he criminal justice system has long functioned on the assumption that crime victims should behave like good Victorian children—seen but not heard. The Crime Victims' Rights Act sought to change this by making victims independent participants in the criminal justice process.' Two decades later, the National Crime Victim Law Institute (2022) reported that, contrary to the law, too many victims can still struggle to be heard.

One of the reasons for that struggle is prohibitive legal fees. To alleviate this barrier, the US Office for Victims of Crime sponsors legal clinics, in 2023, supported by a financial grant the Equal Justice Works' Crime Victims' Advocacy Program (CVAP).This programme is staffed by a cohort of 21 Attorney Fellows based at host organisations across the USA 'to increase access to legal services for crime victims and, particularly, for victims who identify as Black, Indigenous, and People of Color' (National Crime Victim Law Institute 2023b).

Another barrier is the somewhat divided opinions amongst courts on the ambit of the right to confer. In re Wild, 994 F.3d 1244, 1327 (11th Cir. 2021), the majority [rewrote],

> the CVRA to add a blanket post-indictment limitation and [read] out of the statute any ability for crime victims to judicially enforce their conferral rights outside of a preexisting criminal proceeding.

Conversely, Hull J (dissenting (In re Wild, 955 F.3d 1196 (11th Cir. 2020)) held that the majority were incorrect 'to leave the victims "emptyhanded'. Hull J observed,

> Given the undisputed facts that the U.S. Attorney's Office completed its investigation, drafted a 53-page indictment, and negotiated for days with Epstein's defense team, the Office egregiously violated federal law and the victims' rights by (1) not conferring one minute with them (or their counsel) before striking the final [deal]; (2) intentionally and unfairly concealing the [deal] from the victims, as well as how the upcoming State Court plea hearing would directly affect them, and (3) affirmatively misrepresenting the status of the case to the victims after the [deal] was executed.

A third barrier concerns the writ of mandamus. Courts have determined that a court must find three requirements before a writ will issue,

> (1) the party seeking issuance of the writ [must] have no other adequate means to attain the relief he desires; (2) the petitioner must satisfy the burden of showing that [his] right to issuance of the writ is clear and indisputable; and (3) even if the first two prerequisites have been met, the issuing court, in the exercise of its discretion, must be satisfied that the writ is appropriate under the circumstances. (See *Cheney v. United States District Court for the District of Columbia*, U.S., 124 S.Ct. 2576, 2587, 159 L.Ed.2d 459 (2004); *Will v. United States*,389 U.S. 90, 95, 88 S.Ct. 269, 274, 19 L.Ed.2d 305 (1967))

Mindful of these requirements, courts have granted the writ on occasions. In re *W.R. Huff Asset Management Co.* 409 F.3d 555 (2d Cir. 2005) the Second Circuit Court applied the 'plain language test' then concluded that the US Congress had "chosen [the mandamus remedy] as a mechanism by which a crime victim may appeal" a trial court's denial of relief under the *Crime Victims' Rights Act* 2004. Moreover, a *Crime Victims' Rights Act* mandamus petitioner 'need not overcome the hurdles' associated with a traditional mandamus proceeding. Likewise, the Ninth Circuit Court (see *Kenna v. United States District Court for the Central District of California* 435 F.3d 1011 (9th Cir. 2006) @ 1017 stated that the traditional mandamus requirements were not required because the Crime Victims' Rights Act,

> … contemplates active review of orders denying victims' rights claims even in routine cases. … The [mandamus provisions create] a unique regime that does, in fact, contemplate routine interlocutory review of district court decisions denying rights asserted under the statute.

Contrary, in re *Antrobus* (0519 F.3d 1123, 1125 (10th Cir. 2008) a 1124-25) the 10th Circuit Court commented,

> [W]here Congress borrows terms of art in which are accumulated the legal tradition and meaning of centuries of practice, it presumably knows and adopts the cluster of ideas that were attached to each borrowed word in the body of learning from which it was taken and the meaning its use will convey to the judicial mind unless otherwise instructed.

Hence, after applying the 'plain English test', the Court applied the 'traditional' mandamus requirements. Likewise, in *Dean* 527 F.3d 391 (5th Cir. 2008), the 5th Circuit Court applied the traditional requirements. So divergent were the courts' opinions that Tobolowsky (2015) has described the status of the law as the 'mandamus muddle', that could be resolved by legislative amendment if the US Congress had the will. Until such amendment is made, or the issue is resolved before the United States Supreme Court, 'courts will likely continue to construe the timing of the conferral right differently' (Cook 2021, p. 568) while also independent legal representatives continue to petition for the enforcement of victims' rights.

6.6 Japan

The Japanese criminal justice system operates on adversarial principles but without juries as 'tribunals of fact'. In 2009, Japan adapted the German law giving victims status as a co-accuser in serious criminal cases (Matsui 2020). As well, the Japanese state funds the victim's lawyer if he/she cannot afford the legal fees. These reforms are attributed to the lobbying of a defence lawyer whose family and firsthand experiences revealed to him the ordeals victims face in a system too heavily weight against them.

6.7 Ireland

The Gillen Review (2019) in Northern Ireland examined the question of whether the adversarial court processes of that country ought to provide publicly funded legal representation for victims of serious sexual offences. For many victims, Gillen (2018, pp. 127–128) observed in a preliminary report, 'the absence of a legally trained advocate acting on their behalf is both shocking and upsetting. Complainants are often left feeling vulnerable and exposed, merely seen as "collateral damage" in a process to which they are not a party and have no independent voice.' He continued, 'The adversarial focus that underpins cross-examination at trial provides a risk of re-traumatisation for complainants. The use of advocates who are legally trained means that complainants are likely to see less use of the myths and misconceptions that may be invoked currently by defence teams. These are damaging on many levels' (Gillen 2018, pp. 127–128).

Since the Gillen Review (2019), Northern Ireland has introduced a Sex Offences Legal Officers programme that is cost free for victims of serious sex offences. These legal officers may provide advice before a victim reports the offence, and during proceedings, may make submissions regarding disclosure of medical records and sexual history (for a discussion on pros and cons of this programme see Iliadis et al. 2021a).

6.8 Scotland

In Scotland, to avoid unnecessary intrusions on the privacy and dignity of victims of sex offences there are prohibitions in relation to counselling and medical records, and physical property (e.g. mobile phone). The Scottish Appellate High Court Justiciary considered the existing law in *RR v Her Majesty's Advocate & LV* [2021] HCJAC 21. The Court acknowledged that victims of crime have a right 'to respect for private and family life'. The Court held, 'In the absence of statutory intervention, the system of criminal prosecution remains an adversarial one between the Crown and the accused. The [victim's] status is still that of a witness to the facts libelled.' For this and other reasons given, the Court found, 'it is the duty of the Crown to ascertain a [a sex offence victim's] position in relation to a section 275 application [i.e., to elicit evidence of the victim's bad character or sexual history] and to present that position to the court, irrespective of the Crown's attitude to it and/or the application.' Thus, until the right to legal representation becomes the law, victims of sex offences must rely on the prosecutor to voice their views—a situation that has proven unsatisfactory (see, e.g., Raitt 2010).

Since then, the First Minister announced in March 2023 that her government would introduce a bill that, amongst other reforms, would provide for free, independent legal representation for victims of sex offences (Scottish Government 2023). Victims would, therefore, counsel when courts are hearing applications (mostly made by the accused) to lead evidence of their sexual history in court or so-called 'bad character'. The reform follows a recommendation made in a cross-justice review on improving the management of sexual offences. The review emphasised the importance of victims being provided with automatic independent legal representation to better protect their rights.

6.9 Victims' Right to Independent Legal Representation in India

There have been many reforms to victim-centred laws in India (Nagpal & Rawandale 2023; Pradeep 2021), but it has often been the criminal courts that have driven change. For example, in the case of *Delhi Domestic Working Women's Forum v Union of India* 1995 SCC (1) 14, the Court gave specific guidelines on assisting victims of sexual assault access justice. The Court referred to *Modem Legal Studies Rape and the Legal Process* by Jennifer Temkin (1987), and specifically cited Temkin's assertion that '[c]hanges in the substantive law might also be helpful in producing new ways of thinking about [sexual assault]'. Acknowledging the importance of a victim-centric approach, the Court held it is necessary victims of 'sexual assault cases [are] provided with legal representation'. The Court continued, 'Legal assistance will have to be provided at the police station since the victim of sexual assault might very well be in a distressed state upon arrival at the police station, the guidance and support of a lawyer at this stage and whilst she was being questioned would be of great assistance to her.' In addition, the Court recommended that a list of legal advocates willing to assist victims of sexual assault should be kept at police stations; and that the police should ask a court to appoint a legal advocate, which should happen expediently, so as not to further burden the victim.

In Indian law, the victims' right to independent legal representation is found in sections 301 and 302 Criminal Procedure Code, which govern the conduct of criminal prosecutions before all courts. Section 301 provides for legal representation for the 'aggrieved person' (i.e. the victim) in a criminal case in any criminal court. The victim's legal representative, however, is required to act on the directions of the Public Prosecutor or Assistant Prosecutor who has the responsibility of conducting the prosecution. There is a further limitation because the victim's legal representative and may 'submit written arguments after the evidence is closed in the case' only with the permission of the Court. Hence, a victim cannot initiate a criminal prosecution, introduce evidence or cross-examine witnesses. Section 302 provides for an exception in cases before the Magistrates Court. The section authorises a magistrate who is hearing a case to 'permit the prosecution to be conducted by any person other than a police officer below the rank of inspector' to conduct the prosecution personally or by a legal representative. Thus, the victim is conceived as a 'third party' in criminal proceedings before a magistrate.

In *J.K. International v. State (Govt. of NCT of Delhi) & Ors*. [(2001) 3 SCC 462], the Supreme Court considered sections 301 and 302. The Court held that the 'scheme envisaged in the Code of Criminal procedure does not preclude the victim (in person or through a legal representative) from 'ventilating' their grievance, even if the police conducted the investigation and laid the charge, or the Public Prosecutor has authority over the conduct of the prosecution. ... a private person who is aggrieved by the offence involved in the case is not altogether debarred from participating in the trial.' Notable also are the comments of the Supreme Court in *Dhariwal Industries Ltd. v. Kishore Wadhwani* [(2016) 10 SCC 378] that it would be open to a magistrate to consider a victim's request to prosecute criminal cases before the Magistrates Court. Moreover, such permission should be granted if it 'serves the ends of justice'. The Supreme Court, however, pointed out that whenever a public prosecutor was conducting the prosecution, the victim (or their legal representative) should not be permitted to undermine the public prosecutor's role (see also *Shiv Kumar vs Hukam Chand And Anr* (1999) SC CR R 789), which Hemant Gupta J said is "to assist the Court to do justice rather than to be vindictive and take side with any of the parties" (*Amir Hamza Shaikh & Ors. v. State of Maharshtra & Anr.* [(2019) 8 SCC 387]).

The role of a victim's legal representative has been explored in other cases. Whether a victim's legal representative, for instance, should be given a free and independent hand to conduct prosecution arose in *Amir Hamza Shaikh & Ors. v. State of Maharshtra & Anr*. [(2019) 8 SCC 387]. The Supreme Court observed,

> The rights of victims, and indeed victimology, is an evolving jurisprudence and it is more than appropriate to move forward in a positive direction, rather than stand still or worse, take a step backward. A voice has been given to victims of crime by Parliament and the judiciary and that voice needs to be heard, and if not already heard, it needs to be raised to a higher decibel so that it is clearly heard.

In reaching its conclusion, the Court also noted,

> In *Mallikarjun Kodagali*, this Court approved the Justice Malimath Committee, wherein the victim's right to participate in the criminal proceedings which includes right to be impleaded, right to know, right to be heard and right to assist the court in the pursuit of truth had been recognised.

The Court held,

> ... though the Magistrate is not bound to grant permission at the mere asking but the victim has a right to assist the Court in a trial before the Magistrate. The Magistrate may consider as to whether the victim is in a position to assist the Court and as to whether the trial does not involve such complexities which cannot be handled by the victim. On satisfaction of such facts, the Magistrate would be within its jurisdiction to grant of permission to the victim to take over the inquiry of the pendency before the Magistrate.

To what extent a victim's legal representative can participate at a criminal trial was considered by the Supreme Court in *Rekha Murarka v. State of West Bengal & Anr.* [(2020) 2 SCC 474]. The Supreme Court's decision rested on the word "assist" (see section 24(8) Criminal Procedure Code), which the Court determined Parliament intended to mean a victim's legal representative role was to support the prosecutor rather than be a co-prosecutor. a legal representative can suggest questions of cross-examination to the Public Prosecutor but cannot directly examine or cross-examine witnesses. Furthermore, an independent legal representative could also bring victim's questions to the court's attention then the court might invoke its powers in relation to criminal procedure and evidence and out the questions to a witness.

Section 372 of the Code of Criminal Procedure allows victims who are dissatisfied with a judgement or order to seek review by a higher court. Pursuant to this section, only the victim has a right of appeal (see *State of Karnataka v. Malleshnaika*, 5 September, 2023). The section acknowledges the importance for victims of judicial review to ensure access to justice (Shekhar and Ranjani 2023). Victims have recourse if they believe there are errors or injustices in a lower court's decision. This section indicates victims' interests and the state's interests can operate independent of each other without jeopardising the accused's interests.

In summary, the law provides victims with participatory rights, but these rights have been shaped through the criminal courts. Court rulings have, on the one hand, acknowledged victims' rights to participate but, on the other hand, confined these rights. Victims are not co-prosecutors. When their interests' conflict with the Public Prosecutors, the Public Prosecutor's interests will prevail. Victims can initiate prosecutions in the Magistrates Court but not in any court where the Public Prosecutor is in control of prosecutions. Victims have no right to cross-examine witnesses but can avail themselves of other avenues to pose their questions. Variously, courts have justified their stances as necessary to ensure that victims' rights do not unduly compromise accused persons' rights, and to mitigate the risk that public justice should become *vindictive justice*—both issues that Professor Chockalingham has consistently put forth as paramount, though he also asserts that a better balance than currently exists, can be struck.

6.10 Victims' Right to Independent Legal Representation in Australia

Australia on colonisation inherited the British common law and the adversarial criminal justice system. Traditionally, therefore Australia's domestic law paid little attention to crime victims (Kirchengast 2011). Since the 1980s, however, there has been a greater focus on victims' rights and their needs, but the implementation of the state- and territory-based instruments has been patchy, so many victims still do not have their rights fulfilled (O'Connell 2015, 2020, 2021).

In 2007, Cummins J observed that a modern criminal justice system should ensure a 'fairer balance between the rights of offenders and the rights of victims' (*DPP v Dupas* [2007] VSC 305). Later as the head of the Victorian Law Commission, Cummins J recommended that victims should be acknowledged and treated as genuine participants in the criminal justice system. In a report on victims and criminal justice, the Law Commission noted the progress made to achieve this in South Australia.

Prior to the election in March 2006, the Labor Government in South Australia declared that if re-elected it would introduce law to create a Commissioner for Victims' Rights. The Government did not specify the commissioner's functions, but after being re-elected the Attorney-General introduced amendments to the Victims of Crime Act 2001 that listed the commissioner's functions and authorities. These amendments were enacted and came into operation in July 2018. Controversially, the commissioner can, in person or through legal counsel, appear in criminal proceedings as provided in the Victims of Crime Act or another Act. A further amendment provided for the victim to approve a representative to exercise his or her rights, and that representative may be the commissioner or legal counsel selected by the commissioner. These laws, coupled with other state laws, have led to victims being represented throughout the criminal justice process.

The first Commissioner for Victims' Rights (O'Connell 2012, 2017, 2020) asserted that independent counsel is warranted out of procedural fairness. He claimed victims should not be bystanders in a system that would collapse without their cooperation. Table 1 presents the distinct stages in the criminal justice process in South Australia, and the issues for which the Commissioner for Victims' Rights engaged legal representatives for victims. Overwhelmingly, feedback from the counsel (who were prominent defence counsel) was positive. None declared any undue infringement of the rights of accused persons. Several reported they gained a better insight into victims' interests, which they valued. Most observed a notable change in prosecutors and defence counsel attitudes towards victims. One lawyer said he had had strong reservations but would now be a strong advocate; and another said lawyers for victims held prosecutors to account and made their decisions more transparent.

Overall, most lawyers who had represented victims accepted the reform as necessarily modernising the adversarial criminal trial consistent with changed public standards.

Victims also reported 'remarkable' changes in how they were treated by prosecutors and others, and importantly, many felt their voices were heard because they had 'their lawyers'. Some judicial officers embraced the 'reform'. In *Steele's case*, for instance, Gray J in the Supreme Court ruled that victims' families were interested persons entitled to be heard on applications to revoke or vary court orders on the detention or conditions of release of mentally incompetent offenders.

Iliadis (2020) studied the role and functions of the Commissioner for Victims' Rights in South Australia, which also cover the commissioner's engagement with independent legal representation for victims. She noted, 'Police officers, prosecutors, magistrates and judges, and defence counsel, despite initial wariness, and even opposition, have recognised the potential to improve the administration of justice by having a "third voice."' (p. 120) Most of the respondents in her study said the commissioner's interventions in person and through legal counsel had not undermined the adversarial process. Though she noted the advantages to those victims who had received funded legal representation, she also pointed to ways the commissioner's

Table 1 Key stages in criminal proceedings where victims may benefit from independent legal representation

Stage	Sub-stage/Issue	Notes/Examples
Charge/plea bargaining	Withdrawal of charge	9A of the Victims of Crime Act—a victim of serious offence entitled to be consulted in relation to certain decisions, and S32A of the Act empowers a victim to appoint an 'approve representative', such as legal counsel, to exercise a right
	Variation of charge	
Criminal proceedings	Stay of proceedings	*R v Lowe* (attempted murder, South Australia)—the Court approved a lawyer representing the victim to make submissions after the accused applied to stay proceedings
	Suppression order	R v Peet (3 counts of murder, South Australia)—a lawyer applied successfully in the Magistrates Court for a suppression order to protect the privacy of a surviving sibling, and later the Supreme Court upheld the order
	Protected communications	S14 of the Victims of Crime Act prohibits unnecessary intrusion on a victim's privacy. District Court granted permission for the victim of a sexual assault to be represented by legal counsel during a *voir dire* to decide if Medicare records are protected
Sentencing	Victim impact statements	S10 of the Victims of Crime Act—a victim is entitled to have impact of offence considered by sentencing court S32A of the Act empowers a victim to appoint an 'approve representative', such as legal counsel, to exercise this right
	Mentally incompetent offenders	S10 of the Victims of Crime Act—a victim is entitled to have impact of offence considered by sentencing court. Courts have endorsed victims making impact statements in these cases prior to the court imposing the 'sanction'. S32A of the Act empowers a victim to appoint an 'approve representative', such as legal counsel, to exercise this right
Post-Proceedings/ Sentence	Revocation or Variation of 'Licence' (Mental Incompetence)	R v Steele [2012] SASC 162 – Gray J held that the family of a deceased person (who under South Australian law are crime victims) could be represented by legal counsel on the offender's application to vary the licence order
	Revocation of Anti-Violence Order (Domestic Violence)	Before varying or revoking an intervention order, the Magistrates Court must allow each person protected by the order a reasonable opportunity to be heard on the matter. For this purpose, that person may be represented by legal counsel, which happened in a case after the police refused to assist the victim challenge an application to revoke an order

Note: This table illustrates procedural stages where independent legal representation can amplify victims' voices and safeguard their rights limited budget for legal services restrained interventions through counsel. She observed that the commissioner funding cases 'ad hoc' and not being able to offer funded counsel to all victims, risked creating a 'hierarchy' of victims. Notwithstanding, Iliadis' study (2020) favours O'Connell's (2017, 2020, 2021, 2023) assertions that the inroads made are *prima facie* significant in facilitating a better balance, albeit not a complete balance, of the competing *triangulation of interests*. Kirchengast et al. (2019) concluded,

> South Australia's experience rejects the notion that victims ought to be relegated as witnesses for the prosecution and instead suggests a significant step toward victims gaining more comprehensive participatory rights in that state's criminal justice system. (p. 19)

Two Australian states—Queensland and New South Wales—already have law that gives victims of sexual assault the right to be legally represented when challenging defence applications for the disclosure of their counselling notes and other confidential therapeutic records. These laws, however, do not extend to legal representation during the criminal trial. Though the impact of these laws victims has not been adequately evaluated, Braun (2014) suggests they make the process less harmful for victims.

In addition, there are three pilot programmes offering specialised and trauma-informed legal services for victims of sexual assault. In Victoria, Legal Aid, Djirra, and the Women's Legal Service collaborated to provide a state-wide Victims Legal Service that offers legal information for victims of sexual assault through an existing Helpline, and targeted advice and case work for victims seeking to protect confidential communications (which in some cases has led to victims being represented in court). This pilot also provides tailored support for Aboriginal victims to report sexual assault to police. In Western Australia, the Women's Legal Service, Aboriginal Family Legal Services, and Ruah Legal Services collaborated to provide state-wide, integrated, specialised, and trauma-informed legal services for victims, at known points of victim disengagement and withdrawal from the legal process. And, in the Australian Capital Territory, the Women's Legal Centre and Victim Support ACT established the ACT Sexual Assault Legal Service to provide legal assistance (including legal representation) to support victims to engage with the criminal justice system. The pilot also offers 'wrap-around services' for victims, including financial assistance, counselling, and specialist support. The over-arching aim of the pilots is to identify ways "to provide legal services for sexual violence victims and survivors that do not add to their trauma" (Dreyfus and Rishworth 2023). Although these pilot programmes are a positive development, anecdote indicates that they are under-funded, and there is little funding allocated for an empirically sound evaluation.

Notwithstanding the ongoing pilots, *With You We Can* is amongst those who continue to campaign for victims of sex offences to be assisted by independent legal representation throughout the criminal justice system. The non-government organisation is calling on governments to fund legal representation to enhance victims' treatment in the legal process and reduce, even prevent, re-traumatisation. Although this would be an important step in the right direction, and one that should be taken, it would leave victims of other offences behind.

In 2016, the Victorian Law Reform Commission opposed permitting victims to be independently represented, because, the Commission commented, the police and prosecutors are obliged to keep victims informed about the investigation and prosecution respectively, and introducing independent legal representation for victims could result in 'dual representation' (see also on dual representation for the victim Kirchengast et al. 2019). Iliadis and Braun (2021), however, assert that 'this fails to recognise victims have legitimate interests that might compete with the interests of the prosecution, who represent the public interest'. Contrary to the Victorian Law Reform Commission's view, the Victoria Royal Commission into Family Violence (2016) recommended that all Magistrates Courts and specialist family violence division courts should be equipped with 'facilities for access to specialist family violence service providers and legal representation for applicants and respondents'. Iliadis and her colleagues (2021b) pointed out that the Royal Commission, however, fully enunciate its recommendation, but it did identify independent legal representation as an 'imperative to make the court experience safer and more accessible for [intimate partner violence] victims'. Furthermore, the Royal Commission (2016) suggested that independent legal representation for victims during contested proceedings on family violence protection orders would serve to 'alleviate the burden' victims experienced.

7 Benefits of Independent Legal Representation

Independent legal representation for crime victims offers several crucial benefits, ensuring their rights and well-being throughout the criminal justice process. Several studies have found that victims' satisfaction with the criminal justice system also improves. Alternatively, fear of re-traumatisation can lead to a decrease in the number of victims willing to report crime and fulfil their roles and responsibilities as a witness. Such disengagement is detrimental to the criminal justice system. As Karmen (2010) suggested, the criminal justice system would collapse without the cooperation of victims.

Experiences of trauma can be a barrier to effective victim participation. These experiences can be exacerbated by the criminal trial process: for instance victims often face aggressive and inappropriate questioning during trials (Symons 2014; Skinner and Smith 2021). In a preliminary report, for example, the Gillen review (2018, p. 127), commented,

> Research suggests that providing legal representation to complainants to support them through the criminal justice process can be effective at reducing secondary trauma, reducing attrition and thus may improve low conviction rates. It is the most effective way of supporting complainants during trials.

In various countries, independent legal representatives provide support, aid, and advice that prevent trauma-inducing experiences. Research confirms that the presence of a victim's lawyer has 'a highly significant effect on victims' level of confidence when giving evidence and meant that the hostility rating for the defence lawyer was much lower' (Backik et al. 1998, pp. 17–18).

Most victims are lacking legal literacy, so legal representatives can guide victims through process and procedures to ensure, their privacy rights, as well as other rights, are respected and fulfilled. For example, in Canada, victims of sexual assault can have independent legal representation to advise them on applications for access to medical and therapy records by invoking their own privacy and equality rights. According to Canadian Crown Counsel, '[in regard to disclosure of medical records for victims of sexual assault] everyone takes it more seriously [when there is independent counsel for the victim' (Mohr 2002, pp. 16–17).

Between 2018 and 2020, England ran a Sexual Violence Complainants' Advocate scheme. This engaged lawyers to provide legal advice and support to victims of sexual violence in Northumbria (a mainly rural county). In their final report, Smith and Daly (2023) identified 'a clear legal basis for providing (limited) legal advocacy' to rape victims. The researchers found that victims benefitted from more considered and relevant evidence requests, and that there were over time fewer requests. They also found that the victims who were able to use the scheme had positive experiences and had an increased sense of confidence in the criminal justice process. Furthermore, all participants (i.e. police, Crown Prosecution Services, participating lawyers, support workers, and other stakeholders) agreed the scheme had no impact on the accused's right to a fair trial.

Hence, independent legal representation allows victims to actively participate, ensuring their voices are heard and their interests protected (O'Connell 2017, 2020, 2021). However, victims' independent legal representation, not only benefits them but also supports the state's prosecution efforts and leads to better substantive justice outcomes (O'Connell 2021). There is, as the UNODC noted in reference to the rights and needs of victims of human trafficking, 'a clear relationship between the victims' access to legal representation and successful prosecution outcomes'.

8 Conclusion

Professor Chockalingham said, 'Justice is a delicate and complicated task' (2016, p. 3). Crime victims' access to justice is not a mere aspiration; it is a fundamental right. By addressing barriers, providing support, and promoting legal literacy, societies can bridge the gap between victims and justice. Empowering victims contributes to a fairer and more compassionate legal system that, given the importance of victims in the administration of justice, they deserve.

Despite the dramatic expansion of victims' rights in international and domestic laws, victims still feel alienated and ignored, as well as revictimised by the criminal justice process. This chapter proposed independent legal representation as a remedy. Independent legal representation for victims is an existing concept in countries with traditionally inquisitorial justice systems and an evolving concept in international and adversarial justice systems.

Independent legal representation would ensure victims are fully informed about their rights, role, and responsibilities in the criminal justice system, ensure they are meaningfully engaged in decision-making that affects them, and advance their participatory rights. Independent legal representatives would not have the constraints or conflicts that oblige prosecutors to be objective and impartial, but rather they would afford greater support for victims' interests throughout the criminal justice process, including pre-trial and during trial.

Although the jurisdictional examples demonstrate the independent legal representation is possible in an adversarial criminal justice system, they also give rise to a crucial question, which is funding for that representation. The Commissioner for Victims' Rights provided funds 'ad hoc' to enforce victims' procedural rights and ensure their voices were heard. If victims are to gain the right to independent legal representation, this issue must be resolved. International guidelines recommend that victims be given access to legal aid, which should be considered.

Independent legal representation for crime victims is not a luxury; it is a necessity that brings benefits as shown by jurisdictions with legal systems that have integrated victims' interests, which can serve as models for others. Learning from successful approaches is essential. Empowering victims, respecting their rights, and providing compassionate support, a more just and inclusive criminal justice system is possible—that is a system where victims are not 'bystanders', relegated to witnesses for the state, but rather active participants in seeking equal and equitable access to justice for all.

The jurisdictional examples as well as empirically sound, though limited, research findings and anecdotal measures outlined will be welcomed by many victims, victim support workers, and others urging reform. Notwithstanding, whether such reform in adversarial criminal justice systems is, at least in the 'eyes' of traditionalists, yet to be shown to be doctrinally and procedurally sound, especially for those presumed innocent but accused. This chapter, however, suggests this can be achieved without unduly impacting the rights of those presumed to be innocent.

International Instruments

Basic Principles and Guidelines on the Right to a Remedy and Reparation for Victims of Gross Violations of International Human Rights Law and Serious Violations of International Humanitarian Law (2005) <https://www.ohchr.org/en/instruments-mechanisms/instruments/basic-principles-and-guidelines-right-remedy-and-reparation#:~:text=In%20accordance%20with%20its%20domestic,violations%20of%20international%20humanitarian%20law>

Convention against Transnational Organized Crime (2000) and Protocols

Declaration of Basic Principles of Justice for Victims of Crime and Abuse of Power (1985). <https://www.ohchr.org/en/instruments-mechanisms/instruments/declaration-basic-principles-justice-victims-crime-and-abuse>
Declaration on the Protection of All Persons from Enforced Disappearance (1992)
International Convention for the Protection of All Persons from Enforced Disappearance (2006)
Rome Statute
Rules of Procedure and Evidence
UN Model Legislative Provision to Support the Needs of and Protect the Rights of Victims of Terrorism (2022) <https://www.un.org/counterterrorism/sites/www.un.org.counterterrorism/files/220204_model_legislative_provisions.pdf>
UN Principles and Guidelines on Access to Legal Aid in Criminal Justice Systems (2013) <https://www.unodc.org/documents/justice-and-prison-reform/UN_principles_and_guidlines_on_access_to_legal_aid.pdf>
Universal Declaration on Human Rights (1948) <https://www.ohchr.org/sites/default/files/UDHR/Documents/UDHR_Translations/eng.pdf>

Regional Instruments

Council of Europe Convention on preventing and combating violence against women and domestic
Council of Europe Convention on the Protection of Children against Sexual Exploitation and Sexual Abuse
European Union Victims' Rights Directive 2012/29/EU

Domestic Instruments

Code of Criminal Procedure (Austria)
Code of Criminal Procedure (India)
Code of Judicial Procedure (Sweden)
Crime Victims' Rights Act 2004 (USA)
Criminal Justice (Victims of Crime) Act 2017 (Ireland)
Victims of Crime Act (South Australia) 2001
Victims, Witnesses, and Justice Reform (Scotland) Bill 2023
Victims' Status (Legal Proceedings) Act (Netherlands)

Case Law

Amir Hamza Shaikh & Ors. v. State of Maharshtra & Anr. [(2019) 8 SCC 387]
Antrobus (0519 F.3d 1123, 1125 (10th Cir. 2008)
Attorney General's Reference (No. 3 of 1999) HL 14 December 2000
Bremer Vulkan Schiffbau und Maschinenfabrik v South India Shipping Corporation Ltd [1981] AC 909
Cheney v. United States District Court for the District of Columbia, U.S., 124 S.Ct. 2576, 2587, 159 L.Ed.2d 459 (2004)
Dean, 527 F.3d 391 (5th Cir. 2008)
Delhi Domestic Working Women's Forum v Union of India 1995 SCC (1) 14
Delhi Domestic Working Women's Forum v Union of India 1995 SCC (1) 14
Dhariwal Industries Ltd. v. Kishore Wadhwani [(2016) 10 SCC 378]
DPP v Dupas [2007] VSC 305
J.K. International v. State (Govt. of NCT of Delhi) & Ors. [(2001) 3 SCC 462]
Kenna v. United States District Court for the Central District of California 435 F.3d 1011 (9th Cir. 2006)
Perez v France, Admissibility and merits, ECHR [2004] application number 47287/99
R v Steele (No.2) [2012] SASC 162
Rekha Murarka v. State of West Bengal & Anr. [(2020) 2 SCC 474]
RR v Her Majesty's Advocate & LV [2021] HCJAC 21
Shiv Kumar vs Hukam Chand and Anr (1999) SC CR R 789)
State of Karnataka v. Malleshnaika, 5 September, 2023
W.R. Huff Asset Management Co. 409 F.3d 555 (2d Cir. 2005)
Wild, 955 F.3d 1196 (11th Cir. 2020)
Wild, 994 F.3d 1244, 1327 (11th Cir. 2021)
Will v. United States,389 U.S. 90, 95, 88 S.Ct. 269, 274, 19 L.Ed.2d 305 (1967))

References

Amaral S, Bhalotra S, Prakash N (2021) Gender, crime and punishment: evidence from women police stations in India. CESifo Working Paper No. 9002. https://doi.org/10.2139/ssrn.3827615
Backik I, Maunsell C, Gogan S (1998) The legal process and victims of rape, Rape Crisis Centre, Dublin, & School of Law, Trinity College. http://www.drcc.ie/wp-content/uploads/2011/03/rapevic.pdf
Bacik I, Maunsell C, Gogan S (1998) The victim in the criminal justice system. Dublin Rape Crisis Centre. drcc_1998_analysis_legal_process_for_rape_vicims_1998.pdf
Braun K (2014) Legal representation for sexual assault victims — possibilities for law reform? Curr Issues Crime Crim Justice 25(3):819–837. https://www.austlii.edu.au/au/journals/CICrimJust/2014/6.pdf
Carrington K, Guala N, Puyol MV, Sozzo M (2020a) How Women's Police Stations empower women, widen access to justice and prevent gender violence. Int J Crime Just Soc Democr 9(1):42–67. https://doi.org/10.5204/ijcjsd.v9i1.1494

Carrington K, Sozzo M, Guala N, Puyol MV (2020b) How Women's Police Stations prevent gender violence. Centre for Justice Briefing Paper, April. https://research.qut.edu.au/pgv/wp-content/uploads/sites/249/2020/04/Briefing-Paper-Carrington-V3-20042020-Revised.pdf

Cherif Bassiouni M (2006) International recognition of victims' rights. Hum Rights Law Rev 6(2):203–279. https://doi.org/10.1093/hrlr/ngl009

Chockalingham K (2016) Comments. In: Gawai MB (ed) Verbatim Report: seminar on sentencing in criminal cases for High Court Justices heading criminal division. 4–6 March. NJA, Bhopal, MP. https://nja.gov.in/Concluded_Programes_2015-16/Verbatim_Reports/P-.976%20Verbatim%20Report.pdf

Cook LK (2021) A victim's right to confer under the crime victim's rights act. Campbell Law Rev 43:543

Cousins A (2020) Closing the justice gap for adult and child sexual assault rethinking the adversarial trial. Palgrave McMillan, Sydney

Dagras M (2021) The protection of victims under international criminal law. August 19. https://doi.org/10.2139/ssrn.3908146

Derrington JS. (2018) Access to justice in modern legal practice - what does it mean. https://www.fedcourt.gov.au/digital-law-library/judges-speeches/justice-s-derrington/s-derrington-j-20180530

Doak J (2005) Victims' rights in criminal trials: prospects for participation. J Law Soc 32(2):294–316. https://doi.org/10.1111/j.1467-6478.2005.00325.x

Doak J (2008) Victims' rights, human rights and criminal justice: reconceiving the role of third parties. Hart Publishing, Oxford

Dreyfus HM, Rishworth HA (2023) Supporting victims and survivors of sexual violence-piloting new legal services models. Media Release. Government of Australia: Attorney-General's Department. https://ministers.ag.gov.au/media-centre/supporting-victims-and-survivors-sexual-violence-piloting-new-legal-services-models-20-09-2023

European Parliament (2026) Victims of crime: Improved legal protection and support systems. Press Release, 21 May, Ref.: 20260513IPR43311. https://www.europarl.europa.eu/news/en/press-room/20260513IPR43311/victims-of-crime-improved-legal-protection-and-support-systems

Fenwork H (1997) Procedural 'rights' of victims of crime: public or private ordering of the criminal justice process? Mod Law Rev 60(3). https://doi.org/10.1111/1468-2230.00083

Gillen J (2018) Preliminary report into the law and procedures in serious sexual offences in Northern Ireland, vols 1–2. Department of Justice, Belfast

Gillen J (2019) Report into the law and procedures in serious sexual offences in Northern Ireland. Department of Justice, Belfast. https://niopa.qub.ac.uk/bitstream/NIOPA/9384/1/gillen-report-may-2019.pdf

Herman J (1997) Trauma and recovery: the aftermath of violence - from domestic abuse to political terror. Basic Book

Hodgson J (2005) French criminal justice: a comparative account of the investigation and prosecution of crime in France. Hart Publishing, Oxford

https://pure.manchester.ac.uk/ws/portalfiles/portal/216121711/FULL_TEXT.PDF

Hunter G, Jacobson J, Kirby A (2013) Out of the shadows: victims' and witnesses' experiences of attending the Crown Court. Victim Support, London

Iliadis M (2020) Adversarial justice and victims' rights reconceptualising the role of sexual assault victims. Routledge, London, UK

Iliadis M, Braun K (2021) Sexual assault victims can easily be re-traumatised going to court — here's one way to stop this. The Conversation, March 25. https://theconversation.com/sexual-assault-victims-can-easily-be-re-traumatised-going-to-court-heres-one-way-to-stop-this-157428

Iliadis M, Smith, Doak J (2021a) Independent separate legal representation for rape complainants in adversarial systems: lessons from Northern Ireland. J Law Soc 48(2):250–272. https://doi.org/10.1111/jols.12295

Iliadis M, Fitz-Gibbon K, Walklate S (2021b) Improving justice responses for victims of intimate partner violence: examining the merits of the provision of independent legal representation. Int J Comp Appl Crim Justice 45(1):105–114

Jassal N (2020) Gender, law enforcement, and access to justice: evidence from all-women police stations in India. Am Polit Sci Rev 114(4):1035–1054. https://doi.org/10.1017/S0003055420000684

Karmen A (2010) Crime Victims: An Introduction to Victimology. Cengage Learning.

Khan KAA, Rudy D (2010) The right of the Civil Parties to participate v. the right of the Accused to a fair and expeditious trial: challenges at the ECCC? Justice and Reconciliation in Cambodia. http://otjr.crim.ox.ac.uk/materials/papers/41/KhanandRudy_TheRightofCivilPartiesvTheRightoftheAccused.pdf

Killean R (2021) Legal representation for sexual assault complaints. In: Killean R, Dowds E, McAlinden A (eds) Sexual violence on trial. Routledge, London, UK, Chapter 14

Kirchengast T (2011) The integration of victim lawyers into the adversarial criminal trial. In: Lee M, Mason G, Milivojeic S (eds) Proceedings of the 4th Annual Australian and New Zealand Critical Criminology Conference, Sydney Institute of Criminology, Sydney Law School, University of Sydney, 1–2 July 2010, pp 1–6

Kirchengast T (2017) Victimology and victim rights international comparative perspectives. Routledge, London

Kirchengast T, Iliadis M, O'Connell M (2019) Developing charter rights through the office of commissioner of victims' rights: integrity, access and justice for victims of crime. Monash Univ Law Rev 45(1):1–28

Kury H, Kilchling M (2011) Accessory prosecution in Germany: legislation and implementation. In: Erez E, Kilchling M, Wemmers J-A (eds) Therapeutic jurisprudence and victim participation in justice, international perspectives. Carolina Academic Press, Durham, North Carolina, pp 41–65

Laxminarayan M (2014) Psychological effects of criminal proceedings through contact with the judge: the moderating effect of legal system structure. Psychol Crime Law 20(8):781–797

Lord V (2015) All women police units in the US: been there. Done that. Do it again. In: Shekhar B (ed) Creating a space for women & child victims of crime. Department of Criminology and Criminal Justice, Manonmaniam Sundaranar University, Tirunelveli, India, pp 55–62

Matsui S (2020) Victim participation in the criminal process in Japan. Hastings J Crime Punish 1:303. https://repository.uclawsf.edu/hastings_journal_crime_punishment/vol1/iss3/4

McAsey B (2011) Victim participation at the international criminal court and its impact on procedural fairness. Aust Int Law J 18:105

McDonald S (2021) Access to justice for victims of crime. Victims of Crime Research No. 12. https://www.justice.gc.ca/eng/rp-pr/cj-jp/victim/rd12-rr12/p4.html

Mohr R (2002) Words are not enough: sexual assault – legislation, education and information. Department of Justice, Canada

Mullen T (2016) Access to justice in administrative law and administrative justice. In: Palmer E, Conford T, Guinchard A, Marique Y (eds) Access to justice: beyond the policies and politics of austerity. Hart Publishing, Oxford, pp 60–104. https://media.bloomsburyprofessional.com/rep/files/9781849467346sample.pdf

Nagpal M, Rawandale C (2023) Tracing journey of crime victim's position under Indian law with evolutionary insights from the United States' federal code on victims' rights. Cogent Arts Humanit 10:2. https://doi.org/10.1080/23311983.2023.2286071

National Crime Victim Law Institute (2022) Advocating for Survivors - Back to the Basics. NCVLI Happenings: Fighting for victims through legal advocacy, education and public policy, July

National Crime Victim Law Institute (2023a) Increasing Victims' Access to Justice: Recognition of Victims' Right to Counsel. NCVLI Happenings: Fighting for victims through legal advocacy, education and public policy, August

National Crime Victim Law Institute (2023b) Attorney Fellows Mobilize to Increase Access to Legal Services for BIPOC Crime Victims. NCVLI Happenings: Fighting for victims through legal advocacy, education and public policy, October

O'Connell M (2012) Commissioner for victims' rights: strengthening victims' rights. In: Morosawa H, Dussich JP, Kirchhoff GF (eds) Victimology and human security: new horizons. Wolf Legal Publishers, Netherlands

O'Connell M (2015) The evolution of victims' rights and services in Australia. In: Wilson D, Ross S (eds) Crime, victims and policy: international contexts, local experiences. Palgrave McMillan, Houndmills, Basingstoke, Hampshire, pp 240–277

O'Connell M (2017) Victims' rights: integrating victims in criminal proceedings. https://aija.org.au/wp-content/uploads/2017/08/OConnell2.pdf

O'Connell M (2020) Improving access to justice: procedural justice through legal counsel for victims of crime. In: An international perspective on contemporary developments in victimology, a festschrift in Honor of Marc Groenhuijsen. Springer Switzerland

O'Connell M (2021) The Commissioner for Victims' Rights, South Australia – integral to strengthening the rights of victims of crime. In: Shekhar B et al (eds) Global perspective of victims of crime & victim assistance: best practices from across the globe. Bloomsbury Publishing

O'Connell M (2023) In reply: Can we accommodate independent legal representation for complainants of sexual violence in an adversarial system? 18 August. Level 1, Law Lounge, New Law Building, Eastern Avenue, Camperdown campus. Unpublished

Ostermann AC (2003) Communities of practice at work: gender, facework and the power of habitus at an all-female police station and a feminist crisis intervention center in Brazil. Discourse Soc 14(4):473–505. http://www.jstor.org/stable/42888584l

Payne S (2009) Redefining justice: addressing the individual needs of victims and witnesses. Petty France, London. https://library.college.police.uk/docs/moj/sara-payne-redefining-justice.pdf

Pizzi WT (1999) Victims' rights: rethinking our "Adversary System". Utah Law Rev 2:349–368

Pizzi WT, Perron W (1996) Crime victims in German courtrooms: a comparative perspective on American problems. Stanford J Int Law 32(1):37–64

Pradeep C (2021) Concept of victim justice: is it an aspiration for progressing society. LawSikho iPleaders. https://blog.ipleaders.in/concept-victim-justice-aspiration-progressing-society/

Raitt EF (2010) Independent legal representation for complainers in sexual offence trials, Research Report for Rape Crisis Scotland

Schafer S (1967) The victim and his criminal: Victimology. Submission to the President's Commission on Law Enforcement and Administration of Justice. https://www.google.com.au/books/edition/_/4uPTjld8C50C?hl=en&gbpv=1

Scottish Government (2023) Independent legal representation for sexual offence victims. News. https://www.gov.scot/news/independent-legal-representation-for-sexual-offence-victims/

Shekhar B, Ranjani R (2023) Access to justice for victims of crime in India: an analysis of Section 372 CrPC. J Victimol Victim Justice 6(1):64–80. https://doi.org/10.1177/25166069231160434

Skinner T, Smith O (2021, Sept 1) Independent legal representation is a necessity for victim-survivors. Institute for Policy Research, University of Bath

Smith O, Daly E (2023) Final Report: Evaluation of the Sexual Violence Complainants' Advocate Scheme, Loughborough University and Northumbria Police and Crime Commissioner, December. https://needisclear.files.wordpress.com/2020/11/svca-evaluation-final-report-1.pdf

Stern V (2010) The Stern Review: A Report by Baroness Vivien Stern CBE of an independent review into how rape complaints are handled by public authorities in England and Wales. Home Office, Government Equalities Office, London

Symons S (2014) Independent Legal Representation for Victims of Sexual Assault: Consideration of a Proposed Amendment to the Victims of Crime ACT 2001 (SA). Unpublished

Tobolowsky P (2015) Mandamus Muddle: The Mandamus Review Standard for the Federal Crime Victims' Rights Act. Univ Denv Crim Law Rev 5:123

UK Parliament (2024) Magna Carta https://www.parliament.uk/magnacarta/#:~:text=Magna%20Carta%20was%20issued%20in,as%20a%20power%20in%20itself

United Nations Development Programme (2004) Access to justice practice note. UNDP, New York

United Nations Development Programme (2005) Programming for justice: access for all: a practitioner's guide to human rights-based approach to access to justice. UNDP, Bangkok

USHistory.org (2024) Independence Hall Association, a nonprofit organization in Philadelphia, PA
Victorian Law Reform Commission (2016) Victims of Crime in the Criminal Trial Process, Final Report, November
Victorian Royal Commission into Family Violence (2016) Royal Commission into Family Violence, Volume I–VII: Report and Recommendations. Royal Commission into Family Violence, Victoria
Wemmers J (2013) Victims' rights are human rights: the importance of recognizing victims as persons. Temida. https://ssrn.com/abstract=2364886

Unveiling the Layers: An Analysis of the Intersectional Factors Contributing to the Victimization of Contemporary Devadasis in India

M. Priyamvadha, V. Bharathi Harishankar, D. M. Padma Priya, and Harshaa Vardhini Narasimhan

Abstract The practice of the Devadasi system dates back to the third century in India. The system has undergone many transitions from its origin till today including social, cultural, and economic transitions, which lead to derogatory evil practices against women. The review of the literature identifies the factors that led to the transition from sacred service to modern-day prostitution. During the ancient period, the girls even from sophisticated and influential families were dedicated to Gods, but their status was eroded over time. During that period, the Devadasis were occupational groups and were not segregated based on caste. Even though there are many sociological factors, the caste system and male domination are the most influential factors for the continuation of this practice. For various reasons, the young girls were dedicated to temples due to hereditary practices. Even though many studies were conducted in the area of the Devadasi cult, this study mainly identified the gap in the literature and focused on the sociocultural aspect and the art form of Devadasi system in the present context. At present, the devadasi system is prevalent in Tamil Nadu, Andhra Pradesh, Telangana, Maharashtra, and Karnataka. This study involved extensive interactions with stakeholders related to the Devadasi system to understand intersectional factors contributing to the victimization. This chapter is based on the project conducted by the authors of the chapter for the National Commission for Women, Government of India.

M. Priyamvadha (✉)
Department of Criminology, University of Madras, Chennai, India

V. B. Harishankar
Avinashilingam Institute for Home Science and Higher Education for Women, Coimbatore, India

D. M. P. Priya
Department of Women Studies, University of Madras, Chennai, India

H. V. Narasimhan
Queen's University, Belfast, UK

© The Author(s), under exclusive license to Springer Nature Singapore Pte Ltd. 2026

G. S. Bajpai et al. (eds.), *Beyond the Gavel: A Paradigm Shift in Global Criminal Justice*, https://doi.org/10.1007/978-981-95-4487-5_13

Keywords Devadasi • Cultural exploitation • Abuse • Victimization • Sexual exploitation

1 Introduction

The Devadasi system is an old practice in Hinduism where young girls are dedicated to temple deities and expected to serve the temple and the community for their entire lives. This practice has faced significant criticism and debate because of its patriarchal nature and exploitation. The Devadasi system has a long and complex history in Indian religious traditions. Traditionally, these women were supposed to serve the god through dance, music, and rituals.

They had a distinct social role and enjoyed economic stability, education, and artistic growth. But the system's vulnerability to exploitation, especially the forced prostitution of some Devadasis, led to strong condemnation during the British colonial era and after India's independence. The British government and reform movements worked to suppress the Nautch dance associated with the system. Although the practice was banned in 1982, the deep-rooted presence along with social inequalities and economic hardships has allowed the system to persist in various forms and still affects many women and girls, especially from marginalized communities. This study explores the contemporary reality of Devadasi system in Tamil Nadu, Andhra Pradesh, Telangana, Karnataka, and Maharashtra and the intersectional factors that contribute to the continued victimization of these women.

2 History of Devadasi System in India

The Devadasi meaning "Servant of God" refers to women dedicated to serving deities in Hindu temples, particularly in South India. The intricate history of this practice blends religious devotion, social structures, economic dependency, and exploitation, sparking societal reform efforts. To understand this tradition, it is necessary to explore its evolution from its origins to its contemporary issues. Initially, the system was held in high regard. Historical evidence suggests that the origin of the Devadasi system can be traced back to pre-vedic period, where music and dance played a central role in temple rituals. Inscriptions from the sixth century CE mention women who engaged in these artistic expressions, such as dance and music, as part of religious worship (Marglin 1985). By the time of the Chola and Vijayanagara dynasties, the practice had developed into a formalized institution. Women dedicated to temple service were typically well-versed in classical art forms such as Bharatanatyam, music, and poetry. They held a respected social status and often enjoyed benefits of financial security, receiving land, jewelry, and patronage from the royal court and affluent donors. Their performances were believed to contribute to the spiritual sanctity of the temple, benefiting both the deity and the broader community (Allen 1997).

During this period, the role of Devadasis was predominantly artistic and spiritual. Figures from ancient literary traditions, such as Amrapali and Madhavi, were esteemed for their intelligence, beauty, and artistic mastery, reflecting the high regard in which these women were held. However, with changing socioeconomic and political conditions, the Devadasi system began to weaken. The decrease in royal patronage and temple funding diluted the financial stability of the Devadasis.

Additionally, during the nineteenth and twentieth centuries, colonial influence and Victorian moral frameworks led to a shift in public perception, with many beginning to associate the practice with immorality. As power structures within the system evolved, Devadasis became increasingly reliant on temple priests and affluent benefactors, making them vulnerable to exploitation. This shift led to growing concerns regarding the system's ethical implications, prompting social reform movements. Prominent figures, such as Muthulakshmi Reddy, played a role in advocating for the abolition of the practice due to which the Madras Devadasis (Prevention of Dedication) Act was enacted in 1947, which criminalized the dedication of young girls to temple service and seeking to rehabilitate those already affected. Similar legislative measures were later implemented in other regions of India.

The legacy of the Devadasi system remains a subject of scholarly debate. While some scholars emphasize its cultural and artistic contributions, others focus on its historical links to gender-based exploitation. The challenge lies in preserving the rich artistic heritage associated with the tradition while ensuring the dignity, safety, and autonomy of women. It is essential to bridge the gap between the idealized portrayal of the Devadasi and the lived experiences of those within the system; the latter is very crucial for a nuanced understanding of this complex historical institution.

3 Devadasi System in Ancient Times

In ancient India, the Devadasi system was categorized into seven types. A girl dedicated to the temple by her family was known as a "Dutta Devadasi." If a woman was abducted and made a Devadasi, she was called "Hruta Devadasi." When a woman was sold to the temple for this role, she became a "Birkrita Devadasi." If a woman willingly became a Devadasi, she was referred to as a "Bhrutya Devadasi." A woman who was devotionally offered as a Devadasi was called a "Bhakta Devadasi." When a woman, after reaching a certain level of competence, was offered to the temple, she was known as "Alankara Devadasi." If a Devadasi was paid for her dance and music, she was called "Gopika" or "Rudraganika." In the present day, most Devadasis belong to categories like Dutta Devadasi (offered by a family member), Hruta Devadasi (sold to the temple or priest), and Bhakta Devadasi (devotionally offered). Some beliefs like the one that dedicating a sick girl would cure her also contributed to the system's longevity.

4 Dedication Process

The term Devadasi is derived from Sanskrit meaning "servant of the deity." Traditionally, young girls were initiated into this system through rituals similar to Brahmin marriage ceremonies.

Before puberty, a girl would be symbolically "married" to the god through a ceremony called "tali" tying or "pottukattu." After puberty, another ceremony called "cadanku" would be performed, often under the patronage of landlords and temple trustees. Then a nuptial ritual would be performed to signify her union with the deity, making her a "nityasumangali" (one who is never a widow). After this, the Devadasi could choose a patron, often a Brahmin or high-caste landlord, who would provide for her. These patrons sometimes became her sexual partners, but the Devadasi's relationship with them was not akin to that of a wife, and her children had no inheritance rights (Anandhi 1991).

5 Prevalence of Devadasi System

The Devadasi system was most prevalent in the southern states of India, including Maharashtra, Karnataka, Andhra Pradesh, Telangana, and Tamil Nadu, though it was also present in states like Gujarat, Goa, Assam, and Odisha (Colundalur 2011). In Karnataka, it was more common in the northern districts like Dharwad, Belgaum (now Belagavi), Bagalkot, and Bijapur, which are together known as the "3B" districts (Orchard 2007). In Maharashtra, it was more prevalent in the border areas near Karnataka, like Kolhapur, Sangli, and Solapur. Devadasis in Tamil Nadu were temple-linked: Thanjavur, Madurai, and Kanchipuram were the notable centers. In Andhra Pradesh, it was common in districts like Karimnagar, Warangal, and Nizamabad. Devadasis had different regional names such as "Maharis" in Kerala; "Natis' in Assam; "Basavis" in Karnataka; "Bhavanis" in Goa; "Kudikar" on the West Coast; "Bhogam- Vandhi" or "Jogin" in Andhra Pradesh; "Thevardiyar" in Tamil Nadu; "Murali," "Jogateen," and "Aradhini" in Maharashtra. In Karnataka, old Devadasis are called as "Jogati" and young Devadasis as "Basavi."

6 Review of Literature

The emergence of Devadasi system is cited between third century and twelfth century, and the tradition has come through many transitions in the course of history. During every transition, the tradition has suffered socially, culturally, and economically to such an extent that contemporary Devadasi practice is now only associated with social evils. The Devadasi system of dedicating young girls to temples was present in some parts of India as early as 300 A D. It became an established institution in Hindu by 700 A D. The origin of Devadasi system can be traced to fifth century AD. There are some references in Skanda Purana. In the "Purushottam Ksetra Mahamtya" in Skanda Purana and Bamadeva Samhita, it is evident that Devadasis were present and they used to serve God by dancing in rituals and festivals. In Nityasumangali: Devadasi Tradition in South India, Saskia C. Kersenboom contextualizes the roles of a Devadasi both in day-to-day life and in the temple rituals.

Citing the Devadasi as a multivalent concept, Kersenboom points out how a Devadasi balances two opposite forces of "life enhancing, fertile" and auspicious aspect as a nitya sumangali and a "life-destroying, deadly" aspect as a ritual woman. Kalpana Kannabiran traces the origins of the Devadasi abolition movement in the Madras Presidency to the social reform movement. As Kannabiran writes, "one of the crucial elements of the crusade was the broadening of the term prostitution not only to refer to sexual intercourse for monetary gain but also to serve as a metaphor for social depravity and moral corruption in general."

Kunal Parker traces the process by which dancing girls came to be criminalized as prostitutes. "Crucial in this process was the representation of dancing girls as a professional group, rather than as a caste, which might have its own laws concerning marriage and property inheritance. The representation of dancing girls as a professional group characterized by the activities of dancing and prostitution brought them under the purview of Hindu law and allowed them to be seen as a group that had fallen from caste because of their practice of prostitution" (Parker 1988). Historical studies refer to Devadasi system as "Sacred Prostitution" and it was a part of the society. However, now, the Devadasi system is a form of open prostitution and many poor people dedicate their daughters to the system in the name of appeasing the gods (Colundalur 2011). Under the pretense of religion and culture, the Devadasi system has now become widely synonymous with sexual exploitation: To guarantee that there is a continuous stream of exploitation through sex slaves and child prostitution (Deane 2022). Sriram captures this duality in his book The Devadasi and the Saint: "On the one hand, the (devadasi) community was the storehouse of arts. On the other it was the repository of all evil and every conceivable vice." (Sriram 2007).

This divided opinion is the result of multiple historical factors including Christian preachers, colonial moralists, and Indian social reformers. "...these people had no hesitation in condemning all Devadasis as prostitutes and their art as sinful." (Sriram 2007). Amita Kanekar's A Spoke in the Wheel is the latest addition in the literary representation of a Devadasi. Through the central character, Upali and the Devadasi,

Sutanuka, the author, explores how women are oppressed in the name of religion and traditions. The conversation between Upali and the temple priest regarding Sutanaka's love for the sculptor, Devadina, reveals the many faults of the Devadasi system. "The girl may be happier, you say, but is that all that matters? What of the sacred laws before which we all are helpless? If she flouts the law, there will be calamity- on her, on her community, on this temple."

In their study on the novel, Smriti Thakur and Alpana Saini point out how practitioners of religion "mould sacred laws according to their convenience which become in one or another way, the medium of women's exploitation, specifically, for those women who are engaged in practices like devadasi. Simultaneously, Kanekar shows the fact that these religious practitioners, who pretend to serve society, in actuality, are the culprits of society who mislead people in the name of religion." Devkant Barooah's poem "Devadasi" (1980) evokes the real dedication of the body and soul of the Devadasi as the handmaiden of God and how destiny intervenes to push them to their lowly state. Dalrymple (2008) says that "the Devadasi system is centuries old, and the women once enjoyed lives of great privilege." They were invited to all ceremonies and their presence was considered auspicious. The social, cultural, economic, and political changes made them prostitutes (Orchard 2007).

The Devadasi system continues to maintain a cycle of exploitation, especially for young girls who are inducted into the practice as early as age 11 or 12 years. These girls attain puberty by the ages 12 or 13, and by the age of 15, they would have acquired their first sexual encounter, often with no prior knowledge about protective measures or reproductive health. As a result of this ignorance, they get more ingrained in the system, which also makes them more susceptible to early pregnancies and STDs. Furthermore, these children are usually from traditional rural families and are deprived of access to education, which perpetuates a cycle of social marginalization, socioeconomic deprivation, and illiteracy (Advika and Arthi 2021).

Many of the studies focus on the history of the Devadasi system. Some of the studies perceive the Devadasi system as a by-product of the caste system and other studies focus on the HIV AIDS perspectives. The studies, by and large, do not address the issue of rehabilitation. It is very important to study the awareness about existing legislations, policies, and schemes for Devadasis among stakeholders. To provide effective rehabilitation, it is equally important to identify the problems faced by the stakeholders in the field.

7 Contributing Factors to the Devadasi System

Social troubles regularly have multiple underlying factors that make a contribution to their endurance, many of which can be rooted in society's shape. The "Devadasi system," diagnosed as one of the most giant social evils, is supported by different factors, which may be widely categorized into social, cultural, nonsecular, and financial classes. These contributing factors are discussed below and are classified based on their severity.

8 Poverty

Poverty is the main cause of many social problems, along with the Devadasi system. Initially, the practice of dedicating girls was pushed by means of religious ideals, but through the years, poverty has become a major factor in influencing the selection process to commit young girls. Poor households, struggling financially, frequently choose to dedicate their daughters as Devadasis, who may additionally later pose for intercourse paintings either domestically (ordinarily for top-caste people) or in brothels or some other place. The economic benefits of prostitution, which can provide sizable profits, tempt poor households to use the religious component of determination to justify this practice. Additionally, dedicating a female as a Devadasi allows families to keep away from the economic burden of paying a dowry. By dedicating a daughter, households also obtain financial assistance, because the female contributes financially, often playing the role of a son in the household. Though poverty is a first-rate element, it's far intertwined with several different impacts. Furthermore, the Devadasi system receives nonsecular validation, which permits mother and father to apply religion as a tool to gain economic advantage through their daughters who earn through prostitution (Colundalur 2011).

9 Religious and Superstitious Beliefs

The Devadasi system is deeply intertwined with Hindu spiritual practices. In a few communities, dedication of girls is rooted in blind faith, wherein households believe that dedicating their daughters will get them benefits including wealth, fitness, or the begetting of a male infant. In some cases, the dedication is executed to treat a member of the family's infection or incapacity. There is likewise a perception that if a woman develops matted hair (jat), she must be dedicated to the temple.During disaster times, which includes disease outbreaks or financial distress, families may additionally lodge to determination, hoping that the goddess will offer healing or economic remedy (Kamat 2016). This harmful practice is perpetuated, while superstition merges with poverty, leading to social injustice (Evans and Kirsti 1998).

10 Caste System

The Devadasi system is most prevalent among lower-caste communities. There is a strong correlation between poverty and caste, which regularly forces the parents to devote their daughters to the Devadasi system. The system frequently persists in Scheduled Castes, a non-Brahmin group. Devadasis are also from diverse social backgrounds. However, by the early twentieth century, educated upper-caste people distanced themselves from this cruel practice.

Today, the system is largely limited to Dalit communities, apart from its hereditary practice. Devadasis are frequently the daughters of girls who themselves are Devadasis. In a few cases, girls are dedicated to retaining the subculture, while their households face economic difficulties (Shiva Kumar 2009). Although poverty is an important component, some scholars argue that the exercise was historically an outcome of the caste practice, with upper-caste individuals enforcing it on the lower castes. In any case, poverty and caste are intertwined elements that perpetuate the system to accelerate.

11 Hereditary Practice

The Devadasi system is frequently passed down through generations. Many Devadasis are daughters or granddaughters of ladies who practiced the equal system. The lifestyle is regularly maintained inside lower-caste households, where women are devoted as a manner of existence, continuing the legacy of their ancestors. While some families have been as soon as involved within the exercise because of necessity, in current times, some non-Devadasi families also dedicate their daughters in hope of gaining financial benefits (Orchard 2007). In a few areas, the practice is resumed by using families that once abandoned it, especially when facing economic or health-associated difficulties (Shiva Kumar 2009).

12 Social Pressure

Social strain also plays a role in the continuation of the Devadasi system. In a few cases, higher-caste men exert pressure on lower-caste families to commit their daughters, frequently turning into the primary to sexually make the most of them. Additionally, temple priests, who preserve impact over the network, offer "spiritual sanction" to households, encouraging them to dedicate their women. Once a female is devoted, she is predicted to provide sexual services to higher-caste men, monks, and other powerful figures in society (Colundalur 2011). While this pressure exists, it is important to notice that in many instances, the exercise of determination is in general pushed through economic elements in preference to direct social coercion.

As an end result, the contributing factors—religious beliefs, caste pressures, and monetary wishes—are all intertwined.

13 Devadasis in Prostitution

The Devadasi system, which has a long history, has gone through many changes over the years..

While sex work was never initially the primary profession of Devadasis, many of them had one or two patrons during their lifetime (Orchard 2007). However, the Devadasi system has become increasingly associated with prostitution and the connection between the two is significant (Rural Education and Action for Change 2013). According to Dalrymple (2008), the Devadasi system has ancient roots, and in earlier times, women in the system enjoyed privileges. They were invited to various ceremonies and their presence was seen as auspicious. However, social, economic, and political shifts led to these women being forced into prostitution (Orchard 2007). After the British took control of temple revenues, the financial support for Devadasis was cut off, leading to a decline in their social and economic status. As a result, prostitution became one of the few remaining options for survival ("Law Making, Cultural Shifts and Life of Devadasis," 2013).

In the past, Devadasis provided sexual services to kings, landowners, and other powerful individuals. Over time, however, they began to entertain a broader range of people and eventually became involved in prostitution (Moni 2001). A major factor in this shift was the loss of royal patronage, which caused a significant decrease in the income of Devadasis, pushing some into begging and prostitution (Rout n.d.). Historically, the dance and artistic skills of Devadasis had little to do with obscenity, making prostitution seem like a more attractive alternative (Geetanjali et al. 2000). The system, which was initially based on cultural and religious traditions, gradually lost its sacred meaning as modernization and westernization diminished the religious significance of the Devadasi role, contributing to many Devadasis turning to sex work (Evans and Kirsti 1998).

In modern times, some Devadasis engage in sex work in brothels in cities like Mumbai, Pune, Kolhapur, Miraj, and Sangli, where a considerable number of commercial sex workers are former Devadasis (Rural Education and Action for Change 2013). The dedication of young girls to the Devadasi system is often determined by their parents, who make this decision when the girls are too young to have a say in the matter. These girls should be viewed as victims of a system that forces them into exploitation. In some cases, brothels are run by older, retired Devadasis who have practiced sex work and now recruit young girls from their home villages to join the trade. These women, familiar with the local communities, know which families or castes are likely to accept the offer of money for their daughters. The advance given for the girls is adjusted against the money the girls will earn through sex work. Over time, the financial success of both non-Devadasi prostitutes and Devadasis encourages poor lower-caste families to dedicate their daughters. Unfortunately, many of these girls never return to their families, while others may return only when they are old or ill (Rural Education and Action for Change 2013).

Although the Devadasi system initially centered around cultural practices like dance and music, today, the act of dedication has little to do with these traditions. The system has essentially become a way to feed young girls into the sex trade, with religion used as a guide to mask the practice's harmful effects.

14 Objectives of the Study

- To identify the factors contributing to victimization of the Devadasi system in Tamil Nadu, Andhra Pradesh, Telangana, Karnataka, and Maharashtra.
- To examine the processes involved in the rescue and rehabilitation of Devadasis.
- To recommend policy measures for the rehabilitation of Devadasis.

15 Methodology

The entire gamut of this study includes stakeholders such as health workers, social workers, government officials, personnel of nongovernmental organizations, representatives from the judiciary, law enforcement agencies, and correctional administration in five states of India namely, Karnataka, Maharashtra, Andhra Pradesh, Telangana, and Tamil Nadu. The factors surrounding the Devadasi system and its associated evils are sensitive and delicate issues. Hence, only people who know about handling or combating this evil practice were selected as a sample for the study. Purposive sampling, a kind of nonprobability sampling technique, is characterized by the use of judgment and a deliberate effort to obtain data from the sample collected for the study. The total sample size of the study is $N = 205$.

16 Results and Discussion

Abuses are classified into five categories: verbal abuse, physical abuse, financial abuse, sexual abuse, and sociocultural abuse. The study shows that verbal abuse and sociocultural abuse are more prevalent than the other types of abuse. According to respondents, name-calling and insults are the leading forms of verbal abuse. In sociocultural contexts, stigma/labeling and discrimination are at the top. Sexual abuse follows sociocultural abuse. Abuse can manifest in various ways, frequently with multiple forms of abuse happening simultaneously for individuals.

17 Verbal Abuse

Verbal abuse involves words, actions, or alternative methods to instigate fear, shame, emotional strain, or distress. Victims face threats of punishment, denial, or confinement. Other forms of verbal abuse consist of, but are not restricted to, belittling, patronizing, embarrassing, mocking, swearing, making severe remarks, etc.

Nevertheless, evaluating the effects of these types of abuse can be challenging, since comparable actions or phrases might be more distressing to certain people than to others. Cultural standards and expectations seem to influence the way these types of abuse affect victims considerably. Verbal mistreatment is a prevalent type of abuse experienced by Devadasis. They are often called bitch. Devadasi women frequently encounter verbal hostility when they refuse requests from clients seeking sexual services.

18 Physical Abuse

Physical abuse is defined as the application of physical force that inflicts discomfort on another individual. This abuse may or may not lead to bodily injury, physical pain, or impairment. The people who experience this kind of treatment suffer from it. Physical abuse includes actions like hitting, violently shaking someone, pushing them hard, kicking them, punching them, or hitting them with an object or weapon. Each of these actions aims to cause harm or show power over the victim. Deliberately exposing someone to extreme weather, excessive physical confinement, forced isolation, and neglecting to provide adequate medical care. Physical mistreatment by family, relatives, neighbors, strangers, and even their clients is quite prevalent among Devadasis. They receive no assistance from law enforcement agencies, even in cases of severe attacks or assaults.

19 Sexual Abuse

Any undesirable type of sexual conduct, actions, assault, or harassment toward individuals constitutes sexual abuse. It may involve verbal or suggestive actions, touching, sexual relations, invasion of personal space, being compelled to perform humiliating sexual acts. The reproductive function of young girls before development inhibits and increases the likelihood of obstructed labor. The health risks are additionally exacerbated by inadequate nutritional and health assistance from both family and community. The surge in growth during adolescence is diminished by poor nutrition, and psychological stress can result in psychosomatic issues; additionally, these girls are prone to experiencing three times more complications than older women. Thus, the Devadasi women are at extreme risk, which leads to health and psychological ailments, social stigma, and ostracization from the society.

20 Financial Abuse

Financial abuse encompasses the exploitation of an individual's financial resources or property through means such as deception, fraud, theft, or coercion. It can entail fraud, scams, the improper use of money or property, persuading someone to purchase a product by offering money, theft of cash or belongings, abusing bank or credit cards, misapplying joint accounts, forging signatures on pension checks or legal papers, and misusing power of attorney. Any small amount of money earned by the Devadasis is misappropriated by their family and friends. Financial exploitation is regarded as a significant type of exploitation since Devadasis generate income through sexual services. The primary offenders of financial exploitation are the family members of the Devadasis. Since the dedication of Devadasis to the temple, their family members have been exploiting them financially, leaving them in a state of vulnerability. The minimal financial aid provided by the government to the Devadasis as a pension is also exploited by their family members.

21 Sociocultural Abuse

The fictional wives of the deity are socially hated and morally stigmatized and confront the extra challenge of facing widowhood. All these factors can cause Devadasis to experience depression, which may appear as irregular alterations in their behavior. Over time, they are prone to experience psychosomatic disorders and might be overlooked in the community. In addition to other mistreatments, the Devadasis indicated that those involved often mistreat them.

22 Rescue, Rehabilitation, and Reintegration

The places of rescue of Devadasis include brothels, red-light areas while being trafficked from family/neighbors/friends, temples, domestic labor, court referrals, and villages: 27.9% from family, 23.0% from temple, and 18.0% from brothels are the major places from where the rescue has taken place. Most of the dedications take place with the strong support of the family and are associated with temples (Graph 1). Then later, they can be found in brothels or in the commercial sex industry in their place or somewhere far away, like in red-light areas: 14.8% of rescues have been from red-light areas. As per the respondent's opinion, 6.6% of Devadasis have been rescued while being trafficked for prostitution and 1.6% of them have been

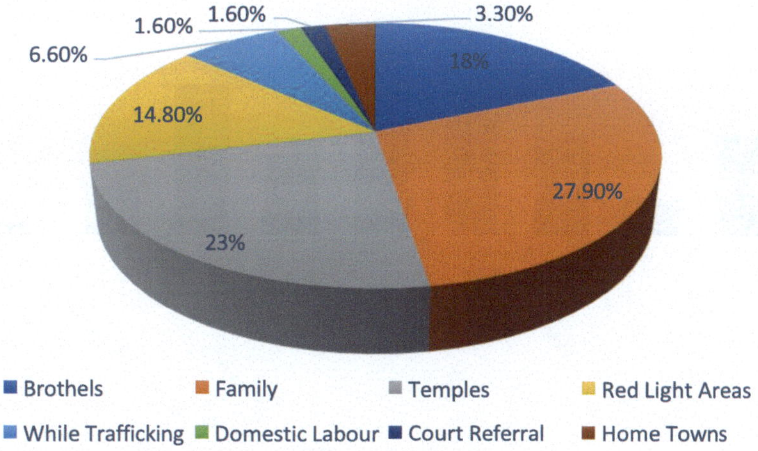

Graph 1 Recuse of Devadasis. *Source*: NCW Report, 2016 (Self-cited)

rescued by respondents from domestic labor. Some other times, rescue has taken place through court referral (1.6%) and also from their home towns (3.3%).

There are many campaigns undertaken by NGOs to rescue and rehabilitate Devadasis and integrate them back into society. A new effort has begun with small teams taking up "jat" removal or haircutting campaigns in the towns of Kolhapur, Gargoti, and Nipani. So far, about 50 women in several towns and villages have been officially released from their state as Devadasis, and several have been married. Many of the activists' plan to continue these campaigns by linking propaganda against the Devadasi system with propaganda for the need for a united struggle by Dalits against all the injustices that beset their lives. It remains true, however, that the current phase of anti-Devadasi campaigning contrasts with the early period, not only in that its leadership is primarily caste Hindu and middle class, but also in that its style has mostly involved lobbying, rallies, seminars, and conferences without much follow-up. The desire to throw off traditional forms of religion endorsed by patriarchal enslavement has not yet crystallized among the masses of low-caste workers, agricultural laborers, and poor peasants in the border areas between Karnataka and Maharashtra. In Karnataka and Maharashtra, most stakeholders undertake awareness-building and rehabilitation work. The NGOs work in the red-light areas and home-based brothels. They often conduct awareness-raising camps, health camps, HIV prevention camps, etc. During an interview with a Devadasi in Solapur, we saw many condom boxes; when we asked about it, they said NGOs would provide them condoms regularly. The situation is similar in many places. So, it is understood that NGOs work in brothels to support the Devadasis and not in rescues. Perhaps, in a way, some of the NGOs are indirectly supporting the Devadasi system for their benefit. The availability of information about dedications and secret ceremonies by the family members makes it even more difficult to trace the dedicated girls.

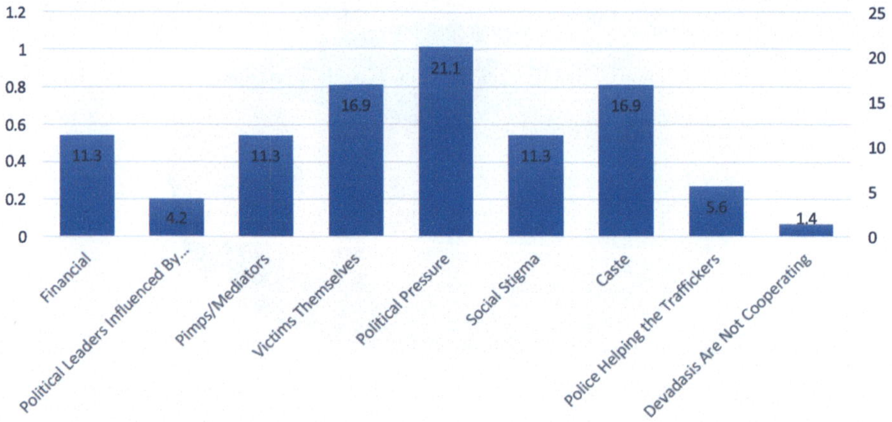

Graph 2 Problems faced while rescuing. *Source*: NCW Report, 2016 (Self-cited)

23 Problems Faced While Rescuing

The above graph outlines the problems faced by respondents during their rescue operations (Graph 2). The actual size of the sample is 205, but a few questions in this head do not apply to all respondents. Hence, the total number of respondents is 71. As shown in the table, the respondents said that political pressure (21.1%) is a hindrance while rescuing the Devadasis. Here, the term political pressure does refer to actual politicians, but it refers to the influential social groups of that locality that politicize the issue for their own vested interest: 16.9% is because of the caste of the victim, and 16.9% of victims themselves create problems because few of them are ready to be rescued; they are happy with the life they are living. Another 11.3% lack proper financial support; 11.3% is due to the influence of pimps and mediators, which has a great impact on rescue; and 11.3% is because of the problem of stigma attached to Devadasis. Even though they are rescued and rehabilitated, society views them only as Devadasis.

24 Rehabilitation of Devadasis

In both Andhra Pradesh and Karnataka, rehabilitated Devadasis are entitled to a variety of State benefits. These include monthly pensions, assistance with housing, free healthcare, and education for their children. Due to the combination of corruption and prejudice, they often find it difficult to access these benefits. Many people do not know their rights..

The Karnataka government provides entitlement certificates to Devadasis to help them access benefits. In Maharashtra, a job training program runs through District Training Centers to improve Devadasis' skills in areas like tailoring, knitting, weaving, candle making, envelope manufacturing, and petty shops. Much of the work of these organizations has been done through sanghas and self-help groups, which help these women to access benefits, subsidies, and legal support. For economic independence, micro-credit loans are available based on the interests and skills of each Devadasi. This program aims to build confidence and self-esteem. Rehabilitated Devadasis associated with such groups have proven effective agents in preventing dedication ceremonies from taking place. However, due to the limited resources of self-help groups, they are not always as successful as they could be in improving the lives of former Devadasis.

25 Need for Reintegration

Reintegrating Devadasis into the community is a complex challenge that requires community engagement due to the Devadasi system's deep roots in local traditions. An effective reintegration program should adopt a psychosocial framework that addresses three key areas: Human Capacity, Social Ecology, and Culture and Values. This approach will help create supportive environments for Devadasis returning to their families and communities. Numerous existing challenges associated with the elimination of the Devadasi system can be addressed through a balanced approach that takes into account each core aspect of the framework while promoting community engagement. An inclusive support system should assist Devadasi girls and women in managing psychosocial challenges, addressing physical health concerns, and overcoming economic hardships.

26 Refusal to Reintegrate

The above diagram explains the refusal of Devadasis to get reintegrated: 62% of respondents believed that Devadasis were not ready to reintegrate and 14% of respondents said that Devadasis were ready to reintegrate (Graph 3). Social stigma,

Graph 3 Refusal to reintegrate. *Source*: NCW Report, 2016 (Self-cited)

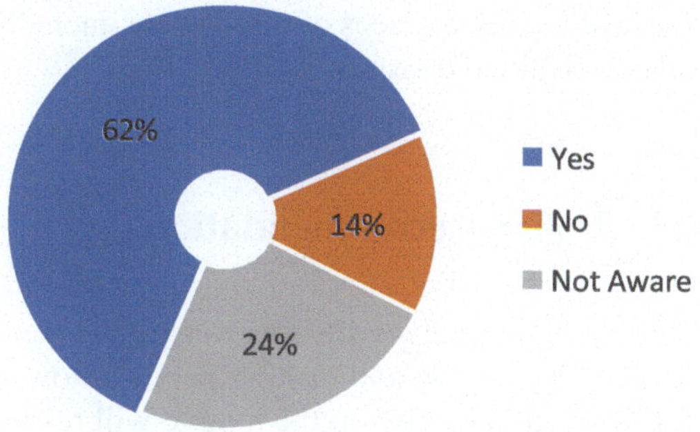

isolation, and discrimination from society force these poor souls to reject the option of reintegration. Twenty-four percent of respondents were not aware of any of the reintegration programs for Devadasis. According to the stakeholders, the reasons for refusing to reintegrate are refusal from the family, social stigma, family's hatred toward the Devadasis, Devadasis' hatred toward their family, feeling comfortable in sex work, providing financial support to family, lack of legal support, getting trapped by sex traffickers, liking toward luxurious life, dedicated themselves to temples, the lack of awareness of the existing reintegration programs, and the lack of job opportunities available for rehabilitated Devadasis in the society.

27 Prevention Strategies

The practice of dedication is preventable. Ninety percent of them responded positively that the practice of dedicating girls as Devadasis in the temple is completely preventable and 10% of the respondents were not sure whether the total eradication of the system is possible. Despite the positive opinion of stakeholders on prevention, dedications still happen. The reason behind this is that the age-old practice is deeply rooted in society, and changing the minds of the people overnight through legislation is not possible. The other common reasons for dedication are gender, lower economic status, lower social status, lower caste, lower level of education, the hereditary practice, and the reluctance to lose the status of "nithyasumangali." If all the above-mentioned causes are addressed properly, then there is a chance of a reduction in the number of dedications in temples. There are different ways to prevent the dedication. The eradication of superstitious beliefs and the provision of proper education are the main ways to liberate them. According to the respondents, awareness building among family and temple priests will greatly impact dedication. Most parents dedicate their female child as a Devadasi to support their families financially; if they are economically stable, they can earn and support their family. The next important thing, according to the respondents, is the prevention of Devadasis' children from entering into the same profession. The respondents argue that authority should frame up a Vigilance Committee to avoid further dedications. Several NGOs are active in the fight against the Devadasi system. They have primarily been working to raise awareness among the Devadasis and local villages about the health consequences of this system, including the spread of HIV and other sexually transmitted diseases.

28 Policy Recommendations

Devadasis themselves are not aware of the legislation. Creating awareness about the existing legislation and making people know about the stringent punishment given for dedication of girls to the temple will result in eradicating the Devadasi system.

Periodical amendments in the existing legislation will help to curb the problem extensively. Steps should also be taken for proper implementation of the existing legislation. Monitoring mechanisms should also be in place for proper implementation. Speedy trials through fast-track court will help in a long way to avoid unnecessary delay in proceeding with the case. Some of the stakeholders argue that the actual number of Devadasis is less compared to the statistics available from the government and NGOs. A baseline survey needs to be conducted to find out the actual needs of the Devadasis. The government should have a proper mechanism to identify the exact number of Devadasis in each state of India to effectively prepare, plan, prevent, and rehabilitate the existing Devadasis and to curb this menace permanently. The policies, programs, and schemes of the government should reach the beneficiaries without any hassle. The lack of official statistics and information about the socio demographic profile of the Devadasis hinders the government from making effective policies for the welfare of the Devadasis as well as for complete eradication of the Devadasi system. There is an urgent need to focus on the rehabilitation of Devadasis in order to empower them and to prevent them from getting into prostitution. The immediate need of the Devadasis during and after rehabilitation should be the focus of the government to provide them the sustainable standard of living. The stakeholders' policy recommendations include increasing the pension scheme, preferring Devadasi children in government jobs, providing free education for the children of Devadasis until they complete their education, and providing free hostels for Devadasi children.

29 Intersectional Factors of Victimization Class and Caste

The Devadasi system, a deeply complicated tradition, is seen mainly among marginalized communities, especially among Dalits and other lower caste groups. It limited the possibilities available for Devadasis on socioeconomic margins, exposing them to utilization. Poverty and illiteracy are the key factors of being in this evil practice. Stakeholders opine that the Devadasis are unaware of different forms of abuse and recognizing the abusive situation as a crime will make them understand their vulnerability to come out of this profession..

Sensitization programs, periodical skill development training, and stable employment opportunities will ensure a better quality of life for Devadasi to keep themselves away from this practice.

30 Gender and Patriarchy

The conceptualization of gender-encompassing patriarchal ideologies leads to the mistreatment of women in society. The double jeopardy that includes gender, lower caste, and economically unstable status intertwined with a patriarchal mindset restricts women from claiming their rights to enjoy equal status in society. This interconnected vulnerability leads to further victimization of Devadasis in society. This cultural milestone confirms the idea that the value of women is linked to their objectification and commercialization of the physical body, which facilitates a change in their existence that prefers men's control over their lives. The widespread social norms discourage women by demanding their agency, creating an environment where Devadasis are vulnerable to different forms of harassment, including physical and sexual violence.

31 Religion and Culture

The Devadasi system associated with specific religious beliefs and practices is prevalent under the cover of the age-old tradition. This unconducive contemporary environment makes it very difficult for Devadasi women to challenge the deep-rooted system and to liberate themselves from the clutches of evil social practices in society. To uphold their rights, it needs enormous individual and political will to eradicate this kind of cultural practice. This requires a coordinated effort from all the stakeholders who strive to make a conducive society for women to enjoy equal status and freedom.

32 Impact of Victimization

Multidimensional hunting of contemporary Devadasis manifests itself in serious, far-reaching consequences that can destroy their physical, emotional, and socioeconomic welfare. The sensitivity to a variety of health problems in contact with Devadasis for sexual abuse and exploitation increases sensitivity, including sexually transmitted infections (STI), unwanted pregnancies, and other serious health complications. Lack of access to health services further increases these risks, leading to long-term health dilemmas. The vicious cycle of violence cannot be untangled unless there is an effort to eradicate poverty and eliminate both discrimination and social stigma. The plight of contemporary Devadasis is pathetic and many are trapped in an uncertain existence and lack of hope to live a dignified life. Physical, emotional, and sexual abuse can lead to psychological trauma, which can seriously affect their mental health and general well-being. Many Devadasi women experience anxiety, depression, and posttraumatic stress disorder (PTSD), which complicates their ability to imagine life beyond their current circumstances.

33 Conclusion

A nuanced expertise of the intersectional elements contributing to the victimization of current Devadasis is essential for developing guidelines and policies that deal with this grave menace. Many Devadasis are innocent about their rights and the existing support system, leaving them powerless ahead of exploitation. This ignorance about their rights not only inhibits their ability to seek help but also perpetuates a cycle of victimization. The stakeholders can foster a movement in the direction of a greater equitable and just society, empowering these women to reclaim their rights and dignity by way of tackling the underlying socio-financial, cultural, and other demographic dynamics that sustain the Devadasi system. Additionally, raising public awareness, improving access to education and economic opportunities, and providing adequate support systems can significantly reduce their vulnerability to exploitation and abuse.

References

Advika M, Arthi R (16 July 2021) The Devadasi System: A Tale Of Exploitation And Religious Sanction. IJLLR. https://www.ijllr.com/post/the-devadasi-system-a-tale-of-exploitation-and-religious-sanction

Allen M (1997) The Hindu conception of personhood. State University of New York Press. Amitha, K. (200...5). A Spoke in the Wheel. New Delhi: Harper Collins

Anandhi S (1991) Women's question in the Dravidian movement. Soc Sci 19

Bharathi VH, Priyamvadha M (2016) Exploitation of women as Devadasis and its associated evils. National Commission for Women, New Delhi

Colundalur N (2011) Devadasis are a crushed community. The Guardian

Dalrymple W (2008) Serving the Goddess: The dangerous life of a sacred sex worker. The New Yorker

Deane T (2022) The Devadasi system: an exploitation of women and children in the Devadasi system: an exploitation of women and children in the name of god and culture the name of god and culture. J Int Women's Stud 24(1) https://vc.bridgew.edu/cgi/viewcontent.cgi?article=2883&context=jiws

Devkant B (1980) Devadasi. Indian Literature 23

Evans, Kirsti (1998) Contemporary Devadasis empowered auspicious women or exploited prostitutes. Bull John Rylands Library 80(3)

Geetanjali M, Ajay M, Rima S (2000) Protecting the rights of sex workers: the Indian experience. Health Hum Rights 5(1)

Kamat K (2016) The Yellamma Cult. Retrieved from http://=www.kamat.com/kalranga/people/yellamma/yellamma.html

Marglin FA (1985) Wives of the god-kings: the rituals of the Devadasis of Puri. Oxford University Press

Moni N (2001) Anthropological perspectives on prostitution and AIDS in India. Econ Polit Wkly 36(42)

Orchard T (2007) In this life: the impact of gender and tradition on sexuality and relationships for Devadasi sex workers in rural India, sexuality and culture. Sex Cult 11(1)

Parker K (1988) A corporation of superior prostitutes. Anglo-Indian Legal Concep Stud 32(3)

Rout J. Dancing Girls (Devadasis) at the Temples- with special reference to the Jagannath Temple, Puri, and Orissa, India"
Rural Education and Action for Change (2013) A report on diagnostic study on prostitution in Rayalaseema region of Andhra Pradesh and impact of preventive measures. Ministry of Women and Child Development Govt. of India, Andhra Pradesh
Shiva Kumar N (2009) Finally, an end to the devadasi system. Times of India
Sriram V (2007) The Devadasi and the saint: the life and times of Bangalore Nagarathnamma. C, 2nd edn. Oxford University Press, Chennai

Ways to Advance Safety and Justice for Victims: New but Essential Content for Teaching

Irvin Waller

Abstract This chapter starts with numbers of victims of homicide, gender-based violence, and violence against children. It recalls the UN magna carta for victims from 1985 and the goals to reduce violence and improve access to justice agreed by all governments.

It challenges professors of victimology to teach new courses to the next generations of victimologists to be the catalysts in reducing violence significantly and realizing universal rights for victims.

It presents an overview of the knowledge of what has reduced violence, how it gets implemented, and how to build political will to get sustained investment. The knowledge identifies proven examples of programs and cities that have reduced violent crime by 50% within 3 years. It sets out standards for access to justice for persons who are victims of crime as well as ways in which victim rights are being delivered, which show what is possible. It stresses the need to measure whether victims are getting that access to justice and so provide targets for programs.

It shows how victimologists can shift governments from a failing criminal justice system to effective violence prevention and access to justice for victims.

Keywords Victim rights · Victimization prevention · Activist victimology · Teaching · Evidence-based · UN sustainable development goals

---

This chapter draws on Waller (2019), Waller (2020a, 2020b), and Monette and Waller (2024).

I. Waller (✉)
University of Ottawa, Ottawa, ON, Canada
e-mail: iwaller@uottawa.ca

© The Author(s), under exclusive license to Springer Nature Singapore Pte Ltd. 2026

G. S. Bajpai et al. (eds.), *Beyond the Gavel: A Paradigm Shift in Global Criminal Justice*, https://doi.org/10.1007/978-981-95-4487-5_14

1 Introduction

There has never been a more important time to teach students the knowledge needed to reduce crime and victimization significantly and advance access to support, reparation, and justice for victims. This knowledge has important components of what has been proven to reduce crime and what best practices exist for justice for victims, but also how that knowledge can be put to work and how to build the political will for change and sustained investment.

Globally each year, half a million victims are murdered (United Nations Office for Drugs and Crime 2023), an estimated 25 million women are raped (extrapolated from Waller 2019, pp. 9–10), and one billion children are victims of violence (World Health Organization 2017). These are outrageous numbers given our knowledge.

These statistics reflect victims who suffer injuries, pain, trauma, financial loss, and more. The victims are often the most vulnerable and disadvantaged. Where these tragedies have reached epidemic proportions, they threaten economic development and reduce the Gross Domestic Product. They threaten democracy and rule of law (Inter-American Development Bank 2018). The impact of this violence on its victims is massive and progress to support, repair, and get justice for these victims is still a patchwork in developed countries and hardly started in middle-income and developing countries. In sum, there is significant work to be done to build the political will to invest in providing services, reparation, and justice for victims of crime.

The next generation of victimologists are needed to get the changes that will guarantee the most effective policies to stop crime before it happens. With present knowledge, we should be able to reduce the rates of victimization by 50% in the next 5 years, but this will still leave massive numbers of victims, who need access support, reparation, and right to be heard.

So the next generations are needed to get to know and share practices proven to prevent violence by tackling the risk factors that lead to violence. They are needed to get to know the best practices that already exist to support, repair, and access justice. They are needed to understand and teach the essentials for getting those proven practices put into action. They are needed to master and share ways to persuade decision makers and the public to establish guarantees to basic justice and to invest in saving lives and increasing GDP.

Dr. Chockalingam is a titan of the world victimology movement, whose commitment to stopping victimization and providing rights for victims in Tamil Nadu, India, and the world is an inspiration to all current and aspiring victimologists. No other criminologist or victimologist can match his collaboration with the iconic politician and Supreme Court Justice Eier in the world's most populist country, his influence over the State Superior Court Justice Malimath report on victim support and rights, his role in getting compensation in Tamil Nadu and his spectacular academic career including the head of the new University in Tirunelveli and encouraging innovative programs in victimology at Indian universities.

The next generation of victimologists must be inspired by his exemplary role model and successful life work. Through the collaboration and innovation of so many, we have achieved so much, but still much more work is needed (Waller 2011, 2019).

This chapter is a clarion call for professors to help the next generation of victimologists to be activists to accelerate progress toward dramatically reducing victimization and multiplying basic rights and services for victims. The opportunities for rapid advances are made possible by the extent of our knowledge, examples of good practice, and international exchanges but also by government commitment to act now to transform our world to get results through the Sustainable Development Goals. Getting action now is more possible than academics think, because of the new affordability of social media, modern ways to communicate, and willingness of young generations to engage with these tools and so shape the world rather than let others shape it.

2 UN General Assembly Resolution on Prevention of Victimization and Justice for Victims

In 1985, the United Nations General Assembly (UNGA) adopted a land mark resolution 40/34 on Basic Principles of Justice for Victims of Crime and Abuse of Power (UNGA 1985) where the governments of the world agreed for the first time to focus on the prevention of victimization and adopted fundamental principles of justice for victims of crime and abuse of power. The resolution was justified on the basis of the disturbing prevalence of violence, its painful impact on victims, and the lack of access to rights when dealing with criminal justice. These basic principles of justice in the UNGA resolution are often referenced as the victim magna carta.

Since 1985, much progress has been made. We have more than 40 years of accumulated victimological knowledge on the prevalence and impact of victimization and, the actions that have prevented victimization. We have initiatives for victim care and rights that set a new meaning for normal such as the European Commission Directives for Victims (2012).

In 2015, all the governments of the world at the UNGA committed to significant transformations to achieve by 2030 measurable targets that form the Sustainable Development Goals. These include targets in SDG 5 for the reduction in victims of violence against women and in SDG 16 to the reduction of victims of violence and homicide. They also include a goal on access to justice, that includes an indicator on increasing victim reporting to police, but does not yet identify whether victims are accessing services, reparation, or right to be heard.

The SDGs include the commitment to reduce dramatically the number of victims of violent crime in SDGs 16.1, 5.2, 16.2 by 2030 (UNGA 2015b). "Transforming Our World: The 2030 Agenda for Sustainable Development" (UNGA 2015a) requires a new way of doing business. There are essentially four new ways that we must get to know and understand. They are result based, build on progress in a network of domains, use evidence, and focus on transforming policies in both advanced and developing nations.

The indicator for homicide is measured regularly and considered reliable enough to make comparisons over time and between countries (United Nations Office for Drugs and Crime 2023). So this is a clear example of a focus on results. The indicators on sexual violence and violence against children will require the use of surveys such as the gold standard victimization survey known as the Intimate Partner and Sexual Violence Survey developed by US Centers for Disease Control (2011; Together for Girls 2026).

It is not so clear yet how governments will meet their commitments. So victimologists must focus on helping governments to invest now in the actions that will achieve those targets. They must build on the shoulders of Professor Chockalingam's leadership. Several intergovernmental agencies such as the World Health Organization, the UN Office on Drugs and Crime, UNICEF, UN Women, and UN-Habitat agree that the rates of prevalence and impact for victims are unacceptable as well as the importance of harnessing the knowledge to prevent crime and victimization. But there has been little focus on access of justice for victims. Few governments have started to invest to make the transformations needed to achieve the targets.

The commitment to transformations in the Sustainable Development Goals (SDGs) is a first step, but professors must help the next generation to put their laws and money where their mouth is. Victimologists must use science, model practices, and social media to build on, and emulate. They must engage politicians and become policy leaders now to get transformations so that effective upstream prevention and victim rights become the new normal by 2030.

3 Professors Must Teach What Has Reduced Victimization Before It Happens?

Victimologists must get to know the science, how to implement it, and how to convince policy makers to invest in it. I have now written a book to share this knowledge with victimologists, policy makers, faith-based organizations, and nongovernmental organizations, entitled the "Science and Secrets for Ending Violent Crime" (Waller 2019). The book makes the evidence-based case for a major shift from overuse of criminal justice and incarceration to effective solutions that prevent violent crime and victimization before it happens. It is based on a careful analysis of the science available from many academic sources as well as websites like crimesolutions.gov of the US department of Justice (n.d.) and info violence from the World Health Organization (n.d.) (Waller 2019, pp. 23–36). It explains the conclusions in terms that are easily understandable by politicians, victim advocates, and the public. Here are some of the highlights:

The book explains the essentials for this science to be applied. It focuses on guidelines, agreed at UN bodies such as United Nations Office for Drugs and Crime, UN-Habitat Safer Cities (2024), and World Health Organisation (2016, 2017) that are little known but are essentials for governments to successfully implement that science and achieve sustained reductions in victimization. These have been integrated into an impressive model for national governments (EuroSocial 2014).

It shares some inspiring examples of cities that have acted consistently with these essentials to achieve dramatic reductions in homicides within as little as 3 years. It highlights the success of Glasgow in Scotland who achieved a 50% reduction within 3 years and has sustained the decline over much longer. The Glasgow model is being adopted by the Mayor of London, UK (Mayor of London 2026). The largest Canadian Province now requires every municipality to have a community safety and well-being plan (Ontario Community Safety and Police Act 2019).

It shows how cities have planned their ways to reduce street violence significantly and importantly, why those cities succeeded when so many have not. The seven Essentials for Success (Waller 2019, pp. 117–122) are as follows:

1. Establishing a permanent violence and crime reduction board for the city
2. Being informed by violence prevention science and data
3. Having an integrated crime prevention plan
4. Mobilizing sectors able to tackle causes
5. Having adequate and sustained funding
6. Developing standards and training for human talent
7. Having public support and engagement¨

3.1 More of the Same, Not Enough

Chapter 1 in Waller (2019) reminds us of the horrendous numbers of victims of violence and the pain and loss from the impact of violence.

The dominant system of police, courts, and corrections provides some accountability to potential offenders, through certainty of detection where it exists, but lengthening prison sentences to achieve general deterrence is not effective. The history of rates of incarceration in the USA shows that extraordinary high rates of incarceration in States like Louisiana are associated with higher rates of homicide and not the reverse.

The failure of more incarceration in the USA to bring homicide rates down to levels close to other rich democracies confirms that more police and prison use is not enough to achieve significant reductions in victimization.

3.2 Consensus Among Prestigious Clearing Houses on Proven Preventive Practices

Part II of Waller (2019) presents the science of effective solutions. It uses an encyclopedic analysis of clearing houses and registries of what has been proven to reduce violence (Waller 2019, chapter 2). This included well-established clearing houses such as crimesolutions (US Department of Justice) and violence-info (World Health

Organization). Since the publication of the book, two other sources have come to the same general conclusions—the recent Toolkit (Youth Endowment Fund n.d.) in the UK and now in Spanish and Portuguese, Plataforma para desarrollo de soluciones efectivas en seguridad y justicia (BID). All summarize the best available evidence on proven ways to prevent violent crime. Many of the evaluations are based on several random control trials of the same smart innovation.

The analysis identified a short list of practices that are proven to have reduced violent crime before it happens more effectively and cost-efficiently than the dominant law enforcement and incarceration policies that primarily react after violent crime has happened. Many of these upstream practices have been shown to be highly cost-effective, often returning much more than US $7 for every US $1 invested in savings in losses to victims and to taxpayers, who pay less for unnecessary police and prisons.

3.3 *Practices Proven to Have Reduced Youth Violence by Tackling the Causes*

Chapter 4 (Waller 2019) discusses a range of practices for which there is evidence that they stop violence by young males. Here are some examples.

3.3.1 Youth Outreach

Projects that engage street workers to outreach to young men at risk of engaging in violence have achieved reductions 50% better than the traditional systems of police, courts, and corrections. In the UK, youth inclusion programs are the best illustration. These formed a key part of the Glasgow strategy where rates of violence across the city were reduced by 50% within 3 years. Under the name of Community Violence Intervention, they are the key ingredient in cities like Boston that achieved a 50% reduction across the city within 2 years. The funding of these programs across the USA are likely the main reason for reductions in homicide rates in the last few years across many cities in the USA.

Cognitive Behavioral Interventions

Programs that aim to regulate emotional decisions by helping children in their early teens. The Canadian program known as Stop Now and Plan (2015) teaches children with behavioral problems, and their parents, how to make better choices "in the moment." This achieves reductions in excess of 30% with estimated cost savings over $30 for every dollar invested.

3.4 *Activities Focused on Gender-Based Violence*

Some of the proven practices to stop youth violence also stop gender-based violence. Chapter 5 discusses the evidence for others that focus particularly on gender-based violence. Here are two examples.

3.4.1 Changing Male Attitudes

Sexual and intimate partner violence can be reduced significantly by changing male norms that encourage or tolerate violence against women. Victimologists can promote bystander intervention in their universities. Similar programs in teen years in schools such as programs adding responsibility to the focus for schools on reading, writing, and arithmetic. Intentionally changing community attitudes also achieve reductions in the range of 50%.

3.4.2 Empowering Women

Several activities that empower women reduce rates of violence against women. These include providing independent income, training in self-defense and knowing their rights, access to all female stations, and physical protections on transportation and streets.

3.5 *Activities Focused on Preventive Policing*

In chapter 3 (Waller 2019), the limits of standard policing are emphasized, but also a few preventive policing strategies that work are discussed.

3.5.1 Certainty of Detection

Though more police and expenditures on police do little to reduce crime. Improving certainty of detection is established as important to reducing violence. This applies to violence itself but also factors that influence violence such as alcohol, other drugs and guns. It also applies to traffic crime such as speeding and lack of use of seat belts which can lead to as many deaths and injuries as street and gender-based violence. Both problem-oriented policing and situational crime prevention use certainty to reduce crimes against property significantly.

3.5.2 Diversion and Focused Deterrence

One of the truisms is that the more a person gets involved with arrests and convictions, the more they get involved in arrests and convictions. So, programs to divert offenders from the system get some reductions in violence though rarely as much as the practices that tackle violence earlier.

Focused deterrence combines police action to threaten arrest with outreach as discussed above. The research shows that these combined programs reduce arrests for those targeted, but do not measure the spill effect of severe sanctions on those who refuse the outreach services. It is better to adopt programs like youth inclusion.

4 Professors Must Teach the Essentials for Using Proven Prevention

But solid science confirming proven solutions is not enough to save lives, protect women and children or avert physical and psychological trauma. Decision makers must implement the solutions on a scale sufficient to save thousands of lives and horrendous number of rapes and violence against children.

This implementation must be part of a larger coordinated, targeted and sustained effort to get reductions in violence in just a few years. It requires national and state actions as well as local government.

4.1 Consensus on Essentials at ECOSOC

What have governments identified as the essentials for that science to be used locally and for measurable goals to be achieved? In chapter 7, Waller (2019) identified seven essentials for successful implementation that are in common between different UN Agencies. For Latin America, an important framework was developed that built on these UN guidelines, the experience of 8 Latin American countries and the experience of EU countries. It identified similar essentials but emphasized the importance to teaching the planning skills that are needed to justify and implement programs based in evidence nationally and locally (EuroSocial 2014).

4.2 Office for Violence Prevention

The first essential for success is establishing a permanent violence and crime reduction board for the city. This responsibility center is the energy behind developing and implementing crime prevention plans.

4.3 *Success Requires Skilled Community Safety Planners*

For innovations to be successful, they will require developing standards and training for human talent capable of planning and implementing effective solutions. The World Health Organization published a tool. The Canadian Centre for Safer Communities (2024) has developed training courses available on the web.

4.3.1 Comprehensive Planning Strategy Focused on Outcomes

Having an integrated crime prevention plan is key to coordinate and oversee crime prevention The UN Guidelines stress the need for a local plan that mobilizes various community and economic sectors to prevent crime. The plan must be based on diagnoses of local crime problems and should include performance standards, targeted solutions, training protocol, and outcome evaluations.

4.3.2 Informed by Violence Prevention Science

At this point most decision makers and victimologists are not aware of the violence prevention science that is discussed above. This must change if significant reductions in victimization are to be achieved.

4.3.3 Mobilizing Sectors Able to Tackle Causes

Because of the nature of the risk factors that lead to crime, the violence prevention office must mobilize talent able to help solve the problems. These individuals might include social workers, educators, health professionals, employment specialists, and sports figures as well as criminal justice system workers (Waller 2019; UN-Habitat Safer Cities 2024; ECOSOC 2002; World Health Organization 2016; Youth Violence Commission 2020; Ontario Ministry of Community Safety and Correctional Services 2020).

4.3.4 Public Involvement

Lastly, it is crucial to have public support and engagement. The public can play many roles in applying violence prevention science. They can become mentors, take precautions, and help map crime. They can also be advocates to get the permanent board and funding needed to implement violence prevention strategies. For instance, mothers and parents of at-risk young men tend to be successful actors in effecting change at the local and national levels.

4.4 Adequate and Sustained Funding

The next essential for successful crime prevention is to have the investment to achieve the targets. Crime prevention requires adequate resources, including funding for structures and activities. A good rule of thumb is to start with the equivalent of 10% of expenditures on police and prisons.

Chapter 9 (Waller 2019) shows how several cities have implemented actions consistent with these guidelines to achieve a 50% reduction in just a few years. Bogota in the 1990s established a planning group that diagnosed the risk factors for homicides and then implemented a series of policy initiatives to reduce homicide over 10 years by 50%. This in turn inspired the Glasgow model where a violence reduction unit diagnosed the problems leading to policy initiatives that reduced homicide by 50% within 3 years. Cardiff is another model where a diagnosis of the risk factors for young men coming to hospital emergency rooms led to reductions of 42% in hospital admissions for intentional injuries and 32% reduction in police records of violence.

5 Professors Must Teach Ways to Build Political Will to Use Proven Prevention

Chapter 12 of Waller (2019) discusses a range of practical ways to raise awareness among the public and decision makers.

"What we treasure, we can measure" and "what gets measured gets done." Unfortunately spending on more of the same and expecting different results has not worked. So focusing on outcomes must become the rule for the future.

The history of these movements in other countries is that innovation starts in the right direction but is eventually eaten for breakfast by a swing back to the status quo of policing, courts and incarceration. So, e-marketing must be accompanied by proof of success.

5.1 Making the Compelling Case

5.1.1 Big Benefits from Smart Investment

Chapter 10 in Waller (2019) brings together the human and economic case for smart investment in prevention. The compelling case for investing in proven prevention is in part the victimological argument that it stops the pain, injury and trauma to victims. But it is also the economic argument that reducing violence generates economic activity. In 2024, 18 governments in Latin America and the

Caribbean established the Alliance for Justice, Security and Development (2024) in major part because they were losing so much GDP to violence. "The economic impact of crime and violence in Mexico for the year 2021 has been estimated at about $192 billion US dollars, which corresponds to 14.6% of the national GDP. By reducing violence 50% by 2030, we estimate savings of at least US$110 billion dollars".

5.1.2 Significant Reductions in Violence Are Affordable and Achievable

How to Get Buy-in

It identifies how to foster sustainable and smarter investments by policy makers. It makes a giant step further forward to getting this knowledge used by using my several decades of experience in the USA and elsewhere, including India, to get buy-in. Prevention is a big shift but includes the benefits of savings to taxpayers, reductions in mass incarceration, and meeting the visions of many victims to stop violence (see Waller 2019, pp. 183–200).

So how do we make the transformations to make our communities safer. Effective violence prevention is not only more affordable and successful than policy makers think; a modest equivalent of 10% of what they spend on police, courts, and corrections will do it and often before the next election! Violence prevention is achievable, because voters, contrary to what the media tells us, want much more than reaction, they want prevention (see Waller 2019, pp. 221–228). Yes, they want tough on crime, but they also want tough on causes.

Think of a World Where Victimologists Helped Reduce Violence by 50% by 2030

The stakes are high. The science and successes show that a 50% reduction in violent crime is achievable by 2030 (Waller 2019). Globally, this reduction saves 250,000s lives from homicide for the target in SDG 16.1, more than 10 million women from rape for the target in SDG 5.2, and half a billion children from violence for the target in SDG 16.2. Yes, if we follow the life work of Professor Chockalingam, we can counter the crisis of epidemic proportions with getting policy makers to transform their policies, laws, and investments.

The innovations needed are in the interests of governments by spending money better, managing cities to make cities safer, investing in disadvantaged families, and legislating support for affordable, popular, and cost-effective preventive solutions. In high violence countries and communities, it will increase GDP and well-being (Inter-American Development Bank 2018; Waller 2019).

The Challenge for Activist Victimologists

Victimologists now must get to know the science and model practices as well as use social media and political engagement. They must spear head decisive action, in partnership with UN agencies and pathfinder governments, by five initiatives:

1. Get to know the science, the essentials for success, and how to get buy-in.
2. Raise awareness among politicians and the public of effective solutions and strategies, using modern communication tools.
3. Train and foster the human talent to implement effective strategies successfully.
4. Act locally to deliver effective solutions.
5. Work collaboratively to convince policy makers to invest now, including policy proposals based on effective solutions and strategies (Waller 2019).

There are several movements with which victimologists can collaborate (Waller 2019, pp. 221–238). Most of these movements are focused on getting decisive actions now from governments to achieve the results agreed in the Sustainable Development Goals (2021). Many of the movements are planning to advocate for transformations at the UN Congress on Crime Prevention and Criminal Justice in Kyoto in April 2020.

Across Latin America, ILANUD is working with seventeen or more Latin America countries and with cities within those countries to mobilize action to reduce their epidemic levels of violence, using science, tools and best practices. ILANUD is the Latin American institute working on crime prevention and criminal justice as part of the program network of institutes associated with United Nations Office for Drugs and Crime.

Peace in our cities campaign (2019) calls on mayors, local authorities, civil society, the private sector, and other partners to halve violent victimization in their cities by 2030. They recognize that we now have the tools, evidence, and best practices to curb violence but also address the structural inequalities and injustices that perpetuate it.

The Coalition of Faith-Based Organizations, Spirituality, held a major event in the Grace Cathedral in San Francisco where the UN Charter was first signed 74 years ago. It is exploring ways in which faith-based organizations can contribute to crime prevention and the criminal justice system. It will submit a declaration to the UN Congress on Crime Prevention and Criminal justice with a view to encouraging the transformations needed to achieve the objectives of SDG 16.

In the USA, several movements are pressuring governments to do something about gun violence (Waller 2019, pp. 233–235). March for our Lives for instance has proposed a plan for a Safer America. In Latin America and increasingly globally feminists are calling for governments to pay attention and solve the issues of violence against women.

Chapter 11 (Waller 2019) shows that significant reductions in violence are achievable and importantly affordable.

The evidence from violence prevention science shows the economic benefits from reducing victimization and increasing GDP. Smart community safety planners need to get the education and training to know how to argue how smart investments in well planned prevention will achieve reductions in victimization, taxes saved and increases in economic activity.

5.2 Raising Awareness

We are living in the social media age where it is possible to share messages cheaply with followers who can repeat the message. It is also possible to send messages directly to the decision makers.

Contrary to beliefs of too many decision makers, the majority of the public including victims want prevention not punishment. Victimologists must learn to work with the activist movements clamoring for prevention of victimization and help use evidence-based arguments on what is effective and cost benefit justifications for investment.

5.2.1 Mechanisms for Policy Shift

Victimology Can Build on International Progress

Examples like Glasgow and Boston illustrated that good planning and smart investment can achieve 50% less violent crime within 3 years. National policies such as the violence reduction unit program in the UK illustrate success. Significant progress has been achieved. More action is needed, particularly to get proven solutions used and sufficient of the essentials to get national wide and city-wide reductions to meet the SDG targets.

Two international movements are important. Peace in our cities (2019) is a network of cities across the globe that are committed to halving violence by 50% before 2030. It provides a community of practice with networking between the cities who are the members. While some members like Palmira in Colombia have already achieved the goal, many of the members have not yet profited from the science or the essentials for implementation that are needed to achieve their goal.

UN-Habitat has its own Safer Cities program; it has guidelines and a global network of 80 or so cities. Though many have respected some of the essentials for success, there are few that are able to demonstrate significant reductions in gender-based and street violence. They have created a small group of peer experts to advise on tools to help more cities reduce violence.

There is an opportunity for victimology to partner with both these networks in Latin America to help them make more use of the proven solutions, get the essentials for success implemented, and particularly help decision makers do what will save lives, stop gender-based violence, and make communities significantly safer and so prosperous.

Nationally, the US White House (2023a, b) has started to fund gun violence reduction programs based on evidence and has started a national program, which includes a national office for gun violence prevention chaired by the Vice President who has a background in enforcement and prevention. It includes efforts to provide more accountability through law enforcement and more responsible gun ownership. But it breaks new ground in the USA by adopting strategies recommended internationally. These include a state office for violence prevention and use of evidence-based strategies. Two of the evidence-based strategies expand US funding for community violence initiatives and hospital intervention with funding from the US Victims of Crime Act.

In the USA, Thomas Abt is an example of what a criminology professor can do. He is the founding director of the Center for the Study and Practice of Violence Reduction (VRC) and an associate research professor in the Department of Criminology and Criminal Justice at the University of Maryland. He collaborated with the City of Boston in a 3-day workshop with leaders in the city and folk from different communities. This resulted in the mayor launching an evidence-based program, where she promised a 20% reduction in shootings and homicides within 3 years. He is collaborating with other cities.

In the UK, recommendations from the Youth Violence Commission focused on cloning the Glasgow Violence Reduction Unit, where the unit diagnosed the problems, which it addressed with proven solutions and achieved a 50% reduction in violence within 3 years of implementing the solutions. Approximately 20 regions have a VRU, though the extent to which the essentials are in place is not clear. The Home Office (n.d.) provides some modest funding and is undertaking a systematic evaluation of the process and the outcomes. The early results focus on hospital admissions for intentional injuries, which show some reductions. Manchester has demonstrated important reductions.

The Mayor of London was inspired in 2018 to establish his own violence reduction unit. It was inspired by Glasgow and brought together leaders from health, police, local government, probation, and community organizations to tackle violent crime and its underlying causes (Mayor of London, 2026). It has 15 or more staff, including a small research team, and a budget of $20 million with $10 million from the city and the remainder from central government.

Canada's largest province has added community safety to the title of its police act and now requires every municipality to develop a community safety plan to reduce risk factors that contribute to "crime, victimization, addiction, drug overdose, and suicide." For instance, the Mayor of Toronto recently said "People in our city deserve to be safe … Then let's use a public health, a scientific approach; what has worked in the past? How could we expand those and then we track the results. Cities like Glasgow have done it." Montreal now has a university chair for gun violence prevention.

5.2.2 Commissions to Recommend Change

In many countries and cities, commissions are established to review the state of knowledge, best practice, and listen to public concerns. In the USA, the Council on Criminal Justice is an independent group that has made several recommendations for change. In the UK, the Youth Violence Commission is another example.

Legislative committees are another way of making actionable recommendations.

5.2.3 Partnering with Activist and Lobby Groups

Victims of violence and parents of murdered children are an important group to push for reductions in victimization. Javier Sicilia is one example, where the father of a murdered child mobilized marches in Mexico to argue for change. In Bogota in the 1990s, it was the mothers of murdered children who kept pressure on successive mayors to keep the actions that were reducing homicides. There are also international movements often started in the USA that have an impact internationally such as MeToo and Black Lives Matter.

These movements want results, but are often not aware of the prevention science. In collaboration with smart community safety planners, they can get to know the science and how to implement it and so influence proven ways to get the results that they want.

6 Professors Must Teach Ways To Advance Rights for Victims

The international statistics represent too many millions of tragedies, where victims were unjustly subjected to suffer loss, injury, trauma, and much more. Too many of these victims in developed countries do not get their legislated rights to services, reparation for the harm, or being heard when their interests are affected. Many suffer hardship when assisting with the prosecution of an offender. The situation is catastrophically worse in middle-income and developing countries.

6.1 What Are The Rights for Victims of Crime?

In the developed world, the European Union, Japan, the UK, and the USA are among the leaders in improving justice, reparation, and assistance for victims of crime, but there is still a long way to go to secure universal and effective recognition of, and respect for, the rights of victims.

Other countries, particularly with high levels of interpersonal violence, have started to make improvements, but much less progress has been achieved. The high rates of violence cause harm, losses, and injustice. Increasingly, violence is recognized as stopping economic development and impeding rule of law in their own countries while contributing to uncontrolled migration and organized crime to developed countries.

In the last 50 years, the leading developed countries have achieved

- National surveys of victimization, including violence against women.
- Best practice to inform, assist, and protect victims of crime after victimization, including for victims of gender-based violence, human trafficking, and cybercrime.
- Systems of reparation to victims, including health care, compensation from the state, restitution from offenders, civil settlements, and restorative justice.
- Ways for victims to be heard in the criminal justice process and seek remedies where rights are not respected.

We have accumulated significant knowledge and best practices on how to meet the needs rights for victims of crime, but much more is needed. Groenhuijsen did much to show the progress in the handbook on international victim rights legislation (Groenhuijsen and Letschert 2009). *Rights for Victims of Crime* (Waller 2011) makes the case for much greater investments to *rebalance justice*. It uses the latest in scientific research, best practice across the world, and international human rights norms. Though many proposals focus on the USA, there are lessons for every continent. It presents this victimology to policy makers, justice professionals, and advocates for victims. But much more must be done by victimologists to get the investments and legislation that are so overdue.

In the USA, the Victims of Crime Act (VOCA) in 1984, Violence against Women Act (AWA) in 1994, and the Victtim Rights Act in 2004 have advanced funding, services, and rights for victims of crime. VOCA provides more than $4 billion annually for States and local government to establish services, compensation, and actions for vulnerable victims such as domestic violence.

In the EU (2012), the directive has been adopted and is being implemented (European Commission 2012). This sets standards across more than 25 countries reaching potentially 500 million people or more than 70 million victims. The standards include services, restitution, restorative justice, information, and a limited right to participation.

Australia and the UK have victim commissioners. Canada has a Federal Ombudsman for Victims of Crime. Japan has implemented a comprehensive program for victims of crime (Waller 2011).

The achievements of the last 50 years show that we know what to do, because it has been done somewhere already, but we are not doing it widely enough. The challenge is how to achieve these targets by expansion of best practice in the developed world and make strategic investments to achieve them in the developing world.

These require accelerating the transformations in policy to put what we know to work. Reductions in violence are particularly important as by definition they reduce the need for services and rights after victimization.

In preparation for the celebration of 40 years since the adoption of the UN Declaration, United Nations Office for Drugs and Crime contracted for a new Handbook on Justice for Victims of Crime and Abuse of Power. The draft discussed at an expert meeting in 2014 covered everything from impact of victimization to victim rights to services.

It included a list of items for policy reform that included national legislation to create a central agency to provide assistance and fair treatment, making victim rights as human rights, establishing Ombudspersons nationally to protect rights of victims in dealings with government, and a Special rapporteur at the UN.

There are three policy initiatives that are strategic to accelerating the shift toward universal remedies and demonstrable respect for standards:

The European Union has adopted a victim rights directive that sets out minimum standards across all country members to be met by 2015. Its implementation has been evaluated several times. These measure the extent to which victims are receiving the respect and rights in the directive. These evaluations show an implementation gap and recommend ways to improve achievement of the standards. The EU is providing "expertise, training, guidance, and support."

The National Crime Victim Law Institute has identified 10 Common Victim Rights, which shows important progress across the USA on rights obtainable within the justice system. They span rights to air treatment to restitution. However, their analysis shows variations between states on these rights. Also, they do not cover core supports for victims such as assistance, compensation, or fair treatment by law enforcement.

The Office for Victims of Crime was established in 1984 to enhance services for victims of crime. Its main function is to provide financial support for services and state compensation. It is committed to professionalization through training and sharing best practices. In 2004, the USA adopted a federal crime victim rights act that established a short list of rights, directives on how they were to be implemented, and ways to enforce the rights. An initial evaluation on whether the rights were provided led to recommendations on training. The most recent law identifies who is responsible for implementing the rights.

The Office for Victims of Crime includes a history of victim rights in the USA as a background resource for the annual crime victim rights week. This covers

- The creation and growth of local, state, and national victim service organizations
- The passage of key federal and state legislation
- Notable court decisions
- Groundbreaking reports and studies
- Advances in victim assistance approaches

6.2 Measuring and Other Ways to Get Victims Their Rights

These are all steps in the right direction. Unfortunately, victims often do not get the right or service in the laws, because legislators have rarely provided for adequate funding, an effective remedy, or a way to evaluate the implementation.

Surveys in Europe and North America show that victims are not using services that are available, because they are not informed or linked to the services. A recent survey in the UK showed victims who reported to police would not do so again.

6.3 Rights for Victims of Crime in a Model Law

Experts on victimology from across the globe set out ways to meet the needs of victims through services and implementable rights. Among rights proposed are the following (some proposed as a constitutional amendment are in italics):

- Be notified of all critical proceedings and developments in your case
- Be notified of the status of the alleged or convicted offender
- *Reasonable notice of, and shall not be excluded from, public proceedings relating to the offense*
- *Proceedings free from unreasonable delay*
- *Be heard at any release, plea, sentencing, or other such proceeding involving any right established*
- Be present at all hearings at which the defendant is entitled to attend
- *Reasonable notice of the release or escape of the accused*
- *Restitution* to be paid by the offender in cases that result in a conviction
- *Due consideration of the crime victim's safety and privacy,* before, during, and after the trial
- Apply for victim compensation in cases involving violent crime
- Be treated with dignity and respect
- Right to pursue legal remedies if your rights are violated

Some of these rights would need to respect at least the special needs of children, women, Aboriginal Peoples, and disabled.

One significant way to make these rights enforceable is to make them measurable. What gets measured gets done. We need to build on progress such as England and Wales has set standards; the European Union calls for data; the US GAO monitored the Crime Victims Rights Act.

The UN has spun off the International Criminal Court that provides extensive rights to information, protection, participation, and restitution (Waller 2011). However, at this stage, the number of prosecutions has been limited, but there is need for further research to identify how to measure the extent to which victims get the extensive access to protection, support, reparation, and being heard.

6.4 *Building Political Will To Provide Basic Rights for All Victims*

In the last 50 years, much has been achieved to set out principles for victims to get rights, but in the USA and even in the European Union, there is still a long way to go to get these implemented. Many of the advances have been achieved by nongovernmental groups, such as the US National Organization for Victim Advocacy. Some has been achieved by organizations set up by the parents of murdered children, who are very active for a period of time but slowly lose momentum. In the USA, mothers against guns and the group working on Marsy's Law are important exceptions.

Just like in building political will to reduce victimization, courses for victimologists need to help victimologists understand the compelling case for change, some of which is identifying individual cases, which illustrate not only the tragic consequences of violence to its victims but also how policing, criminal courts, and corrections ignore the basic interests of victims.

Victimologists must acquire the passion and skills to use e-marketing and the media to build the political will to support actions to achieve significant law reform in support of victim rights, including sustained and adequate funding.

7 Conclusion

United Nations Office for Drugs and Crime (2023) said that the international community must take decisive steps now to significantly reduce all forms of violence and related death rates, if they are to achieve the targets in the UN Sustainable Development Goals—SDG16 and 5—by 2030. The international community must also be mobilized to realize protection, support, reparation, and justice for victims of crime.

This chapter identifies the decisive action needed now to significantly reduce violent crime by 2030 as required by SDG 16.1. 5.2, and 16.2. Professors must get to know the knowledge, how to get it implemented, and how to build political will to get effective investments. They must then take on the task of inspiring the next generations of victimologists to acquire and use this knowledge and skills. The knowledge identifies proven examples of programs and cities that have reduced violent crime by 50% within 3 years. So the teaching must share this knowledge and how to get it used and build the political will for adequate and sustained investment at the city, country, and ultimately the world scale.

This is the key to important and compelling benefits, starting with significantly fewer victims killed, injured, and traumatized within 5 years. It is women and children protected from sexual and intimate partner violence. It is improved feelings of safety and greater prosperity. It is increased GDP and better rule of law, and fewer pockets of fragility. It is also investments in the futures of young disadvantaged males rather than violations of their human rights in the belief that repression is the only way to less violence, when prevention science is a better way.

It also sets out standards for access to justice for persons who are victims of crime. There is an urgent need to teach the ways victim rights are being delivered, which show what is possible. It stresses the need to measure whether victims are getting that access to justice as well as stronger legislation. It discusses ways to build political will to make these happen.

With this teaching, next generations of victimologists can accelerate the transformations needed. They can partner with UN agencies and pathfinder governments and cities, particularly by becoming active with the groundswell of movements calling on governments to shift from a failing criminal justice system to effective violence prevention and access to justice for victims

References

Alliance for Justice, Security and Development (2024). https://www.iadb.org/en/who-we-are/topics/modernization-state/citizen-security-and-justice/alliance-security-justice-and-development#:~:text=The%20Alliance%20is%20formed%20by,in%20Latin%20America%20and%20the

Canadian Centre for Safer Communities (2024). https://safercities.ca/

Centers for Disease Control and Prevention (2011) National Intimate Partner and Sexual Violence Survey, Summary Report, Atlanta

ECOSOC 2002 Resolution 2002/13 Action to promote effective crime prevention

European Commission (2012) https://commission.europa.eu/strategy-and-policy/policies/justiceand-fundamental-rights/criminal-justice/protecting-victims-rights/victims-rights-eu_en#victims-rights-in-the-eu

European Union Directive for Victims of Crime, 2012 https://eur-lex.europa.eu/eli/dir/2012/29/oj/eng

EuroSocial (2014) Regional model for a comprehensive violence and crime prevention policy. http://www.sia.eurosocial-ii.eu/files/docs/1461686840-DT_33-_Modelo%20regional%20Prevencion%20Violencia%20(ENG).pdf

Groenhuijsen M, Letschert R (eds) (2009) Compilation of international victim rights instruments. Wolf Legal Publishers, Nijmegen

Home Office, UK (n.d.). https://www.gov.uk/government/publications/violence-reduction-units-year-ending-march-2023-evaluation-report/violence-reduction-units-2022-to-2023

Inter-American Development Bank (2018) Smart spending on citizen security: beyond crime and punishment. https://flagships.iadb.org/en/DIA2018/chapter-7-smart-spending-citizen-security-beyond-crime-and-punishment

Mayor of London, 2026, https://www.london.gov.uk/londons-homicide-rate-capita-lowest-records-began-havingrecorded-its-lowest-homicide-figures-eleven

Monette A, Waller I (2024) How to shift government policy from punishing to saving lives, chapter 48. In: Heide KM (ed) The Routledge international handbook of juvenile homicide. Routledge, New York, pp 782–785

Ontario Community Safety and Police Act (2019)

Ontario Ministry of Community Safety and Correctional Safety (2020) Community safety and well being planning: a shared commitment in Ontario, Toronto

Peace in our cities (2019). https://www.sdg16.plus/peace-in-our-cities/

Stop Now and Plan (2015). https://pmc.ncbi.nlm.nih.gov/articles/PMC4208980/

Together for Girls (2026) A systematic review of the global and regional estimates of the prevalence of sexual violence against children
UN Habitat Safer Cities (2024). https://unhabitat.org/network/global-network-on-safer-cities
United Nations General Assembly (1985) Resolution 40/34 on basic principles of justice for victims of crime and abuse of power. https://www.un.org/documents/ga/res/40/a40r034.htm. Accessed 15 Aug 2019
United Nations General Assembly (2015a) Transforming our world: The 2030 agenda for sustainable development. sustainabledevelopment.un.org A/RES/70/1
United Nations General Assembly (2015b) Sustainable development goals. https://sustainabledevelopment.un.org/
United Nations Office on Drugs and Crime (2023) Global study on homicide. United Nations, Vienna
United Nations Sustainable Development Goals (2021) Final list of proposed sustainable development goal indicators. https://unstats.un.org/sdgs/indicators/Global%20Indicator%20Framework%20after%202023%20refinement_Eng.pdf
US Department of Justice (n.d.). Reliable Research. Real Results. | CrimeSolutions, National Institute of Justice (ojp.gov)
US White House (2023a) Office of gun violence in White House. https://www.whitehouse.gov/briefing-room/statements-releases/2023/09/21/president-joe-biden-to-establish-first-ever-white-house-office-of-gun-violence-prevention-to-be-overseen-by-vice-president-kamala-harris/
US White House (2023b) Safer states agenda US White House. OGVP-Safer-States-Policy-Agenda.pdf (whitehouse.gov)
Waller I (2011) Rights for victims of crime. Rowman and Littlefield, Lanham
Waller I (2019) Science and secrets of ending violent crime. Lanham, Rowman and Littlefield
Waller I (2020a) Activist victimology from principles in 1985 to practical transformations by 2030. In: Shekhar B, Sahni SP (eds) Global perspective of victimology and criminology: yesterday, today and tomorrow. Bloomsbury
Waller I (2020b) What can we achieve by 2030? Rights for victims of crime in the era of sustainable development goals. In: Joseph J, Jergenson S (eds) An international perspective on contemporary developments in victimology. Springer, Cham
Waller I, Monette A (2021) Necessary actions for cities to reduce violence by 50 percent by 2030. https://safercities.ca/evidence-on-crime-prevention/#sectionpol ver video https://youtu.be/VieVtFqFKwY?si=HNJWuM38PD118YHg
World Health Organisation (2016) INSPIRE: Seven Strategies to Ending Violence Against Children https://www.who.int/activities/preventing-violence-against-children
World Health Organization (2017) https://www.who.int/activities/preventing-violence-against children
World Health Organization, Violence Info. (n.d.). https://apps.who.int/violence-info/about/
Youth Endowment Fund, London, UK. https://youthendowmentfund.org.uk/toolkit/
Youth Violence Commission 2020 Final Report Keir Irwin-Rogers, The Open University, July 2020

Compensation for Victims of Crime in Poland Since the Dawn of the Twentieth Century

Emil W. Pływaczewski and Ewa M. Guzik-Makaruk

Abstract This chapter provides an analysis of compensation for victims of crime in Poland since the dawn of the twentieth century in the criminal codes then in force and in the Act of July 7, 2005, on state compensation to victims of certain criminal acts (the so-called compensation act). In the twentieth century, Poland had three criminal codes: the Criminal Code of 1932, the Criminal Code of 1969, and the Criminal Code of 1997. The 1932 Criminal code had the fewest compensatory regulations, but the situation of victims of crime was slightly improved by the 1969 Criminal Code.

The Criminal Code that is currently in force is far from perfect, but it most fully fulfills the compensatory function of criminal law. The so-called Compensation Act, passed in 2005, was the first to implement the idea of a state compensation fund for victims of crime. Initially, many hopes were pinned on it, but during the nearly 20 years of its history, many of its shortcomings became evident. These shortcomings even led to the phenomenon of secondary victimization, and the fund itself is used to a limited extent.

Another institution is the Victims Assistance and Post-Penitentiary Assistance Fund, which has been in operation since 2012 and is independent of the so-called Compensation Act. It focuses on assistance to victims and witnesses, prevention of crime, and post-penitentiary assistance. The authority in charge of the fund is the Minister of Justice.

Keywords Victimology • Criminology • Polish criminal law • Functions of criminal law • Compensation to victims of crime • Polish compensation system • Victims • Criminal justice system

E. W. Pływaczewski (✉) · E. M. Guzik-Makaruk
National Police Academy in Szczytno, Szczytno, Poland
e-mail: ewa.guzik@tlen.pl

© The Author(s), under exclusive license to Springer Nature Singapore Pte Ltd. 2026
G. S. Bajpai et al. (eds.), *Beyond the Gavel: A Paradigm Shift in Global Criminal Justice*, https://doi.org/10.1007/978-981-95-4487-5_15

We dedicate this study to the esteemed Jubilarian, Professor K. Chockalingam, the Master and Educator of many generations of criminologists and victimologists—Lawyers. Professor Chockalingam is an outstanding representative of criminological sciences, and his extensive activity and rich scientific and organizational achievements testify to his exceptional activity and versatility of interests.

In a congratulatory letter sent to Professor Emil Pływaczewski on the occasion of his 70th birthday, Professor K. Chockalingam pointed to the more than 25-years long history of mutual academic contacts related to reciprocal visits to Poland and India, and participation in numerous international conferences and congresses. Separately, Professor K. Chockalingam also expressed good wishes on behalf of his wife Dr. Vijayalakshmi Chockalingam and his sons Dr. C. Raj Kumar and Ravi Kumar Chockalingam (Guzik-Makaruk et al. 2023). Professor Ewa M. Guzik-Makaruk participated in important events and assisted in Professor K. Chockalingam's visits to the University of Białystok in 1995 and 1998.

The Jubilarian is a pioneer of victimology in India, and a monograph he edited, titled "Readings in Victimology. Towards a Victim Perspective in Criminology" (Madras 1985), made an important contribution to the development of the foundations of victimology in that country. Over the past 40 years, since the publication of that monograph, Victimology has strongly developed in India, especially at the O.P. Jindal Global University, headed by Jubilarian's son (Sahni et al. 2017).

It should be noted that in recognition of his scientific contributions to Criminology and Victimology during the last several decades, Professor Chockalingam was presented with several awards, in particular the American Society of Criminology's Distinguished International Scholar Award (1995). The same award was given to Professor Emil Pływaczewski (1997).

The scientific and teaching path of the Jubilarian and Professor Emil W. Pływaczewski is also connected with the Tokiwa University in Mito, Japan, where the Jubilarian spent 6 years. He worked as the Deputy Director of the Tokiwa International Victimology Institute for 2 years and finally as the Director of the International Center of the Tokiwa University.

The authors of this text have dedicated it to Professor K. Chockalingam and sincerely express the hope that its reading will give him pleasure and satisfaction, since the issue of compensation for victims of crime is also important to him.

1 The Restitutive Function from a Historical Perspective

In the twentieth century, Poland had three criminal codes. The first code in effect in independent Poland was the Criminal Code of 1932. It was an extremely progressive code, modeled on the best European standards. Unfortunately, its successor, the Criminal Code of 1969, was based on the socialist (Soviet) experience. Today, the not-quite-successful Criminal Code of 1997 remains in force.

The Penal Code of 1932 combined elements of the sociological and classical schools of law, but the catalog of principal and additional penalties did not include any restitutionary measures. Only with a conditional suspension of the enforcement of a penalty, which is shaped on the Franco-Belgian model, it is stipulated that the court may oblige the convict to compensate for the damages caused by the crime, if the convict's economic situation allows it.

On the basis of the Criminal Code of 1969, the functions of criminal law presented in the doctrine were framed within a narrower or broader catalog. Usually, it was limited to highlighting two functions of criminal law, namely, the guarantee function and the protective function, leaving out the justice function. The justice function was part of the protective function. Sometimes, the catalog of functions of criminal law included the protective, guarantee, repressive, and preventive functions.

A. Marek, on the other hand, identified three functions of criminal law: protective, guarantee, and preventive-educational (Marek 1986, pp. 12–13). K. Buchała included in the catalog of functions of criminal law, successively, the protective function, the preventive educational function, the repressive function, the prophylactic-safeguarding function, and the guarantee function, referring to the belief, quite unanimous in the doctrine, that the protective function is "the basic function of criminal law" (Buchała 1980, p. 20). Fifteen years later, K. Buchała and A. Zoll identified only two functions of criminal law: the protective function and the guarantee functions (Buchała and Zoll 1995, pp. 11–14). Another prominent representative of the Polish doctrine of criminal law, W. Świda, similarly took a two-pronged view of the functions of criminal law (Świda 1989, pp. 13–14). It follows that during period when the Criminal Code of 1969 was in force, the doctrine did not attach importance to the restitutive function.

However, it should be noted that that Criminal Code contained some provisions that included the restitutive function of criminal law. For example, when conditionally discontinuing criminal proceedings, the court could oblige the offender to repair all or part of the damage caused by the crime, and if the offender was charged with a crime against property, the court would be obligated to require repair of the damage. TThe offender's failure to repair the damage would be the basis for the mandatory resumption of the conditionally discontinued proceedings.

Another example of reference to the restitutive function was the provisions regarding the penalty of restriction of liberty. When imposing the penalty of restriction of liberty, the court could oblige the offender to repair all or part of the damage caused by the crime and/or to apologize to the victim.

The compensatory function was also evident with the conditional suspension of the enforcement of sentence. The court could oblige the convict to repair all or part of the damage caused by the crime and/or to apologize to the victim. With regard to the perpetrator of theft of collective property, the repair of the damage was an obligatory condition for the application of that probationary institution. Failure to comply with the obligation to repair the damage was a prerequisite for the mandatory order of execution of the sentence.

2 Compensation in the Current Criminal Code of 1997

A. Marek, cited above, presented a much broader catalog of functions of criminal law in his first textbook, which already included the solutions contained in the new Criminal Code of 1997. In addition to the previously indicated functions, namely, the protective, guarantee, and preventive-educational functions, he also mentioned such functions as affirmative motivational, justice, and restitutive. With regard to the restitutive function, A. Marek emphasized that it was formed under the influence of the idea of protection of human rights, including the demands of victimology. In other words, criminal law should, through an appropriate system of penal measures, enable the perpetrator of a crime to strive to repair the harm caused to the victim (Marek 1997, pp. 14–16).

The restitutive (compensatory) function is also emphasized—in addition to the protective and guarantee function—by J. Giezek, who pointed out that it gained importance after the entry into force of the Criminal Code of 1997, the essential characteristic of which is the strengthening of the role and standing of the victim. This author emphasizes that the compensatory function is fostered not only by the regulations provided by the substantive criminal law, but also by certain procedural solutions, such as the institutions of mediation or settlement, as a result of which the accused voluntarily accepts liability (Giezek 2010, p. 26).

The Criminal Code of 1997 is a piece of legislation that most fully fulfills the restitutive function of criminal law to date. It contains the broadest catalog of compensatory institutions, capturing for the first time in the history of criminal legislation the obligation to repair a damage as a penal measure. IAs of July 1, 2015, Chapter Va titled "Forfeiture and Compensatory Measures" was added to the Criminal Code. Compensatory measures are an obligation to repair in whole or in part the damage caused by the crime, a compensation for the harm suffered, exemplary damages to the victim or the Victims Assistance and Post Penitentiary Assistance Fund.

The Victims Assistance and Post-Penitentiary Assistance Fund has existed since 2012. It is a state fund that focuses on assistance to victims and witnesses, prevention of crime, and post-penitentiary assistance. The authority in charge of the Fund is the Minister of Justice.

The Fund's resources are used for the following:

1. Give assistance to people who are victims of crime and their loved ones, especially medical, psychological, rehabilitative, legal, and material assistance.
2. Training for bodies that conduct criminal proceedings.
3. Funding for alternative conflict resolution methods, in particular mediation in family, minor, and criminal cases.
4. Education in the field of violence and crime prevention, in particular for police officers and employees of educational and health-care entities.
5. Post-penitentiary assistance to former inmates released from prisons and detention centers, as well as their loved ones.
6. Psychological assistance to witnesses and their loved ones.

7. Undertaking, organizing, and commissioning scientific research on the situation and needs of victims of crime, witnesses, and convicts, as well as the causes and conditions of crime and its prevention.
8. Activities to support families at risk of dysfunctionality, in particular in the area of prevention and therapy of addiction and codependency, and conflict resolution in the family.

3 Compensation According to the Act of July 7, 2005, on State *Compensation* to Victims of Certain Criminal Acts (So-Called Compensation Act)

Polish victimologists have sought to establish the institution of compensation for many years. First, the Crime Victims Assistance Foundation was registered in 1985 as a substitute for a state compensation system. Poland became the only country in the Eastern Bloc with such an institution. When the new Penal Code of 1997 was drafted, the decision was made not to introduce compensation due to the fact that it was provided by the aforementioned Foundation.

It was only Poland's accession to the European Union and in particular the need to implement the 2004 EU Council Directive relating to compensation for victims of crime that made it necessary to adopt a law on state compensation. State compensation funds were in place in most Western European countries as early as the 1960s. In general, compensation was awarded only to victims of violent crimes. In 1983, countries of Western Europe signed the European Convention on the Compensation of Victims of Violent Crimes, which indicates the minimum conditions for the establishment of a compensation system.

While the compensatory function in the criminal code is linked to obligations imposed on the offender, the Compensation Act imposes certain obligations on the state. The Act is not only an expression of the restorative function, but also of the protective function of criminal law, since the state has a duty to protect citizens and their interests, and when it does so improperly, it should bear the associated consequences.

It is worth mentioning that the original wording of the Compensation Act was amended in 2009. The amendments made by the Act of April 3, 2009 enlarged the set of persons entitled to compensation to include victims of unintentional crimes. In addition, it was assumed that compensation funds could also be spent on medical benefits, including rehabilitation.

The provisions of the Compensation Act have been analyzed in detail by both representatives of doctrine and practitioners, who have tended to take a critical stance toward them (Bieńkowska 2009, 2011).

In 2012, the results of the first research on the operation of that act were presented. The research was conducted by L. Mazowiecka, a prosecutor in the Prosecutor General's Office, with the primary goal of finding out how court rulings on state compensation are shaped in practice, as well as whether the institution of state compensation itself is understood by those entitled to it and the bodies conducting the proceedings (Mazowiecka 2012b).

The research has shown that the scale at which the possibility to apply for compensation is used is small. During the analyzed period of 2005–2009, on average, courts processed only 96 applications for compensation annually. This shows a glaring disproportion between the prediction of the originators of the legislation that nearly 13,000 people may apply for compensation annually and the actual situation. At the same time, with the number of compensations awarded steadily decreasing (in 2005, no compensations were awarded at all, in 2006 there were 30, in 2007—49, in 2008—47, and in 2009—26) the value of individual compensations increased. In 2006, it averaged PLN 1780 (USD 445) and in 2009, it was already PLN 6670 (USD 1668). However, one should bear in mind that, as envisioned by the originators of the legislation, the burden on the State Treasury caused by the compensation payments was to be PLN 70 million (USD 1,750,000), but it actually averaged only 0.2% of the expected amount (Mazowiecka 2012a, p. 19).

The results of the research lead to a clear conclusion, which L. Mazowiecka articulated as follows: obtaining compensation on the basis of the current legislation not only does not alleviate the phenomenon of primary victimization, as postulated by victimology, but, on the contrary, is a source of secondary victimization (Mazowiecka 2012a, p. 22). Similar conclusions were also reached several years later (Mazowiecka 2016, p. 132).

E. W. Pływaczewski formulated some conclusions of a more general nature, exposing the role of criminological research and the importance of its results for optimizing the legal solutions. The results of such research are sometimes very inconvenient for politicians, as they disclose all sorts of discrepancies in both regulations and the practice of their application. With a common-sense approach, the postulated changes should be made as soon as possible. However, usually, this is not the case. In general, the reason for omissions in this regard is a lack of political will due to opportunism, budget problems, etc. This short-sighted "strategy" generates even more costs in the long run, not to mention the broader social damage. The pathological state of law caused by the Compensation Act has persisted for many years (Pływaczewski 2015, p. 35).

It seems that the demands of various groups, including the scientific community, have been recognized to some extent, because, despite the marginal practical significance of the Compensation Act, the legislature decided to amend it again in 2016, which should be considered a positive development. The need for changes arose from an assessment of the courts' jurisprudential practice related to the implementation of the Compensation Act. What was also important was information on the activities of the Commissioner for Human Rights for 2012, together with comments on the state of the observance of human rights and freedoms.

The Commissioner expressed serious concern, based on his observation of the effectiveness of the implementation of the Compensation Act, and stated that the Act not only fails to guarantee effective assistance to victims of crime, but often results in their secondary victimization. Thus, he confirmed the results of previous research.

The Commissioner called for consideration of measures that would rectify this undesirable state of law so that the rights of victims of crime and their dignity would be properly protected.

The purpose of the amendment was to broaden the scope of the Act's subject matter, eliminate or amend vague provisions that contradict the international law that is binding to Poland, or add norms that would increase the maximum amount of compensation.

An analysis of the Act's provisions has shown that many are inconsistent with the law of the European Union and many contradict each other. The contradictory nature of the provisions has made access to state compensation illusory in practice.

Many of the amended solutions are rooted in acts of international law, which identify the way to help victims of crime in national legislation. The first of these legal acts is the European Convention on the Compensation of Victims of Violent Crimes of November 24, 1983, which, unfortunately, Poland, as a member of the Council of Europe, has not ratified to date.

Its originators of the amendments assumed that the anticipated and expected legal effect of the proposed Compensation Act would be an increase in the number of successful applications for compensation and an increase in the amounts awarded in these cases. Unfortunately, the amendments to the Act have not yielded the expected results. According to the Crime Victims Assistance Foundation, the institution of compensation was hardly used between 2005 and 2021. On average, about PLN 140,000 (USD 35,000) were paid out as compensation annually, although the originators of the legislation predicted that it would be PLN 70 million (USD 1,750,000). The expectation was that compensation would be claimed by 12,800 people annually, but courts actually award about 30 compensations per year.

4 Conclusion

The Polish legislature, by means of successive amendments, expands the compensation solutions, thus improving the standing of the victim in the criminal process. It was only the current Criminal Code of 1997 that emphasized the compensatory (restorative) function of criminal law. The first Polish law implementing the concept of a state compensation fund for crime victims was not enacted until 2005. By way of comparison, it is worth pointing out that in India, the first initiatives in this area were taken as early as the mid-1990s as part of the work of the Indian Society of Criminology in the form of The Victims (Criminal Violence) Compensation Bill, 1996.

As A. Marek rightly notes, the belief that criminal law should also fulfill a compensatory (restitutive) function was gradually formed under the influence of the development of the idea of human rights, including the demands of victimology, which emphasizes the need for criminal law to take into account the interests of victims of crime. In particular, criminal law should, through an appropriate system of penal measures, enable the perpetrator of a crime to strive to remedy the harm caused to the victim (Marek 2001, p. 17).

An adequate criminal-law response, in addition to strengthening the public sense of justice and the preventive impact, should also give moral satisfaction to the victim of the crime. Financial compensation is as important to the victim of a crime as the criminal punishment of the perpetrator, and should make up for the damage or harm suffered by the victim as a result of the crime. Thus, the compensatory function of criminal law is focused primarily on the interest of the victim.

The discussion of the shape of compensation for victims of crime is complemented in an excellent way by the view of the Esteemed Jubilarian, who almost 40 years ago recognized the need to combine dogmatic research with the social context to which it relates.

He pointed to the need to analyze the effectiveness of the existing laws and the obligation to confront the legislation with the practice of its application in the real society. In terms of the assistance to the victims of crime, it would be most desirable to construct a holistic system that would involve representatives of the nongovernmental sector in addition to the state component (Chockalingam 1985, pp. 73–90).

References

Bieńkowska E (2009) Prawa ofiar przestępstw [The rights of crime victims]. Lex a Wolters Kluwer

Bieńkowska E (2011) Państwowa kompensata przysługująca ofiarom niektórych przestępstw. Komentarz [State compensation for victims of certain crimes. A commentary]. Lex a Wolters Kluwer

Buchała K (1980) Prawo karne materialne [Substantive criminal law]. Państwowe Wydawnictwo Naukowe

Buchała K, Zoll A (1995) Polskie prawo karne [Polish criminal law]. Wydawnictwa Prawnicze PWN

Chockalingam K (1985) The problems of victims and their families. In Chockalingam K (ed) Readings in victimology. Towards a victim perspective in criminology. Ravi Raj Publications

Giezek J (2010) Pojęcie i funkcje prawa karnego [The concept and functions of criminal law]. In: Bojarski M (ed) Prawo karne materialne. Część ogólna i szczególna [Substantive criminal law. The general and specific parts]. Wydawnictwo LexisNexis

Guzik-Makaruk EM, Laskowska K, Filipkowski W (eds) (2023) Człowiek, społeczeństwo i państwo z perspektywy nauk kryminologicznych. Księga jubileuszowa z okazji 70-lecia urodzin prof. zw. dr. hab. dr. h.c. Emila W. Pływaczewskiego [Man, society, and state from the perspective of criminological sciences. A jubilee book on the occasion of the 70th birthday of Professor Emil W. Pływaczewski]. Wydawnictwo Instytutu Wymiaru Sprawiedliwości

Marek A (1986) Wiadomości wstępne [Introductory information]. In: Marek A (ed) Prawo karne. Zagadnienia teorii i praktyki [Criminal law. Theoretical and practical problems]. Państwowe Wydawnictwo Naukowe

Marek A (1997) Prawo karne. Zagadnienia teorii i praktyki [Criminal law. Theoretical and practical problems]. C.H. Beck

Marek A (2001) Prawo karne [Criminal law]. CH Beck

Mazowiecka L (2012a) Kompensata państwowa w Polsce [State compensation in Poland]. Niebieska Linia 2(79):15–20

Mazowiecka L (2012b) Państwowa kompensata dla ofiar przestępstw [State compensation for crime victims]. Lex a Wolters Kluwer

Mazowiecka L (ed) (2016) Nowe środki ochrony i pomocy dla ofiar [New measures for the protection of and assistance to victims]. Wolters Kluwer

Pływaczewski EW (2015) Funkcja restytucyjna (kompensacyjna) prawa karnego z perspektywy teorii i praktyki [The restitutive (compensatory) function of criminal law from the perspective of theory and practice]. In: Nowicka I, Mocarska D (eds) Współczesne problemy prawa. Tom 1 [Contemporary problems of law, vol 1]. Wydawnictwo Wyższej Szkoły Policji w Szczytnie

Sahni SP, Dhanda A, Palit M (2017) Victims' assistance in India. Suggesting legislative reform. Ane Books Pvt Ltd

Świda W (1989) Prawo karne [Criminal law]. Państwowe Wydawnictwo Naukowe

Young Adult Recidivists Lodged in Tihar Prisons: A Criminological Analysis

Sajith Mohmad Saleem

Abstract Young adult recidivists are offenders in the age range of 18–21 years. The Young Adult Offenders face unique challenges, usually different from those of the juveniles and the adult offenders. Given the age and developmental factors, if not reformed and rehabilitated at the right time, their tendency to resort to deviancy increases. This study analyzes the factors that result in recidivism among young adult offenders. By analyzing existing research and empirical evidence, this study suggests policy changes and individual treatment plans for young adult recidivists. This study, wherein a total of 250 young adult recidivists were interviewed, showed that substance abuse, cognitive development, age, peer influence, and socioeconomic differences all have a significant impact on the likelihood of recidivism. Furthermore, the effect of deviant associations and social networks on recidivism is investigated, emphasizing the significance of sound social support systems. Further, a qualitative analysis of three case studies of young adult offenders who have been imprisoned more than three times has been covered in detail.

Keywords Young adult offenders · Recidivism · Policy · Imprisonment

1 Introduction

Young adult offenders, who fall in the age bracket of 18–21 (it also extends to the age of 25 in some definitions), are a special category of deviants in the system. They are at the cusp of juvenile delinquency and adult offenders, making their involvement a complex challenge for the system as well as society at large. Although the demographic profile of these young adults varies across cultures and regions, they are disproportionately represented. Young adults accounted for a significant proportion of arrests in the United States, comprising approximately 10% of all individuals arrested in 2018 (Hockenberry and Puzzanchera 2020). Moreover, many reports

S. M. Saleem (✉)
Jindal Institute of Behavioural Science, O.P. Jindal Global University, Sonipat, India

© The Author(s), under exclusive license to Springer Nature Singapore Pte Ltd. 2026

G. S. Bajpai et al. (eds.), *Beyond the Gavel: A Paradigm Shift in Global Criminal Justice*, https://doi.org/10.1007/978-981-95-4487-5_16

have also brought out that most of the young adult offenders are from the most marginalized and vulnerable sections of society (Bureau of Justice Statistics 2021).

Recidivism, the tendency of individuals to reoffend after their initial contact with the criminal justice system, is a complex issue that poses significant challenges for societies worldwide (Snyder & Sickmund 2006). While recidivism rates vary across different demographics and age groups, the focus of this chapter is on young adult offenders, a particularly vulnerable and understudied population. Young adults, typically defined as individuals between the ages of 18 and 25, undergo a critical period of transition marked by cognitive, emotional, and social changes. Understanding recidivism patterns among young adult offenders is essential for developing effective interventions and promoting successful reintegration into society.

Several factors have been predicted to cause criminality among young adult offenders (Ulmer 2001; Wartna et al. 2010). These are worsened for those who engage in crime by social and economic disadvantages such as poor educational possibilities, disadvantaged family circumstances, and insufficient support systems. Such drawbacks impede their ability to build the stability required for crime-free behavior (Prop et al. 2025).

Studies (Sampson and Laub 1993) have established an age-graded theory of informal social control to explain why some continue to engage in criminal behavior while others stop committing crimes in their early adult years. This idea emphasizes the importance of informal social relationships to society (job, family, school, and community) across the lifespan and links them to recovery and reduced recidivism (Oldfield 1996). In simple words, when the social bonds are weakened, there is a tendency for the young adults to engage repeatedly in crime.

Young individuals who engage in repeated criminal behaviors have a disproportionately high prevalence of mental illness, which increases with deeper participation in the judicial system, with some estimates exceeding 95% of adolescent forensic cases reporting mental illness (Livanou et al. 2019). Inadequately addressing the mental health needs of justice-involved youth can impair critical processes in the development of adult role functioning (Arnett 2000). These include building prosocial interactions and support networks, as well as providing educational and employment possibilities (Baumer 1997). It also raises the chance of persistent offending, antisocial behavior, marginalization, and other social and economic consequences. We argue that progress can be made even in environments with limited resources (Rice et al. 2024).

Andrews et al. (1990) identify two categories of risk factors: static and dynamic. Static factors (i.e., age, previous convictions) are aspects of the offender's past that are predictive of recidivism but cannot be changed. Dynamic risk factors, or what Andrews and Bonta commonly refer to as criminogenic needs (e.g., antisocial cognitions, values, and behaviors), are mutable and thus serve as appropriate targets for treatment (Andrews et al. 1990).

Developmental studies have found behavioral and emotional problems to be predictive of later delinquency and substance abuse (Dishion et al. 1999). Similarly, early childhood aggressive behaviors are predictive of later delinquent behaviors and activities (Lloyd et al. 1994) Tremblay and LeMarquand 2001). Attention and hyperactivity problems are linked to later high-risk taking and more violent offending behavior (Elander et al. 2000; Hawkins et al. 1998). Antisocial behaviors and emotional problems in early childhood are markers for later delinquent activities (Wasserman et al. 2003). In addition, childhood depression and attention-deficit hyperactivity disorder (ADHD) are linked to predict involvement in crimes in the future, evidenced through physical aggression and stealing behaviors (Heilbrun et al. 2005; Moffitt and Scott 2008, chap. 35; Ryan and Redding 2004).

The cost-effective and humane management of prisons, particularly considering the dramatic increase in incarceration rates (Mauer 1994), dictates that maximum security prisons be reserved for the highest-risk offenders. Moreover, the design of effective offender treatment programs is highly dependent on the knowledge of the predictors of recidivism (Gendreau et al. 1994).

Studies have shown that recidivism rates among young adult offenders tend to be alarmingly high, warranting increased attention from policymakers, researchers, and practitioners (May 1999; Mears and Travis 2004). One study conducted by Mendel (2018) found that approximately 60% of young adults released from incarceration in the United States were rearrested within 3 years of their release. Another study by Farrington (2019) revealed that young adult offenders had a higher likelihood of reoffending compared to both juvenile and adult offenders.

Recent advancements in rehabilitation programs and reintegration centers have led to a significant increase in recidivism rates. It not only causes problems for the criminal justice system, but it also has an impact on society as a whole, considering the safety of the victims and society (Odedokun 2022).

In India, the number of studies that have focused on young adult offenders who recidivate is rare; therefore, additional research is needed. Continuing these inquiries and identifying what legal and extra-legal factors predict recidivism to detention placement is important in understanding and directing preventative programs. If certain risks, behaviors, and/or disabilities are identified, then early intervention efforts may decrease or help youth desist delinquent offending and subsequent detention or incarceration (Moffitt et al. 2002). Decreasing youth recidivism (offending and imprisonment) is an effective public policy, saving limited fiscal resources and improving public safety (Caldwell et al. 2006; Gatti et al. 2009; Loughran et al. 2009; Soler et al. 2009).

2 The Study

This study is part of a comprehensive and longitudinal study of young adult offenders, titled "Utopia in Correctional Settings." The study is set in Central Jail 5, Tihar Ashram, Delhi, India. Central Jail 5 is one of the very few central prisons in India that only houses young adult offenders aged 18–21 years. All along the year, the population average of Central Jail 5 stays at 1000. The Jail has a special ward to house the recidivists. The population of the ward stays at an average of 250 all year. This implies the recidivist population is 25% of the total.

The study, "Utopia in Correctional Setting," is a Prison Educational Program that covers Life Skills-based Education in the Prison School, Central Jail 5. As a part of the educational program, the young adults in custody are admitted to individual batches of the program. A special batch was created for the recidivists, and the data collected for this study stems from the data collected to assess the effects of the Educational Program.

3 Data Collection

The individual batch of young adult recidivists in the educational program was limited to only 35 individuals. The individuals were called after the educational session and were subjected to a structured interview. The sample for this study is 250. The 250 young adults were subjected to a structured interview that collected demographic and other details. The young adults who were participants in the school were randomly chosen. The rapport formed during the educational program helped with the ice-breaking and the interviews. The structured interview collected demographic, educational, mental health, substance dependence, and personality variables.

4 A Brief Description of the Young Adult Recidivists

The sample of 250 is very diverse. 90% of them are from Delhi, 6% are migrants from Uttar Pradesh, and the remaining 4% are from Rajasthan. The median age of the population was 20 years. Before entering prison, 12% were married and 4% of them had children. Mostly, no school education before prison is observed. 59% of them are illiterate, and only 7% are found to have passed primary school (X Grade).

As mentioned in Fig. 1, 100% of respondents reported using illegal drugs more than thrice a week in the last 6 months leading up to their imprisonment, with Marijuana and Heroin each accounting for about a third of reported drug use. This number increased to about two in three respondents when alcohol intoxication was also considered.

As mentioned in Table 2, many respondents had a significant history of criminal activity before the current incarceration. 84% had prior imprisonment, with about a third having four or more previous times served. 36% of respondents had been convicted earlier for a crime, and 47% had been returned to prison for a parole or probation violation at some point. About a third (34%) had served time in a juvenile correctional facility, and the median age at first arrest was 15.

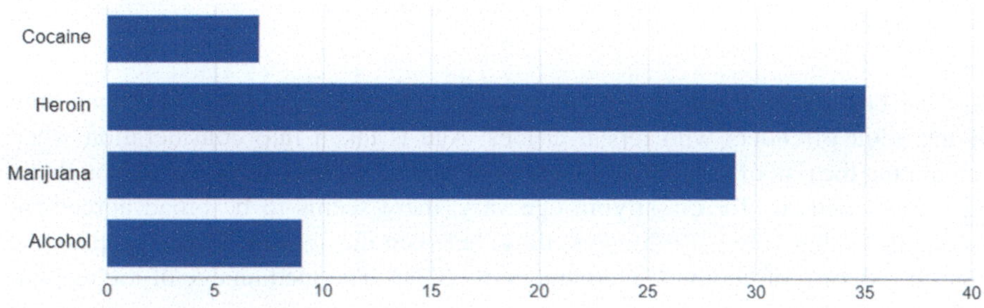

Fig. 1 Drug usage pre-prison (in %)

Table 1 General demographics of the respondents

Health	Physical	Mental	No problems
	42	157	51
Employment	Regular	Unemployed	Student
	98	150	2
Education	Illiterate	Passed V	Passed X
	147	58	18
Marital status	Unmarried	Married	Married with children
	220	30	10
Accommodation	Private	Govt. housing (rain Basera)	Homeless
	147	60	43

Table 2 Types of offenses

Property offenses Under IPC s. 379, 380, 356, 411	165
Bodily offenses Under IPC s. 302, 304, 307, 376, 392, 394, 397	63
Public nuisance Under IPC s. 268	22

As mentioned in Table 1, health issues were also observed. Among the sample, a high 62.8% faced mental health issues. On further assessment by the psychologists in the prisons, mental health disorders such as depressive disorders, manic disorders, anxiety disorders, and disruptive disorders were assessed. Substance abuse disorders were also common among the sample. The physical health concerns extended to poor nutrition, lack of physical activity, and other injuries from violence and self-harm.

As mentioned in Table 1, housing is also a concern among young adult recidivists. Although most of them have a stable house, a significant number are homeless or under the government housing scheme. These make-shift arrangements only fuel substance abuse and further risk them falling back into crime.

4.1 Age

Age has been determined as an element that has drawn much attention concerning young adult offenders who repeat crimes. Age is taken into consideration when calculating the risk of sexual recidivism by actuarial risk measures. Even though the measures' methods for classifying age vary, there seems to be broad agreement among them that younger offenders, those between the ages of 18 and 24, pose the highest risk of reoffending (Smethurst et al. 2021). The median age of the respondents in this study is 20 years.

4.2 Type of Offenses

Studies have found that property offenses have consistently been linked to the highest relative recidivism risk (Yukhnenko et al. 2023). Consequently, a sizable percentage of property offenders in any cohort would raise recidivism rates, and reported and detected property crimes may be responsible for a sizable portion of reported recidivism rates.

In this study, and also as enumerated in Table 2, the respondents throughout their criminal careers had been imprisoned for at least three cases. Of these, 66% were property offenses, 25% were body offenses, and 9% caused public nuisance. The most common, even among the property offenses, was that of theft. Section 379 of the Indian Penal Code (IPC) deals with the offense of theft. The punishment being 3 years also gives rise to chances to reoffend.

4.3 Substance Abuse

100% reported drug usage among the respondents. To be very specific, a famous saying in Indian prisons is "P*aisa, Nasha aur Pyaar*" (money, drugs, and love), showing the apparent risks of substance abuse.

As clear from Fig. 1, use of heroin predicts recidivism and the most pronounced risk was seen for reporting both heroin (injecting) and marijuana. Also, recidivism can be associated with a higher number of substances used before imprisonment. Substance abuse combined with younger age, homelessness, and previous use of drugs can be predictors for recidivism among young adults.

5 Case Studies

Apart from the structured interview, three case studies were conducted among individuals who have been imprisoned more than three times, either in a juvenile facility or in an adult prison. The following case studies have been selected to give a clear picture of a young adult who often resorts to the circle of crime.

5.1 Case Study I

The Individual is the youngest of the five siblings. Mother had been ill for as long as the Individual can remember, and her death in 2009 changed the world for him. The father is observed to be a submissive and straightforward man who could not manage the family after his wife's death. After the loss of his mother, he found no purpose in life, or probably, he managed and decided not to lose himself just for the sake of his mother, but as soon as she passed off, it was like a life that he had always wanted to live. The Individual dropped out of school and started forming deviant associations, cultivating the habit of drugs and alcohol to "ease the pain."

He has been accused of murder as a juvenile. The justification of the crime involves his being framed, which points to his defensive nature. He was with two other friends who were also involved in the incident and have been convicted for the offense and are imprisoned in CJ-3 and CJ-5, respectively. As no evidence could be provided, he was bailed out. He was then accused of Sexual Assault. The justification of the crime involved a narrative where he was framed by the victim's family. He was in a relationship with the victim, which also extended to physical relations. He was bailed out as he compromised the case by promising to marry the victim. Sexual deviancy and low attitudes toward women were observed. In 2008, he was then accused of fraud, damaging the modesty of a woman, and kidnapping. The family of the Individual has now abandoned him, thinking they gave him enough chances. Although the bail has been prepared, the family is not ready to furnish a 'bail bond,' thinking Jail would induce "wisdom" to not commit a crime in the future. If we look closely at the Individual, the loss of his mother and the care he used to receive can be the main reason he turned into a deviant. He also has cultivated low attitudes toward women and believes in rape myths. Now that his family has abandoned him, it will provide a new spectrum and defense to act deviantly.

1. July 2016: Accused under IPC s. 302, where the Individual was in the Children's Home for 45 days and was bailed out by his father.
2. October 2017: Accused under IPC s. 376, where the Individual was in CJ-5, TJ for 120 days, the case was reconciled with the victim's family, and the Individual was bailed out by his father.
3. June (2018): Accused under IPC s. 25, 354, 359, where the Individual was again lodged in CJ-5, TJ and has been serving since.

5.2 *Case Study II*

The family members include the father, one elder brother who has settled outside Delhi, and two younger sisters; the youngest is generally ill, and the other sister is the only member who goes to school. His mother died while he was a kid, and he did not receive any attention or care as a kid; his father is an alcoholic and abusive, which made him form close "relations" outside his family. He was admitted to a government school but never attended any class, eventually dropping out of school. A drug addict who has been shooting up heroin as a kid and continues the same habit. Observed to have a very strained relationship with the family. Has regular conflicts with father.

The first case lodged against him was under IPC S. 377, unnatural act. However, the narrative included how the other person convinced him to have physical relations with him, but then framed him for sexual assault, because the Individual was abusive during the act, which could not be digested by the victim. This throws light on him having normalized the abusive behavior.

The rest of the patterns of crime involve snatching and theft. He has a fixed modus operandi and carries out his operation as a pillion by snatching mobiles, purses, wallets, or phones, and selling them. The money is then used to fulfill the drug expenses. If we look closely, the Individual wants his pleasure to exceed his pain and hence is involved in antisocial acts, which will fuel his antisocial intents.

Also, the uncle, a family member who has been supporting him, has become a source of positive reinforcement; no matter what he does, he believes that this person will bail him out, instilling hopes of acting in any way he wants. This Individual has normalized abusive and deviant behavior because he has been in such an environment for a very long period. The father's role and the omission of the mother's role have led him to where he is today. Although he has no idea of gender or sexuality, he feels same-sex relations are "normal." Has deviant and antisocial contacts inside and outside prison, and would serve them if he is promised drugs and a peaceful life.

1. May 2015: Accused under IPC s. 377, where the Individual was in a Children's home for 30 days and was bailed out by the Individual's uncle.
2. May 2016: Accused under IPC s. 379, where the Individual was lodged in CJ-7 for 45 days and was bailed out again by his uncle.
3. May 2017: Accused under IPC s. 379, where the Individual was lodged in CJ-5 for 30 days and was bailed out again by his uncle.
4. June 2018: Accused under IPC s. 379, where the Individual was lodged in CJ-5 and is currently serving time.

5.3 Case Study III

The Individual is observed to have a normal relationship with the family. The family, including the father, mother, and three elder brothers, is in business. He was also employed, not in his father's business but at his father's friend's place. The Individual was observed to be antisocial and violent as a child, and to teach him lessons, the father gave his responsibility to his friend, who took him under and employed him in his business. The lack of care and attention from his own house alienated him further in his relations with his father's friend. He has dropped out of school for the same reason. The Individual is observed to be a hedonist. He calculates the end of the act and concludes that he might enjoy the activity and hence involves himself in antisocial acts. Thrill-seeking attitude observed. The modus operandi has been snatching, threatening, and then robbing. The looted money is spent on clubbing, alcohol, drugs, travel, and buying fancy stuff. Has been accused of theft thrice and follows the same pattern. The increased self-image and high sense of worth accept his imprisonment and consider it a proud thing he has done.

1. August 2016: Accused under IPC s. The individual was imprisoned for 30 days in a Children's home, where his father bailed him out.
2. January 2018: Accused under IPC s. The individual was imprisoned for 10 days in CJ-5, TJ and was bailed out by his father.
3. June 2018: Accused under IPC s. 379 and is currently imprisoned in CJ-5, TJ.

6 Discussions

If we look at the patterns of crime, it is mostly theft, robbery, being a public nuisance, and public threat. The individuals find out ways to get a hand on "easy money," and as most of them have conflicts and broken relations with their parents, and as they look and form deviant associations, they enter the circle of crime.

The Individuals who have been accused are those members of the group who are slow or are not capable and compatible enough to outrun the law, due to ignorance and lack of financial support. The planners and conspirators of the act are primarily outside the law, as they are already experienced and know how to handle situations that might get them arrested. However, it is also observed that these deviant associations also apply to the bail of the imprisoned, and once they are out, they are asked to serve for the gang. Individuals who have no support from the house find it an opportunity for survival and respect, getting deeper into the rabbit hole of the deviant world. Some Individuals have support from the family, but as it acts as a positive reinforcement, they see that no matter what the gravity of their act is, they will always be supported by their parents, which undermines the purpose of imprisonment. It is also observed that once they are out of prison, they get employed, but as time passes, the influence of the associations draws them back into criminal life.

The pattern observed after imprisonment is that the family sends them to a different location away from their hometown to provide a different atmosphere. That motivation is carried on for some time, but as the deviancy is never dealt with, it always stays there inside, just waiting to explode. Hence, any manipulation by deviant associations leads them to get deviantly motivated, and they fall back on crime. Addiction is also another problem that fuels the deviant attitude; most individuals are addicted to chemical drugs that help them avoid, repress, and forget most of their issues.

7 Conclusion

In conclusion, the issue of young adult recidivism is a complex and multifaceted problem that requires a comprehensive and holistic approach to address effectively. Criminal recidivism among young adult offenders is linked to heroin and marijuana usage, injectable drug use, and polysubstance addiction, not alcohol, opiate analgesics, or hallucinogenic substances. The current findings call for increased emphasis on treatment referrals, evidence-based addiction treatment, and structured follow-up of prisoners' substance use problems. The current findings recommend further investigation into the factors that influence criminal behavior in clients with various substance use patterns.

Several young adults are incarcerated multiple times. In many cases, Jail is useless in improving outcomes for delinquent youth. This study looked at 250 young adult recidivists and focused on the characteristics that predict recidivism. According to the findings of this study, kids who have previously been diagnosed with a mental health concern, are younger, and have a substance use illness are more likely to recidivate. If the goal is to prevent recidivism, which leads to subsequent detention placement, all stakeholders must grasp the elements that can serve as early warning signs for concern and intervention. A community-based mental health screening and referral method could help identify and assist these high-risk youths.

References

Andrews DA, Bonta J, Hoge RD (1990) Classification for effective rehabilitation: rediscovering psychology. Crim Justice Behav 17:19–52

Arnett JJ (2000) Emerging adulthood: a theory of development from the late teens through the twenties. Am Psychol 55(5):469–480

Baumer E (1997) Levels and predictors of recidivism: the Malta experience. Criminology 35(4):601–628

Bureau of Justice Statistics (2021) Crime in the United States: arrests 2018. https://www.bjs.gov/content/pub/pdf/cv18.pdf

Caldwell MF, Vitacco M, Van Rybroek G (2006) Treatment outcomes at the Mendota Juvenile Treatment Center: Reducing recidivism among violent juvenile offenders.

Dishion TJ, McCord J, Poulin F (1999) When interventions harm: Peer groups and problem behavior. *American Psychologist, 54*(9), 755–764.

Elander J, Simonoff E, Pickles A, Rutter M (2000) A longitudinal study of adolescent and adult conviction rates among children referred to psychiatric services for behavioural or emotional problems. *Criminal Behaviour and Mental Health, 10*(1), 40–60.

Farrington DP (2019) The Cambridge study in delinquent development. In D. Eaves, C. D. Webster, Q. Haque, & J. Eaves-Thalken (Eds.), Risk rules: A practical guide to structured professional judgment and violence prevention (pp. 225–233). Pavilion Publishing.

Gatti U, Tremblay RE, Vitaro F, McDuff P (2009) Iatrogenic effect of juvenile justice. Journal of Child Psychology and Psychiatry, 50(8), 991–998.

Gendreau P, Cullen FT, Bonta J (1994) Intensive rehabilitation supervision: the next generation in community corrections? Fed Probat 58:72–78

Hawkins JD, Herrenkohl TI, Farrington DP, Brewer D, Catalano RF, Harachi TW (1998) A review of predictors of youth violence. In R. Loeber & D. P. Farrington (Eds.), Serious and violent juvenile offenders: Risk factors and successful interventions (pp. 106–146). Sage Publications.

Heilbrun K, Goldstein NE, Redding RE (Eds.) (2005) Juvenile delinquency: Prevention, assessment, and intervention. Oxford University Press.

Hockenberry S, Puzzanchera C (2020) Juvenile arrests 2018. https://www.ojjdp.gov/ojstatbb/crime/JAR_Display.asp?ID=qa05261

Livanou M, Furtado V, Winsper C, Silvester A, Singh SP (2019) Prevalence of mental disorders and symptoms among incarcerated youth: a meta-analysis of 30 studies. Int J Forensic Ment Health 18:400–414. https://doi.org/10.1080/14999013.2019.1619636

Lloyd C, Mair G, Hough M (1994) Explaining reconviction rates: a critical analysis. Home Office Research Study 136, Home Office, London

Loughran TA, Mulvey EP, Schubert CA, Fagan J, Piquero AR, Losoya SH (2009) Estimating a dose-response relationship between length of stay and future recidivism in serious juvenile offenders. *Criminology, 47*(3), 699–740.

Mauer M (1994) Americans behind bars: the international use of incarceration, 1992–1993. Sentencing Project, Washington, D.C.

May C (1999) Explaining reconviction following a community sentence: the role of social factors. Research study 192, Home Office, London

Mears DP, Travis J (2004) Youth development and reentry. Youth Violence Juvenile Justice 2(1):3–20

Mendel RA (2018) Transforming juvenile probation: A vision for getting it right. Annie E. Casey Foundation.

Moffitt TE, Scott S (2008) Conduct disorders of childhood and adolescence. In M. Rutter, D. Bishop, D. Pine, S. Scott, J. Stevenson, E. Taylor, & A. Thapar (Eds.), Rutter's child and adolescent psychiatry (5th ed., pp. 579–597). Blackwell Publishing.

Moffitt TE, Caspi A, Harrington H, Milne BJ (2002) Males on the life-course-persistent and adolescence-limited antisocial pathways: follow-up at age 26 years. Dev Psychopathol 14(1):179–207

Odedokun SA (2022) The relationship between dysfunctional family, substance abuse, emotional intelligence, and recidivism among young adult inmates in Agodi Correctional Centre, Ibadan, Nigeria. Eur J Soc Sci Stud 7(5)

Oldfield M (1996) The Kent reconviction survey. Research and Information Department, Kent Probation Service, Kent

Prop LJ, van der Laan AM, Beerthuizen MG, Barendregt CS, van Nieuwenhuizen C (2025) Juvenile sanctions for young adult offenders in The Netherlands: an opportunity for rehabilitation? Child Adolesc Psychiatry Ment Health 19(1):1–15

Rice SM, Baker DG, Purcell R, Chanen A (2024) Offending behaviour and mental ill-health among young people: reducing recidivism requires integration with youth mental health care. J Glob Health 14:03001

Ryan EP, Redding RE (2004) A review of mood disorders among juvenile offenders. *Psychiatric Services, 55*(12), 1397–1407. https://doi.org/10.1176/appi.ps.55.12.1397
Sampson RJ, Laub JH (1993) Crime in the making: pathways and turning points through life. Harvard University Press, Cambridge
Smethurst AJ, Bamford J, Tully RJ (2021) A systematic review of recidivism rates of older adult male sex offenders. Appl Psychol Crim Justice 16(1)
Snyder HN, Sickmund M (2006) Juvenile offenders and victims National Report Office of Juvenile Justice and Delinquency Prevention
Soler M, Schoenberg D, Schindler M (2009) Juvenile justice: Lessons for a new era. Georgetown Journal on Poverty Law & Policy.
Tremblay RE, LeMarquand D (2001) Individual risk and protective factors. In R. Loeber & D. P. Farrington (Eds.), Child delinquents: Development, intervention, and service needs (pp. 137–164). Sage Publications.
Ulmer JT (2001) Intermediate sanctions: a comparative analysis of the probability and severity of recidivism. Sociol Inq 71(2):164–193
Wartna BSJ, Tollenaar N, Blom M, Alma SM, Bregman IM, Essers AAM, Van Straalen EK (2010) Recidivism report 2002–2008. Trends in the reconviction rate of Dutch offenders
Wasserman GA, Keenan K, Tremblay RE, Coie JD, Herrenkohl TI, Loeber R, Petechuk D (2003) Risk and protective factors of child delinquency. U.S. Department of Justice, Office of Juvenile Justice and Delinquency Prevention.
Yukhnenko D, Farouki L, Fazel S (2023) Criminal recidivism rates globally: a 6-year systematic review update. J Crim Justice 88:102115

Conclusion

G. S. Bajpai

Abstract This volume explores the dynamic and evolving relationship between law and society, emphasizing how legal systems must continuously adapt to changing social, moral, and ethical values to ensure justice and fairness. It highlights recent legislative reforms in India that reflect a shift toward transformative justice and address contemporary societal challenges. The work adopts an interdisciplinary approach, integrating insights from criminology, criminal law, and victimology to examine diverse issues such as food fraud, sex trafficking, youth justice, gender-based violence, victim impact statements, and access to justice. The contributions in this volume underline the importance of victim-centric approaches, restorative justice, and evidence-based policymaking. They also analyze the role of forensic science, customary justice, and global perspectives in shaping modern criminal justice systems. Special attention is given to victims' rights, rehabilitation, and the need for institutional reforms such as the establishment of cold case units and enhanced victim support services. Overall, the volume pays tribute to the scholarly contributions of Professor K. Chockalingam while presenting a comprehensive and interdisciplinary understanding of contemporary challenges and developments in global criminal justice systems.

Keywords Criminal Justice System · Criminology · Victimology · Legal Reform · Transformative Justice · Victims' Rights · Social Change and Law · Gender-Based Violence

G. S. Bajpai (✉)
National Law University Delhi, New Delhi, India
e-mail: vc@nludelhi.ac.in

© The Author(s), under exclusive license to Springer Nature Singapore Pte Ltd. 2026

G. S. Bajpai et al. (eds.), *Beyond the Gavel: A Paradigm Shift in Global Criminal Justice*, https://doi.org/10.1007/978-981-95-4487-5_17

Because society and the law have the power to impact and mold one another, their relationship is extremely dynamic and intricately entwined. Every legal modification reflects how society and ideals have changed. A community's moral and ethical ideals are embodied in its laws. For a law to be effective, it must continuously change to create a society that is fair, just, and healthy. A legal system must be able to adjust to the new issues brought about by ever-evolving social circumstances.

In order to blend and balance traditional values with the contemporary ideals of justice and equality, India has recently seen a number of legislative reforms aimed at addressing current societal challenges and bringing about greater uniformity and certainty. The new criminal laws reflect a significant change in India's legal system and a move in the direction of transformative justice.

Every human being is subject to the general control structure of society. It is important to remember that these control systems occasionally undergo improvements that serve as a guiding principle to preserve social order by restricting actions that violate the rights of an individual or group of individuals. The festschrift *Beyond the Gavel: A Paradigm Shift in Global Criminal Justice* serves as a tribute to Professor K. Chockalingam's contributions.

The subthemes in the first part *Criminology: Unveiling the Mechanisms of Deviance* brings forth a wide range of debates, from analyzing food fraud to youth crime. *Pamela Kerschke-Risch* discusses how food crime is a global problem that impacts consumers in many different ways. The financial, health, and ethical repercussions for individuals impacted are examined and illustrated by the author(s) using a variety of fraud cases, all seen through the victimological lenses. In a world where the public is so unaware of the issue of food fraud and how the harm is so difficult to measure financially, this research goes on to suggest that those affected by serious food fraud must be given help in the form of victims' assistance.

Dr. (Prof.) Dipa Dube and Dr. Ankita Chakraborty support an intricate view of sex trafficking that places the victims' rights and dignity at the center of all action. They advise including extensive victim support services and community-based rehabilitation that prioritize victim integration and empowerment rather than criminal prosecution. It addresses the underlying socioeconomic factors that contribute to sex trafficking while simultaneously preserving autonomy. It encourages a compassionate approach while balancing prosecuting the crime as well as rehabilitating the victims.

Frieder Dünkel unfolds how the extension of youth justice to young adults up to age 21 or even older is a recent reform trend in both Europe and the USA. This reform movement is grounded in developmental and social evidence regarding the transition of an individual from childhood to adulthood, while also bringing to light new neuroscience evidence regarding brain maturation during this age. The second broad theme *Criminal Justice: Navigating the Dynamic Landscape* highlights the importance of combining academic fields in order to build governmental policies and crime control tactics, while looking at it from a victimological view-point.

Dr. Upma Gautam, Dr. Deeksha Bajpai Tewari, and Dr. Priya Das conducted a study in 2020 to inspect the relevance of socioeconomic correlates in comprehending the policy measures for reducing sexual violence against women in India. The study found that the number of police officers per lakh of the population and the number of police officers per 100 square kilometers have an impact on the country's rape statistics, and that enhanced monitoring and surveillance play a favorable role in reducing sexual assaults. In light of these findings, their current study examines the effects of female police officers and female help desks in reporting rape cases. The establishment of Mahila Thanas, where women who have been abused can report occurrences to female police officers, was one of the most ambitious attempts to feminize the Indian police force. This chapter thereby argues that increased feminization of the police force has been shown to improve women's reporting of experiences of gendered sexual violence. This necessarily addresses a major problem faced by the system today—underreporting.

Prof. (Dr.) Purvi Pokhariyal and Ms. Deepa Dubey while promoting dialogic processes for all stakeholders involved, such as the gravity of "victim impact statements" (VIS) in the criminal justice delivery system, they also examine the influence of legal education and the function of jurists in mediating the Dialectics of Law in the criminal justice system. It investigates and concludes that a dialogic process improves victim representation and advances rehabilitative jurisprudence. *Prof. (Dr.) G.S. Bajpai and Ms. Prerna Deep* extensively discuss the complex function and significance of victim impact statements in the criminal justice system. It centers on observations from the common law jurisdictions. The effects of victim impact statements on sentencing, victims' psychological health, the several difficulties that arise in this situation, and the legal foundation in that area are the main subthemes of this study. They also emphasize on the intricacies of the adversarial system, where victims' rights have superseded their participation.

Dr. Vipin Vijay Nair contributes to the current academic discussion regarding the improvement and growth of victim support services. This chapter probes into the findings from Rehabilitation & Protective Homes in India in an effort to empower victims on their path to rehabilitation by providing them with comprehensive assistance through PAR. In this sense, it promotes the parties' active involvement in order to jointly address their problems and concerns.

The third part *Criminal Law: Navigating the Jurisprudential Landscape* widens our horizons: by bringing into frontline discussion varied criminal law matters from around the world.

Professor B.B. Pande explains to us how the future equilibrium of the interface between forensic science and criminal justice is going to change as a result of the normative legitimization and infusion of forensic science on the one hand, and its extensions to new precrime phases on the other. *Dr. Heru Susetyo* brings forth an interesting debate in the Indonesian criminal justice system. Even if they are voluntary, lewd activities between unmarried men and women in Aceh are considered crimes and are punishable by law (jinayat), in contrast to other parts of Indonesia. The provision of alternate remedies through customary courts begs the question of whether this is a breach of individual human rights or a way to accommodate Acehnese local wisdom. The author arrives at a pivotal jurisprudential question—Is customary justice a legal aberration or just a component of local wisdom?

Prof. Jing Cao, Jan Van Dijk and Marc Groenhuijsen talk about China's compliance to the 1985 United Nations Declaration on the Basic Principles of Justice for Victims of Crime and Abuse of Power, which is undeniably a landmark text in the global advancement of victims' rights. Their study evaluates the evolution and present status of victims' rights in China in relation to the Declaration's standards using a multifaceted methodology that includes legal research, semistructured interviews with criminal justice officials and other stakeholders, and a comprehensive survey of Beijing residents on their experiences with crime and the police. They conclude that in spite of China making significant strides in codifying victims' rights since the new Law was adopted in 1996, difficulties still exist, especially in guaranteeing victims empathetic treatment, sufficient state compensation, and social assistance.

Prof. Sarah Agnela's study examines how forty-four ship crew members interviewed at an off-duty crew recreation center in a UK port evaluated the maritime work environment in relation to maritime piracy, along the East African coast. This chapter delves deep into the pirate issue that occurred along the East African coast between 2005 and 2015, revealing the conflict and contradiction between Somalia's failed economy and the booming global shipping industry that operated side by side in the same region.

Prof. Beulah Shekhar and Rithin Joseph present an intriguing proposal—the need for a dedicated cold case center in India. With a focus on the advantages, such as increased investigative efficiency, justice for victims and their families, and re-established public trust in the criminal justice system, this study uses a qualitative research design, to investigate the necessity and design of a dedicated cold case center in India. Their analysis demonstrates how advanced forensic methods, data analytics, and digital forensics may be used to uncover new leads and insights into cold cases. India can learn a lot from the success stories of cold case units in nations like the USA, South Korea, and Australia, where tenacious and modern investigation techniques have produced breakthroughs in long-unsolved cases. The mechanism for the establishment of a cold case center is explained in depth, which includes integrating state-of-the-art forensic research, fostering more interagency collaboration, and allocating resources specifically to the backlog of unsolved cases.

The final part *Victimology: Illuminating the Voices of the Silenced* highlights the struggles of a victim in their pursuit of justice, and how it is significantly dependent on the workings of the criminal justice system.

Michael O' Connell examines the idea of access to justice, the legal underpinnings of crime victims' entitlement to it, and the obstacles that victims face in their pursuit of it. The importance of independent legal representation for victims during criminal proceedings is also covered in this chapter, which comes to the conclusion that one of the best ways to empower victims is to give them the freedom to decide whether, when, and how to exercise their rights. Additionally, while delving deeper into victim's participatory rights in India, he suggests that victims have better access to justice when they have independent legal representation.

Prof. M. Priyamvadha, Dr V. Bharathi Harishankar, Dr D.M Padma Priya, and Ms. Harshaa Vardhini Narasimhan show us the Devadasi system in its current setting. This study primarily focuses on the social element and the art form of the

Devadasi system in Telangana, Maharashtra, Karnataka, Tamil Nadu, and Andhra Pradesh. In order to comprehend the intersectional elements influencing victimization, this study entailed extensive interviews with stakeholders associated with the Devadasi system.

Irvin Waller pushes victimology professors to develop new courses for the upcoming generation of victimologists, who will be the driving forces behind a major decrease in violence. It gives a summary of what is known to have decreased violence, how it is put into practice, and how to create political will to secure sustained funding. The study cites places and initiatives that have successfully decreased violent crime by 50% in just 3 years. It also lays out intricate guidelines to have access to justice and how victim rights are being upheld, demonstrating what is feasible.

Prof. Emil W., Pływaczewski, and Ewa M. Guzik-Makaruk analyze the compensation for victims of crime in Poland since the twentieth century. They scrutinize the criminal codes and the Act of 2005 on state compensation to victims of certain criminal acts. Of its nearly two decades of existence, many of its flaws have now been exposed. The fund itself, for instance, is used to a limited degree, and such flaws contribute to the phenomena of secondary victimization.

Sajith Mohmad Saleem assesses how compared to juvenile and adult criminals, young adult offenders typically confront distinct problems. Given their age, they are more likely to turn to deviance if they are not reformed and rehabilitated in a timely manner. The causes of recidivism among young adult criminals are examined in this study. According to this study, which involved interviewing 250 young adult recidivists, the chance of recidivism is significantly influenced by a number of factors, including age, peer pressure, substance abuse, cognitive development, and socioeconomic disparities.

A celebration of Professor K. Chockalingam's contributions to the area of criminology and victimology is presented in *Beyond the Gavel: A Paradigm Shift in Global Criminal Justice.* Criminal justice, criminology, victimology, and criminal law are the four main essences examined in this volume, which offers notable insights into the difficulties and changes influencing the contemporary judicial systems. The significance of having interdisciplinary approaches in crime deterrence and criminal policymaking is highlighted in this volume.

The manufacturer's authorised representative in the EU is Springer Nature Customer Service Centre GmbH, Europaplatz 3, 69115 Heidelberg, Germany. If you have any concerns regarding our products, please contact ProductSafety@springernature.com

Printed and bound by CPI Group (UK) Ltd, Croydon, CR0 4YY
07/10/2026
02229349-0008